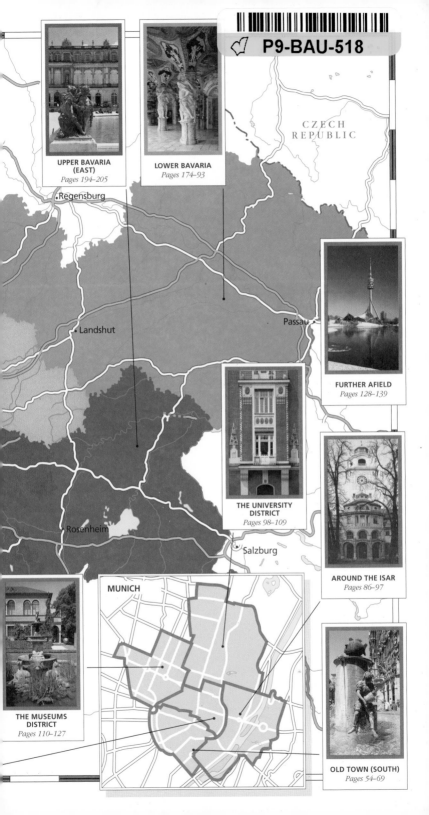

EYEWITNESS TRAVEL

MUNICH
& THE BAVARIAN ALPS

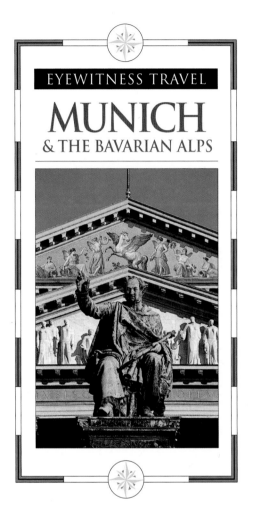

EYEWITNESS TRAVEL

MUNICH
& THE BAVARIAN ALPS

IZABELLA GALICKA
KATARZYNA MICHALSKA

DK

LONDON, NEW YORK,
MELBOURNE, MUNICH AND DELHI
www.dk.com

PRODUCED BY Wydawnictwo Wiedza i Życie S.A., Warsaw
CONTRIBUTORS Izabella Galicka, Katarzyna Michalska
CONSULTANT Sergiusz Michalski
ILLUSTRATORS Lena Maminajszwili, Bohdan Wróblewski, Piotr Zubrzycki
PHOTOGRAPHERS Dorota and Mariusz Jarymowiczowie
CARTOGRAPHERS Magdalena Polak, Dariusz Romanowski, Kartographie Huber (Munich)

JACKET DESIGN AND GRAPHICS Paweł Kamiński
GRAPHIC DESIGNER Paweł Pasternak
EDITORS Robert G. Pasieczny, Dorota Szatańska
TECHNICAL EDITOR Anna Kożurno-Królikowska
DESIGNERS Ewa Roguska, Piotr Kiedrowski

Dorling Kindersley Limited
EDITOR Lucilla Watson
TRANSLATOR Mark Cole (Linguists for Business)
DTP DESIGNERS Jason Little, Conrad Van Dyk
PRODUCTION Sarah Dodd

Reproduced by Colourscan, Singapore
Printed and bound by L. Rex
Printing Company Limited, China

First American Edition 2002
10 11 12 13 10 9 8 7 6 5 4 3 2

Published in the United States by DK Publishing,
375 Hudson Street, New York, New York 10014

Reprinted with revisions 2006, 2008, 2010

Copyright 2002, 2010 © Dorling Kindersley Limited, London
A Penguin Company

Published in Great Britain by Dorling Kindersley Limited.

A catalog record of this book is available from the Library of Congress

ISSN 1542-1554
ISBN 978-0-7566-3187-1

FLOORS ARE REFERRED TO THROUGHOUT IN ACCORDANCE WITH EUROPEAN
USAGE; IE THE "FIRST FLOOR" IS THE FLOOR ABOVE GROUND LEVEL.

Front cover main image: The skyline of Old Town, Munich

MIX
Paper from
responsible sources
FSC
www.fsc.org   FSC™ C018179

**The information in this
DK Eyewitness Travel Guide is checked regularly.**
Every effort has been made to ensure that this book is as up to date
as possible at the time of going to press. Some details, however,
such as telephone numbers, opening hours, prices, gallery hanging
arrangements and travel information are liable to change. The
publishers cannot accept responsibility for any consequences arising
from the use of this book, nor for any material on third party
websites, and cannot guarantee that any website address in this
book will be a suitable source of travel information. We value the
views and suggestions of our readers very highly.
Please write to: Publisher, DK Eyewitness Travel Guides,
Dorling Kindersley, 80 Strand, London WC2R 0RL, Great Britain.

◁ **Theatinerkirche in Munich with Victory Arch in foreground**

CONTENTS

HOW TO USE
THIS GUIDE **6**

**Gothic figure of a Dancing Moor
from the Stadtmuseum, Munich**

INTRODUCING
MUNICH
AND THE
BAVARIAN ALPS

DISCOVERING MUNICH
& THE BAVARIAN ALPS
10

PUTTING MUNICH
& THE BAVARIAN ALPS
ON THE MAP **12**

A PORTRAIT OF THE
BAVARIAN ALPS **16**

**View of Munich, with the Neues
Rathaus in the foreground**

A verdant, flower-filled meadow near Schwangau, in the Allgäu

Pork salamis

The Propyläen in Munich,
designed by Leo von Klenze

The Frauenkirche,
one of Munich's most
prominent landmarks

HOW TO USE THIS GUIDE

This guide will help you to get the most out of your stay in Munich and the Bavarian Alps. The first section, *Introducing Munich and the Bavarian Alps,* locates the city and the region geographically and gives an outline of its history and culture. The subsequent sections, *Munich Area by Area and The Bavarian Alps*

Area by Area, describe the main sights and attractions. Feature spreads, with maps, illustrations and drawings, focus on important sights. Information about accommodation and restaurants is given in *Travellers' Needs,* while the *Survival Guide* provides useful tips on everything you need to know, from money to getting around.

MUNICH AREA BY AREA

In this guide, Munich has been divided into five central areas and a Further Afield section. Each area is described in an individual section, giving the names of all the main sights and attractions. The sights are numbered on the area maps.

Sights at a glance lists the buildings in a particular area by category: churches, museums and art galleries, historic buildings, and streets and squares.

All pages relating to Munich have red thumb tabs.

A locator map shows at a glance where you are in relation to the city plan.

1 Area Map
For easy reference the sights in each area are numbered and located on an area map, as well as on the Munich Street Finder on pp148–53.

2 Street-by-Street Map
This gives a bird's-eye view of a particularly interesting sightseeing area described in the section.

Stars indicate the sights that no visitor should miss.

A suggested route takes in some of the most interesting streets in the area.

3 Detailed Information
All the important sights of Munich are described individually. The address, telephone number, opening hours, admission charges, how to get there and disabled access are given for each sight.

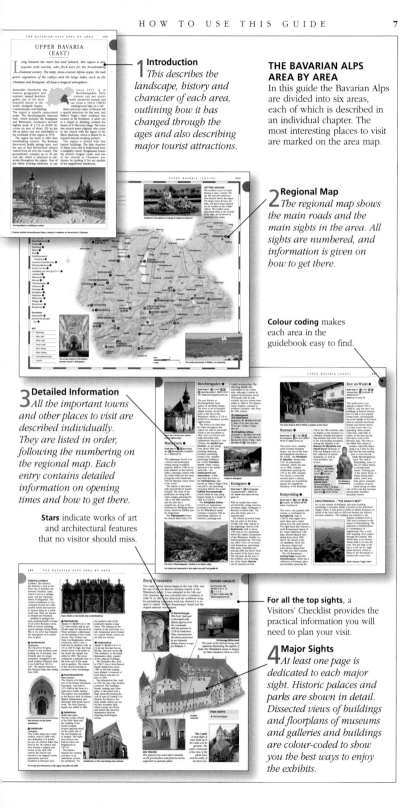

THE BAVARIAN ALPS AREA BY AREA

In this guide the Bavarian Alps are divided into six areas, each of which is described in an individual chapter. The most interesting places to visit are marked on the area map.

1 Introduction

This describes the landscape, history and character of each area, outlining how it has changed through the ages and also describing major tourist attractions.

2 Regional Map

The regional map shows the main roads and the main sights in the area. All sights are numbered, and information is given on how to get there.

Colour coding makes each area in the guidebook easy to find.

3 Detailed Information

All the important towns and other places to visit are described individually. They are listed in order, following the numbering on the regional map. Each entry contains detailed information on opening times and how to get there.

Stars indicate works of art and architectural features that no visitor should miss.

For all the top sights, a Visitors' Checklist provides the practical information you will need to plan your visit.

4 Major Sights

At least one page is dedicated to each major sight. Historic palaces and parks are shown in detail. Dissected views of buildings and floorplans of museums and galleries and buildings are colour-coded to show you the best ways to enjoy the exhibits.

INTRODUCING MUNICH & THE BAVARIAN ALPS

DISCOVERING MUNICH & THE BAVARIAN ALPS

Frescoes on the Old Town Hall, Lindau

As well as the natural beauty of the region's river valleys, alpine pastures, peaks, lakes, nature reserves and dense forests, Munich and the Bavarian Alps boast a rich architectural heritage. The region's wonderfully ornate castles and grand palaces are testament to the wealth and lavish lifestyle of former kings and noblemen, while its fine Baroque churches and monasteries are evidence of the ecclesiastical wealth enjoyed by the church. The following pages highlight the most popular sights in Bavaria.

Muncheners making the most of the city's many cafés and bars

MUNICH

- **World-class art galleries**
- **Café culture**
- **Breweries and beer gardens**

Bavaria's capital is chic, cosmopolitan and stylish and its districts have their own distinct character. Take a stroll around the old town, **Marienplatz** *(see pp56-57)*, with its shopping streets or venture along the **Isar** *(see p87)* and through the quaint **Englisher Garten** *(see p106)*. Café culture forms an integral part of Muncheners' lives and there are coffee houses such as **Dallmayr** *(see p277)* and little cafés around **Gärtnerplatz** *(see p64)* where you can have the obligatory *Kaffee und Kuchen* (coffee with cake). Equally characteristic are Munich's various beer gardens and the brewery cellar taverns such as

Hofbräuhaus *(see p84)*. Take in the art museums on Prinzregentenstraße and in the Museum District, as well as the privately owned galleries in the University District.

UPPER BAVARIA (NORTH)

- **Schleißheim Palace**
- **Picturesque monasteries and Baroque churches**
- **Fabulous forests and rivers**

The northern part of Bavaria has a striking landscape full of forests and rivers. In particular, the scenic area of the Altmühl river valley, where hops are grown, is great for cyclists and hikers. A must-see is **Schleißheim Palace** *(see pp172–3)*. This Baroque masterpiece has gardens laid out in geometric form, with topiary and canals. For more Baroque treasures visit the **Asamkirche Maria de Victoria** in Ingolstadt *(see p166)* and Scheyern's **Mariä Himmelfahrt** with its Baroque Basilica *(see p165)*.

Be inspired by churches at **Kapuzinerkirche Hl.** in Eichstätt *(see p163)* and the **Kloster Indersdorf** *(see p171)*.

LOWER BAVARIA

- **Blue Danube river cruise**
- **Renaissance castle, Burg Trausnitz**
- **Crystals Museum**

The wonderful River Danube winds its way through Passau and much of Lower Bavaria. Take a river cruise in **Passau** *(see pp188–91)* to see the Old Town from the river or visit the gorge by boat between **Weltenberg and Kelheim** *(see p182)*. The **Crystals Museum** in Riedenburg *(see p183)* boasts the largest emerald from the Alps and the world's largest ever rock crystal formation, from the United States. For a sense of Renaissance court life visit **Burg Trausnitz** *(see p181)* and admire the frescoes, tapestries and fine pillars, as well as great views.

Cruising the Danube near Kelheim, Lower Bavaria

UPPER BAVARIA (EAST)

• **Beautiful Königssee**
• **Lavish Palace of Herrenchiemsee**
• **Pretty painted villages**

The picture perfect lake, **Königssee** *(see p200)* has a mysterious deep green colour, a red onion-domed pilgrimage church and boat tours to experience the Wall of Echoes – as each boat pauses, the sound of the boat's horn is echoed back from the cliffs. King Ludwig II's most extravagant palace, at **Herrenchiemsee** *(see p202)*, was an attempt to recreate the palace of Versailles. This showpiece is worth a visit for its lavish interior and museum about Ludwig's life. In many of the local villages in Upper Bavaria look out for examples of the famous **Lüftlmalerei** *(see p212)*, the art of painting house façades with naïve rural scenes. These pretty paintings date from the 17th century.

King Ludwig II's magical Neuschwanstein castle in the Allgäu

Königssee and the pilgrimage church of St Bartholomä

UPPER BAVARIA (SOUTH)

• **Lakes and the Alpine Road**
• **Ancient town centres**
• **Franz-Marc-Museum**

One artist inspired by the beauty of Bavaria was Franz Marc. The **Franz-Marc-Museum** at Kochel am See *(see p219)* is worth a visit for over 150 examples of the

artist's work. The south's beautiful Five Lake District is made up of Ammersee, Stamberger See, Pilsensee, Wesslinger See and Wörthesee. Locals swim and sail here in summer. The **Alpine Road** *(see p220–21)* links ancient towns, some with well-preserved architecture, from Lindau to Berchtesgaden. Cross 105 bridges, 10 viaducts and 15 tunnels on the 450km (280 miles) of roads stretching along the German Alps.

ALLGÄU

• **Fairytale Neuschwanstein**
• **The Romantic Road scenery**
• **Nerve-racking ski jumps**

Enjoying a spectacular mountain setting, the fairytale castle **Neuschwanstein** *(see p230)* is not to be missed. The castle sits on a craggy rock surrounded by thick pine forests and was built for King Ludwig II, who was inspired by Wagner's operas. The **Romantic Road** *(see p292)* is a popular route for cyclists, hikers and coach parties. Launched in the 1950s, Germany's first tourist route runs between Würzburg and Füssen, taking in medieval towns, famous churches, the Danube and the ancient Roman Via Claudia route. For high ski jumps that will literally take your breath away, visit **Oberstdorf** *(see p232)*.

NORTHERN SWABIA

• **Historic Augsburg**
• **Castles, forests, rivers and valleys**
• **Roman ruins**

This northwestern region of Bavaria is rich in historical towns, architectural treasures and fabulous castles. From the vast forest of Augsburg Westliche Wälder to the Danube flood plains, the landscape is varied and great for walking. The historic town of **Augsburg** *(see p248–53)* with its canal bridges has a suitable nickname of "Venice of the North". Here, visit the **Fuggerei** *(see p252)*, commissioned by rich local merchants who also built the castles of the southwest, or stop by the **Roman Museum** *(see p251)* for coins and other finds from local ruins and the **Roman Via Claudia** *(see p246)*.

The pretty village of Ulm on the River Iller, in Northern Swabia

Putting Munich and the Bavarian Alps on the Map

Southern Bavaria, the southernmost part of Germany, consists of three administrative regions: Upper Bavaria (Oberbayern), Swabia (Schwaben) and Lower Bavaria (Niederbayern). The region borders the Czech Republic, Austria and, across Lake Constance, Switzerland. To the north it is bounded by the Danube, and the south by the Alps. Munich, on the River Isar, is the capital (Land), with 1.3 million inhabitants.

Aerial view of the Deutsches Museum in Munich

KEY

✈	Airport
⛴	Ferry
═══	Motorway
═══	Major road
───	Railway
─∙─	National border

0 km   100

0 miles   100

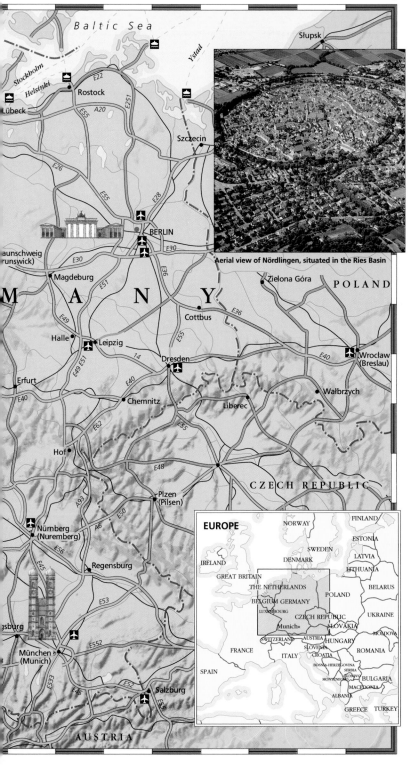

Baltic Sea

Słupsk

Stockholm

Helsinki

E22

Lübeck

Rostock

E55

A20

E251

E251

Szczecin

E26

E55

E28

BERLIN

E30

Aerial view of Nördlingen, situated in the Ries Basin

aunschweig
(runswick)

E30

Magdeburg

E51

Zielona Góra

POLAND

M

A

N

Y

E36

E49

Cottbus

E36

Halle

Leipzig

E55

Wrocław
(Breslau)

E49 E51

14

Dresden

E40

Erfurt

E40

Chemnitz

Liberec

Wałbrzych

E40

E62

E55

Hof

E48

CZECH REPUBLIC

A93

Plzen
(Pilsen)

E50

Nürnberg
(Nuremberg)

A6

E56

E45

Regensburg

E53

jsburg

E552

München
(Munich)

E533

E552

Salzburg

E26

E52

E55

AUSTRIA

EUROPE

NORWAY

FINLAND

SWEDEN

ESTONIA

IRELAND

DENMARK

LATVIA

LITHUANIA

GREAT BRITAIN

THE NETHERLANDS

BELARUS

BELGIUM GERMANY

POLAND

LUXEMBOURG

UKRAINE

CZECH REPUBLIC

Munich

SLOVAKIA

MOLDOVA

SWITZERLAND

AUSTRIA

HUNGARY

FRANCE

SLOVENIA

CROATIA

ROMANIA

ITALY

BOSNA-HERZEGOVINA

SERBIA

SPAIN

MONTENEGRO

BULGARIA

MACEDONIA

ALBANIA

GREECE

TURKEY

Central Munich

Central Munich boasts a variety of architectural styles, and each of the five areas has its own unique atmosphere. Marienplatz, and the Old Town around it, abounds in old-world architecture, and is the main tourist area. Along the River Isar, green areas are flanked by grand 19th-century urban thoroughfares. The great thoroughfare of Ludwig-straße/Leopoldstraße sets the tone for the northern quarter, which includes the picturesque Schwabing and Englischer Garten districts. The suburb of Maxvorstadt to the northeast has a wealth of museums and art galleries.

Lenbachhaus
The home of the 19th-century portrait painter Franz von Lenbach is built in the style of an Italian villa and is fronted by a picturesque garden.

Asamkirche
Also known as the Church of St Johann Nepomuk, it is named after the Asam brothers who built it. The finest work of their careers, it is also one of the most oustanding examples of European Baroque architecture.

New Town Hall
The coat of arms on the New Town Hall features the monk who symbolizes Munich. The city took its name from the legendary monks (München meaning "monk settlement") who settled there.

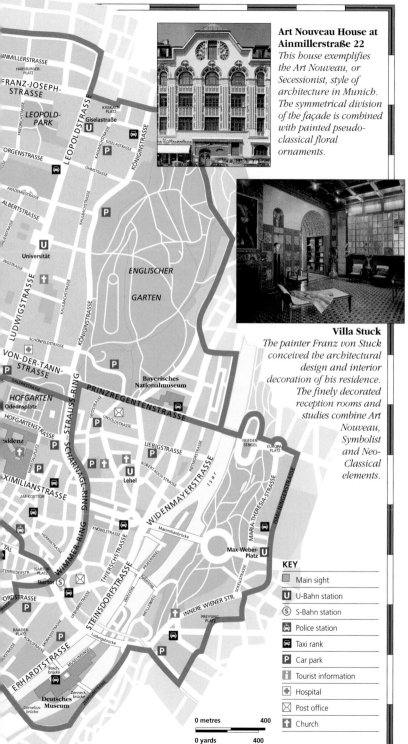

Art Nouveau House at Ainmillerstraße 22
This house exemplifies the Art Nouveau, or Secessionist, style of architecture in Munich. The symmetrical division of the façade is combined with painted pseudo-classical floral ornaments.

Villa Stuck
The painter Franz von Stuck conceived the architectural design and interior decoration of his residence. The finely decorated reception rooms and studies combine Art Nouveau, Symbolist and Neo-Classical elements.

KEY

▢	Main sight
U	U-Bahn station
Ⓢ	S-Bahn station
🚖	Police station
🚕	Taxi rank
P	Car park
i	Tourist information
✚	Hospital
⊠	Post office
✝	Church

0 metres 400
0 yards 400

A PORTRAIT OF THE BAVARIAN ALPS

T*hree out of every four Germans say they would like to live in Bavaria, especially southern Bavaria. As it is one of the most picturesque and also one of the most prosperous parts of Europe, this is not so surprising. For many foreigners, Bavaria is quintessentially German; this is not, however, strictly true, as Bavaria has always nurtured its own distinct political framework and culture.*

Southern Bavaria is inhabited by three main groups of people: a branch of the Swabian tribes of Württemberg, in the western region, who are the descendants of the legendary Baiuvarii; the Upper Bavarians, in the central region, and the Lower Bavarians, centred in the eastern region.

To this day, there are still distinct regional differences in the Bavarians' dialect, folklore and cuisine and, arguably, in their mentality as well. The shared characteristics that they have are a love of tradition, a certain conservatism and a strong sense of loyalty to the Free State of Bavaria (Freistaat Bayern).

White and sky-blue, the colours of the Bavarian flag

Bavarian culture and customs were developed as much in court circles as by the peasantry. This development on two social levels has left its mark on the character of the people and their traditions. The latter include an affinity with the soil, and a tendency to a certain stubbornness and defiance coupled with warm hospitality and friendliness. These qualities are combined with tolerance and at times a fondness for absolute rulers and politicians ranging from men such as Maximilian I, Maximilian I Josef and Franz-Josef Strauss to eccentrics and dreamers such as Ludwig II.

Summer in the old quarter of Lindau

◁ **A beer hall during Oktoberfest – Munich's famed beer festival**

Peaceful sub-alpine landscape

THE LANDSCAPE
OF THE BAVARIAN ALPS

When they look up at the sky, the Bavarians see the colours of their national flag – white and sky-blue. On clear days the sky takes on a Mediterranean translucence; this may be because Bavaria is the bridge between northern Europe and the Mediterranean region. Munich is in fact much closer to Venice than it is to Berlin.

Bavaria's mild climate and varied scenery combine to create an idyllic landscape. Lush green meadows populated with grey and brown Alpine cattle alternate with thick woodland, countless brooks and streams, rocky outcrops, lakes and

Bay window of a house in Garmisch-Partenkirchen

rolling hills, against which rise majestic Alpine peaks. When the famous *Föhn* (warm Alpine wind) blows, the Alps can be clearly seen from as far as 100 km (60 miles) away.

The local architecture complements the scenery perfectly. Picture-postcard towns and villages, large monasteries, castles and palaces, and village churches with their onion domes fit together in perfect harmony. A typical feature of the region is the way in which high art is combined with kitsch. Exquisite Baroque churches and monasteries with ephemeral frescoes stand side by side with simple peasant art, while the splendid Neo-Classical architecture of the Wittelsbachs contrasts with the enchanting fairy-tale castles of Ludwig II.

RELIGION, TRADITION
AND CULTURE

Bavaria is a land of defiant, ritualised Catholicism, which once effectively blocked the march of Protestant Germany to Rome. It is no surprise then to find that Bavaria

Nativity scene on a house in Hindelang – a 20th-century example of Lüftlmalerei (the Bavarian art of façade painting)

has its own conservative ruling party, the CSU, and that in place of the ubiquitous "Guten Tag", the people here greet each other with "Grüß Gott" ("Greetings to God"). The Bavarian national anthem, which is played every day when the local television station closes for the night, begins with the words: "God be with you, land of Bavaria."

Catholic ritual is omnipresent – during the celebration of Sunday Mass, at innumerable church fairs, and during processions and pilgrimages. However, piety expresses an affirmation of life rather than prudishness. Many stereotypes are attached to the Bavarians: among the best known are green hats with feathers in them, short *Lederhosen* and knee-socks, beer-mugs joyfully held on high.

Folk traditions have survived too: perhaps nowhere else in the world is there such a proliferation of folk festivals and music groups. Almost everywhere you

Futuristic style of the BMW works in Munich

Decoration for a maypole

can see the characteristic but regionally differentiated men's *Trachten*, which includes a short jacket with bone buttons, and the women's *Dirndl*, with their wide, low-cut dresses and a narrow waistcoat. Simplified versions of these costumes are also worn as everyday clothing, even by Bavarian politicians. More refined and lavish versions are worn when attending official functions or going to the opera.

Beer-drinking is another integral part of Bavarian folk tradition. Some 1,100 breweries work to quench beer-lovers' thirst. Bavaria has some of the oldest breweries in the world (including the Weihenstephan brewery), and it was the first place where a ducal decree (1516) banned the

use of any other ingredients than barley, hops and water in beer-making. The best way to drink beer is from a large, litre mug, known as a Maß, or "measure", preferably in a beer garden beneath a chestnut tree, in the cellars of a monastic brewery, or in a marquee to the strains of folk music, as during the famous Oktoberfest.

THE SOURCES OF BAVARIA'S WEALTH

For centuries farming and trade have been the main source of Bavaria's wealth. It is the largest supplier of farm produce in Germany. It also has the largest hop harvest in the world. After World War II Bavaria's economy expanded enormously, with some of Germany's largest companies based here, such as Audi, BMW and Siemens. Bavaria has chemicals, aircraft, printing, electronics and tourism industries.

The Maß – the best way to drink beer

Landscape of the Bavarian Alps

Southern Bavaria is one of Germany's most picturesque and scenically varied regions. To the south it is bordered by the Alps, with their breathtaking limestone peaks and verdant slopes. To the north it is bounded by the Danube, with its marshy flood plains. The region's landscape consists of undulating hills and many lakes and mountain streams, which were formed by glaciers during the Ice Age. Much of the terrain takes the form of pasture and fields, or is covered in forests, while industrialization has remained unobtrusive.

Alpine meadows are covered in lush grass which produces high-quality hay and provides rich grazing for cattle.

A hop plantation *in Hallertau, which is the largest hop-producing region in Bavaria. Wooden poles overgrown with hops are a characteristic sight.*

Mountain peaks with breathtaking escarpments are a common sight.

Mountain streams *have over millennia cut their way through the Alpine rocks, creating scenic gorges. The picturesque Wimbachklamm is accessible to hikers.*

Local buildings harmonize with the surrounding landscape.

SOUTHERN BAVARIAN LAKES

Huge glaciers that melted centuries ago left many lakes in southern Bavaria. Their limpid waters attract watersports enthusiasts and swimmers. This breathtakingly beautiful environment is ideal for walking and many other outdoor activities.

This marina *on Chiemsee, also known as the Bavarian Sea, is one of the finest spots in southern Bavaria for amateur yachting.*

The Zugspitze, *rising to a height of 2,962 m (9,718 ft), is the highest German peak.*

PLANTS AND ANIMALS OF THE BAVARIAN ALPS

Southern Bavaria's varied natural scenery has remained largely unspoiled thanks to careful protection and clean air. Animals and plants occur in several bands of vegetation. While in the higher parts of the Alps only mosses and lichens grow, at altitudes of under 1,500 m (4,900 ft) there is an abundance of flora and fauna. The forests contain a wealth of plants, animals and birds, while the extensive meadows and marshes are covered in various grasses, and the clear waters of the rivers and lakes are home to many species of fish. The parks and nature reserves help to preserve endangered species.

The grey-brown Alpine cow *is especially common in the Allgäu, a region known for its dairy products.*

Goats *are able to negotiate rough terrain and steep slopes and are a common sight on mountain hikes.*

Marmots *peep out from mountain screes and crevasses, emitting their characteristic whistling call.*

Ravens *appear in large flocks over ploughed fields, searching for worms and leftover grains of corn.*

Trout *is the most common species of fish to be found in Bavaria's mountain streams. They thrive in the clear, unpolluted waters.*

Butterflies *share the flowery Alpine meadows with bees, gadflies and grasshoppers. The most colourful of the butterflies is the peacock butterfly.*

Forests *are thick and extensive, many of them in a pristine state.*

Edelweiß *is an increasingly rare sight in the Alps. This protected Alpine flower is a favourite decorative motif in the Bavarian national costume.*

The gentian *is the "national" flower of Bavaria. It is honoured in song and is used in making the famous gentian schnapps.*

Architecture of the Bavarian Alps

Statue in Michaelskirche in Munich

The architectural landscape of southern Bavaria features a large number of churches and monasteries. These noble buildings, in perfect harmony with the surrounding landscape, are topped by onion-domed towers. Although each architectural era created a legacy of fine buildings, it was during the Baroque period (the late 16th to the early 18th century) that the region flourished architecturally. New churches were built, and existing ones endowed with stunning ornamentation. In southern Bavaria architectural splendours were built in the 19th century, including the fairy-tale residences of Ludwig II.

Altenstadt basilica *is one of Bavaria's many Romanesque buildings.*

GOTHIC

The Gothic style of architecture is widely represented in Bavaria, although its impact in Europe went far beyond this region. As well as in surviving town houses, the Gothic style in Bavaria is seen in fortified residences and religious buildings. A specific regional characteristic is the wide nave of Gothic churches. The oldest Gothic church was built in Laufen. The largest is the Frauen-kirche in Munich, and the most resplendent is the Martinskirche in Landshut. The use of pointed arches and ribbed vaulting made it possible to create much higher, light-filled spaces. Gothic architecture reached its apogee in the mid-15th century.

The Chapel of St Sigismund *in Blutenburg Castle is a typical example of late Gothic religious architecture.*

Entrance to the church of St Ulrich and St Afra, Augsburg

RENAISSANCE AND MANNERISM

The Renaissance reached Bavaria from Italy via Augsburg, where in 1510 the Renaissance chapel of the Fugger family was built. This set the style for town houses (as at Neuburg and Augsburg). At the end of the century, Renaissance style was overtaken by Mannerism, which departed from Classical forms. One of the main Mannerist architects was Elias Holl.

The window is set under a broken pediment.

Carvings contrast with the austere façade.

The façade *of the Arsenal at Augsburg, designed by Joseph Heintz the Elder in 1607, is a fine example of Mannerism, distinguished by a flat façade and the rejection of Classical proportions.*

The Archangel Michael overcoming Satan *displays dramatic poses typical of Mannerism.*

BAROQUE

No architectural style left such a strong impression on southern Bavaria as did the Baroque. Its highly decorated, almost theatrical style held a special appeal, and it was expressed in skilfully articulated spaces to which abundant ornamentation was added. The first Baroque buildings were by Italian architects, but a local school was soon producing work of the highest quality. The Bavarian Baroque reached its height with the Asam brothers *(see pp66 & 68–9)*.

The vaulting *of Passau Cathedral is a fine example of late Baroque forms derived directly from Italy. Despite the excessive stuccowork and elaborate fresco decorations, the main architectural elements are still discernible.*

The façade *of the church of Berg am Laim illustrates the typical Baroque rhythm of architectural elements, accentuated by cornices, pilasters and columns.*

The windows *of the Neues Schloss in Schleißheim are framed and decorated with rosettes and mock-antique masks. Doorways and windows with exuberant ornamentation were highly characteristic of Baroque architecture.*

NEO-CLASSICISM

The Neo-Classical style developed in France in the 18th century. After 1806, when Bavaria proclaimed itself a kingdom, it was adapted to serve the purposes of the Napoleonic Empire Style. Neo-Classicism reached the peak of its splendour after 1816, but was confined to Munich. Ludwig I intended to rebuild the city to turn it into "Athens on Isar". To this end the court architect Leo von Klenze designed many fine buildings, with references to ancient Greece and the Italian Renaissance.

The Prinz-Carl-Palais, *by the architect Karl von Fischer, is a typical example of early Neo-Classical architecture. It is fronted by an imposing portico with Ionic columns supporting a tympanum.*

This capital *of a column in the portico of the Glyptothek is decorated with typically Ionic scrolled volutes.*

An akroterion is a decorative element often used in Classical architecture.

The tympanum *of the Propyläen contains sculptures of Otto I among kings of the Greeks. Otto I abdicated before the building was completed. The people mocked: "Do not glorify the day before the sun is down – the proof is the Propyläen."*

Sculptures in a style evoking the glory of ancient Greece were carved by Ludwig Schwanthaler.

Monasteries and Abbeys

A surprising feature of the Bavarian Alps is the large number of monasteries and abbeys that are to be seen here. The first Benedictine monastery was founded in the early Middle Ages. In the 11th and 12th centuries monastic establishments were built in the foothills of the Alps. The next period at which such building activity flourished was the Baroque, when medieval abbeys were rebuilt and new ones, such as Ottobeuren and Ettal, were constructed. In the 18th century, with the spirit of the Enlightenment, fine libraries with valuable collections of books were built. The secularization of more than 160 monasteries in 1803 led to the destruction of a large part of Bavarian monastic culture.

Figure of the emperor in Kaisersaal

Altarpieces *often take the form of large statues of saints or of one of the Church Fathers. They are a prominent feature of church interiors.*

Heilig-Kreuz-Kapelle
The Chapel of the Holy Cross is one of the few monastic chapels open only to monks. Such chapels were used for gatherings and for silent prayer away from the outside world. Their decoration is no less lavish than that of the rest of the monastery.

The church interior *is graced by numerous altars, and the architectural features, mouldings, paintings and furniture combine to form a unified whole.*

The Library *reflects the scientific and cultural aspirations of Bavarian churches. The walls are lined with decorated shelves that harmonize with the leather-bound volumes they hold.*

The ceremonial hall was designed for official gatherings.

The Kaisersaal, *or imperial hall, was one of the abbey's countless reception rooms. It underlines the abbey's close association with the concept of a Christian Empire.*

OTTOBEUREN ABBEY

Ottobeuren, which has been described as the "Swabian Escorial", is one of the largest monastic establishments in Europe. The church is attached to a vast complex with rows of rooms built around three courtyards, as well as numerous ancillary buildings.

The staircase, *a feature of conscious pomp and elegance, shows the importance that abbeys attached to the appearance of public reception areas.*

Ottobeuren Abbey *blends with the sub-Alpine landscape in a way that is characteristic of many Bavarian monasteries, with their red roofs and their tall belfries. In spring and summer, the entire building stands in striking contrast to the lush greenery with which it is surrounded.*

Art of the Bavarian Alps

Late Gothic miniature in Passau Museum

Art in the region developed against the background of the major trends in European art. The ecclesiastical and ducal protectorate, and later that of free cities, led to the development of important artistic centres in Munich, Augsburg, Landshut and Passau. Schools of painting, sculpture and craftsmanship developed as early as the Gothic period, and the Renaissance and Mannerism also left their mark. But it was in the Baroque period that the arts of fresco, stucco and sculpture reached their peak. Folk elements meanwhile were always a feature of Bavarian art, taking the form of votive images, roadside shrines and mural paintings on village houses.

This man with a shield *is a late Gothic figure from Ottobeuren Abbey.*

ROMANESQUE AND GOTHIC ART

Romanesque art is characterized by a stylization rooted in Byzantine art. As well as the crafts and sculpture, southern Bavaria has interesting examples of mural painting. The windows of Augsburg Cathedral are among the finest in Europe. The Gothic period, which continued until about 1520, brought in a new style, primarily in the way that human figures were depicted, with flowing garments and expressive gestures. By about 1500 Gothic painting and sculpture had their greatest exponents in Jan Polack and Erasmus Grasser.

Masks are placed at the intersections between panels.

Bas-reliefs are of allegorical and Old Testament subjects.

Door handles take the shape of lions' masks.

The Moriskentänzer *is one of ten expressive carvings by Erasmus Grasser of Moors in a court dance. According to custom, the men would dance in sophisticated poses, and capture the ladies' attention with elegant gestures. These sculptures are a rare example of secular subject matter in Gothic art.*

The bronze doors *of Augsburg Cathedral show the influence of Byzantine art. They initially consisted of four wings, with a total of 224 reliefs. Only 35 remain today.*

GREAT ARTISTS

One of Erasmus Grasser's Dancing Moors

1400	1450	1500	1550
	1450–1518 Erasmus Grasser	**c.1540–99** Friedrich Sustris	**c.1570–163** Hans Krumpe
	c.1460/65–1524 Hans Holbein the Elder	**c.1500–62** Christoph Amberger	
		1516–73 Hans Mielich	
		c.1548–1628 Peter Candid de Witte	**c.157 16** Hans Reich
	c.1435–1519 Jan Polack	**1473–1531** Hans Burgkmair	
		c.1550–1620 Hubert Gerhard	

RENAISSANCE AND MANNERISM

The southern Bavarian Renaissance was influenced by Italy and the Netherlands, but it developed its own elements. The crafts flourished, and in sculpture and painting new themes, such as genre scenes, classical mythology and portraiture, appeared. The most prominent artists of the time were the Augsburg painters Hans Holbein the Elder, Hans Burgkmair and Christoph Amberger. Mannerism developed in the mid-16th century, its most outstanding exponents in southern Bavaria being Hans Krumper and Hans Reichle.

This portrait of Felicitas Welser *by Christoph Amberger is typical of Renaissance portraiture in that it shows a certain rigidity of pose combined with a care to capture the sitter's individuality and accurately depict the costume. The coloration reveals a Venetian influence.*

This ornamental cup *dating from 1570–80 was made in one of Augsburg's famous goldsmiths' workshops. The work of Augsburg goldsmiths graced many churches and grand houses in Europe.*

BAROQUE

During the Baroque period the walls of churches, monasteries and palaces were lavishly covered with stucco mouldings and *trompe-l'oeil* paintings. An important centre for such art was Wessobrunn. From the 18th century the prominent Asam brothers began working in Bavaria *(see p66)*. *Lüftlmalerei*, paintings on the walls of houses *(see p212)*, is a typically Bavarian phenomenon. Fine Rococo sculpture was produced by Ignaz Günther and Johann Baptist Straub, while the court artist François Cuvilliés refined the art of Rococo decor to perfection.

This traditional wardrobe *is from the renowned furniture-making centre in Bad Tölz. The distinctive furniture made here was covered in folk paintings. Sideboards, beds and the carts associated with the St Leonard's Day festival can be seen in the town's local history museum.*

This amber sculpture *from the Bürgersaal in Munich by Ignaz Günther embodies all the elements of the late Baroque: pathos, levity and dynamism.*

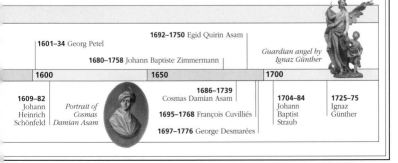

1601–34 Georg Petel	**1692–1750** Egid Quirin Asam	Guardian angel by *Ignaz Günther*
	1680–1758 Johann Baptiste Zimmermann	

1600	**1650**	**1700**

1609–82 Johann Heinrich Schönfeld	*Portrait of Cosmas Damian Asam*	**1686–1739** Cosmas Damian Asam	**1704–84** Johann Baptist Straub
		1695–1768 François Cuvilliés	**1725–75** Ignaz Günther
		1697–1776 George Desmarées	

Traditions of the Bavarian Alps

Landshut Wedding newly-weds

Bavaria is a land where old local traditions and folklore are cultivated and revered. Almost every town and village has its own local holiday, with folk bands, beer-drinking and general merriment in the streets. These events variously involve folk dancing and fire-work displays. The Catholic tradition is strong in the region, the countless religious feast days and church processions often coinciding with fairs. Many places also commemorate local historical events.

PASSION PLAYS

Once every ten years the mountain village of Oberammergau becomes the centre of the Easter mystery plays *(Passionsspiele)* that are performed over four months from late May to early October. This tradition dates back to 1633.

At that time, so as to ward off the plague, the villagers vowed to act out scenes from the Passion of Christ. Initially these were staged outside the church, but since 1930 they have been held in a special open-air theatre with seating for 4,800. The performances, lasting from morning until late afternoon with a break in between, take place five days a week. According to tradition, the actors must be residents of Oberammergau by birth. The lavish decorations and the costumes, of which there are over 1,000, are provided by the local populace. The scenes, accompanied by a choir and music, are performed by amateur actors in a natural and expressive way. Against the backdrop of mountains they have the realism of *tableaux vivants.*

The Passion plays have gained world renown, and tickets must be booked well in advance. A similar tradition exists in certain other Bavarian villages.

THE MAYPOLE

On 30 April each year, small groups of people can be seen beside fires, drinking beer and watching over a long, barkless tree trunk. Recovering a tree trunk stolen by the inhabitants of the neighbouring village is rewarded by a large number of barrels (or today, cases) of the Bavarians' favourite drink. Next day the trunk is decorated and ceremonially raised in the village square.

According to tradition, the maypole, the pride of every local community, ensures a successful year. The custom of raising the maypole, the tree of life, goes back to medieval times. Usually painted in the Bavarian colours of white and blue, maypoles are decorated with the emblems of local crafts and crowned with a large wreath. Traditions include dancing round the maypole and climbing up it to reach the prizes tied to the wreath.

Residents of a small town joining forces to raise the maypole

LANDSHUT WEDDING

In 1475, Landshut saw the wedding of Georg, son of Ludwig the Rich, and Princess Jadwiga of Poland, daughter of Casimir Jagiellon. The celebrations lasted eight days, and went down in history as one of the most sumptuous in medieval Bavaria.

Since 1903 the Landshut Wedding (Landshuter Fürstenhochzeit) has been re-enacted every four years on three weekends in June and July. About 100,000 visitors come to enjoy this historic drama. Medieval costumes are worn during the young couple's triumphal procession, which is accompanied by court dances and by tests of the skills of knights and squires.

Christ stumbling under the Cross during the Oberammergau Passion play

THE OKTOBERFEST

This famous beer festival, the world's largest, began in 1810, when Princess Theresa von Sachsen-Hildburghausen married Ludwig (later to become King Ludwig I), the heir to the Bavarian throne. Horse races were organized in a meadow on the edge of Munich, which was named the Theresienwiese in honour of the young lady. It was decided to make this a regular event, and gradually it became customary to organize agricultural shows, which were combined with equestrian events and shooting contests. To these were added roundabouts, beer tents and fireworks, thus giving rise to the present Oktoberfest (it was moved from October to September due to the weather).

Today the Oktoberfest attracts some 6 million visitors from all over the world. Year after year the record for amounts of beer, sausages and roast chickens consumed at the festival is broken. The Oktoberfest opens with a grand procession of waggons of the city's seven main breweries accompanied by folk bands. On the stroke of noon, the city's mayor broaches a barrel of beer to open the two-week revelry surrounding the city's fair.

Folksong and beer – the world-renowned Oktoberfest

THE CHRISTMAS FAIR

Advent, which comes from the Latin *adventus*, "the coming", is the period in the Christian calendar leading up to Christmas. It starts on the fourth Sunday before 24 December. In Bavaria this period is marked with a number of rituals.

Advent candles are lit in churches and in people's houses, and special biscuits known as *Plätzchen* are baked. In the larger towns and cities, market stalls are set up for the Christmas fairs, which are known as *Christkindlmarkt* or *Weihnachtsmarkt*. They begin with the ritual raising of a huge Christmas tree in the brightly illuminated market squares.

Wooden decorations, Nativity figures and all sorts of delicacies and gifts are displayed for sale round the tree. The air is filled with the delicious aroma of freshly baked gingerbread and roasted almonds. The rituals also include drinking hot wine (*Glühwein*) in the frosty air. St Nicholas and the Wicked Witch distribute apples and nuts to children, and the holiday atmosphere is heightened by the joyful singing of carollers. The best Christmas fairs in southern Bavaria are those that are held in Munich, Augsburg and Landsberg.

BAVARIAN FOLK COSTUME

To many people, traditional Bavarian folk costume epitomizes Bavaria. Nowhere else in Europe is traditional costume so widely celebrated, and no other national costume has become so well known in Europe. The traditional men's *Tracht* includes: *Lederhosen*, leather shorts held up by leather braces and sometimes tied up at the knees; the *Janker*, a waistcoat of rough cloth with bone buttons; the *Gamsbart*, a hat with a goat's hair tassel, and asymmetrically tied shoes. Women wear the *Dirndl*, a blouse with puffed sleeves, a corset, a waistcoat, a crimped skirt and an apron. Jewellery and ornaments are an important element of Bavarian costume. Men's trousers are decorated with chains with pendants and their shirts have letters, medallions, coats of arms and embroidery. The women wear intricate necklaces and richly decorated chokers.

Bavarian in national costume

Illuminated tree, the focal point of a Christmas market

MUNICH & THE BAVARIAN ALPS THROUGH THE YEAR

Turnfest mascot

The Bavarian calendar is filled with picturesque rituals, historical spectacles, festivals and trade fairs. The type of event depends on the season, and in Bavaria they are varied indeed. The snowy winter is the season for skiers and tobogganists, while hikers enjoy walking along the scenic and well-marked trails. From springtime onwards, colourful paragliders can be spotted as they soar over mountain peaks, and the appearance of sails heralds the start of the yachting season on the lakes. The summer attracts mountaineers, hikers and watersports enthusiasts. Almost everyone can be seen during the famous Oktoberfest, which starts in the middle of September.

SPRING

Spring comes early here. At the beginning of April, fruit trees are in blossom, Alpine meadows become carpeted with flowers, mostly crocuses, and the melting Alpine snow creates rushing streams. Numerous festive ceremonies mark the Easter period in Bavaria. Easter traditions centre on the symbolism of the egg. Houses are decorated with ornamental twigs with Easter eggs hanging from them, while excited children are up early searching for eggs. In May, the blossom of chestnut trees forms a canopy over reawakening beer-gardens.

Crocus from a meadow

MARCH

Starkbierfest *(between Ash Wednesday and Good Friday)* Munich. The Festival of Strong Beer commemorates the strong ale that was drunk by Pauline monks as they observed the Lenten fast.

APRIL

Biennale *(April/May)*, Munich. Germany's largest contemporary music festival.

Augsburger Plärrer *(two weeks after Easter)*, Augsburg. Biannual event (also held in September). The largest folk festival in Swabia, the counterpart to the Oktoberfest.
Auer Dult (Maidult) *(from the last Saturday in April)*, Munich. Renowned fair held in the Mariahilfplatz in the city's Au district.
Internationale Jazzwoche *(last two weeks in April)*, international jazz festival that takes place in Burghausen.

MAY

Trachten- und Schützenfestzug *(first Sunday in May)*, Passau. Large procession of folk groups and bands from Bavaria and Austria open this annual fair.
Maibaumaufstellen *(May 1)*. Virtually every Bavarian community honours the custom of Raising the Maypole *(see p28)*.

Typical Fronleichnam (Corpus Christi) procession

Maibockausschank *(May 1–14)*, Munich. The occasion when the strong Bockbier is broached. It begins in the Hofbräuhaus to the sounds of a children's orchestra.
Fronleichnam *(Thursday after Trinity Sunday)*. According to Catholic tradition, this religious festival in honour of Corpus Christi is marked by countless processions. The most picturesque are in Lenggries and Bad Tölz.

The Augsburger Plärrer – the biggest traditional holiday in Swabia

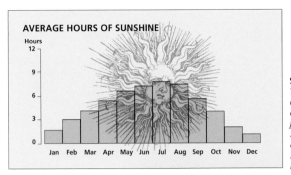

AVERAGE HOURS OF SUNSHINE

Hours

Sunshine
The greatest number of sunny days are concentrated in the period from June to September. May can also be sunny. December is the least sunny month.

SUMMER

On summer days the blue skies over Bavaria reach an almost Mediterranean intensity. Cascades of flowers hang from balconies and window boxes. Bathers and watersports enthusiasts are drawn to the crystal-clear rivers and lakes. Almost every resort has its own summer festival, and these celebrations are particularly impressive when they are held by a lakeside. They feature regattas, firework displays and angling contests.

Agnes Bernauer Festspiele in Straubing

JUNE

Stadtgeburtstag *(one weekend in June)*, Munich. Festival commemorating the foundation of the city.
Filmfest München *(last week in June)*, Munich. One of Europe's liveliest and most important film festivals.
Tollwood Festival *(four weeks June–July)*, Munich, Olympic Park. Festival of jazz, rock and theatre.

JULY

Kaltenberger Ritterspiele *(first 3 weekends in July)*, Kaltenberg Castle, near Landsberg. Jousting tournaments re-enacting medieval traditions.
Münchener Opernfest-spiele *(1–31 July)*, Munich. Festival of classical opera, ballet, singing and music.

Poster for the
Auer Dult fair

Landshuter Hochzeit *(every four years, the next in 2009)*, Landshut. Spectacle commemorating the marriage of Georg, son of Ludwig the Rich, and Princess Jadwiga *(see p28)*.
Schwäbischwerder Kindertag *(1st Wednesday and Sunday in July)*, Donauwörth. Children dressed in historical costume re-enact important events in the history of the town.
Agnes Bernauer Festspiele *(every four years, the next in 2011)*, Straubing. Historical theatre festival telling the story of Duke Albrecht III and Agnes Bernauer, an Augsburg barber's daughter.
Memminger Fischertag *(early July)*, Memmingen. Trout-angling competition.

AUGUST

Auer Dult (Jakobidult) *(July/August)*, Munich. One of three annual fairs held in the Au district of Munich.

Schleißheimer Schloß-konzerte *(July/August)*, Schleißheim. Concerts of classical music.
Gäubodenfest *(around mid-Aug)*, Straubing. Folk festival combined with an agricultural and industrial fair, Bavaria's second largest after the Oktoberfest.
Allgäuer Festwoche *(mid-August)*, Kempten. Exhibition of the Allgäu region's economic and cultural achievements, also including an important folk festival.
König-Ludwig-Feier *(24 Aug)*, Oberammergau. Festival commemorating the death of Ludwig II, who drowned in the Starnberger See. There is singing, dancing and speeches.

Sunflowers, symbols of summer, a common sight in Bavaria

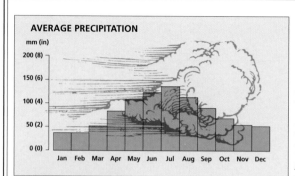

AVERAGE PRECIPITATION

mm (in)

- 200 (8)
- 150 (6)
- 100 (4)
- 50 (2)
- 0 (0)

Jan Feb Mar Apr May Jun Jul Aug Sep Oct Nov Dec

Rain and snowfall
Although the autumn drizzle is the most unpleasant, the heaviest rainfall occurs in summer. Intensive snowfall is common in winter, particularly in the Alps and the foothills.

One of the vast beer tents at the Oktoberfest

AUTUMN

Bavarian autumns are often warm and sunny. The forests turn every shade of red and gold, and mushroom-pickers return with baskets filled with many species of edible fungi. The mountain pastures echo to the sounds of herded cows and sheep.

In autumn the sky becomes dull and overcast, and the shortening days are chilly and damp. The first overnight frosts set in, and mornings often start with a blanket of thick fog, which causes problems for road and air traffic.

SEPTEMBER

Oktoberfest *(16 days leading up to the 1st Sunday in October)*, Munich.
The city's world-famous beer festival, held in the Theresienwiese fairground. Sample beer from all over the world, accompanied by

traditional Bavarian entertainment *(see p29)*.
Viehscheid *(second half of September)*. Traditional celebration of the cattle being brought down from summer pastures in many areas, including Hindelang, Oberstdorf and Königssee.

OCTOBER

Oktoberfest *(see September)*.
Auer Dult (Herbst Dult) *(third Saturday in October)*, Munich. The third of the annual fairs held in the Au district of Munich.
Systems *(third week in October)*, Munich. International IT and telecommunications fair held on the grounds of the Neue Messe in Munich.
Medientage München *(around mid-October)*, Munich. Fair dedicated to the mass media. Discover the latest trends in multimedia and communications.

NOVEMBER

Leonardifahrten und Leonardiritte *(1st Sunday in November)* throughout Bavaria. In many areas, such as Bad Tölz, Schliersee, Murnau and Benediktbeuern, processions on horseback or in painted carts take place in honour of St Leonard, regarded by Bavarians as the patron saint of horses. In Bad Tölz the horses re-enact Christ's journey on the road to Calvary in a procession after receiving a blessing.
St Martin's Day *(11 November)* throughout Bavaria. In almost every town and village processions are held in which children take part, carrying lanterns. Pretzels that they have been given hang from the lanterns. The processions are often led by a horse-rider in a long cloak who represents St Martin.

Bavarian women in a painted cart on St Leonard's Day

AVERAGE MONTHLY TEMPERATURES

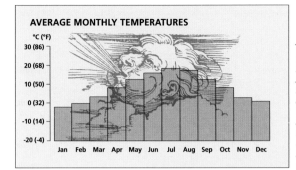

°C (°F)
30 (86)
20 (68)
10 (50)
0 (32)
-10 (14)
-20 (-4)

Jan Feb Mar Apr May Jun Jul Aug Sep Oct Nov Dec

Temperatures
Temperatures are highest in the summer, although temperatures rarely exceed 30°C (86°F). Winters are frosty and snowy, although they can be mild. The coldest temperatures are naturally in the mountains.

WINTER

As autumn draws to a close, people light the Advent candles on the Advent wreaths in their homes every week, while the smell of baking biscuits wafts through the air. At the beginning of December skiers set out on excursions, and if the lakes and canals are sufficiently thickly frozen, they are soon covered with skaters. Winters in southern Bavaria are unpredictable. They may be icy and snowy, or mild and snow-free. December is marked by the carnival spirit. Village carnivals are colourful affairs. At events associated with driving off winter with witchcraft, masks and costumes are a common sight.

The Skifasching (skiing carnival) in Firstalm

PUBLIC HOLIDAYS

Neujahr *New Year*
Epiphany (6 January)
Karfreitag *Good Friday*
Ostern *Easter*
Maifeiertag *May Day*
Christi Himmelfahrt
Ascension
Pfingsten *Whitsun*
Fronleichnam
Corpus Christi
Mariä Himmelfahrt
Assumption (15 August)
Nationalfeiertag
German Reunification Day (3 October)
Allerheiligen *All Saints*
(1 November)
Weihnachten *Christmas*
(25/26 December)

DECEMBER

Tollwood *(throughout December)*, Munich. A major music and arts festival held in Theresienwiese.
Christkindlmarkt *(early December to Christmas Eve)*, throughout southern Bavaria. A Christmas fair inaugurating the Christmas season with the ritual raising of the Christmas tree in the town or village square.

Oberstdorf in winter during the Four Ski-Jump Tournament

Sylvester *(31 December)*. Sumptuous balls and receptions mark the New Year, which is ushered in with lavish firework displays.

JANUARY

Four Ski-Jump Tournament *(1–4 January)*, Oberstdorf, Garmisch-Partenkirchen. Famous ski-jumping tournament.
Schäfflertanz *(Epiphany to Shrove Tuesday)*, Munich. The Dance of the Coopers street festival held every seven years (the next in 2012) to commemorate the passing of the plague in the 15th century.

FEBRUARY

Tanz der Marktfrauen *(last day of Carnival)*, Munich. Market women of the Viktualienmarkt dress up and perform a dance.
Skifasching *(last Sunday of Carnival)*, Firstalm. Bavaria's renowned skiing carnival, including a competition for the best fancy dress. Also held in Garmisch-Partenkirchen.

THE HISTORY OF MUNICH AND BAVARIA

*O*ver the centuries, despite its location in the heart of Europe, southern Bavaria gradually built up its distinct character, becoming a geographically and culturally unified entity. Although it never played a leading role, it was one of the strongest duchies in Germany. The Wittelsbach dynasty ruled Bavaria until 1918, when the Free State of Bavaria (Freistaat Bayern) was proclaimed. After World War II Bavaria opposed centralization.

EARLY SETTLEMENT

The first farming communities settled in southern Bavaria in the 4th millennium BC. Traces of their presence, in the form of the foundations of peasant huts, were found near Kelheim in the 1960s. During the period of the Altheim culture (about 3900–3500 BC), peasant settlements were often surrounded by fortified ditches. During the Bronze Age (1800–1200 BC) the pace of cultural development accelerated, and a wealth of items from burials and many everyday tools of that period have been discovered. During the Hallstatt period, iron began to be used in preference to bronze.

Lion statue outside the Residenz in Munich

THE CELTS

The Hallstatt period was marked by the appearance in Bavaria of the Celts, whose origins are not clear to this day. The Celts were distinguished by their loose tribal and family ties. The Vindelici tribe of Celts settled in the territory between the rivers Inn and Lech, and their capital was Manching, near Ingolstadt. The Bavarian Celts maintained links with the Mediterranean world, particularly with the Etruscans. They imported Etruscan, and sometimes Greek, luxury goods. Many later Bavarian towns, among them Regensburg (Ratisbon), Kempten, Straubing and Passau, were founded by the Celts.

THE ROMAN EMPIRE

In 15 BC the Roman army, under Drusus and Tiberius, conquered the Celts and reached the Danube. This became the frontier of the Roman Empire and a fortified wall was built to defend it. Southern Bavaria was divided into the provinces of Raetia and Noricum. The city of Vindelicorum, today Augsburg, was founded by the Emperor Augustus, whose name it still bears. It became the administrative centre of this part of the Roman Empire.

TIMELINE

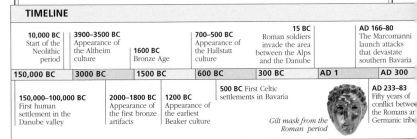

10,000 BC Start of the Neolithic period	3900–3500 BC Appearance of the Altheim culture	1600 BC Bronze Age	700–500 BC Appearance of the Hallstatt culture	15 BC Roman soldiers invade the area between the Alps and the Danube	AD 166–80 The Marcomanni launch attacks that devastate southern Bavaria
150,000 BC	**3000 BC**	**1500 BC**	**600 BC**	**300 BC**	**AD 1**	**AD 300**
150,000–100,000 BC First human settlement in the Danube valley	2000–1800 BC Appearance of the first bronze artifacts	1200 BC Appearance of the earliest Beaker culture	500 BC First Celtic settlements in Bavaria	*Gilt mask from the Roman period*	AD 233–83 Fifty years of conflict between the Romans and Germanic tribes

◁ Portrait of Ludwig I, king of Bavaria (1786–1868)

THE END OF THE ROMAN EMPIRE

After two centuries of peaceful development, Raetia and Noricum were attacked by two Germanic tribes, the Marcomanni and the Alamanni. The first attacks were repulsed by Emperor Marcus Aurelius, but the province suffered destruction in the mid-3rd century by invasions and civil war. Towards the end of the 3rd century stability returned for about 100 years, but after AD 400 a new wave of Germanic invasions toppled Roman control.

From those war-torn and troubled times there are records of the activities of the early Christians – St Afra, the martyr who was burned in Augsburg, and St Severinus, who revived missionary activity in the region.

Roman stella from Augsburg

THE GREAT MIGRATION AND EARLY CHRISTIANITY

The origins of the Bavarians are still imperfectly known. Most historians believe that a new tribe, whom the Romans knew as the Baiovarii, appeared south of the Danube, in the area of present-day southern Bavaria, in 450–550. They are thought to have originated from a Germanic tribe centred in Boiohaemum, what is today the Czech Republic. The Baiovarii were joined by remnants of other Germanic and Celtic tribes and by Romanized people. At the same time, settlers started appearing to the west of the River Lech. The Alamanni tribes became the neighbours of the Baiovarii to the west, while to the north, the region a few dozen kilometres beyond the Danube was conquered by the Franks. This situation continued virtually unchanged to the present day, with the addition of the territories beyond the River Lech and Bavaria's acquisition of the Franconian lands after 1803.

Most of the inhabitants of the region retained their pagan beliefs for some time, and Christianity took hold only very slowly. Irish, Anglo-Saxon and Frankish missionaries started preaching in the region in the early 7th century. At the turn of the 7th century, numerous bishops were active in Bavarian lands: Emmeram in Ratisbon, Korbinian in Freising, and Rupert in Salzburg. In 739 there were bishoprics in Ratisbon, Freising, Passau and present-day Salzburg. They were set up and run by the Anglo-Saxon missionary bishop, St Boniface. It is noteworthy that the importance of their sees continued for the next millennium. A key role in the establishment of Christianity and the nurturing of cultural development from the late 7th century and throughout the 8th century was played by the many Benedictine monasteries, particularly by those of Weltenburg and Benediktbeuern.

Roman mosaic with hunting scenes from a villa near Westerhofen

TIMELINE

450–550 Emergence of the Bavarian tribes	**476** Fall of the Roman Empire	**555** Garibald I becomes Duke of Bavaria	**c. 620** First monastery founded in Weltenburg

400	450	500	550	600	650

400–476 Pressure from Germanic tribes overthrows Roman rule in Bavaria	**482** Death of the missionary St Severinus in Bavaria	**c. 630** Lex Baiuvariorum, the first book of Bavarian law, is written

Fragment from a Longobardi helmet

RULE OF THE BAVARIAN TRIBES

The Duchy of Bavaria was founded in the mid-6th century. The ruling Agilofing dynasty probably originated from the territories of the Merovingian state to the west, and was its vassals. The first known Duke of Bavaria was Garibald I (555–91). According to the *Lex Baiuvariorum*, the first legal code issued in those lands, the ducal throne was to belong to the Agilofing dynasty for all time.

Being dependent on the powerful Merovingians and weaker than the Frankish dukes to the north, Bavaria's Agilofing rulers were forced to resort to constant manoeuvring to retain their position. One of the ways in which they managed to preserve their rule was by strategic marriages with the Allaman, Longobardi and Frankish dynasties. Their activity within the state was limited to military leadership, while in peacetime they took charge of the judiciary. Despite this, the Agilofing dukes played a major role in Bavaria's development. Not only did they lay the foundations of the future state of Bavaria by ensuring its territorial unity, but they also played an important role in championing Christianity.

The main centre of ducal and ecclesiastic power was Ratisbon, on the River Danube. The duchy itself grew slowly and by peaceful means, and almost unnoticed it expanded into

The Cross of Tassilo from the church in Polling

Chalice of Tassilo, c. 777

what was later to become Austria. Under the rule of Tassilo III (748–88), the last ruler of the Agilofing dynasty, the duchy extended as far as Carinthia. However, the growing might of the Agilofing dynasty and of its state alarmed the Frankish ruler Charlemagne, who defeated Tassilo in 788 and in so doing put an end to the Bavarian tribes' first state. Bavaria lost its independence and became part of the Frankish state, while Tassilo himself was confined to a monastery.

After the division of the Frankish empire under the terms of the Treaty of Verdun in 843, Bavaria became one of the centres of the East Frankish Empire (which was the embryo of the later Germany). The Emperor Arnulf of Carinthia resided in Ratisbon at the end of the 9th century.

Initial from an illuminated manuscript, depicting the martyrdom of St Emmeram, Bishop of Ratisbon

A fibula decorated with a geometric pattern

788 Tassilo III is overthrown by Charlemagne

907 Hungarian tribes overrun Bavaria

938 Emperor Otto's campaign against Duke Eberhard of Bavaria

750	800	850	900	950	1000

739 Bishoprics established in Freising and Passau

738 St Boniface begins evangelizing Bavaria

843 Division of the Frankish empire

899 Death of Emperor Arnulf leads to a period of instability

954 Hungarian tribes invade Swabia

Friedrich Barbarossa bestowing power on the Ottonians and Wittelsbachs

THE EARLY MIDDLE AGES

At the end of the 8th century, rulers proceeded to unify the Bavarian tribes and founded a new duchy. Throughout the 9th century the Bavarian dukes were in conflict with the Saxons, who took the Bavarian throne in 919. These conflicts ended in their defeat, and in the 10th century the German kings decided to appoint their own vassals to the Bavarian ducal throne, or to rule the duchy directly.

The following centuries brought a degree of stability with the rule of the Welf dynasty. Duke Henry the Lion founded Munich in 1158 and with the support of Bavaria and his possessions in Saxony waged a war against the Emperor Friedrich Barbarossa. He was finally defeated in 1180, and Bavaria lost the lands east of Salzburg. The same year, Friedrich Barbarossa conferred the title of Duke of Bavaria on Otto I Wittelsbach. This powerful dynasty was to rule Bavaria right up until 1918, a record length of time for any German dynasty. The Wittelsbachs gradually built up their family possessions in central Bavaria, repelling successive attacks by rival families. In 1214 they annexed part of the Rhineland Palatinate, and by 1253 Bavaria was one of the largest ducal territories in the fragmented German empire.

THE LATE MIDDLE AGES

Under Ludwig IV of Bavaria, the duchy was at the height of its powers. Ludwig added the Margravate of Brandenburg, the Tyrol and part of the southern Netherlands to Bavaria. In 1314 he became king of Germany, and 14 years later he was crowned Holy Roman Emperor. External glory was reflected in internal changes. The Emperor introduced civic and land laws, and built up an administrative system with new central institutions.

From the end of the 14th century, tax affairs were decided by representatives of three ranks: knights, clergy and burghers. From the 15th century this group assumed the form of an assembly called the Landtag or Landschaft. After the death of Ludwig IV, Bavaria was shaken by an endless succession of conflicts and local wars.

Late Gothic sculpture from Ottobeuren Abbey

TIMELINE

1070 Bavaria is ruled by the Welfs		**1180** Otto Wittelsbach is made Duke of Bavaria	**c.1200** The final edition of the *Nibelungenlied* appears in Passau		**1328** Ludwig IV of Bava becomes German empe
1100	**1150**	**1200**	**1250**		**1300**
Romanesque stained glass from Augsburg Cathedral	**1158** Foundation of Munich by Duke Heinrich de Löwe			**1255** Munich becomes the capital of the duchy	**1317** Fire destroys a large part of Munich
		1214 The Palatinate is incorporated into Bavaria			

The sons of Ludwig IV attempted to divide the state into small duchies ruled by each of them. In spite of the poverty and sacrifice brought by the resulting wars, this situation had a positive aspect. The division and rivalry of the various ducal courts encouraged the development of culture.

Landshut underwent a period of splendour and in 1475 it was the venue of the sumptuous wedding of the daughter of Casimir Jagiellon, king of Poland (*see p28*). However, in the Swabian territories on the River Lech, territorial disintegration continued in the 15th century. A leading role was played by the empire's principal city, Augsburg. The territory under the control of the Bishop of Augsburg also held a prime position.

Renaissance tombstone from the church in Oettingen

imperial parliament in Augsburg, the Protestants presented the articles of their faith, known as the Confessions of Augsburg, to the Emperor. Some Bavarian Protestants were forced to renounce their faith, while the following edict of 1571 finally removed all supporters of the Reformation from Bavaria. In the war of 1546–7 between Karl V and the Protestant dukes, Bavaria took the Emperor's side. The first Bavarian Jesuits fought actively against the Reformation. The great Michaelskirche in Munich was built in the late 16th century as a symbol of Bavarian Catholicism. In return for their allegiance to Rome, the younger sons of the Wittelsbachs were given sees in the west and north of the Empire, thus further strengthening the position of the Wittelsbachs on the German political scene.

THE RENAISSANCE AND COUNTER-REFORMATION

In 1506 the Bavarian states forced the adoption of a regulation that forbade the division of duchies: from then on, the throne passed to the eldest son. The Bavarian duchies were strengthened by the fact that their lands were not affected by the German peasants' wars of 1524–6.

The rulers of Bavaria were firmly opposed to the Protestantism that was spreading through the territories of Swabia and Franconia. In 1530, at the

Handing the Confessions of Augsburg to Emperor Karl V

1385 The first residence in Munich is built by Duke Stephan III

1516 The dukes of Bavaria issue the Reinheitsgebot, the world's first decree, enforced to this day, on brewing beer

1530 Protestants submit the Confessions of Augsburg to Karl V at the imperial parliament

| 1350 | 1400 | 1450 | 1500 | 1550 |

1369 The population of Munich exceeds 10,000

Martin Luther, father of the Reformation

1506 The states of Bavaria issue a decree forbidding the division of the country

1517 Luther's 95 "theses" launch the Reformation

1555 The imperial parliament declares the Religious Peace of Augsburg

THE AGE OF MAXIMILIAN I

Duke Wilhelm V, who came to the throne in 1579, brought the state to the edge of bankruptcy, abdicating in 1598 in favour of his son Maximilian I (1573–1651). During his 54-year reign, Maximilian reorganized the administration of the state and the military, streamlined the fiscal system and reigned in a kind of early absolutism. In the face of worsening religious and political conflicts in the empire, which ultimately led to the outbreak of the Thirty Years' War, Maximilian I took charge of the Catholic camp. In 1618 he supported the Habsburgs against the rebellious Bohemian state, and Bavarian troops played a decisive role in the defeat of the Bohemians at the Battle of White Mountain in 1620.

Bust of Maximilian I

As a reward for his part in this victory, Maximilian I was given the title of Prince Elector in 1623. The lands of the Upper Palatinate, which were added to Bavaria, were subjected to a brutal regime of re-Catholicization. During the second part of the Thirty Years' War, attacks by Swedish and Franco-Swedish forces caused a great deal of devastation and severely impoverished the country.

Finally, thanks to French support, Maximilian succeeded in retaining all conquered lands and the title of Elector at the peace congress in Münster. Pro-French policy would dominate Bavarian policy from then up until German Unification in 1871.

Maximilian's style and method of rule were emulated by later Bavarian leaders, including Duke Maximilian Montgelas and Franz-Josef Strauß. Bertel Thorvaldsen's equestrian statue of Maximilian in Munich commemorates his achievements.

DREAMS OF POWER

Maximilian II Emanuel, who married the daughter of the Polish king Jan III Sobieski, was known as the "White Knight". One of the most colourful figures in Bavaria's history, he had dreams of great conquests and of winning the crown. He allied himself with the Viennese court, and took part in the Battle of Vienna, where the Turks were defeated, in 1683. He was rewarded with the regency of the southern Netherlands. Entangled in the Wars of the Spanish Succession, he changed sides and in 1702 formed an alliance with Louis XIV.

However, in 1704 the Franco-Bavarian

Maximilian Emanuel receiving a Turkish emissary after his victory at Vienna

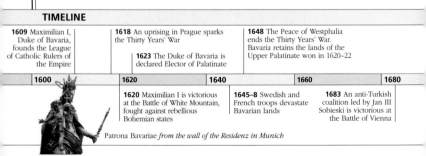

Patrona Bavariae from the wall of the Residenz in Munich

army was defeated by Habsburg troops and Maximilian II Emanuel fled to France. Bavaria then suffered ten years of harsh Austrian rule during which protests by desperate peasants were suppressed with bloodshed.

Rococo window arch at the Residenz in Munich

Maximilian II Emanuel did not return to the elector's throne until a peace treaty was signed in 1714. Although he was a prominent patron of the arts and a popular leader, his lengthy and turbulent rule had weakened Bavaria's position.

REFORM, ANNEXATION AND ENLIGHTENMENT

Rococo monstrance from Passau

In 1740–45, despite Maximilian II Emanuel's disastrous anti-Habsburg policy, his son Karl Albrecht made a further attempt to become involved in the Austrian succession. As Karl VII, Emperor of the Holy Roman Empire, he was, however, unable to repel the troops of Maria Teresa. At the Treaty of Füssen in 1745, his successor Maximilian III Joseph was forced to renounce claims to the Austrian throne.

During the long and peaceful reign of Maximilian III Joseph, in which the ideology of enlightened absolutism was put into practice, there were important agricultural reforms, as well as the foundation of the Bavarian Academy of Sciences in 1759. Another development was the famous Nymphenburg porcelain factory.

The king's death in 1777 ended the direct Wittelsbach line. Emperor Joseph II's orders to annexe Bavaria caused Prussian objections and led to the accession of Karl Theodor, an indirect descendant of the ruling family of the Palatinate. Karl Theodor continued his predecessor's policy of enlightenment, while the spirit of scientific enquiry was cultivated in Bavarian abbeys, which contributed to knowledge and culture.

With the outbreak of the Napoleonic Wars (1799–1815), Bavaria tried to remain neutral but was unable to protect its possessions in the Palatinate from French occupation.

Ornamental interior of the church of Weltenburg Monastery, one of many built in the Baroque period

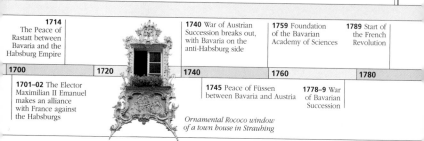

1714 The Peace of Rastatt between Bavaria and the Habsburg Empire		**1740** War of Austrian Succession breaks out, with Bavaria on the anti-Habsburg side	**1759** Foundation of the Bavarian Academy of Sciences	**1789** Start of the French Revolution
1700	**1720**	**1740**	**1760**	**1780**
1701–02 The Elector Maximilian II Emanuel makes an alliance with France against the Habsburgs		**1745** Peace of Füssen between Bavaria and Austria	**1778–9** War of Bavarian Succession	

Ornamental Rococo window of a town house in Straubing

The Wittelsbach Dynasty

In 1180 Bavaria was given in lien to Otto I Wittelsbach, whose family ruled Bavaria until 1918. In 1329 the family was divided into a Bavarian and Palatinate line, which branched out even further. The Wittelsbachs occupied the German imperial throne on two occasions (in 1328 and 1742). In 1806 Napoleon proclaimed Maximilian I Joseph king. The family traditionally patronized the arts, which reached their apogee in the 19th century. The decline of the Wittelsbach dynasty began with Ludwig II, the "dilettante" king, and finally ended with the abdication of Ludwig III.

Wilhelm IV (1508–50) periodically shared his rule with his brother, Albrecht IV.

Otto II (1231–53) reformed the administrative and judicial system.

Otto I (1180–83) was the first Wittelsbach on the Bavarian throne.

Ludwig II, the Severe (1253–94) shared power with his brother Henry XIII. He moved the duchy's capital from Landshut to Munich.

Stephan II (1347–75) was one of six sons of Ludwig IV, who shared power among themselves.

Albrecht III, the Pious (1438–60) secretly married Agnes Bernauer, a baker's daughter, who was drowned in the Danube on his father's orders.

1150	1225	1300	1375	1450	152

1150	1225	1300	1375	1450	152

Ludwig I of Kelheim (1183–1231) extended Bavarian territory into the Rhineland Palatinate. He was stabbed on the bridge at Kelheim by an unknown assassin.

Johann II (1375–97), son of Stephan II, built the new Residenz in Munich with his three co-ruling brothers.

Ernest (1397–1438) ruled Bavaria for over 40 years, averting wars and conflicts.

Albrecht IV, the Wise (1467–1508) was the first humanist to occupy the Bavarian throne. He ended the influence of the Italian Renaissance.

LVDOVICVS.IV. IMP.P.F. AVG:DVX.BOIOR. ✝1347.

Ludwig IV of Bavaria (1294–1347) was crowned king of Germany in 1314. He became Emperor in 1328, and this brought him into conflict with the Pope.

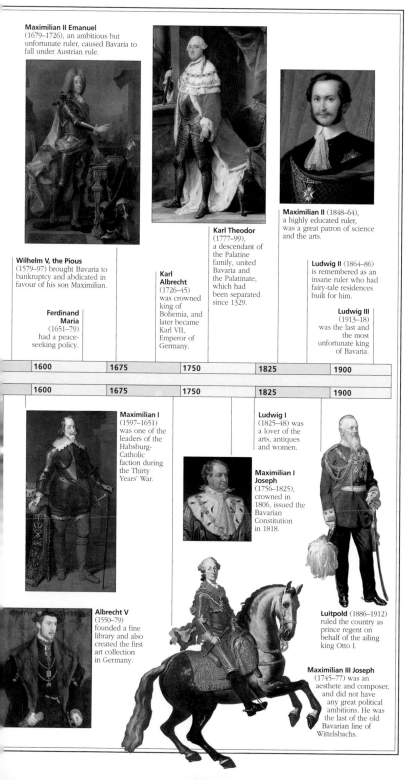

Maximilian II Emanuel (1679–1726), an ambitious but unfortunate ruler, caused Bavaria to fall under Austrian rule.

Wilhelm V, the Pious (1579–97) brought Bavaria to bankruptcy and abdicated in favour of his son Maximilian.

Ferdinand Maria (1651–79) had a peace-seeking policy.

Karl Albrecht (1726–45) was crowned king of Bohemia, and later became Karl VII, Emperor of Germany.

Karl Theodor (1777–99), a descendant of the Palatine family, united Bavaria and the Palatinate, which had been separated since 1329.

Maximilian II (1848–64), a highly educated ruler, was a great patron of science and the arts.

Ludwig II (1864–86) is remembered as an insane ruler who had fairy-tale residences built for him.

Ludwig III (1913–18) was the last and the most unfortunate king of Bavaria.

1600	1675	1750	1825	1900
1600	1675	1750	1825	1900

Maximilian I (1597–1651) was one of the leaders of the Habsburg-Catholic faction during the Thirty Years' War.

Ludwig I (1825–48) was a lover of the arts, antiques and women.

Maximilian I Joseph (1756–1825), crowned in 1806, issued the Bavarian Constitution in 1818.

Albrecht V (1550–79) founded a fine library and also created the first art collection in Germany.

Luitpold (1886–1912) ruled the country as prince regent on behalf of the ailing king Otto I.

Maximilian III Joseph (1745–77) was an aesthete and composer, and did not have any great political ambitions. He was the last of the old Bavarian line of Wittelsbachs.

The Wittelsbach rulers of Bavaria

GOLDEN AGE OF THE WITTELSBACHS

The modern state of Bavaria was established at the beginning of the 19th century and it has survived more or less intact to this day. In 1803 Napoleon dissolved the German Empire's old territorial structures, and with his approval in 1803–06 Bavaria doubled its territory, incorporating the Swabian lands up to Ulm, and the Franconian lands. In 1806 Maximilian Joseph, again with Napoleon's approval, was crowned king, acquiring the title of Maximilian I Joseph.

Territorial expansion was accompanied by far-reaching internal reforms. In 1803 Maximilian I Joseph and his aide Count Maximilian Montgelas disbanded the monasteries and

Maximilian I Joseph, king of Bavaria

reorganized the country's administration. In late 1813 they deftly switched allegiance from Napoleon to the anti-Napoleonic coalition. Thus, at the Congress of Vienna they were able to retain the bulk of the territory that they had acquired with Napoleon's aid.

From 1815 to 1866 the Bavarian kings manoeuvred between the Prussians and Austrians, managing to conduct an independent foreign policy. This ended when the Prussians defeated the Bavarian-Austrian alliance.

In the latter half of the 19th century Bavaria made significant cultural and political advances. Education was developed and the re-established University of Munich flourished. Thanks to Ludwig I, Munich acquired impressive new parks, gardens and buildings. The visual arts and drama flourished, briefly overtaking those of Vienna and Berlin. Maximilian I Joseph's reign saw great progress in science and industry, and the emergence of "Maximilian" architecture. Ludwig I's patronage of the arts was continued by his grandson Ludwig II.

In 1866 Bismarck forced Bavaria to join the Prussian camp, which was supported by groups from the state bureaucracy and Franconian Protestant quarters.

Cartouche with Bavarian crest

TIMELINE

1803 Montgelas dissolves the Bavarian monasteries	**1813** Bavaria joins the anti-Napoleonic coalition	**1818** Bavaria becomes a constitutional monarchy	**1848** The revolution in Munich leads to the abdication of Ludwig I	
1800	**1815**	**1830**	**1845**	
1805 Bavaria forms an alliance with Napoleon	**1806** Bavaria becomes a kingdom	**1815** At the Congress of Vienna, Bavaria retains almost all its territorial gains from the Napoleonic period	*The dancer Lola Montez, mistress of Ludwig I*	

UNDER PRUSSIAN RULE

Their country's participation on the victors' side in the Franco-Prussian war of 1870–71 won many Bavarians over to the idea of a unified Germany. Ludwig II, who ruled Bavaria at the time, increasingly avoided any involvement in politics and escaped more and more into the world of Wagner's music, tales of chivalry and fairy-tale castles. The day-to-day running of the country was left to an anonymous group of government officials in Munich.

When the regency was taken over by Prince Luitpold after Ludwig II's tragic death, little changed. Luitpold, a popular ruler, attempted to offset political dependency on Berlin with a liberal cultural policy which contained a distinct anti-Prussian element. Under Luitpold's rule, Munich enjoyed the highest period of cultural and artistic development that it has ever experienced. Luitpold's son and heir, Ludwig III, who was thoroughly pro-Prussian, quickly lost his popularity.

After Germany's defeat at the end of World War I, on 7 November 1918 the rule of the Wittelsbachs in Munich was overthrown, and the Free State of Bavaria (Freistaat Bayern) was proclaimed. This has been Bavaria's official name ever since. Between February and May 1919 the far-left Bavarian Soviet Republic ruled Munich and part of Bavaria. This weakened Bavaria's moderate forces and radicalized the right, which started to embrace extremist groups, such as Hitler's. In the general ferment of the Weimar

Ludwig II, much admired among Bavarians

Republic, Bavaria became a bastion of stability, with a slightly dictatorial right-wing government. The failure of Hitler's attempted putsch in 1923 helped to stave off Nazism for a while, but the mild sentences imposed on the leaders of the fascist Brownshirts only helped to increase their popularity.

From 1923 to 1933 the country was ruled by the Bavarian People's Party, whose policy was to oppose that of liberal and "red" Berlin. However, attempts to weaken Prussia's position in the Reich were unsuccessful, and political and cultural decline ensued. From 1918 to 1933 Munich's position as a cultural metropolis was taken over by Berlin.

Cartoon from a 1908 issue of the satirical journal *Simplicissimus*

The Castles of Ludwig II

King Ludwig II of Bavaria, fondly known as "Kini" to his subjects, has remained a cult figure to this day. With his mad fantasies and lack of interest in politics, he seemed to come from another world. The king's passions were architecture and music, and his friendship with Richard Wagner influenced his entire life. He dragged the country into financial ruin as he built one magnificent country home after another, all the while dreaming of new ones. Gradually he became withdrawn and, deemed insane, was finally removed from power. At the age of 42 he drowned in the Starnberger See in mysterious circumstances.

This turret is reached by a spiral staircase leading from a picturesque gallery.

Ludwig II's Night Sleigh Ride
This painting by Richard Wenig, and the actual sleigh, can be seen in the Marstall-museum in Nymphenburg. The king adored his nocturnal escapades, which helped him avoid the harsh realities of daylight.

Throne Room of Neuschwanstein Castle
The Throne Room was designed in Byzantine style. It is decorated with gilded mural paintings, mosaics and a huge chandelier. A splendid gold and ivory throne planned for Ludwig II (see p230) was never made.

The Minstrels' Room is a lavishly painted official reception room.

NEUSCHWANSTEIN CASTLE

The castle was built in 1868–86. Assisted by the painter and designer Christoph Jank, Ludwig II fulfilled his vision of an old German castle, although he only lived here for 172 days.

The Linderhof Grotto
Built in the park, complete with stalactites, the grotto covers a lake 3 m (10 ft) deep. Ludwig II reached it in a gilded barge, which rocked on artificially created waves (see pp216–17).

Hall of Mirrors in Herrenchiemsee Palace

This showcase gallery was built in 1879–81 along the side of the palace facing the garden. Almost 100 m (328 ft) long, it outstrips the Hall of Mirrors at Versailles, on which it is based. The ceiling frescoes glorify Louis XIV, and night-time concerts (see p202) were illuminated with 1,848 candles placed in the gilded candelabras and chandeliers.

Moorish Hall in Schachen

With its fountain, rich carpets, ottomans, gilded candelabra and vases, the hall of this palace conjures up The Tales of the Thousand and One Nights (see p217).

The upper courtyard leads into the main part of the castle, containing the reception room and apartments.

The gatehouse, flanked by turrets and set with crenellations, is decorated with the royal coat of arms.

LUDWIG'S CASTLES

Ludwig II was obsessed with creating the perfect residence. In Alpine surroundings he built Neuschwanstein Castle *(see p240)*. His fascination with the world of the Bourbons was expressed in the Linderhof *(see pp216–17)* and Herrenchiemsee *(see p202)* palaces.

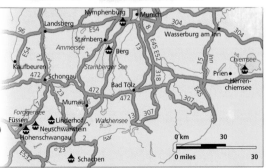

Adolf Hitler signing the Munich Agreement

IN THE SHADOW OF THE NAZIS

The rulers of Bavaria underestimated the danger of the burgeoning Nazi movement. The participants in Hitler's 1923 putsch were given light sentences, with Hitler spending only eight months behind bars. In 1925 the NSDAP (Nazi Party) was reactivated, and in 1926 the ban on public speeches by Hitler was lifted. By 30 January 1933 Hitler had seized power, and in March he overthrew the Bavarian government and stripped Bavaria of its autonomy. Munich became Capital of the Movement; the Führer wanted it to become the Reich's ideological and cultural centre. The first concentration camp was built in nearby Dachau. During the Winter Olympics in Garmisch-Partenkirchen and the Summer Olympics in Berlin in 1936, the Nazis were at pains to present a positive image to the world. In 1937 Hitler embarked on an overt clamp-

Concentration camp prisoner's shirt

down in cultural policy. An exhibition of Degenerate Art was held in Munich, and later in other cities, its aim being to stigmatize modern "degenerate" art. The Haus der Kunst was built for annual exhibitions of German art. The large-scale redevelopment of Munich began, and the Königsplatz became the venue for Nazi rallies.

In 1938 the Munich Agreement, by which Czechoslovakia was partitioned, was signed and two years later the first Allied bombs fell on Munich. Hitler was associated with Bavaria until the end of his life, frequently visiting its capital and his residence near Berchtesgaden. Relatively few Bavarians spoke out against Hitler, a notable exception being the White Rose student group, and the opposition movement did not play a significant role here. In April 1945 an attempt was made to organize the final resistance here, but Hitler's "Alpine Fortress" ultimately proved to be of no use.

Hikers at the Kehlsteinhaus, the surviving part of Hitler's residence

TIMELINE

	1934 Hitler abolishes independence of German states, including Bavaria	30 April 1945 American troops enter Munich		14 June 1958 Celebrations mark Munich's 800th anniversary	1972 20th Olym Games hel Mur
	29 September 1938 Munich Agreement	1 October 1946 The first elections in Bavaria bring victory to the CSU			

1930	1935	1940	1945	1950	1955	1960	1965

30 January 1933 Hitler becomes Chancellor of the Reich		1 September 1939 German attack on Poland launches World War II	14 September 1949 Appointment of the government of the Federal Republic of Germany	1957 The population of Munich reaches 1 million	1966 Constructi the Munich U-Bahn an S-Bahn begins
		February 1936 – the 4th Winter Olympics are held in Garmisch-Partenkirchen			

Oktoberfest – the world's best-known beer festival

MODERN BAVARIA

The ravages of war were less severe in Bavaria than they were in other parts of Germany. In April and May 1945 Bavaria was occupied by American troops and until 1949 it formed part of the American occupation zone. Despite a great influx of displaced people, most of Bavaria's inhabitants were spared the worst of postwar deprivation because of the agricultural strength of the region. The Federal Republic of Bavaria, set up in 1949, made efforts to take an independent position as the region with the best preserved sense of historical and geographical identity, and constantly opposed any attempts at centralization. One of the external manifestations of this trend towards autonomy was the success that the local

Christian Democrats had in keeping their own organization distinct from the CDU (Christian Democratic Union), and in setting up their own CSU (Christian Social Union). It ruled Bavaria continuously from 1949. The main figure in the CSU, until his death in 1988, was the temperamental Franz-Josef Strauß, an unquestioned leader of the German right.

The CSU, appealing to regional tradition even to the extent of anti-Prussian separatist sentiment, skilfully pursued a policy of industrialization after 1960. Electronics and computer manufacture developed strongly, as did the car manufacturers BMW and Audi. During the 1972 Summer Olympics, the region glittered not only with its celebrated modern architecture, but also with its openness and liberalism. The Olympic ideal of peace was, however, marred by bloodshed in an attack by Palestinian separatists.

Franz-Josef Strauß

In the years leading up to the reunification of Germany, Munich was regarded as "Germany's secret capital". But 1989 and the revival of Berlin's role means that Munich and Bavaria now face fresh challenges.

FC Bayern Munich, one of the world's best soccer teams

1974 The 10th World Soccer Championship finals are held in Munich

1980 Pope John Paul II visits Altötting during his pilgrimage to Germany

1992 The opening of Munich's new airport

The BMW logo, one of the symbols of modern Bavaria

2008 Munich celebrates its 850th birthday

1975	1980	1985	1990	2000	2005	2010	2015	2020

Poster for the Munich Olympics

1988 Death of Franz-Josef Strauß

3 October 1990 Reunification of Germany weakens Bavaria's political role

2004 Munich hosts the EuroGames

2006 Germany hosts the FIFA World Cup. The opening ceremony is held in Munich's Allianz arena

MUNICH
AREA BY AREA

Munich at a Glance

Munich is Germany's third-largest city, and
before the fall of the Berlin Wall it was
dubbed the "unofficial capital of the country".
Another name for it was the "village with a
million inhabitants". Its metropolitan bustle,
prosperity and high-tech industries exist alongside a rural, traditional atmosphere. The city
has many parks, including the landscaped
Englischer Garten, with the pretty River Isar
that flows through it, and on fine days there
are splendid views of the Alps, all of which
combine to give the capital of Bavaria its
unique atmosphere. It is also a city of culture.
Munich has many historic
monuments as well as
outstanding museums
and art galleries and
several theatres.

Alte Pinakothek
Susanna and the Elders *by Albrecht
Altdorfer is one of the gallery's
masterpieces of German
Renaissance art* (see pp118–21).

The Glyptothek
*Peace, a Roman
copy of a sculpture
by Cephisodotus, is
one of the many
classical sculptures
on display in the
Glyptothek, built by
Ludwig I specifically
to house such works
of art* (see p116).

**THE MUSEUMS
DISTRICT**
(See pp110–27)

Theatinerkirche
*This elegant
Baroque church
with its twin-
towered façade is
a prominent
feature of the city's
skyline* (see p79).

**OLD
TOWN
(SOUTH)**
(See pp54–69)

Asamkirche
*The interior of the
Church of St Johann-
Nepomuk exemplifies
Baroque illusionism.
Space, architectural
elements, stuccowork,
frescoes and the inter-
play of light and shadow
combine to create the
illusion of wave-like
motion* (see pp66–7).

0 metres   750

0 yards   750

Siegestor
Based on the Arch of Constantine in Rome, this is a monument to the Bavarian army. It is crowned by a statue symbolizing Bavaria riding in a chariot drawn by four lions (see p104).

THE UNIVERSITY DISTRICT
(See pp98–109)

Bayerisches Nationalmuseum
This museum contains interiors taken from elsewhere in Bavaria and preserved in their entirety. An example is the Gothic Weberstube from Augsburg (see pp108–9).

Friedensengel
The Angel of Peace, standing on the right bank of the Isar, can be seen from afar. The column, 18m (59 ft) high, is topped by a gilded bronze angel (see p92).

AROUND THE ISAR
(See pp86–97)

LD TOWN (NORTH)
ee pp70–85)

Maximilianeum
This building, in what is known as the Maximilian style, now houses the Bavarian parliament (see p91).

The Residenz
The Brunnenhof is one of the seven courtyards in the Residenz. It takes its name from the Mannerist Wittelsbach Fountain (Brunnen) that stands in the centre (see pp74–7).

OLD TOWN (SOUTH)

Three gates, the Karlstor, Sendlinger Tor and Isartor, mark the boundary of the southern part of the Aldstadt (Old Town). Marienplatz is the main square in this district, and it is also the central point of the whole of Munich. Marienplatz was once a market square, and it has witnessed all of the most important events in Munich's history.

Both tourists and local people come to admire the many fine

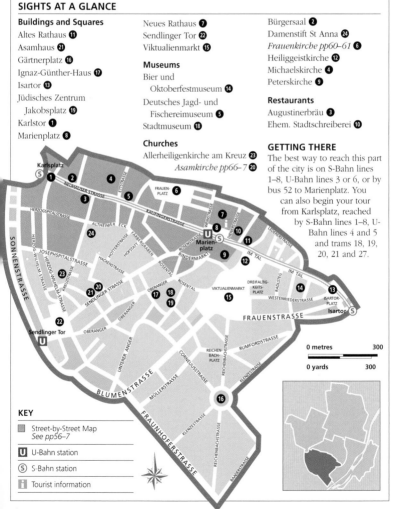

Putto from the plinth of the Mariensäule

historic buildings, including the Frauenkirche, with its distinctive outline, and Peterskirche, the city's oldest church. South of Marienplatz is the Angerviertel. Because it was safe from flooding by the River Isar, this area was chosen by the legendary monks who founded Munich and gave the city its name. Life in the Angerviertel centres around the Viktualienmarkt, which has been held here for almost 200 years.

SIGHTS AT A GLANCE

Buildings and Squares
Altes Rathaus ⑪
Asamhaus ㉑
Gärtnerplatz ⑯
Ignaz-Günther-Haus ⑰
Isartor ⑬
Jüdisches Zentrum
 Jakobsplatz ⑲
Karlstor ①
Marienplatz ⑧

Neues Rathaus ⑦
Sendlinger Tor ㉒
Viktualienmarkt ⑮

Museums
Bier und
 Oktoberfestmuseum ⑭
Deutsches Jagd- und
 Fischereimuseum ⑤
Stadtmuseum ⑱

Churches
Allerheiligenkirche am Kreuz ㉓
Asamkirche pp66–7 ㉔

Bürgersaal ②
Damenstift St Anna ㉔
Frauenkirche pp60–61 ⑥
Heiliggeistkirche ⑫
Michaelskirche ④
Peterskirche ⑨

Restaurants
Augustinerbräu ③
Ehem. Stadtschreiberei ⑩

GETTING THERE
The best way to reach this part of the city is on S-Bahn lines 1–8, U-Bahn lines 3 or 6, or by bus 52 to Marienplatz. You can also begin your tour from Karlsplatz, reached by S-Bahn lines 1–8, U-Bahn lines 4 and 5 and trams 18, 19, 20, 21 and 27.

KEY

▢	Street-by-Street Map *See pp56–7*
U	U-Bahn station
Ⓢ	S-Bahn station
ℹ	Tourist information

◁ **The Fish Fountain on Marienplatz, which has been redesigned with 19th-century elements**

Street-by-Street: Around Marienplatz

Virgin on the Mariensäule

Ever since Munich was founded, Marienplatz has been the city's architectural and commercial hub. The geographical centre of the city is marked by the Mariensäule (Column of the Virgin), from which all distances in Munich are measured. The square and the streets around it, which have been pedestrianized since the Munich Olympics in 1972, are always full of visitors. In one hour up to 18,000 tourists and shoppers pass through this area, rising to 22,000 on Saturdays.

Karlstor
This gate was retained when the old city walls were demolished in 1791 **①**

Asamkirche ↓

Bürgersaal
The austere façade of this church is decorated by a statue of the Madonna and Child by Franz Ableitner set over the portal **②**

Neuhauser Straße
is Munich's largest shopping street. It is filled with typical 19th-century buildings and with cafés and shops that enjoy the highest turnover in the whole of Germany.

Augustinerbräu
This pub, one of the oldest in Munich, has elaborate interior decoration and a picturesque beer-garden courtyard **③**

STAR SIGHTS

★ Frauenkirche

★ Michaelskirche

★ Neues Rathaus

KEY

– – – Suggested route

★ Michaelskirche
The nave of the Church of St Michael, roofed by impressive barrel vaulting, is separated from the presbytery by a triumphal arch **④**

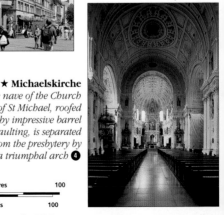

| 0 metres | 100 |
| 0 yards | 100 |

Deutsches Jagd- und Fischereimuseum
The German Hunting and Fishing Museum, located in a former Augustinian church, is reached from the presbytery side **5**

LOCATOR MAP
See Street Finder, maps 3, 5 & 6

★ Frauenkirche
The figure of the Madonna and Sorrowful Christ comes from a 13th-century basilica. The Baroque gates were carved by Ignaz Günther **6**

★ Neues Rathaus
The figures in the New Town Hall's chiming clock enact a joust and perform the Dance of the Coopers **7**

Peterskirche
The high altar of the Church of St Peter is decorated with a figure of the saint carved by Erasmus Grasser. Around it are the four Church Fathers, by Egid Quirin Asam **9**

Altes Rathaus
The tower of the Old Town hall was reconstructed after World War II on the basis of plans dating from 1493 **11**

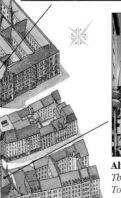

KAUFINGERSTR.

ROSENSTR.

MARIENPLATZ

RINDERMARKT

Heiliggeistkirche

Karlstor ❶
Karl's Gate

Karlsplatz 5. **Map** 3 A2 (5 A2).
Ⓢ or Ⓤ *Karlsplatz-Stachus.*
🚊 *18, 19, 20, 21, 27.*

A vestige of the medieval
town's fortifications, this
gate stands at the western
entrance to the Old Town.
Originally known as the
Neuhauser Tor, the gate
received its present name in
1791 in honour of Elector Karl
Theodor, who recommended
the demolition of the old walls
to enable the city to expand.

Initially, the Karlstor had
three towers. The tallest of
them, the central tower, was
destroyed in 1861 when the
gunpowder that was stored
there exploded. The gate
was rebuilt, to a Neo-Gothic
design by Domenico Zanetti.
The bronze figures in the
walls of the arches were
taken from the old fountain
in Marienplatz in 1865.

**The medieval Karlstor, seen
from the Old Town**

Bürgersaal ❷

Neuhauser Str. 14. **Map** 3 A2 (5 B3).
Tel 21 99 720. Ⓢ or Ⓤ *Karlsplatz-
Stachus.* 🚊 *16, 17, 18, 19, 20, 21,
27.* **Lower church hall** ◯ *8am–
8pm daily.* **Upper church hall**
◯ *11am–1pm daily.*

The name of this church
reflects its original purpose as
the headquarters of the Marian
congregation. It was designed
by Giovanni Antonio Viscardi
and consecrated in 1778. The
rather austere façade fronts a
two-storey interior. The **lower
church** contains the tomb of
the beatified Rupert Mayer, a
staunch fighter against the

The dazzling interior of the Bürgersaal, featuring 19th-century frescoes

Nazis. The **upper church**,
which was the main meeting-
place of the Marians, glitters
with Rococo stuccowork by
Joseph Georg Bader and
paintings by Anton von
Gumpp, among others.
During World War II the
interior was damaged by fire,
and some of the decoration
has been restored. Surviving
original features include the
bas-relief on the high altar by
Andreas Feistenberger, dating
from 1710, the famous
Guardian Angel of 1763 and
the group of figures crowning
the pulpit by Ignaz Günther.

Augustinerbräu ❸
Augustine Brewery

Neuhauser Str. 27. **Map** 3 A2 (5 B3).
Tel 23 18 32 57. Ⓢ or Ⓤ *Karlsplatz-Stachus.* 🚊 *16, 17, 18, 19,
20, 21, 27.* ◯ *9am–midnight.* 🔟

Two adjoining houses with
picturesque 19th-century
façades form part of the
oldest brewery in Munich.
The Augustinerbräu was
founded by Augustinian

Alfresco seating outside the Augustinerbräu

monks and was mentioned as
early as 1328. The historic
interior of the brewery hall is
a fine and today rare example
of the aesthetics and atmosphere of a Munich restaurant
pre-dating World War I. An
unusual feature is the
Muschelsaal (Shell Hall),
whose walls are lined with
seashells, pebbles, decorative
mouldings, busts and antlers.
The brewery is divided into a
restaurant and beer hall, with
a delightful beer garden.

Michaelskirche ❹
St Michael's Church

Neuhauser Str. 6. **Map** 3 B2 (5 B3).
Ⓢ or Ⓤ *Karlsplatz-Stachus.*
🚊 *18, 19, 20, 21, 27.* ◯ *7am–
4:30pm Mon–Fri; 8am–4pm Sun.*

The founder of this church,
built for the Jesuit order,
which was active in this area
from 1559 onwards, was Duke
Wilhelm V. Construction began
in 1585, but when the tower
collapsed in 1590, it was
decided to enlarge the transept
and to add a choir to designs
by Friedrich Sustris.
The Michaelskirche,
which aimed to
bolster the Counter-
Reformation and
reinforce the Jesuits'
presence, is the largest
late-Renaissance reli-
gious building north
of the Alps. It is remi-
niscent of the church
of Il Gesú in Rome.
The three-tier
façade, with its
double doorway,
is an outstanding

example of Mannerist architecture. Between the pilasters there are windows and rows of niches containing the figures of Bavarian and imperial rulers engaged in the expansion and defence of Christendom. The ground floor is dominated by a bronze figure of St Michael slaying the Dragon, with a figure of Christ the Saviour on his shield, made by Hubert Gerhard in 1585. The two portals, designed by Friedrich Sustris, lead in to a strikingly spacious interior. The barrel vaulting over the nave spans the second-largest space after St Peter's Basilica in Rome. The elongated choir ends with the massive high altar, where a painting by Christoph Schwarz depicts the fall of the rebellious angels. In the crypt beneath the choir lie members of the Wittelsbach family, including Maximilian I and Ludwig II, and the church's founder. Beside the church is a monastery and a college. The latter was built in 1585–97, also by Sustris. It is known as the Alte Akademie.

Statue from the Michaelskirche

Deutsches Jagd- und Fischerei- museum ❺
German Hunting and Fishing Museum

Neuhauser Str. 2. **Map** 3 B2 (5 B3). *Tel* 22 05 22. Ⓢ or Ⓤ Marienplatz. 🚋 16, 17, 18, 19, 20, 21, 27. ⏰ 9:30am–5pm Fri–Wed; 9:30am–9pm Thu. ♿

The largest collection of field sports equipment in the world is displayed in a white Augustinian basilica. The building's ecclesiastical origins are concealed by the shops in the aisle, through which the museum is entered from the street. The church was built in the late 13th century. It was rebuilt several

times, and became the first building in Munich to be decorated in the Baroque style. In 1911 it was convert- ed into a concert hall, and in 1966 the collection of the German Hunting and Fishing Museum, founded in 1938, was moved here from Schloss Nymphenburg. The collection includes hunting weapons, bags and sleighs, and 1000 stuffed animals and birds in re-creations of their natural surround- ings. There are also trophies and pictures of hunting scenes. The angling section illustrates the development of fishing tackle, and shows numerous specimens of fish.

Frauenkirche ❻

See pp 60–61.

Neues Rathaus ❼
New Town Hall

Marienplatz 8. **Map** 3 B2 (6 D3). *Tel* 23 300. Ⓢ or Ⓤ Marien- platz. 🚻 🔲 **Viewing tower:** ⏰ Nov– Apr: 10am–5pm Mon–Fri; May–Oct: 10am–7pm daily. **Clock chimes:** Nov–end Feb: 11am & noon; Mar–Oct: 11am, noon & 5pm.

In the second half of the 19th century, the civic authorities decided to build new headquarters for them-

selves. The chosen site was the south side of Marienplatz and 24 houses were demo- lished to clear a large plot of land. Construction lasted from 1867 to 1909. This monu- mental building with its six courtyards is a prime example of German pseudo-historical architecture, in this case mock-Netherlands Gothic. The decoration of the façade abounds in sculptures alluding to Bavaria's legends and history, images of local saints and many allegorical figures. The steeple is topped by a bronze figure of the Münchner Kindl (Munich Child), the symbol of the Bavarian capital. The clock in the tower is the fourth-larg- est chiming clock in Europe. Every day a concert is played on its 43 bells, with coloured copper figures dancing to its rhythms. The figures dance in two scenes – a knightly tournament of honour of the wedding of Duke Wilhelm V and Renata of Lotharingia, and the Schäfflertanz, or Dance of the Coopers (see pp32–3), which is performed in the streets of Munich to this day to commemorate the passing of an epidemic of the plague in 1515–17. In the evening, in the bays of the tower's seventh storey, appear the figures of a night- watchman blowing on his horn and the Angel of Peace blessing the Münchner Kindl. The spectacular viewing tower commands a fine view of the city.

The Neues Rathaus, a highly ornamented 19th-century public building

Frauenkirche ❻

A medallion from the façade

The Frauenkirche, the largest Gothic building in southern Germany, was built in just 20 years from 1468–88, a record time for the period. It stands on the site of an earlier Romanesque parish church.

The imposing triple-naved brick building was begun by Jörg von Halsbach, and was continued after his death by Lucas Rottaler. The domes that crown the west towers, rising to a height of almost 100 m (330 ft), were not completed until 1525. Since 1821, the Frauenkirche has been the seat of the archbishopric of Munich and Freysing.

The onion domes crowning the towers are typical of the Renaissance.

The façade has a rather severe aspect. The towers have blind windows at their angles and are pierced by arched doors and windows that echo the shape of the central portal.

Entrance

View of the Church
With its twin towers, the church's distinctive silhouette is Munich's oldest and best-known symbol. By law, no new building that may obscure the view of the church is allowed.

STAR FEATURES

★ Emperor's Tomb

★ Stalls

★ Statue of St Christopher

★ Emperor's Tomb
A Mannerist canopy of black marble covers the tomb of Emperor Ludwig IV of Bavaria. The sarcophagus is surrounded by the figures of four kneeling knights, personifications of War and Peace, and putti.

Chorhauptkapelle
This painting by Jan Polack (c.1510), in the main chapel of the choir, shows the Virgin protecting members of the patrician Sänftl family.

VISITORS' CHECKLIST

Frauenplatz 1. **Map** 3 B2 (5 C3).
Ⓢ or Ⓤ *Marienplatz.*
52 19. ◯ 7am–7pm
Sat–Wed, 7am–8:30pm Thu,
7am–6pm Fri. 2pm daily.
Tower Apr–Oct:
10am–5pm, except Sun
and public holidays.

★ Statue of St Christopher
This carved statue, made in a local workshop c.1525, is an example of the dramatic style of the late Gothic period.

★ Stalls
Like the other figures that decorate the stalls, this bust of St James was made by Erasmus Grasser.

Cathedral Interior
Legend tells that the cathedral's builder wagered with the Devil that no window could be seen from within. From the spot where the Devil made his footprint, only a wall of pillars is seen.

"Memminger Altar"
This altar was built in 1994, incorporating reliefs by Ignaz Günther and a Rococo Madonna.

Marienplatz, Munich's bustling and historic central square

Marienplatz ❽
St Mary's Square

Map 3 B2 (6 D3).
Ⓢ or Ⓤ *Marienplatz.* 🚊 *Dec.*

Ever since the city was planned by Heinrich der Löwe, Marienplatz has been Munich's focal point. Until 1807 it was a market-place. It acquired its present name in 1854, when Munich's citizens asked the Virgin Mary to protect them from a cholera epidemic. For centuries the square was the place where major public events, proclamations, tournaments and executions took place. Today it is the venue for the famous Christkindlmarkt (Christmas Fair), which is held in the days leading up to Christmas. The square is dominated by the Neues Rathaus (New Town Hall).

Crowds of tourists and local people gather in the square every day to watch the mechanical figures on the clock tower perform their concert. The Mariensäule (Column of the Virgin) in the square was erected in 1638 in gratitude for the end of the Swedish invasion.

The golden statue of the Virgin (1590) is by Hubert Gerhard and the four putti around the plinth (1638) are by Ferdinand Murmann. The putti are shown overcoming hunger, war, heresy and pestilence. Another attraction of the square is the 19th-century Fischbrunnen (Fish Fountain), which was rebuilt after being destroyed in World War II.

Peterskirche ❾
St Peter's Church

Rindermarkt 1. **Map** 3 C, D2 (6 D3).
Ⓢ or Ⓤ *Marienplatz.* **Church**
◻ *7am–7pm daily.* **Tower** ◻
9am–7pm Mon–Sat, 10am–7pm Sun & public hols (to 6pm in winter).

St Peter's Church, standing on the highest point of the Old Town, is Munich's earliest public building. Built in the 12th century, the basilica formed part of the monastery from which the city received it's name (*Mönchen* meaning "monks"). In 1278–94 it was replaced by a new church in the Gothic style. In the 14th century the twin towers of the west front were replaced with a single tower. In the 17th century the church was redecorated in Baroque style, and in the 18th century was remodelled in the Rococo

The Peterskirche, with its famous tower, Munich's oldest church

style. The stuccowork is by Johann Baptist Zimmermann and others. The church's famous tower, known as Alter Peter (Old Peter), has eight clocks, seven bells and a viewing gallery that offers a splendid view over the Old Town. The interior of the church has unusually lavish decoration. The high altar is crowned with a statue of St Peter (1492) by Erasmus Grasser, surrounded by the Church Fathers (1732) by Egid Quirin Asam. The choir contains five figures (1517) by Jan Polack with scenes from the life of St Peter.

Late Gothic side entrance to the Ehem. Stadtschreiberei

Ehem. Stadtschreiberei ❿
Former City Writers' Guild

Burgstraße 5. **Map** 3 C2 (6 D3).
Tel *24 21 04 44.* Ⓢ or Ⓤ
Marienplatz. **Restaurant**
◻ *11am–10pm daily.*

A visit to Munich's oldest surviving town house is the perfect excuse to enjoy a beer and some food in a late Gothic cloistered courtyard. In 1510 the town council bought this pair of houses between Burgstraße and Dienerstraße. The house on Burgstraße, rebuilt in 1551/2, housed the offices of the city writers' guild (Stadtschreiberhaus) from 1552–1612. The house has an interesting façade with a large window in the centre. The perfectly preserved large main doorway conceals the entrance passage.

For hotels and restaurants in this region see pp262–5 and pp276–9

To the right of the façade is a small late Gothic side entrance framed by a donkey-back arch. The façade, which had been under restoration, was unveiled in 1964, revealing most of the restored Renaissance decoration executed by Hans Mielich in 1552. An attractive addition to the courtyard is a late Gothic tower with a spiral staircase.

Altes Rathaus ⓫
Old Town Hall

Marienplatz 15. **Map** 3 C2 (6 D3).
Ⓢ or Ⓤ *Marienplatz*. ⬛ to visitors. **Spielzeugmuseum Tel** 29 40 01. ◯ 10am–5:30pm daily. ⬛

The original Old Town Hall, dating from 1310, was replaced by a new one in 1464 which is known today as the Altes Rathaus (Old Town Hall). It was built by Jörg von Halsbach, who also built the Frauenkirche. The town hall was rebuilt on many occasions, most recently in 1861–4, when it acquired its present Neo-Gothic character. In 1877 and then in 1934 two gateways were cut through in order to accommodate the increasing flow of traffic.

Clock on the tower of the Altes Rathaus

The oldest part of the building is the tower of 1180–1200, part of the original city fortifications. Since 1983 it has housed the **Spielzeugmuseum** (Toy Museum), which as well as antique doll's houses, tin cars and copper soldiers contains a display tracing the history of the Barbie doll.

The Gothic interior of the Altes Rathaus survives. The ceremonial hall occupying the ground floor has wide wooden barrel vaulting, and a wall with a frieze of 96 coats of arms dating from 1478. There are plans to use this hall to exhibit the Dancing Moors (Moriskentänzer) that Erasmus Grasser carved in 1480. The figures currently on display here are copies of the originals that can be seen in the Stadtmuseum.

The Pentecost, by Ulrich Loth, in the Heiliggeistkirche

Heiliggeistkirche ⓬
Church of the Holy Spirit

Im Tal 77. **Map** 3 C2 (6 D3).
Ⓢ or Ⓤ *Marienplatz*.
◯ 7am–noon and 3–6pm daily.

The Church of the Holy Spirit is one of Munich's oldest buildings, ranking in importance alongside the Cathedral and the Peterskirche. It stands on the site of a chapel, a hospital and a pilgrims' hostel. In the mid-13th century a hospital church was built here. This was replaced by a church in the 14th century. In 1724 the church was decorated in the Baroque style. The fine vaulting and stuccowork are by the Asam brothers. In 1729 a tower was added. Its Neo-Baroque façade dates from 1895, when the hospital next to the church was demolished.

The interior of the church is a fine example of the combination of Gothic and late Baroque elements. The ceiling frescoes depict scenes from the hospital's history. The high altar was made by Nikolaus Stuber and Antonio Matteo in 1728–30 and rebuilt after World War II.

Original elements of the altar include the painting of the Pentecost (1644) by Ulrich Loth and the flanking angels by Johann Georg Greiff. The bronze figures in the vestibule (1608) by Hans Krumpper originally formed part of the tomb of Ferdinand of Bavaria.

Isartor ⓭
Isar Gate

Tal 50. **Map** 3 C3 (6 E4). Ⓢ *Isartor*.
⬛ **Valentinmusäum Tel** 22 32 66.
◯ 11am–5:30pm Mon & Tue, 11am–6pm Fri & Sat, 10am–6pm Sun (open till 10pm first Fri of every month).

Entry into the city from the southeast is through the Isartor. This gate is the only vestige of the city's original fortifications, and it has been preserved in its original form. The central tower was built in 1337, and in 1429–33 two eight-sided towers, connected by walls, were added. In the 19th century arcades were made in the towers. They were decorated with friezes representing the triumphal procession of Ludwig IV of Bavaria after his victory at the Battle of Ampfing (1322).

The southern tower houses the **Valentin-Karlstadt-Musäum**, a museum dedicated to the actor and comedian Karl Valentin (1882–1948), a master of the absurd who wrote theatre sketches and short films. The collections include many of his scenes, among them *The Vesuvius that Doesn't Smoke Because it is Forbidden in the Museum* and *The Hook on which the Artist Hung his Learned Profession.*

The central fortified tower of Isartor

Bier und Oktober-festmuseum ⓮

Sterneckerstr. 2. **Map** 3 C3. *Tel* 24 23 16 07. Ⓢ or Ⓤ *Isartor.* 🚊 17, 18. ◯ 11am–5pm Wed–Sun. 🎫 ♿

A colourful stall at the popular, lively and historic Viktualienmarkt

The building housing the Bier und Oktoberfestmuseum was constructed under the city expansion scheme, spearheaded by Ludwig IV of Bavaria, after the great fire of 1327.

The museum covers both the history of beer and the Oktoberfest, telling the story of how the festival is an important part of Munich's tradition. Visitors can learn how beer was first made in ancient Egypt, as well as how the beer-making process developed in Munich itself. Up until 1870, beer was only brewed in the city during the winter months, as ice from the lakes was necessary for the cooling process. After the invention of refrigerators, beer began to be brewed all year round, with a rapid expansion in the number of breweries in Munich. At one time there were as many as 70 breweries in the ancient city; today just six remain.

A tankard from the Bier und Oktoberfestmuseum

Visitors will also get to see a collection of artefacts from Oktoberfests over the years, including a vast collection of beer tankards. The museum has a restaurant serving beer and typical Bavarian snacks.

Viktualienmarkt ⓯

Food Market

Between Petersplatz and Frauenstr. **Map** 3 C3 (6 D4). Ⓢ or Ⓤ *Marienplatz.* 🚊 52.

This is Munich's oldest and most picturesque market. Since the beginning of the 19th century food of all kinds has been sold here – fruit and vegetables, milk, meat, the finest French wines and cheeses, fish and shellfish and exotic delicacies from all corners of the world, albeit at fairly high prices. All sorts of people, from ordinary shoppers to tourists, can be seen here. Local customs include eating white sausage (Weißwürst), sipping hot soup and drinking beer in a beer-garden around a decorated maypole. The last day of the carnival is famed for the masked dance of the market women. The fountain that was erected to commemorate various German cabaret artists, such as Karl Valentin, emphasizes the popular nature of the square.

Gärtnerplatz ⓰

Road map 3 C3 (6 D5). Ⓤ *Frauenhoferstr.* 🚊 17, 18. 🚌 52. **Gärtnerplatztheater** *Tel* 21 85 19 60, evenings 20 24 11. **Box office** ◯ 10am–6pm Mon–Fri, 10am–1pm Sat. **Jüdisches Museum** St-Jakobs-Platz 16. *Tel* 23 32 81 89. ◯ 2–6pm Tue, 10am–noon, 2–6pm Wed, 2–8pm Thu.

The hexagonal square lying at the intersection of Reichenbachstraße, Corneliusstraße and Klenzestraße is named after the prominent 19th-century architect Friedrich von Gärtner. It is the focal point of the district known as the Gärtnerplatzviertel, which was built in the second half of the 19th century. It was the first large district of purpose-built apartment blocks in Munich to be designed in a unified style.

In 1864–5 a theatre was built on the south side of Gärtnerplatz. It was designed by Franz Michael Reiffenstuel and was known as the Gärtnerplatztheater. It was a slightly less up-market response to the courtly Nationaltheater. Its decorative façade stands out among the somewhat monotonous architecture that surrounds it. The **Gärtnerplatztheater** stages minor operas, operettas and musicals. Nearby is the **Jüdisches Museum** (Jewish Museum), which traces the history of the Jews in Bavaria.

Ignaz-Günther-Haus ⓱

Ignaz Günther House

St-Jakobs-Platz 15. **Map** 3 B3 (5 C4). *Tel* 23 32 29 94. Ⓢ or Ⓤ *Marienplatz.* Ⓤ *Sendlinger Tor.* ◯ 9am–3pm Mon–Fri.

Ignaz Günther (1725–75) was one of Europe's finest Rococo sculptors. He worked throughout southern Germany, but primarily in Munich. His work can be seen in the Peterskirche, Bürgersaal, Frauenkirche, the grounds of Schloss Nymphenburg and Schleißheim Palace as well as the churches and abbeys of Upper and Lower Bavaria. In

The 19th-century Gärtnerplatz, a green space in the city

1754 he became court sculptor to the Wittelsbachs. He moved into the house on St Jakob's Platz in 1761.

The Ignaz-Günther-Haus is a very fine example of late Gothic residential architecture. It still has its small courtyard with a central fountain. The reception room on the first floor has an early 16th-century wooden ceiling. The façade on the side of the Oberanger contains a statue of the Virgin carved by Günther and known as the Hausmadonna. This is a copy of the original, which is housed in the Bayerisches Nationalmuseum in Munich.

The house and studio of the renowned sculptor Ignaz Günther

Stadtmuseum ⑱

Town Museum

St-Jakobs-Platz 1. **Map** 3 B3 (5 C4).
Tel 23 32 23 70. Ⓢ or Ⓤ Marien-platz. Ⓤ Sendlinger Tor.
🕓 10am–6pm Tue–Sun. 📷

Six adjoining buildings house the Town Museum. Two of them, the Marstall and the Zeughaus, were built in the 15th century as granaries but later became the city's stables and arsenal. During the rebellions of 1848 the citizens of Munich broke into the Zeughaus tower. However, the weapons that they found there had rusted and were useless.

In the second half of the 19th century, this arsenal building was used as a display space for the embryonic museum of local history. At this time a major campaign was under way to collect antique objects from the city's inns and attics, hospitals, orphanages, churches and pawnshops.

In addition to the 1,500 objects that were amassed in this way, a huge collection of etchings with a Munich theme was purchased. The Museum of History finally opened in 1888. As the collection grew, a total of four additional wings were added to the original buildings. The museum was given its present name in 1954.

The Stadtmuseum as it is today is divided into specialized sections, each of which operates independently, organizing various temporary exhibitions. As well as permanent exhibitions of old weapons, crafts, folk art, townscapes and collections of posters, there are the collections of the Puppet Theatre and Museum of Musical Instruments, the Photographic Museum and the Fashion Museum. Amateur filmmakers can view the rare film archives of the Film Museum, which enjoys international renown, especially for reconstructions of silent films. Those interested in interior design will be drawn to the Urban Interiors section. Undoubtedly the most valuable and intriguing items in the museum are the ten famous Moriskentänzer (Dancing Moors), made by Erasmus Grasser in about 1480. These were originally designed for the ceremonial hall of the Old Town.

Jüdisches Zentrum Jakobsplatz ⑲

Jewish Centre Jakobsplatz

St.-Jakobs-Platz 16. **Map** 3 B3 (5 C4).
Ⓢ or Ⓤ Marienplatz. **Tel** 23 39 60 96. 🕓 Jewish Museum 10am–6pm Tue–Sun. 📷 www.juedisches-zentrumjakobsplatz.de www.juedisches-museum.muenchen.de

The recently inaugurated Main Synagogue Ohel Jakob, the Jewish Community Centre of Munich and Upper Bavaria, and the Jewish Museum, constitute a prestigious new centre for the Jewish community at St. Jakobsplatz. Commissioned with the design of the entire complex were the Saarbrücken based architects Wandel, Hoefer and Lorch.

The Jewish Museum is housed in a cube-shaped, free standing building. The transparent ground floor lobby, glazed on all sides, emphasizes the museum's role as a place for open discussion. Three floors of exhibitions, plus a library and a learning centre, all offer extensive information on Jewish culture and history and highlight important aspects of contemporary Jewish life.

The Synagogue, also cube-shaped, is crowned by a light-flooded roof. The Community Centre contains the administrative department, the rabbinate, conference rooms, a kindergarden, a public full-time school, a youth and arts centre and a kosher restaurant. With this combination it reflects the religious, cultural and social demands of contemporary life.

Model of a shop with wax figures, an exhibit at the Stadtmuseum

Asamkirche ⑳

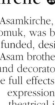

The Asamkirche, or Church of St Johann-Nepomuk, was built in 1733–46. It was funded, designed and executed by the Asam brothers, the most famous builders and decorators of the time. Drawing on the full effects of Baroque artistic expression, they created a mysterious theatrical illusion of another world.

Angel on the confessional The façade, set upon a plinth that imitates natural stone, gives no hint of the splendour within. The nave, with its low-key lighting, is full of striking architectural details, rich stuccowork and masterpieces of fresco painting.

Count Zech's Epitaph
This fine Rococo epitaph, made by Ignaz Günther in 1758, depicts the Grim Reaper taking away someone's life. It stands in the church vestibule.

Statues above the Doorway
The arch over the doorway depicts St John Nepomuk surrounded by cherubs and two angels symbolizing the Secrecy of the Confession and the Profession of Faith.

Church Interior
The exquisite combination of architecture, painting, light and shadow draws attention away from the proportions of the interior. The nave is 28 m (92 ft) long and just 8.80 m (29 ft) wide, proportions that were dictated by the relatively small ground space available.

Bas-relief on the West Doors
The top right-hand carving on the doors of the west façade depicts St John Nepomuk being thrown into prison.

STAR FEATURES

★ High Altar

★ Painted Ceiling

Entrance

★ Painted Ceiling

The ceiling is covered with accomplished trompe-l'oeil paintings executed by Cosmas Damian Asam in 1735. They depict scenes from the life and martyrdom of St John Nepomuk.

VISITORS' CHECKLIST

Sendlinger Str. 32. **Map** 3 A3.
🚇 *Sendlinger Tor.* 🚋 16, 17, 18, 27. 🚌 52, 152. ⏰ 8am–5:30pm daily. ✝ 5pm Mon–Fri; 6pm Sat, 9am, 10:30am Sun

Detail of the Gallery
The undulating gallery that encircles the interior divides the walls of the nave and the high altar into two distinct parts.

★ High Altar

The high altar contains a glass sarcophagus in which lies a robed wax figure of a prelate representing St John Nepomuk.

Pulpit
The pulpit is reached directly from the adjacent presbytery to the east. It is surrounded by a relief with scenes from the life of St John the Baptist and symbols of the Evangelists.

Façade of the Asamhaus, lavishly decorated with allegorical scenes

Asamhaus ㉑

Assam House

Sendlinger Str. 34. **Map** 3 A3 (5 B4). U *Sendlinger Tor.* 16, 17, 18, 27. 52, 152. to visitors.

It would be difficult to find a more unusual artist's home. While Cosmas Damian Asam decided to settle in the suburban Maria Einsiedel Palace, which he renovated, his brother Egid Quirin Asam purchased four adjoining properties on Sendlinger Straße in 1729–33. He converted them into his own residence, with a church and presbytery in addition.

This was the first time that an artist had built his own house next to a church of his own design (there was even an interior window looking from the house towards the high altar).

Egid Quirin Asam added stucco decorations to the medieval façades, depicting Christian and Classical motifs – personifications of the fine arts, poetry and music are watched over by St Joseph, patron saint of craftsmen, who is surrounded by symbols of Faith, Hope and Mercy. A relief depicting Perfection and the initials IHS crowning the entire imagery symbolize the Christian concept of heaven.

On the left the artist gives a vision of the world of Antiquity, whose ideals were adopted by Baroque artists. Thus Pallas Athenae leads a childlike figure into the world of art and science under the

aegis of Pegasus, with Apollo watching over them all. These visions are complemented by the world of sensations, which are represented by Cupid, satyrs and fauns.

Sendlinger Tor ㉒

Sendlinger-Tor-Platz. **Map** 3 A3 (5 A4). U *Sendlinger Tor.*

The southern end of the bustling thoroughfare known as Sendlinger Straße passes through a large Gothic city gate that is overgrown with vines.

The Sendlinger Tor was first mentioned in 1318 and, with the Karlstor and Isartor, this gate is all that remains of the secondary city fortifications that were built in 1285–1347 during the reigns of Ludwig II the Severe and Ludwig IV of

Bavaria. An important trade route to Italy via Innsbruck once passed along here.

The tall gatehouse that formerly stood in the centre of the Sendlinger Tor was demolished in 1808. The octagonal tower which then functioned as a gatehouse dates from the end of the 14th century. In 1906, because of the increasing volume of traffic, the three arches were converted into a single large arch, with pedestrian arches made through the side towers.

Beyond the gate is Sendlinger Tor Platz, a square named after the tower. It is one of Munich's crossroads, with pedestrian subways leading to the metro station. The Sonnenstraße, which continues from here, was the first 19th-century thorough-fare to be built along the

The medieval Sendlinger Tor, now overgrown with vines

course of the old city walls. Its name, meaning "sun street", reflects its bright, open design compared with the narrow, shady passages of the Old Town. Sendlinger-Tor-Platz has a park on the west side with St Matthew's Church rising over it.

Baroque tombstone set into the façade of the Allerheiligenkirche

Allerheiligenkirche am Kreuz ㉓
All Hallows' Church

Kreuzstr. 10. **Map** 3 A3 (5 B4).
U Sendlinger Tor, Karlsplatz-Stachus.
○ 8am–8pm daily.

All Hallows' Church was built in 1478 by Jörg von Halsbach, and was the first cemetery church in the parish of St Peter. In the past, four streets converged here, hence the name "am Kreuz" ("at the crossing").
    The church's bare brick walls, Gothic vaults and tall steeple make it a prominent landmark in Kreuzstraße. The interior was refurbished during the Baroque era, so that the only vestiges of its Gothic appearance are the web vaulting over the nave, fragments of a fresco of Christ in a mandorla and a crucifix made by Hans Leinberger in 1520.
    Fine examples of the transitional style of art that developed between the Mannerist period and led into the Baroque can be seen in the tomb of the banker Gietz

(1627) by Hans Krumpper, and in the depiction of the Virgin appearing before St Augustine on the high altar, which was created by Hans Rotten-hammer in 1614.
    Today Aller-heiligenkirche is a Uniate (Greek Catholic) church.

Baroque doorway of the Damenstift St Anna

Damenstift St Anna ㉔
Church of St Anne

Damenstiftstr. 1. **Map** 3 A2 (5 B3).
U Karlsplatz-Stachus, Marienplatz.
○ 8am–8pm daily.

Princess Henrietta of Savoy, founder of the Theatine Church, brought the Salesian order of sisters to Munich in 1667. During the 18th century the order acquired its own church, which was designed by the Gunetzrhainer brothers. In time the convent passed into the hands of an order of aristocratic ladies, hence the name "Damenstift". Today the building houses a

high school for girls. The façade is in the late Baroque style, as is the opulent decoration of the interior, which was executed by the Asam brothers. After suffering total destruction during World War II, the painting inside the church was restored in sepia, as black-and-white photographs were the only existing record of the original decorative scheme. The paintings depict the oath of angels, the Glory of St Mary and St Anne, and the concert of angels (above the gallery). The realistic group of the Last Supper to the right of the high altar is unusually lifelike. The life-sized statues sitting at the table and gesticulating were probably copied from Spanish originals. This single-nave church, with side chapels behind mighty arches and a presbytery at one end, is a typically Baroque attempt to combine the centrally planned church with the elongated model.

The intersecting interior spaces of the Baroque Damenstift St Anna

OLD TOWN (NORTH)

Royal orb

The northern part of the Old Town (Altstadt) was once defined by the fortified city walls. Today it is enclosed by the Altstadtring (ring road). The principal thoroughfares traversing the Old Town are Theatinerstraße and Residenzstraße. West of Theatinerstraße is the old Kreuzviertel district, with Promenadeplatz its hub.

The Old Town has modern shopping streets, and also many fine 17th- and 18th-century palaces and churches – two of them being the Theatinerkirche and Dreifaltigkeits-

kirche. To the east lies the former Graggenau district. At the Alter Hof (Old Court), the first seat of the Wittelsbach family, there is a maze of medieval streets and buildings, among which is the Hofbräuhaus, Munich's most renowned brewery. The majestic Residenz overlooks the Hofgarten (Palace Gardens).

Max-Joseph-Platz, a stately square surrounded by fine Neo-Classical buildings, marks the beginning of the grand Maximilianstraße, which is a practical example of 19th-century ideals of integral town planning.

SIGHTS AT A GLANCE

Churches
Dreifaltigkeitskirche ⑬
Salvatorkirche ⑦
Theatinerkirche
  (St Cajetan) ⑥

Museum
Literaturhaus ⑪

Garden
Hofgarten ㉓

Restaurants
Hofbräuhaus ⑱

Theatres
Münchner Kammerspiele
  im Schauspielhaus ⑳

Historic Buildings
Alter Hof ⑰
Eilles-Hof ③
Erzbischöfliches Palais ⑧
Feldherrnhalle ⑤

Künstlerhaus ⑫
Marstall ㉑
Münzhof ⑯
Palais Neuhaus-Preysing ⑩
Palais Porcia ⑨
Palais Törring-Jettenbach ⑮
Preysing Palais ④
Residenz (pp74–7) ①
Bayerische Staatskanzlei ㉒

Streets and Squares
Max-Joseph-Platz ②
Maximilianstraße ⑲
Promenadeplatz ⑭

0 metres	200
0 yards	200

GETTING THERE

This part of the city is served by U-Bahn lines 3–6, bus 100 alighting at Odeonsplatz, or tram 19, alighting at the Nationaltheater. You can also begin your tour from the Karlsplatz, which is served by S-Bahn lines 1–8 or U-Bahn lines 4 and 5, and trams 16, 17, 18, 19, 20, 21 or 27.

KEY

▪ Street-by-Street map
  See pp72–3

Ⓤ U-bahn station

🚊 Tram stop

🚓 Police station

◁ **The Theatinerkirche, built on the model of San Andrea della Valle in Rome**

Street-by-Street: Around the Residenz

Painting from the Palais Törring-Jettenbach

The Residenz is set in the most elegant part of Munich, an area characterized mainly by the Wittelsbach residences, numerous Baroque palaces and the fine silhouettes of the Theatinerkirche and the opera house. The streets leading to the Altstadtring are lined with cafés and shops selling luxury goods. This area is also the centre of Munich's cultural life, with several theatres as well as concert and banqueting halls within the residences themselves.

Salvatorkirche
Until the end of the 18th century this old chapel stood in the middle of the city cemetery. It is now a Uniate church ❼

★ Theatiner-kirche
The Baroque coat of arms on the façade of the Theatine Church, designed by Ignaz Günther, features the crests of Bavaria and Saxony ❻

Erzbischöfliches Palais
The façade of the Archbishop's Palace was decorated by the great stuccoist Johann Baptist Zimmermann ❽

Eilles-Hof
The arcades of this enchanting late Gothic courtyard, hidden behind the Residenzstraße, are an oasis of peace ❸

Max-Joseph-Platz
This monument to Maximilian I Joseph was erected in the square ten years after the king's death. He had opposed it, believing that the pose did not convey sufficient majesty ❷

KEY

– – – Suggested route

For hotels and restaurants in this region see pp262–5 and pp276–9

Feldherrnhalle

This hall was built in 1841–44 in honour of Johann Tilly and Karl Philipp von Wrede, the Bavarian field marshals after whom it is named. Their statues stand inside the loggia ❺

LOCATOR MAP
See Street Finder maps 3, 5 & 6

Preysing-Palais

This was the first late Baroque palace in Munich to be decorated with Regency elements. It is also the first work of the court architect Joseph Effner ❹

★ Residenz

The wooden carvings that decorate the interior of the Residenz's Cuvilliés-Theater feature allegories of the arts and mythology ❶

STAR SIGHTS

★ Residenz

★ Theatinerkirche

| 0 metres | 50 |
| 0 yards | 50 |

The Nationaltheater doubles as the National Opera. It was famed for operas by Richard Wagner staged here for Ludwig II.

Residenz **❶**

Baroque vessel in the Silberkammer

The Residenz was the home of the Wittelsbach dynasty up until 1918. The buildings date back to 1385, when the Neufeste was built in the part of Munich enclosed by city walls. In the 16th century the Antiquarium and another wing were added, creating the Grottenhof courtyard. The Kaiserhof was added in the 17th century. After rebuilding in the Baroque and Rococo periods, the ensemble was enclosed by Königsbau and Festsaalbau in the 19th century.

★ **Hofkapelle**
The Princely Chapel, with intricate ceiling stuccowork, was designed by Hans Krumpper in 1601–3.

Staatliches Museum Ägyptischer Kunst
houses a fine collection of Egyptian art.

Kaiserhof

Patrona Bavariae
The 17th-century façade is decorated with a bronze statue of St Mary, patron saint of Bavaria, by Hans Krumpper.

Grottenhof
The courtyard contains a grotto decorated with volcanic crystals and colourful seashells, and a gilded bronze sculpture of Mercury.

STAR FEATURES

★ Antiquarium

★ Hofkapelle

★ Schatzkammer

Nibelungensäle
This mural by Julius Schnorr von Carolsfeld, showing Hagen von Tronje defeating Siegfried, is one of the paintings of the Nibelungenlied.

★ Antiquarium
Built in 1569–71, this great hall is the largest Renaissance ceremonial hall north of the Alps, and the oldest surviving part of the Residenz.

Apothekenhof

Cuvilliés-Theater
The Residenz's old theatre is one of the finest Rococo theatres in the world.

Brunnenhof

★ Schatzkammer
The crown and orb of the Bavarian kings were made by Martin Guillaume Biennais in 1806 when Bavaria was recognized as a kingdom and Maximilian I was proclaimed king. However, the coronation itself did not take place.

★ Schatzkammer
This 17th-century ornamental cup is made of rhinoceros horn and gold-plated silver. It can be admired here alongside numerous other works of art.

Exploring the Residenz

Baroque clock by H. Manlich

A thorough exploration of this unusual palace takes a few days. The first parts to see are the three monumental façades and the many courtyards that are open to the public. The interior of the Residenz is open to the public as the Residenz-museum. It is divided into a section open in the morning and another open in the afternoon. There is separate admission to the Schatzkammer, the Cuvilliés-Theater, the collections of Egyptian art and of coins.

The Grottenhof, which exudes an air of cool Mannerist elegance

THE COURTYARDS

The courtyard that lies on the side of the Residenzstraße features two Mannerist doorways with figures representing the four cardinal virtues: Justice, Prudence, Fortitude and Temperance.

The south doorway leads into the Kapellenhof (Chapel Yard). It is enclosed by the Residenz's tower, built in 1615. The Grottenhof (Grotto Court) is visible through the gates to the right. This Mannerist courtyard, designed by Friedrich Sustris, encloses the Perseus Fountain.

The north doorway leads to the Kaiserhof, the centre of that part of the Residenz that was built in Maximilian style in the early 17th century. This leads in turn to the monumental Apothekenhof, which is closed on its northern side by Festsaalbau (Ceremonial Hall Wing) of 1835–42.

Parallel to the Antiquarium is the elongated octagonal Brunnenhof, with the famous Wittelsbach Fountain by Hans Krumpper and Hubert Gerhard (1611–23). It shows Otto I surrounded by personifications of the rivers of Bavaria.

MUSEUMS AND ROOMS OPEN IN THE MORNINGS

Access to the Residenz-museum is from Max-Joseph-Platz and through Königs-bau, built by Leo von Klenze in 1826–35. Visits start from the vestibule and the two garden halls leading to the Ahnen-galerie (Ancestral Gallery) with its lavish stuccowork and 121 portraits of the Wittelsbachs. After passing François Cuvilliés' porcelain cabinet, visitors reach the Grottenhof and the Antiquarium, the

Tureen from the Silberkammern

The Grüne Galerie, an example of Rococo interiors at their finest

oldest part of the Residenz, which was built in 1568–71 for Prince Albrecht V. The first floor once housed a library and a richly decorated reception hall containing classical sculpture. The final room on this floor is the Schwarzer Saal (Black Hall) of 1590, with trompe-l'oeil paintings on the ceiling. It in turn leads to the Gelbe Treppe (Yellow Stairs), where there is a statue of Venus Italica by Antonio Canova, and rooms in which European and Oriental porcelain and Persian divans are displayed.

Beyond the bedrooms of Maximilian III Joseph and his wife, designed by Cuvilliés in 1763, is the Allerheiligengang (All Saints Passage). It is decorated with 18 paintings by Carl Rottmann, which were moved here from the Hofgarten arcades in 1966. The Charlottentrakt that leads away from here is named after Princess Karoline Charlotte Auguste von Bayern, daughter of Maximilian I Joseph, who once lived in the Residenz.

Next is the 17th-century Trierzimmer (Trier Room). The ceiling was painted by Peter Candida and others and the walls are hung with tapestries dating from 1604–15. The St Georgs-Rittersaal (Knights' Hall) leads to the Reiches Zimmer (Rich Room), built in the 1730s to a design by Cuvilliés, with early Rococo decoration. These rooms also include the Grüne Galerie (Green Gallery), Paradeschlaf-zimmer (Parade Bedroom) and Spiegelkabinett (Mirrored Cabinet).

MUSEUMS AND GALLERIES OPEN IN THE AFTERNOON

A number of rooms are open to visitors all day. They include the Ahnengalerie (Ancestral Gallery) and Porzellankabinett (Porcelain Cabinet), Reiches Zimmer (Rich Room), Päpstliches Zimmer (Pope's Room) and

The Reiche Kapelle, a masterpiece of encrusted ornamentation

Nibelungensäle. The large collections of European porcelain that are exhibited in the seven Porzellankammern (Porcelain Rooms) are open in the afternoon. Also accessible is the lavishly decorated Hofkapelle, designed by Hans Krumpper in 1601–14. It is adjacent to the Paramentenkammern, a treasury of liturgical objects. The royal staircase leads to the Reliquienkammer, which contains an interesting collection of reliquaries from the different workshops of the Augsburg monasteries.

The Reiche Kapelle is a true masterpiece of religious Mannerist architecture. The private oratory of Maximilian I, it was built in 1607 by Hans Krumpper and sparkles with coloured marble, stuccowork, stone plaques and terracotta reliefs, and scagliola (imitation marble).

The Silberkammern and Hartschiersaal nearby house 3,500 pieces of silver plate from the Wittelsbach Service, made in the 18th and 19th centuries. The Steinzimmer (Stone Rooms) beyond are named after their stone walls.

A visit to the 17th-century part of the Residenz ends in the Vierschimmelsaal (Hall of the Four White Horses) and the Kaisersaal (Imperial Hall), where there is a statue of Tellus Bavarica (1594), which once crowned the circular church in the Hofgarten.

SCHATZKAMMER

In 1565, Albrecht V ordered that the jewels of the Wittelsbachs be sold after his death. This led to the creation of a treasure house. To it Elector Karl Theodor added the contents of the Palatinate treasury from Heidelberg, Düsseldorf and Mannheim. Later, religious works of art confiscated after the secularization of the knightly orders, and the insignia of the newly founded kingdom of Bavaria were added.

Decorative chain made in 1575

Highlights include the royal insignia, the cyborium (covered cup) of Arnulf of Carinthia (c.890), the Rappoltsteiner Cup (1540), a statue of St George (1597) and royal insignia of 1806.

Figure of St George (1597), inlaid with precious stones

CUVILLIÉS-THEATER (ALTES RESIDENZTHEATER)

Europe's finest surviving Rococo theatre was designed in 1751–53 by François Cuvilliés in collaboration with Johann Baptist Straub and Johann Baptist Zimmermann.

The predominantly gold and red wood carvings on the balconies, royal loggia and proscenia still survive. The first performance of Mozart's *Idomeneo* took place here in 1781. Destroyed in World War II, the theatre was rebuilt in the Apothekenhof, using the surviving original carvings.

EGYPTIAN COLLECTIONS

Opened in 1970, the Egyptian Art Museum is one of the most recently created state museums in Bavaria. The origins of the collection go back to the 16th century, when Albrecht V acquired a number of Egyptian statues. In the 19th century the rulers of Bavaria purchased Egyptian pieces for the Bavarian Academy of Sciences and the Glyptothek. In the 20th century, personal donations substantially enlarged the collection.

Today the museum contains a fine and extensive collection of Egyptian art from the Old, Middle and New Kingdoms, and from the later Ptolemaic and Coptic periods.

Egyptian bronze statuette

COIN COLLECTION

The Residenz contains the largest coin collection in the world. Its nucleus originated in a collection formed by Albrecht V and Ludwig I. It contains coins and medals dating from all periods and originating from all over the world. Seals, weights and banknotes also form part of the display.

The Neo-Classical National Theatre at Max-Joseph-Platz

Max-Joseph-Platz ❷

Map 3 C2 (6 D2).
Ⓢ *Marienplatz.* Ⓤ *Odeonsplatz.*
🚌 *19.* **Nationaltheater**
Tel *21 85 19 20.* ◯ *10am–7pm Mon–Sat (tickets for performances can also be obtained).*

During the 1820s, Karl von Fischer and Leo von Klenze laid out a grand square outside the Residenz, flanking it with the monumental façades of Neo-Classical buildings: Königsbau to the north, the National Theatre to the east, and the arcaded Törring-Jettenbach Palace to the south. The latter now houses a post office.

In the square is a statue of Maximilian I Joseph, the first king of Bavaria, who drew up the Bavarian constitution, the first in Germany, in 1818. The statue was created by Leo von Klenze and Christian Daniel Rauch.

The building of the **National Theatre**, which doubles as the National Opera, is modelled on a Greek temple. The interior also obeys Classical canons. The large circular auditorium is decorated predominantly in purple, gold, ivory and sky blue. It is surrounded by five-tiered galleries, with the royal box in the centre. The National Theatre became famous for its performances of Wagnerian operas. It was here that *Tristan und Isolde, Die Walküre* and *Rheingold* were first performed. Today it is the venue for opera festivals.

Eilles-Hof ❸

Residenzstr. 13 (also accessible from the side of Theatinerstr. 40–42).
Map 3 C2 (6 D2). Ⓤ or Ⓢ *Marienplatz.* Ⓤ *Odeonsplatz.* 🚌 *19.*

Between the Residenz-straße, Perusastraße and Theatinerstraße runs a network of narrow passages that are filled with small shops and cafés. The peace in this area is broken only by the music of street musicians.

One of the most impressive courtyards in this part of the city is the mid-16th century Eilles-Hof, which once formed part of a monastery. The narrow yard is today surrounded by glazed arched cloisters with late Gothic openwork balustrades. It is one of the last surviving arcaded courtyards that were typical of medieval Munich.

Preysing-Palais ❹

Residenzstr. 27. **Map** 3 C1 (6 C2).

On an irregular plot of land between Theatiner-straße and Residenz-straße, which leads to Odeonsplatz, Count Maximilian von Preysing-Hohenaschau built the first Rococo palace in Munich. It was designed by the court architect Joseph Effner and built in 1723–8. Novel designs were used for the three sides of

the palace (the fourth adjoins Feldherrnhalle). For the first time exuberant mouldings covered the entire façade, partially obscuring the architectural divisions of the building.

The finest example of rich Baroque design at the palace is the grand staircase, in the centre of the north wing. It is reached today via an internal passage that was once a hall and is now lined with elegant shops. The staircase has decorative balustrades and is supported by giant Caryatids, and the walls are covered with lavish stuccowork. No succeeding late Baroque palace has such a wealth of interior décor.

Preysing-Palais, an example of early Baroque exterior decoration

Feldherrnhalle ❺
Field Marshals' Hall

Odeonsplatz. **Map** 3 C1 (6 C2).
Ⓤ *Odeonsplatz.* 🚌 *53.*

On the site of the Schwabinger Tor, a medieval watchtower, the architect Friedrich von Gärtner raised a building that blends perfectly with the old and new towns between which it stands. The aim had been to create a focal point that would close off Ludwigstraße and give the irregular Odeonsplatz a more ordered appearance. At the request of Ludwig I a loggia in honour of the heroes of Bavaria was built, modelled on the famous Loggia dei Lanzi in Florence.

Statue of Count Tilly in the loggia of the Feldherrnhalle

For hotels and restaurants in this region see pp262–5 and pp276–9

HITLER AND THE FELDHERRNHALLE

On 8 November 1923, Adolf Hitler announced the start of the "people's revolution" in the Bürgerbräukeller and ordered the takeover of the central districts of Munich. The following day, a march of some 2,000 people acting on his orders was stopped by a police cordon outside the Feldherrnhalle in Residenzstraße. Four policemen and 16 of Hitler's supporters were shot. The marchers were dispersed, and Hitler fled to Uffing am Starnberger See, but was arrested and imprisoned. When Hitler finally came to power in 1933, he turned what became known as the *Hitler-Putsch* ("revolt") into a central element of the Nazi cult.

The accused in the trial against the participants in the *Hitler-Putsch* of 1923

The Feldherrnhalle was completed in 1844. It consists of an open hall 20 m (65 ft) high with a triple arcade approached by a stairway in the central span. The statues of lions flanking the stairway were added in 1906. The niches in the arcade contain statues of Count Tilly, a renowned military leader in the Thirty Years' War, and of Count von Wrede, a marshal of the Bavarian Napoleonic era. There is also an allegorical memorial to the Bavarian army of Ferdinand von Miller the Younger, built in 1892.

Theatinerkirche 6 (St Cajetan)

St Cajetan's Church

Theatinerstr. 22. Ⓢ *Marienplatz.*
Ⓤ *Odeonsplatz.* 🚋 *19.*
◯ *8am–8pm daily.*

To celebrate the birth of their long-awaited son in 1662, the Elector Ferdinand and his wife Henriette Adelaide of Savoy ordered the construction of a church and monastery for the Theatine order. It was designed by Antonio Barelli of Bologna, who wanted it to be the finest and most highly decorated temple.

Work began in 1663. The church was also designed for use as a court chapel. It was based on Sant' Andrea della Valle in Rome. Thus a building of pure Roman Baroque form rose in Munich. It is a barrel-vaulted cruciform basilica with an apse, a dome over the crossing and arcades opening onto side chapels. From 1675 work was supervised by Enrico Zucalli, who completed the dome, designed the interior and added twin towers which had not formed part of Barelli's original design. Almost 100 years later, the completion of the façade was entrusted to Cuvilliés and his son, who finished the work in 1765.

The distinctive form of the church brought considerable variety to Munich's cityscape. The huge domes of the towers are 70 m (230 ft) high. The volutes on the towers are inspired by those of Santa Maria della Salute in Venice.

The Cuvilliés' late Baroque façade is brought forward and broken up by pilasters and scrolled cornices. It also has niches with the figures of Ferdinand and Adelaide, Maximilian and Cajetan, the patron saint of the church. The portico contains a cartouche with coats of arms, including those of Bavaria and Saxony.

The white interior, which contrasts with the black confessionals and pulpit, is decorated with stuccowork, allegorical figures and putti. The main altar is flanked by twisted columns.

The crypt contains the tombs of the dukes and kings of Bavaria, among them the founders of the church and their son Maximilian Emanuel and his wife Teresa Kunigunda Sobieska.

The Baroque Theatinerkirche, one of Munich's finest buildings

The Salvatorkirche, with the Literaturhaus in the foreground

Salvatorkirche ❼
Church of the Saviour

Salvatorplatz 17. **Map** 3 B1 (5 C2).
Ⓤ *Odeonsplatz.* 🚊 *19.* 🚌 *100.*
⭘ *10am–8pm daily.*

In the late 15th century, the population of Munich increased greatly, and the existing cemeteries at Frauenkirche and Peterskirche were no longer sufficient. A new cemetery was created near the city walls, and cemetery chapels were built – the Kreuzkirche for the parish of St Peter and the Frauenkirche for that of St Mary.

Salvatorkirche was completed in a single year (1493–4). It was built by Lukas Rottaler, who brought the Gothic style to Munich. The combination of brick, stone and terracotta, the intricate fan vaulting and the delicate division of the walls give the church a distinctive

elegance. The whole is complemented by a slender tower ending in a steeple. Vestiges of late Gothic frescoes can be seen over the north door.

In 1829 Ludwig I donated the church to the Orthodox community. The iconostasis (screen) at the end of the nave is in Romanesque style, and the combination of Gothic architecture with Greek Orthodox furniture creates a unique effect. A plaque on the outer wall commemorates those who lie in the cemetery. They include the painter Hans Mielich, the composer Orlando di Lasso, and the architects François Cuvilliés and Johann Baptist Gunetzrhainer.

Erzbischöfliches Palais ❽
Archbishops' Palace

Kardinal-Faulhaber-Str. 12. **Map** 3 B1
(6 D2). Ⓢ Ⓤ *Marienplatz,
Odeonsplatz.* 🚊 *19.* ⭘ *to visitors.*

This palace, which consists of four wings enclosing a courtyard, was commissioned by the Elector Karl Albrecht and built by François Cuvilliés in 1733–7. It became the seat of the archbishops of Munich and Freising in 1821. It is the only surviving urban palace built by Cuvilliés.

The building is fronted by finely moulded pilasters. The tympanum contains the crest of Count von Holnstein, Karl Albrecht's illegitimate son, the division across the coat of

arms indicating his illegitimate status. A bas-relief over the doorway depicts the Virgin surrounded by cherubs.

The interiors of the palace were completed in about 1735 by Johann Baptist Zimmermann to a design by Cuvilliés. They are among the finest examples of late Baroque decoration in Munich. The courtyard contains a statue of Venus by Johann Baptist Straub.

Monumental sculpture on the façade of the Palais Porcia

Palais Porcia ❾

Kardinal-Faulhaber Str. 12. **Map** 3 B2 (5
C2). Ⓢ *Marienplatz.* Ⓤ *Marienplatz,
Odeonsplatz.* 🚊 *19.* ⭘ *to visitors.*

The Palais Porcia was Munich's first first four-winged Italianate Baroque palace. It was built for the Fugger family in 1693–4 by the architect Enrico Zucalli.

The façade is based on that of Bernini's Palazzo Odescalchi in Rome. The rusticated lower storey, which is pierced by a columned doorway, is surmounted by two upper storeys that are divided by pilasters.

In 1733 the Elector Karl Albrecht dedicated the palace to his sweetheart, Princess Porcia. The interior was re-modelled in the Rococo style to a design by François Cuvilliés, with the involve-ment of Johann Baptist Zimmermann. The balustrade of the balcony was replaced by an ornamental grille.

In 1819 the palace was acquired by the Museum

Medallion with the Virgin above the entrance to the Erzbischöfliches Palais

Literary Society, and in 1820 the rear wing was extended by the addition of a ballroom and a concert hall designed by Leo von Klenze.

Over the following century the building was an important centre of musical life in Munich. In 1934 it housed the Bayerische Hypotheken- und Wechselbank. Bombing raids in 1944 unfortunately destroyed the Rococo interior. However, the general design of the vestibule was restored in 1952, and the Rococo statue of Bellony was moved here from the Archbishops' Palace.

Palais Neuhaus-Preysing ⑩

Prannerstr. 2. **Map** 2 B1 (5 C2).
Ⓢ Marienplatz. Ⓤ Marienplatz, Odeonsplatz. 🚋 19. ◐ to visitors.

This palace was built in 1737, probably by Karl Albrecht von Lespilliez. A small attic was added during the Neo-Classical period.

The building is currently owned by Hypo Vereinsbank. The interior was completely destroyed during World War II, although the façade somehow survived. The palace was restored and renovated in 1956–8.

A little further along the same street are two fine late Baroque palaces, also probably designed by Lespilliez: the Palais Seinsheim at No. 7, built in 1764, and the Palais Gise at No. 9, built in 1765.

THE SIEMENSFORUM

The Siemensforum is a showcase that the electronics giant Siemens has built in Munich, and also in Berlin, Zurich, Vienna and Milan. Its purpose is to provide a forum for discussion and information on modern technological advances. As well as organizing congresses, events and exhibitions, the Munich Siemensforum contains a permanent exhibition taken from the Siemens-Museum. The museum was built in 1916 in Berlin to commemorate the 100th anniversary of the birth of Werner von Siemens, the inventor and engineer who founded the company. The museum moved to Munich in 1954.

The history section includes exhibits of the first telegraphic devices, such as the Morse transmitter. The modern section displays modern electronics and micro-electronics, which are presented using the latest multimedia technology.

The Siemensforum, an impressive display of modern technology

Literaturhaus ⑪

Salvatorplatz 1. **Tel** 29 19 340.
During exhibitions ◐ 11am–7pm Mon–Fri, 10am–6pm Sat–Sun.

Munich's great literary traditions and its influential position in the European publishing market were marked by the opening of the Literaturhaus in 1997.

This monumental building, which blends in with the closely aligned façades of town houses and the outline of the Salvatorkirche, dominates Salvatorplatz. Until the beginning of the

20th century this was the site of the city market. In 1887 a large school building designed by Friedrich Löbel was built here, its open ground floor fulfilling the function of a market hall up until 1906.

In 1993 the building, which had been partially destroyed during World War II, underwent renovation and reopened as the Literaturhaus.

The present building skilfully combines the period style of the lower storeys with a light steel and glass structure for the two upper storeys. These provide a breathtaking view on to the dome of the Theatinerkirche and the city's rooftops.

The Literaturhaus is the home of literary institutions and foundations that organize literary conferences and seminars as well as readings, concerts and receptions.

Part of the ground floor hall is occupied by a display area where temporary exhibitions are held. There is a library on the first floor. One of the institution's great attractions is the literary café. Its decor includes an installation by the American artist Jenny Holzer devoted to the Bavarian poet and novelist Oskar Maria Graf.

Façade of the Palais Neuhaus-Preysing with its rich Rococo stuccowork

The Künstlerhaus, built in northern German Renaissance style

Künstlerhaus ⑫
Artists' House

Lenbachplatz 8. **Map** 3 A1 (5 B2).
Tel *59 91 840.* Ⓢ or Ⓤ *Karlsplatz-Stachus.* 🚋 *18, 19, 20, 21, 27.*
Inner Courtyard ◯ *8:30am–5pm Mon–Fri during events.*

The Künstlerhaus, on the southern side of Lenbach-platz, was designed by Gabriel von Seidl and built in 1892–1900. This attractive building, with wings set around an inner courtyard, is in mock northern German Renaissance style, which is characterized by stepped gables and bronze decoration.

The Munich painter Franz von Lenbach made a great contribution to its completion. Having collected funds, he set to work on the interior. The rooms are decorated in Italian Renaissance and Art Nouveau styles.

Despite wartime destruction, the vestibule and the Venetian Room – which today houses a restaurant – have been preserved. The Künstlerhaus is now primarily a conference centre. Small exhibitions are occasionally held in the inner courtyard.

Dreifaltigkeits-kirche ⑬
Church of the Holy Trinity

Pacellistr. 6. **Map** 3 B1 (5 B2). Ⓢ & Ⓤ *Karlsplatz-Stachus.* 🚋 *19.*
◯ *8am–8pm daily.*

In the war of the Spanish Succession (1700–14) the townswoman Anna Maria Lindmayr had a vision in which the city was consumed by the flames of war. To ward off such disaster, the burghers pledged to build a church.

Work began in 1711, and the result is an unusually interesting piece of architect-ure. The design, inspired by the Roman architecture of Francesco Morrominiego, is by Giovanni Antonio Viscardi, and construction was supervised by Enrico Zucalli and Johann Georg Ettenhofer. It was completed in 1718.

The broken façade is set with a multitude of columns, pilasters and cornices, and windows of different shapes are set in surprising places. A niche in the upper storey contains a statue of St Michael by Joseph Fichtl. The plan combines elongated and centralized schemes.

High altar of the Dreifaltigkeitskirche

The interior is profusely decorated with stuccowork and with paintings by Cosmas Damian Asam. The high altar (1717) has a painting of the Holy Trinity, to whom the church is dedicated, by Andreas Wolff and Johann Degler. The Rococo tabernacle of 1760 is by Johann Baptist Straub.

Promenadeplatz ⑭

Map 3 B2 (5 C2). 🚋 *19.*

This elongated rectangular square, whose origins date back to the Middle Ages, was once the site of the salt market, and storehouses for salt and the customs house stood here. At the end of the 18th century, the buildings were demolished and the square was planted with linden trees. Fine palaces and town houses also rose up all round the square.

The square, whose present name dates from 1805, is decorated with 19th-century statues of well-known local and regional figures.

On the northern side is the Bayerischer Hof, a high-class hotel, where many famous people have stayed. In addition to the main building, in the Maximilian style, the adjoining Palais Montgelas also forms part of the hotel. It was designed for the king's minister and the creator of modern Bavaria by the architect Joseph Emanuel von Herigoyen (1811–13). The decoration is by Jean-Baptiste Métivier. The grand interior has been preserved, including the Royal Hall, Montgelas Hall and Library, all in Empire style. It was beside the building on Kardinal-Faulhaber-Straße that Kurt Eisner, first president of the Bavarian Republic, was shot in 1919.

Situated on the other side of the square, at No. 15, is the house belonging to the archi-tect Johann Baptist Gunetzrhainer.

The Neo-Renaissance loggia of the Palais Törring-Jettenbach

Palais Törring-Jettenbach ⓯

Residenzstr. 2. **Map** 3 C2 (6 D2).
Ⓢ or Ⓤ *Marienplatz.*
Ⓤ *Odeonsplatz.* 🚋 *19.* 🕐 *8am–7pm Mon–Fri, 8am–2pm Sat.*

The Baroque palace that originally stood on this site was at odds with ideas of town planning that had inspired the creation of Max-Joseph-Platz, particularly after the Neo-Classical wing of Königsbau and the Opera House were built.

In 1835–8 Ludwig I commissioned Leo von Klenze to rebuild the original palace, extending it and creating a façade based on that of the Ospedale degli Innocenti in Florence. The Baroque doorway was moved inside, as were two of the nine sculptures by Johann Baptist Straub (the remaining seven are in the Bayerisches National-Museum). The new arcade-style loggia was painted in ochre, contrasting with the red walls behind. This aristocratic palace is now one of Munich's main post offices.

Münzhof ⓰
State Mint

Hofgraben 4. **Map** 3 C2 (6 E3).
Ⓢ or Ⓤ *Marienplatz.* 🚋 *19.*
🕐 *8am–4:15pm Mon–Thu, 8am–2pm Fri.*

Two ducal seats in Munich are associated with Albrecht V – the Alter Hof and the mid-14th century Neuveste (now destroyed), which were separated by a stable building. Designed by the architect Bernhard Zwitzel of Augsburg, they were built by Wilhelm Egkl.

The courtyard was surrounded by a three-storey loggia housing the stables and coach-houses. They also contained Albrecht V's library and some of the earliest collections of art in Europe. Despite a marked adherence to the Italian Renaissance, the building shows Albrecht's own interpretation.

When it was rebuilt in the 19th century as the state mint, it was given a Neo-Classical east façade. The north façade, meanwhile, is in the Maximilian style.

Alter Hof ⓱
Old Residence

Burgstr. 8. **Map** 3 C2 (6 D3).
Ⓢ or Ⓤ *Marienplatz.* 🚋 *19.*

The first fortified residence built for the Wittelsbachs within the walls of Munich was constructed in 1253–5. The purpose was to protect them not only from outside invaders, but also from rebellious citizens. In 1328–47 the Alter Hof was the residence of Emperor Ludwig IV of Bavaria. In the second half of the 14th century construction began on a larger residence, and gradually the seat of power was moved there. From the 14th century the Alter Hof only housed the duchy's administrative offices.

This delightful residence is a rare example of medieval secular architecture. The west wing ends with a gatehouse decorated with the crests of the Wittelsbachs, and it retains its original Gothic character. Another original feature is the distinctive bay window known as the Monkey Tower. According to legend, when Ludwig IV was a baby he was carried off by a monkey from the royal menagerie. The monkey climbed to the top of the tower, and it took a long time for it to be coaxed into returning the child.

Monkey Tower in Alter Hof

Renaissance triple-tier arcades create an orderly sense of space in the Münzhof

The Hofbräuhaus – the best-known address in Munich

Hofbräuhaus ⑱

Platzl 9. **Map** 3 C2 (6 E3). *Tel* 22 16 76. Ⓢ or Ⓤ *Marienplatz.* ◯ 9am–midnight daily (to 2am Sat–Sun). ▣

Munich's greatest tourist attraction, and the epitome of the Bavarian lifestyle, is the Hofbräuhaus. An inn, it formed part of the Royal Brewery that was founded by Wilhelm V in 1589. The opening ceremony of the inn in 1830 was attended by Ludwig I. Extended on numerous occasions, the building was given its present Neo-Renaissance exterior in 1896.

The ground floor contains the Schwemme, a large hall with a ceiling painted in 1971. The hall can hold 1,000 drinkers seated at long tables, strains of folk music audible over the talking and laughter.

On the first floor is the vaulted Festsaal, a ceremonial hall seating 1,300, and many smaller side-rooms known as *Trinkstuben*. In summer the beer-garden, with chestnut trees and a bubbling fountain, is a popular place. Every day 10,000 litres (17,600 pints) of beer are consumed here.

Maximilianstraße ⑲

Map 3 C2 (6 D, E2). Ⓤ *Odeonsplatz.* Ⓢ or Ⓤ *Marienplatz.* 🚋 19.

When he came to power, Maxmilian I Joseph continued the passion for building that had gripped his father Ludwig I. His wish to make his own architectural mark on Munich manifested itself in Maximilianstraße. Built in 1852–5, this was a reaction to the outmoded Neo-Classicism of Ludwig-straße. Maximilianstraße was built to connect the Residenz and the Old Town with the green areas along the banks of the Isar. It is divided into two parts, the showpiece square closed off by the Maximilianeum, and the commercial part within the Old Town. The division is further accentuated by the modern ring road. Today, this luxurious boulevard is one of the world's most exclusive and expensive streets.

Friedrich Bürklein, who designed the thoroughfare, created a novel architectural and decorative scheme that combined English Gothic with Italianesque arcades and depended on new skeleton construction methods. The arcades of the imposing Neo-Gothic buildings contain Munich's luxury shops such as Bulgari, Laroche, Hermès, Armani and the eccentric local men's fashion designer Rudolph Moshammer.

The famous Kempinski Vier Jahreszeiten hotel and the Ethnographic Museum are the only buildings not designed by Bürklein.

The opera house, the theatre, the many art galleries, where private views are a social event, and the clientele of the bustling cafés combine to create a thriving urban atmosphere in the area.

Münchner Kammerspiele im Schauspielhaus ⑳
Munich Chamber Theatre

Maximilianstr. 34–35. **Map** 4 D2 (6 F3). *Tel* 23 33 70 00. Ⓤ *Lehel.* 🚋 19. **Box office** ◯ 10am–6pm Mon–Fri, 10am–1pm Sat.

The Schauspielhaus is one of the few surviving Art Nouveau theatres in Germany. It was built in 1900–01 and adjoins the backs of two buildings in Maximilian style. The architect was Richard Riemerschmid and the modern stage equipment was created by Max Littmann.

The interior is also in Art Nouveau style. The walls of the auditorium are bright red with ornamental outlines. The green ceiling has six stucco beams and imaginative floral strands lit by spotlights in the shape of flower buds. The typical Art Nouveau device of softening lines with floral motifs can be seen everywhere – around the stage and the balconies and on door handles. The decorative stage curtain was made in 1971. Equally imaginative and colourful are the foyers on the two floors and the ticket office.

The theatre, which was originally named the Schauspielhaus (Playhouse), was renowned for the con-troversial works performed there, such as Frank Wedekind's *The Awakening of Spring*. The theatre's avant-garde traditions continued in the postwar period.

The interior of the Art Nouveau-style Munich Chamber Theatre

The Bavarian State Chancellery, a pompous presence and the subject of dispute

Marstall ㉑
Royal Stables

Marstallplatz 4. **Map** 3 C1 (6 E2). **Tel** *21 85 20 28.* **U** *Odeonsplatz.* 🚊 *19.*

Leo von Klenze's first major-work on the Residenz was the royal stables, on which he worked from 1817 to 1822. The large hall-like building is based on Renaissance and Baroque palace architecture.

The row of semi-circular windows is topped by medallions depicting horses' heads. Busts of Castor and Pollux, the sons of Zeus who (particularly in the case of Castor) were excellent horse-men, crown the columns at the entrance. The reliefs on the gates depicting the epic battle between the Lapiths and the Centaurs were made by Johann Martin von Wagner in 1821.

Today the Marstall houses the Marstalltheater, which is known for its experimental performances combining theatre with dance and music.

Medallion from the Marstall

Bayerische Staatskanzlei ㉒
Bavarian State Chancellery

Map 4 D1 (6 F1). **U** *Odeonsplatz.*

After a dispute between the city council and the government that went on for almost 30 years, the Bavarian State Chancellery was finally completed in 1992. A design proposed in the 1980s, by which the ruins of the former army museum at the end of the Hofgarten would be linked to a modern archi-tectural complex, seemed too invasive to most of Munich's residents. It interfered with green areas, and the wings of the new building would mean the demo-lition of the 16th-century garden wall. After protests and litigation brought by the town council, supported by art his-torians and building conservationists, the govern-ment altered the original plans.

Hofgarten ㉓
Palace Garden

East side of the Hofgarten. **Map** 3 C1 (6 E1). **U** *Odeonsplatz.* **German Theatre Museum** 🕐 *10am–4pm Tue–Sun.*

The Hofgarten is one of the largest Mannerist gardens

The Mannerist Temple of Diana in the centre of the Hofgarten

north of the Alps. It was laid out in front of the south wing of the Residenz in 1613–17. The geometrically designed gardens are divided by two straight main paths that intersect at right angles. At the intersection is the polygonal Hofgartentempel, or Temple of Diana, built by Heinrich Schön in 1615. The figure of Diana crowning the cupola was completed by Hubert Gerhard in 1594 (the present one is a copy). In 1623 Hans Krumpper remodelled the figure, transforming it into a symbol of Bavaria and adding putti bearing the ducal insignia.

The garden is bounded to the west and north by a gallery built in the reigns of Albrecht V and Maximilian I. The art gallery built in the north of the garden in 1781 was the precursor of the present Alte Pinakothek and Neue Pinakothek. The rooms now house an art gallery and the **German Theatre Museum**, the oldest of its kind in Europe. Its collections illustrate the history of drama in all parts of the world.

The triumphal arch of the entrance gate is Leo von Klenze's first work in Munich. The carvings are by Ludwig Schwanthaler and the frescoes, by Peter Cornelius, depict the history of the Wittelsbachs and Bavaria. The northern arcades feature land-scapes by Richard Seewald of 1962. South of the gardens rises the imposing Festsaal-bau, with von Klenze's huge doorway of 1835–42.

AROUND THE ISAR

The Isar, the river that flows through Munich, is quite attractive in the stretch between two bridges, the Luitpoldbrücke (Prinzregentenbrücke) and Corneliusbrücke. The Prater-insel and Museumsinsel, two islands linked to the city by several footbridges, also con-tribute to a striking townscape.

The main attractions that draw visitors to this part of Munich are in the area of the Luitpoldbrücke, Maximiliansbrücke and Ludwigs-brücke. On the steep right bank of the Isar are the Maximilansanlagen, green

A bust on the façade of the Maximilianeum

areas densely planted with trees and favourite places for walks and cycle rides.

The Maximilianstraße leads to the Maximilianeum, the great parliament building, which appears to be drawn like a theatre curtain across this wide thoroughfare. Everything exudes an air of dignity. Here are the monument to Maxi-milian II, the Ethnographical Museum and the Upper Bavarian gov-ernment building. This section of the Maximilianstraße is flanked by Lehel, the fashion quarter, one of Munich's prettiest districts.

SIGHTS AT A GLANCE

Churches
Annakirche ❶
Klosterkirche St Anna ❷
Nikolaikirche ❿

Museums and Galleries
Alpines Museum ❻
Deutsches Museum
  see pp 94–7 ⓮
Villa Stuck ❽
Völkerkundemuseum ❹

Historic Buildings and Monuments
Friedensengel ❾
Ludwigsbrücke ⓭
Maximilianeum ❼
Monument to Maximilian II ❺
Müllersches Volksbad ⓬
Regierung von
  Oberbayern ❸

Other Sights
Gasteig ⓫

GETTING THERE
The best way to reach this part of the city is on trams 17 and 19 or U-Bahn lines 4 and 5, to Lehel or Max-Weber-Platz. Sights further south are served by tram 18 or S-Bahn lines 1-8, those further north by tram 18 or bus 100.

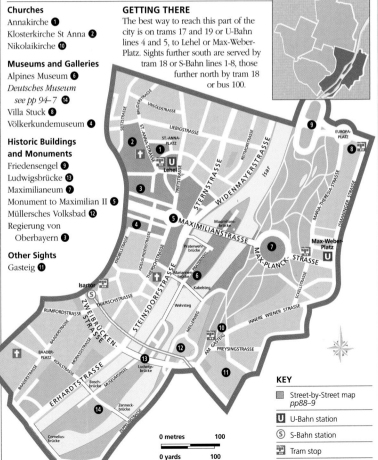

KEY

| Street-by-Street map pp88–9 |
| **U** U-Bahn station |
| **S** S-Bahn station |
| Tram stop |

◁ The entrance to the Müllersches Volksbad, which has several swimming pools and baths

Street-by-Street: Along Maximilianstraße

Maximilian II, with the aid of his court
architect Friedrich Bürklein, translated
his vision of urban planning into
reality in the Maximilianstraße.
Designed in what became known as
the Maximilian style, it opens out from
the Old Town into a kind of forum
flanked by monumental buildings.
It is completed by a circus with a
monument of the king contemplating
his creation. The scheme is
dominated by the Maximilianeum,
the Bavarian parliament building, on the
opposite side of the river.

**Relief from
St Anne's
Church**

Haus der Kunst

S T . - A N N A - S T R .

BÜRKLEINSTR.

S T . - A N N A   S T R .

P F A R R S T R .

Regierung
von Oberbayern
*These Neo-Gothic
buildings house
the government
of Upper
Bavaria* ❸

← **Residenz**

M A X I M I L I A N S T R .

★ **Klosterkirche St Anna**
*The niche in the finial of
St Anne's church holds a
statue of its patron saint* ❷

Monument to Maximilian II
*This statue, 13 m (42 ft) high,
was carved by Ferdinand von
Miller, to a design by Kaspar
von Zumbusch, in 1875.
The king, whose great
ambition was to be a
professor rather than
a monarch, is
surrounded by
figures symbolizing
Peace, Liberty,
Justice and
Strength* ❺

**Völkerkunde-
museum**
*The rich collection of
the Ethnographical
Museum illustrates
the culture and
everyday life of
non-European
peoples* ❹

S T E I N S D O R

The Isar,
although
flanked by
embankments,
retains its
woodland
charm.

0 metres	100
0 yards	100

KEY

– – – Suggested route

STAR SIGHTS

★ Klosterkirche
St Anna

★ Maximilianeum

For hotels and restaurants in this region see pp262–5 and pp276–9

Annakirche

The monumental apse of St Anne's Church, built in Neo-Romanesque style, was painted by Rudolf von Seitz in 1892. It shows the Holy Trinity surrounded by St Mary, St Anne and the Apostles ❶

LOCATOR MAP
See Street Finder maps 4 & 6.

The Maximiliansbrücke

was built in 1904–6 to a design by Friedrich von Thiersch that incorporates Neo-Romanesque decoration. The figure of Athena expresses the idea of Munich as Athens on the Isar.

Friedensengel

★ Maximilianeum

This tympanum in the façade of the Maximilianeum contains scenes of the foundation of a monastery in the Ettal by Ludwig IV of Bavaria in 1330 ❼

Alpines Museum

This museum is dedicated to the Alps and mountaineering displays, including equipment from 1900 ❻

Neo-Romanesque doorway of Annakirche

Annakirche ❶
Parish Church of St Anne

St-Anna-Platz 5. **Map** 4 D2. **U** Lehel.
🚊 17, 19. ⬜ 8am–6pm daily.

A competition for the design
of a parish church for the
Lehel district was held in
1885. The winner was Gabriel
von Seidl. Work began in
1887, continuing until 1892.
The design of the church is
based on that of the Romanesque imperial cathedrals of
the Rhineland, in the great
German nationalist style that
was prevalent after 1871.

The monumental triple-nave
basilica has a square plan, the
transept and apse ending in a
chapel and the west front
having a large tower and a
Neo-Romanesque doorway.
The interior is decorated with
late 18th- to early 19th-
century wall paintings. An
interesting feature is the
hybrid iconography in the
figure of Christ on the west
front, dating from 1910, in
which He is depicted on
horseback holding a bow and
an olive branch.

Klosterkirche St Anna ❷
Abbey Church of St Anne

St-Anna-Platz 21. **Map** 4 D2 (6 F2).
U Lehel. 🚊 17, 19.
⬜ 6am–7pm daily.

In 1725 Lehel, then still a
suburb, was settled by an
order of Hieronymite monks.
A monastery church was built

here in 1727–33.
Designed by Johann
Michael Fischer, it was
a real architectural jewel
for the city: Munich's
first Rococo religious
building. The oval
interior is lined with
scalloped niches that
are separated by arches
supported on pilasters.
The interior decoration
was executed by the
Asam brothers. The
ceiling paintings, which
glorify St Anne, were
executed by Cosmas
Damian Asam and
completed in 1730. In
1737 the Asam brothers
completed the high altar and
most of the side altars,
their stuccowork and
paintings
harmonizing
with the fluid
forms of the
interior. The pulpit
and tabernacle, by
Johann Baptist
Straub, date from
around 1756.

**Cartouche from the
Klosterkirche St Anna**

After suffering
war damage, the interior was
restored on the basis of a
record of colour photographs.

Regierung von Oberbayern ❸
Upper Bavaria Government Building

Maximilianstr. 39. **Map** 4 D2 (6 F3).

This monumental building,
the seat of the government of
Upper Bavaria, is one of the
finest examples of the
Maximilian style. The epony-
mous king, Maximilian II,

**Part of the façade of the Upper
Bavaria Government building**

strove to create a new
architectural style, distancing
himself from the severe
Classicism of his father,
Ludwig I. The result was an
eclectic mixture of elements
drawn from such diverse
styles as English Gothic and
Moorish architecture.

Solid and imposing, the
Regierung von Oberbayern
was built in 1856–64 to a
design by Friedrich Bürklein.
The façade, 170 m (558 ft)
long, was conceived as part
of the grand new city plan.
It is vertically divided into
17 bays of arched windows
arranged above an imposing
arcade. Its strong horizontal
lines and its ornamentation
are highly reminiscent
of those of English
Gothic
cathedrals.
Indeed, the
pseudo-
ecclesiastical
appearance of the
building was
designed to
underline its civic
importance and
dignity. This symbolism is
further reinforced by the
large statue of Justice that
crowns the building.

Völkerkunde-museum ❹
State Museum of Ethnography

Maximilianstr. 42. **Map** 4 D2 (6 F3).
Tel 21 01 36 100. **U** Lehel.
🚊 17, 19. ⬜ 9:30am–5:30pm
Tue–Sun. ⬚

The building that was
eventually to become the State
Museum of Ethnography was
built in 1859–65 to a design
by Eduard Riedel. It is in the
Maximilian style and the
façade is set with eight figures
personifying the virtues of the
Bavarian people: Patriotism,
Diligence, Magnanimity, Piety,
Loyalty, Justice, Courage and
Wisdom.

The building was originally
intended to house the
collections of the Bavarian
National Museum. From
1900 to 1923 it served as the
first main building of the
Deutsches Museum.

For hotels and restaurants in this region see pp262–5 and pp276–9

Caryatids flanking the entrance to the Völkerkundemuseum

Since 1926 it has been the home of the State Ethnographic Museum, the second largest in Germany after that of Berlin.

The collection itself dates from 1782, when curiosities from the collections of Bavarian rulers were displayed in the galleries of the Residenz. The museum collection now consists of some 150,000 pieces relating to the life and culture of non-European peoples. The Far East (China and Japan), South America (Peru) and East and Central Africa are particularly well represented.

Because of the size of the collection, many exhibits are displayed on a rotating basis.

Monument to Maximilian II ❺

Rondo Maximilianstr.
Map 4 D2. 🚊 19.

As you walk along Maximilianstraße you pass a circus that has at its centre a statue of Maximilian II, patron of the arts and industry, and inspirer of the new architectural style to which he gave his name. Maximilian II conceived the urban planning of this part of the city. The monument was erected by the citizens of Munich in homage to their ruler and in honour of the monarchy.

The bronze statue, designed by Kaspar Zumbusch and cast in 1875, stands on a red marble plinth surrounded by personifications of the four royal virtues. Four putti hold the coat of arms of the four tribes of Bavaria: the Franconians, Bavarians, Swabians and Palatines.

Alpines Museum ❻
Museum of the Alps and Mountaineering

Praterinsel 5. **Map** 4 E3.
Tel 21 12 240. 🕙 1–6pm Tue–Fri, 11am–6pm Sat–Sun. 📷

The museum stands in scenic parkland in the southern part of Praterinsel, one of the islands in the Isar in central Munich. The building that it occupies, dating from the late 19th century, was presented to the German-Austrian Mountaineering Association in 1938.

The museum's exhibits illustrate both the scientific and the aesthetic aspects of the Alps. The displays, with a geological section on Alpine rocks and minerals, relate to their exploration and study, and include many paintings and drawings of Alpine scenery.

A book from 1897, Alpines Museum

The museum also houses the world's largest library of books on Alpine subjects, and has a mountaineering archive. An information centre serves the needs of mountaineers intending to set out on expeditions into the Alps.

Maximilianeum ❼

Max-Planck-Str. 1. **Map** 4 E2. 🚇 Max-Weber-Platz. 🚊 18, 19. 🚌 100.

The largest building on Maximilianstraße is, not surprisingly, the monumental Maximilianeum. It was built as a commission from Maximilian II by Friedrich Bürklein in 1857–74 and stands on an elevation on the right bank of the Isar.

The building was the headquarters of a royal fund that gave gifted school students the opportunity to study at university without paying fees. Since 1949 it has been the seat of the Bavarian parliament (and until 1999 the Bavarian senate).

It took 17 years to complete the Maximilianeum, progress being hampered by the sloping terrain of the river bank. The focal point of the slightly concave façade is the tall, triple-arched projecting entrance, topped by the figure of an angel. Wings, arcaded in their lower storey, extend on either side. The terracotta façade is decorated with busts and statues, while coloured mosaics on a gold background fill the semicircular blind windows over the upper storey. The interior is decorated with historical and allegorical paintings by Wilhelm and Friedrich von Kaulbach.

The Maximilianeum, seat of the Bavarian parliament

Die Sünde, a portrait of sin by
Franz von Stuck, in the Villa Stuck

Villa Stuck ⑧

Prinzregentenstr. 60. **Map** 4 F1.
Tel 45 55 51 25. **U** *Prinzregenten-
platz, Max-Weber-Platz.* 🚊 *15, 18,
19, 25.* ⏰ *11am–6pm Tue–Sun.*

Franz von Stuck (1863–1928),
the talented son of a miller
from Lower Bavaria, made a
giddy career for himself in
Munich. He not only achieved
great success as a painter,
sculptor and graphic artist,
but also became a professor
at the Academy of Fine Arts,
was given an aristocratic title
and earned himself the title
"prince of art".

In 1897–8 Stuck built
himself a magnificent home,
to which a large studio was
added in 1913–14. Both the
architectural conception and
the interior decoration of the
house were his own work. In
it, he combined Neo-Classical,
Art Nouveau and Symbolist
elements, thus underlining his
tenet that art and life were
connected.

The house contains finely
decorated reception rooms
which, after the artist's death,
were used for meetings by
Munich's high society. The
walls of the drawing rooms
and studios are covered with
mosaics and paintings in a
Pompeian style. As well as
ostentatious furniture, there
are examples of Stuck's own
sculpture. The museum also
has an Art Nouveau display
and hosts visiting exhibitions.

Friedensengel ⑨
Angel of Peace

Prinzregentenstr. **Map** 4 F1.
🚊 *18.* 🚌 *100.*

High on the right bank of
the Isar stands the Angel of
Peace, a monument raised to
mark 25 years of peace after
the Franco-Prussian War of
1870–71, in which Germany
was victorious.

Commissioned by the city
council, the monument was
designed by the architect
Jacob Möhl in 1891 and built
in 1896–9 by Heinrich Düll,
Max Heilmeier and Georg
Pezold. It stands on
the Maximilian
Terraces, which are
supported by a wall
pierced by three niches.
The central niche is in
the form of a grotto that
acts as a backdrop to the
fountain. The monument
is flanked by a stairway
with a decorative
balustrade. The plinth,
on a tall podium, is in
the form of an open
hall with caryatids and
columns. It contains
portraits of the rulers
and generals of the Franco-
Prussian War.

The monument was
modelled on the Erechtheum
on the Acropolis in Athens.
Inside the hall, gold
mosaics depicting the
allegories of Peace,
War, Victory and
Culture cover a
pedestal from
which rises a
Corinthian column
25 m (86 ft) high.

**The Angel of
Peace**

The golden figure of the
angel, 6 m (19 ft) high and
crowning the column, imitates
the Greek statue of Nike
Paioniosa on Mount Olympus.

Nikolaikirche ⑩
Church of St Nicholas

Innere Wiener Str. 1 **Map** 4 E3.
U *Rosenheimer Platz.* 🚊 *18.*
⏰ *daily.*

Beside the Gasteig Culture
Centre, in the middle of
a small, tranquil wood, stands
the little church of St Nicholas.
Its whitewashed walls and
onion dome bring to mind
the churches of
rural Bavaria.
The building, first
mentioned in 1313,
was originally part of a
leper hospital. It was
rebuilt in the Renais-
sance and Baroque
periods. After suffering
destruction in World
War II, it was restored
and a late Baroque
altar from Garmisch
was added. Adjoining
the church is the
Altöttinger Kapelle, a
chapel with an arcaded
ambulatory. It is a copy of the
famous church at Altötting.
Originally built in Baroque
style, it has been given several
facelifts since then, the latest
being in 1916. The Crucifixion
group once formed part of an
ancient Calvary. The modern
crucifix standing amid the
Baroque figures replaces the
18th-century original one
that was destroyed during
World
War II.

The tiny Church of St Nicholas, which has a provincial atmosphere

The Modernist, fortress-like Gasteig Cultural Centre

showers and baths, there is also a barrel-vaulted men's swimming pool, a domed ladies' swimming pool and a Roman bath. In the basement is a grooming centre for dogs.

The whole building reflects the new concepts of hygiene that were coming into vogue in the late 19th century, together with an interest in Roman bathing traditions. From an architectural point of view, the building is notable for the Neo-Baroque, Art Nouveau and Moorish elements that it incorporates.

Gasteig ⓫

Rosenheimer Str. 5. **Map** 4 E4. *Tel* 48 09 80. Ⓤ Rosenheimer Platz. 🚋 18. ◯ 8am–11pm daily. **Library** 10am–7pm Mon–Fri, 10am–4pm Sat.

Gasteig Cultural Centre is one of the largest of its kind in Europe. Built from 1978 to 1985, it covers more than 23,000 sq m (247,300 sq ft) and stands on the site of the Bürgerbräukeller, the beer hall where Hitler survived an attempt on his life when a bomb was planted there in 1939. The beer hall was demolished in the 1970s.

The modern glass, steel and brick building dominates the surrounding area like a fortress. It houses four major institutions: the Volkshochschule (an adult education centre), the municipal library, the Richard Strauss Conservatoire and the Philharmonia. The semicircular concert hall, with seating for 2,500, is lined with wood to enhance the acoustics. Besides the three other halls – the Carl Orff performance hall, the Small Concert Hall and the Black Box chamber theatre, there are many smaller auditoriums, workshops and rooms that are a focal point in the cultural life of Munich.

The complex contains a large forum where major performances take place, and where there are also shops and cafeterias. The south entrance is graced by a fountain in the shape of an enormous wind instrument.

Müllersches Volksbad ⓬
Müller Baths

Rosenheimer Str.1. **Map** 4 E3. *Tel* 01801–79 62 23. Ⓢ Rosenheimer Platz. 🚋 15, 25. ◯ 7:30am–11pm daily (to 5pm Mon).

Anyone who is keen on swimming or interested in interior design should visit this complex. It was built in 1897–1901 by the engineer Karl Müller to an architectural design by Carl Hocheder. At the time the baths – the first public baths in Munich – were considered to be the finest in Germany.

The men's and women's pools were originally separate. In addition to the many relaxation rooms,

The tower of the Müllersches Volksbad

Ludwigsbrücke ⓭

Zweibrückenstr./Rosenheimer Str. **Map** 4 D3 (6 F5). Ⓤ Rosenheimer Platz, Isartor. 🚋 16, 17.

The history of Munich began at Ludwigsbrücke in 1158, when Heinrich der Löwe destroyed the toll bridge over the Isar belonging to the Bishop of Freiburg. Prince Heinrich wished the Salzstrasse, the salt route that had existed since Roman times, to cross the Isar near the place where Benedictine monks had established a settlement. He therefore built a new toll bridge, and the settlement became a centre of trade, having trading rights and issuing its own coinage.

The present bridge dates from 1935. It is decorated with figures personifying Industry and River Navigation (these were made in 1892 for the previous bridge) and Art (made in 1979).

Beside the bridge, on Museumsinsel, is the Fountain of Father Rhine, built in 1897–1902 by the sculptor Adolf von Hildebrand. The bronze statue of Father Rhine originally formed part of the fountain that stood outside the theatre in Strasbourg. When it was brought to Munich, it was placed in the centre of a fountain and was surrounded by putti standing on plinths.

Deutsches Museum ⑭

The Deutsches Museum, one of the world's oldest and largest museums of technology and engineering, draws over 1.4 million visitors each year. It was founded in 1903 by Oskar von Miller, an engineer. The collections cover most aspects of technology and the museum is also home to the world's largest library of technology. The museum has two other branches in Munich – the Verkehrszentrum for urban transport and the Flugwerft Schleissheim on the history of aviation.

Exterior of the Museum
The building combines Neo-Baroque, Neo-Classical and modern elements.

Decorative Arts
This plate with the portrait of a lady from Ludwig I's "gallery of beauty" is an example of reproduction techniques applied to porcelain. The ceramics section illustrates the development of faience, stoneware and porcelain.

★ Physics
Galileo's workshop features a large collection of the scientific equipment used by the famous astronomer and physicist to establish the basic laws of mechanics.

Second floor

First floor

★ Pharmaceutics
Among the exhibits in this section is a model of a human cell magnified 350,000 times and graphically illustrating how it functions.

Main entrance

Ground floor

MUSEUM GUIDE

The museum's 20,000 exhibits are displayed over six floors. While those on the lower floors include sections on chemistry, physics, and aeronautics, those on the middle floors relate to the decorative arts. The upper floors are devoted to astronomy, computers and microelectronics.

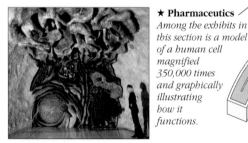

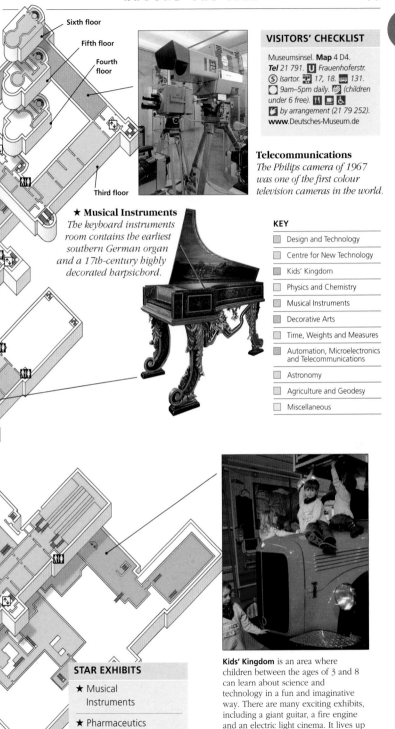

Sixth floor

Fifth floor

Fourth floor

Third floor

VISITORS' CHECKLIST

Museumsinsel. **Map** 4 D4.
Tel 21 791. U *Frauenhoferstr.*
S *Isartor.* 17, 18. 131.
9am–5pm daily. (children
under 6 free).
by arrangement (21 79 252).
www.Deutsches-Museum.de

Telecommunications
*The Philips camera of 1967
was one of the first colour
television cameras in the world.*

★ **Musical Instruments**
*The keyboard instruments
room contains the earliest
southern German organ
and a 17th-century highly
decorated harpsichord.*

KEY

☐	Design and Technology
☐	Centre for New Technology
☐	Kids' Kingdom
☐	Physics and Chemistry
☐	Musical Instruments
☐	Decorative Arts
☐	Time, Weights and Measures
☐	Automation, Microelectronics and Telecommunications
☐	Astronomy
☐	Agriculture and Geodesy
☐	Miscellaneous

STAR EXHIBITS

★ Musical Instruments

★ Pharmaceutics

★ Physics

Kids' Kingdom is an area where
children between the ages of 3 and 8
can learn about science and
technology in a fun and imaginative
way. There are many exciting exhibits,
including a giant guitar, a fire engine
and an electric light cinema. It lives up
to its name because adults can only
enter with the child's permission.

Exploring the Deutsches Museum

To view all the exhibits on every floor in detail would take a whole month since the entire route through the museum is 17 km (10.5 miles) long. With more than 50 sections on offer, it is best to concentrate on just a few areas. The attractive way in which the exhibits are laid out is very effective, and there are plenty of items that visitors can operate themselves, so this is a museum that children will enjoy too. There are also regular demonstrations of working machinery and film shows.

DESIGN AND TECHNOLOGY

The museum contains displays of such classic aspects of engineering as machine-building, mining, metallurgy, and hydraulic and civil engineering. The display of machines and turbines features many prototypes and the first diesel engine. The demonstrations of high-voltage currents and artificial lightning are particularly impressive, as is the re-creation of a mine.

Figures of miners at work in a re-created coal mine from c.1925

PHYSICS, CHEMISTRY AND PHARMACEUTICALS

The physics and chemistry section is outstanding. There are fascinating reconstructions of the laboratories of great scientists and also a collection of the original instruments used in some of the greatest scientific discoveries, as well as many pieces of prototype apparatus.

The exhibits are complemented by interesting demonstrations of the latest technology in optics, nuclear physics and chemistry. In the pharmaceuticals section the

exhibits graphically illustrate the different biochemical processes that take place in the human body.

MUSICAL INSTRUMENTS

This section is displayed in chronological order. The centrepiece of the keyboard instruments section is the earliest harpsichord, which was made in 1561.

The sections on wind, stringed and percussion instruments are equally fascinating. There are also music machines and modern electronic keyboards. In the acoustic hall visitors can try out the synthesizer, creating an almost endless range of weird sounds or analysing their own voice.

DECORATIVE ARTS

The decorative arts are illustrated by a number of thematic displays. The section opens with glass and ceramics manufacturing techniques from the earliest times to the present.

There is an exhibition of paper manufacturing and printing technology, including an impressive display of industrial textile machinery.

The exhibition of the development of film and photography (due to re-open in 2006) begins with Daguerre's original equipment from 1839 and ends with digital technology.

The display of technical toys goes all the way from simple building blocks to the most sophisticated modern modelling kits. On the same floor is a realistic re-creation of Altamira cave, in Spain, with its Stone Age paintings.

A quadrant (an instrument for measuring azimuths) made in 1760

TIME, WEIGHTS AND MEASURES

A fine display of clocks and watches illustrates the problems of measuring time. The clocks begin with the simplest forms, such as sundials and sand-clocks, and progress to highly intricate and lavishly decorated mechanical clocks. There are also gigantic clock-tower mechanisms and elaborately ornamented grandfather clocks from various periods, as well as more modern clocks and watches.

The weights and measures section illustrates the unification of measurements, and shows various types of measuring equipment.

An Augsburg clock with the figure of a dancing bear, 1580–90

ASTRONOMY

With over 180 exhibits, the astronomy section explores such major and still incompletely understood questions as the structure of the universe and the nature of solar energy. It also charts the development of this field of human enquiry with a variety of measuring instruments and models of spaceships, and with models of solar systems and galaxies. It also addresses the problems of radiation and the enigma of black holes. In the observatory visitors can view the stars through giant telescopes.

A highly ornamental brass calculating machine from 1735

AUTOMATION, MICROELECTRONICS AND TELECOMMUNICATIONS

The purpose of this section is to illustrate the genesis and development of modern technology. It opens with the first calculating machines, developed by Blaise Pascal (1642), Gottfried von Leibniz (1700) and Braun (1735), and the first computer, the earliest built by Konrad Zuse in 1941. There is also an interesting display of the latest information technology.

The development of microelectronics is illustrated with models of the simplest diodes, transistors, resistors, condensers and semi-conductors. The importance of crystals in semiconductors and other aspects of modern electronics is also illustrated.

For non-specialists, the use of high-tech applications in everyday life is of particular interest. Broadcasting and the disseminating of information, by means of radio, television, fibre optics and computers, also have important displays.

THE ZEISS PLANETARIUM

One of the world's best-equipped planetariums occupies the sixth floor of the museum. An artificial sky is created by a Zeiss computer-controlled projector. The dome, 15 m (49 ft) across, is used for the projection of images of the sun, the moon and the planets, along with 8,900 stars and 25 constellations and nebulae. You can watch the movements of heavenly bodies as they change position through the year and view them from different points on the earth. There are also laser shows (Cosmic Dreams, Pink Floyd and Laser Magic II), for which special spectacles are provided. Tickets for the Zeiss Planetarium are sold separately.

AGRICULTURE AND GEODESY

This section illustrates the development of farming equipment from the simplest tools to ploughs and modern farm machinery. The geodesic displays show methods of measuring the earth and the development of topography, from early surveying equipment and maps and globes to modern satellite surveying.

CENTRE FOR NEW TECHNOLOGY

On display in this section are the latest developments in the fields of science, technology and social sciences. The Centre promotes itself as a platform from which techno-logical experts can share their knowledge with a wider public on subjects as diverse as research on climate change, new inventions and biomedical discoveries.

The Centre hosts permanent exhibitions as well as tem-porary presentations. Among the items on permanent display is an exhibition charting the emergence and development of career-based education in Germany, which encourages young people to pursue a career in technology.

Due to the very nature of the technological world, the exhibits here are ever-changing, aiming to provide an up-to-date resource on the very latest discoveries. A website (www.deutsches-museum.de/dmznt) keeps track of what is on show.

The Centre for New Technology also contains an interactive visitors' laboratory. After registering, visitors can carry out experiments and take part in modern research – you can even examine your own genetic matter.

Electrochemical telegraph apparatus dating from 1809

THE UNIVERSITY DISTRICT

The area to the north of the Old Town is a varied district in terms both of its architecture and its atmosphere. Ludwigstraße is lined exclusively with elegant Neo-Classical buildings, most of them government offices and public buildings, including the Bavarian State Library and the university.

West and north of Ludwigstraße the atmosphere changes completely. The buildings here are in a variety of styles spanning the 19th and 20th centuries. The area abounds in trendy shops, bookshops and pubs and it is filled with crowds of young

Art Nouveau ornament

students. Full of history and local colour, this area, known as Schwabing, is fascinating to visit. Leopoldstraße, its bustling main boulevard, comes as a great contrast to Ludwigstraße.

To the east of Schwabing is the Englischer Garten, with the museums of Prinzregentenstraße on its southern side. The park is a welcome oasis to the footsore visitor and to those seeking a moment's peace. Here you can rest among abundant greenery, sunbathe (even nude), cool off in the water or enjoy a cold beer in one of the beergardens at the Chinese Tower.

SIGHTS AT A GLANCE

Churches
Ludwigskirche ❺

Museums and Galleries
Archäologische
  Staatssammlung ⓫
Bayerisches Nationalmuseum
  pp108–109 ⓭
Haus der Kunst ⓮
Schack-Galerie ⓬

Historic Buildings
Akademie der Bildenden
  Künste ❽
Bayerische Staatsbibliothek ❹
Jugendstilhaus in
  der Ainmillerstraße ❿
Ludwig-Maximilians-
  Universität ❻
Pacelli Palais ❾
Siegestor ❼

Streets and Squares
Ludwigstraße ❸
Odeonsplatz ❷
Wittelsbacherplatz ❶

KEY

▨ Street-by-Street map
  See pp100–101

Ⓤ U-Bahn station

🚊 Tram stop

🚍 Bus stop

GETTING THERE

This part of the city is best reached on U-Bahn lines 3 and 6, alighting at Universität or Giselastraße. The museums on Prinzregentenstraße are most conveniently reached by tram 17 or bus 100.

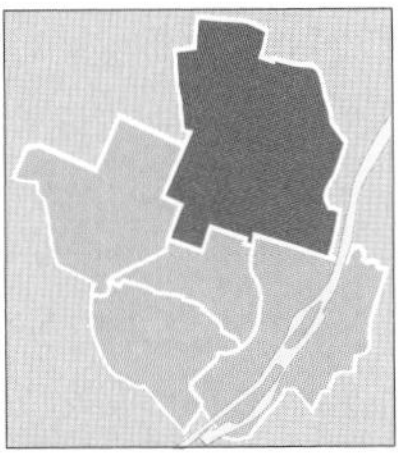

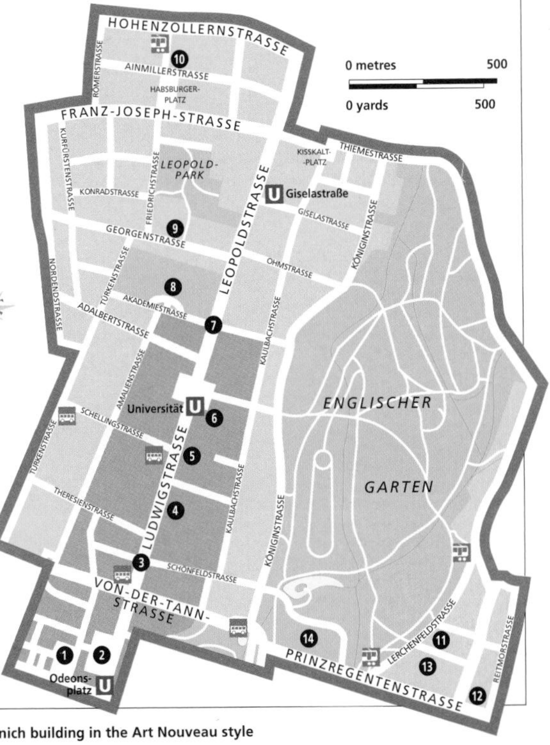

0 metres   500
0 yards   500

◁ **Leopoldstraße 77, a typical Munich building in the Art Nouveau style**

Street-by-Street: Along Ludwigstraße

Sightseeing in this part of the city is fascinating for some but less appealing for others. The district's monumental Neo-Classical architecture was designed to a unified urban plan. There are no shops or pubs here. Instead the streets are lined with palaces whose façades are reminiscent of Italian Romanesque or Renaissance architecture, and the long avenues are punctuated by large squares. It is hard to imagine that the bustling, culturally varied Schwabing district is just next door.

Ludwig-Maximilians-Universität
The university building, looking onto Amalienstraße, has an eclectic façade with an arcaded lower storey ⑥

★ Wittelsbacherplatz
Ludwig I's palace, built on Wittelsbacherplatz in 1825, was briefly the residence of its creator, Leo von Klenze ①

The Monument to Maximilian I
by the Danish sculptor Bertel Thorvaldsen is based on the style of equestrian statues of the Italian Renaissance.

Odeonsplatz
The focal point is the monument to Ludwig I ②

Ludwigstraße
This stretch of the street is flanked by monochrome façades in Italian Renaissance style ③

0 metres	100
0 yards	100

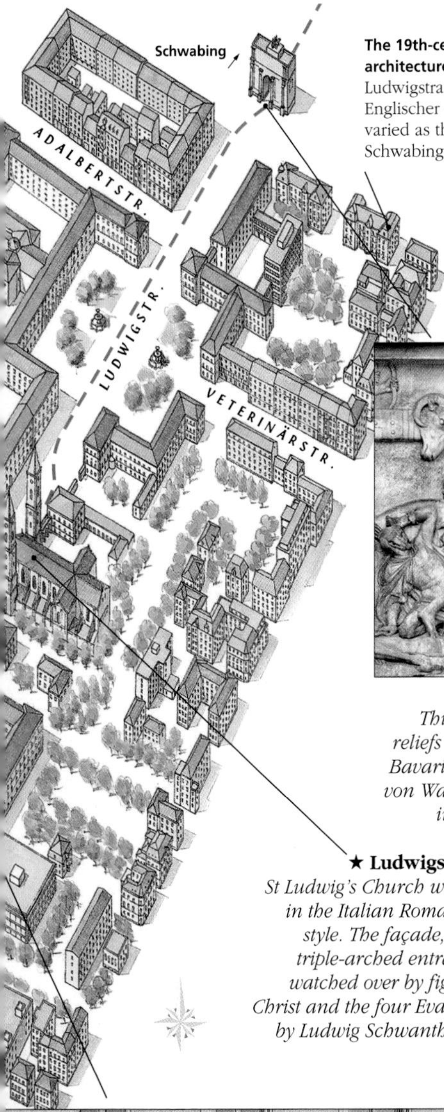

The 19th-century architecture between Ludwigstraße and the Englischer Garten is as varied as the colourful Schwabing district.

LOCATOR MAP
See Street Finder maps 2 & 6

Siegestor
This triumphal arch is decorated with bas-reliefs depicting scenes of battles fought by the Bavarian army. The reliefs, by Johann Martin von Wagner, show the Bavarian troops dressed in the uniforms of Classical antiquity ❼

★ Ludwigskirche
St Ludwig's Church was built in the Italian Romanesque style. The façade, with its triple-arched entrance, is watched over by figures of Christ and the four Evangelists by Ludwig Schwanthaler ❺

KEY

- - - Suggested route

Bayerische Staatsbibliothek
A long flight of steps leads to the entrance of the Bavarian State Library. The balustrade is decorated with statues of Thucydides, Homer, Aristotle and Hippocrates by Ludwig Schwanthaler ❹

STAR SIGHTS

★ Ludwigskirche

★ Wittelsbacherplatz

For hotels and restaurants in this region see pp262–5 and pp276–9

The Palladian façade of Arco-Zinneberg Palace on Wittelsbacherplatz

Wittelsbacherplatz ❶

Map 3 C1 (6 D1).
🚇 *Odeonsplatz.* 🚌 *100.*

This square is situated on Briennerstraße, one of the city's most elegant streets, which leads off from Odeonsplatz. Wittelsbacherplatz was laid out in the 1820s to a design by Leo von Klenze, and is one of Munich's finest squares. It is lined on three sides by Neo-Classical palaces, and the square itself is laid with paving slabs and stones arranged to form various patterns.

Von Klenze lived in the Ludwig-Ferdinand Palais on the south side of the square. From 1878 the palace belonged to Duke Ludwig Ferdinand, after whom it was named. It is now owned by the Siemens corporation.

On the west side of the square is Arco-Zinneberg Palace, also designed by Leo von Klenze, which today houses upmarket shops. To the east is the Odeon and the Palais Méjean, which was rebuilt after being destroyed in World War II.

In the centre of the square stands a monument to the Elector Maximilian I. It was designed by the prominent Danish Neo-Classical sculptor Bertel Thorwaldsen and was unveiled in 1839.

Odeonsplatz ❷

Map 3 C1 (6 D1).
🚇 *Odeonsplatz.* 🚌 *100.*

In the early 19th century, when the Schwabinger Tor was demolished, a decision was made to impose order on the haphazard arrangement of buildings to the north of the Residenz and the Theatinerkirche. In 1817 Maximilian I Joseph approved Leo von Klenze's plan for the Odeonsplatz, unaware that its originator was in fact his son, Ludwig I. The heir to the throne wished to create a magnificent square marking the start of the main thoroughfare to the northern districts and also acting as a triumphal entry point into Munich.

The Odeonsplatz takes its name from the Odeon, a concert hall built by Leo von Klenze in 1826–8 as a counterpart to the Leuchtenbergpalais of 1816–21. Set back from the square, both buildings serve to elongate it.

The equestrian statue of Ludwig I flanked by personifications of Religion, Art, Poetry and Industry in the centre of the square was created by Max Widmann in 1862. It faces the side of the square containing the Market Hall of 1825–6 and the arch

Monument to Ludwig I on Odeonsplatz

leading to the palace court. On the side of the Old Town, the square is bounded by the Feldherrnhalle.

Ludwigstraße ❸

Map 2 D5, 2 E5. 🚇 *Odeonsplatz, Universität.* 🚌 *100.*

One of the most splendid city streets in Europe is Ludwigstraße. It was built from 1815 to 1852, the general plan and the first group of buildings being designed and completed by Leo von Klenze. The street begins at Odeonsplatz, whose Italian Renaissance-style palaces harmonize perfectly with the buildings at the beginning of Ludwigstraße. In 1827 the project was taken over by Friedrich von Gärtner, who was responsible for the buildings south of Theresienstraße, to which he gave Romanesque and Byzantine elements. The principal buildings on this part of the street are the Bavarian State Library, Ludwigskirche and university buildings.

In the mid-19th century, the Feldherrnhalle and Siegestor were added, at the south and north ends of the street respectively. In building this triumphal route, Ludwig I departed from the city's planning rules to satisfy his aesthetic and political ideals.

The Odeon concert hall before it was destroyed in 1944

The fountain in the centre of Geschwister-Scholl-Platz at Ludwig-Maximilians-Universität

Bayerische Staatsbibliothek ❹
Bavarian State Library

Ludwigstr. 16. **Map** 2 E5.
Tel 28 63 80. Ⓤ *Odeonsplatz, Universität.* 🚌 *100.* ◷ *9am–9pm Mon–Fri, 10am–5pm Sat–Sun.* ♿ *telephone in advance.*

The Bayerische Staats-bibliothek, Germany's second largest municipal library after that in Berlin, has its origins in the collections of books that were amassed by Duke Albrecht V and Wilhelm V in the 16th century. It was enhanced from 1663, when the Elector Friedrich Maria ordered that one copy of every new book published in Bavaria or published by a Bavarian abroad should be kept in the library. An enormous addition to the royal collection of books – particularly of early editions – was made when the Jesuit order was disbanded in 1773 and again when the monas-teries were dissolved in 1803.

Today the Bayerische Staatsbibliothek contains almost 6 million volumes, including 71,500 manuscripts, 29,000 maps and almost 20,000 current periodicals.

The library was the first architectural project under-taken by Friedrich von Gärtner, who started in 1832 and completed it in 1843. The building echoes the style of Italian Renaissance palaces. The great interior staircase is flanked by figures of Classical sages carved by Ludwig Schwanthaler and overlooked by figures of the library's founders, Albrecht V and Ludwig I.

Ludwigskirche ❺
St Ludwig's Church

Ludwigstr. 20. **Map** 2 E5.
Ⓤ *Universität.* 🚌 *100.* ◷ *7am–8pm daily (except during services).*

Statue of Hippocrates outside the library

Its façade set with pointed twin steeples, St Ludwig's Church is in sharp contrast to the neighbouring Staatsbibliothek. It was built in the Italian Romanesque style by Friedrich von Gärtner in 1829–43. The niches in the façade contain figures of Christ and the four Evangelists. The wings connect the church to the presbytery and to Friedrich von Gärtner's house. The interior is decorated with Italian Renaissance-style paintings by Peter von Cornelius and his pupils. The painting of the Last Judgment is the second largest in the world after Michelangelo's in the Sistine Chapel.

Ludwig-Maximilians-Universität ❻
Ludwig Maximilian University

Geschwister-Scholl-Platz/ Professor-Huber-Platz. **Map** 2 E4. **Tel** 21 800.
Ⓤ *Universität.* ◷ *7:30am–9pm Mon–Fri.* ♿

This institute of higher education is named in honour of its first sponsors. In 1472 Ludwig der Reiche (the Rich) founded a Jesuit Studium Generale in Ingolstadt. In 1771 it became a university. Maximilian I Joseph moved it to Landshut in 1800 and in 1826 Ludwig I transferred it to Munich. The university has been located on Ludwigstraße since 1840.

Today there are some 60,000 students. The noisy crowds of young people ensure that the streets in the vicinity are always full of life. The university's assembly hall and seminar rooms are set round two quadrangles. The latter are named after Hans and Sophie Scholl and Professor Kurt Huber, who together founded the White Rose movement that opposed Hitler. In 1943 members of the group distributed anti-Nazi leaflets at the university, an event that is commemorated by the "fossilized" sheets of paper in the paving of the main building's courtyard. The group was arrested and most of its members were executed.

The Neo-Romanesque façade of St Ludwig's Church

The monumental Siegestor, crowned by the personification of Bavaria

Siegestor ⑦
Victory Gate

Ludwigstr. **Map** 2 E4.
Ⓤ *Universität.*

Following the early 19th-century fashion for erecting triumphal arches, Friedrich von Gärtner designed the Siegestor for Ludwig I. The monument was built in 1843–50, and with its three grand arches it echoes the architecture of the Feldherrnhalle *(see pp78–9)*. The building stands on Ludwig-straße at the intersection with Leopoldstraße, Schwabing's fine main street.

The design of the Siegestor is based on the Arch of Constantine in Rome. It honours the Bavarian army and its role in the country's victory against Napoleon. The arch is covered in bas-reliefs depicting battle scenes, medallions, personifications of the Bavarian provinces, and figures of Victory at the top of the columns. The arch is crowned by the figure of Bavaria riding in a chariot drawn by four lions. The inscription that was added in 1958 states that the arch, which is "dedicated to victory, destroyed during the war", appeals for peace.

Passing through the Siegestor and entering Leopoldstraße, there is a notable change of atmosphere. The architectural uniformity of Ludwigstraße is replaced by stylistic variety in houses of the late 19th and early 20th centuries. The cafés, restaurants, music shops, book-stores, cinemas and discos here make for a vibrant atmosphere that persists into the small hours. This is the heart of the renowned Schwabing district.

Akademie der Bildenden Künste ⑧
Academy of Fine Arts

Akademiestr. 2. **Map** 2 E4.
Tel 38 520. Ⓤ *Universität.*
♿ ⬤ *to the public.*

During the 19th century Munich was one of the most important centres of painting, although it was regarded as being rather conservative.

Munich's artistic community developed around the Academy of Fine Arts, which was founded in 1808. Many painters who subsequently became famous studied here, including the Germans Wilhelm Leibl and Franz Marc, the German-Swiss Paul Klee, the Russian-born Wassily Kandinsky, and the Italian Giorgio de Chirico.

The Academy of Fine Arts was originally housed in the Jesuit College of Michaels-kirche, moving to its present location in 1886. The architect of the new building was Gottfried Neureuther, who based his design on that of a three-storey Italian palazzo.

The façade is pierced by a series of arched windows and the building is approached by a driveway leading to a grand staircase, with equestrian statues of Castor and Pollux.

Pacelli Palais ⑨

Georgenstr. 8–10. **Map** 2 E3.
Ⓤ *Universität, Giselastr.*
⬤ *to the public.*

This grand city palace provides an opportunity to compare two distinct architectural styles that were prevalent in Munich around 1900. The right-hand half of the building is in a late historical style, with columns, tympanums, small towers, carved loggias and sculptures. The flat but colourful Neo-Classical decoration on the left-hand half is typical of the Munich Art Nouveau style. It is now a private residence.

Art Nouveau decoration on the Pacelli Palais

Jugendstilhaus in der Ainmillerstraße ⑩
Art Nouveau House

Ainmillerstr. 22. **Map** 2 E2.
⬛ 27. ⬤ *to the public.*

The house at Ainmiller-straße 22 was the first residential building in Munich to be given an Art Nouveau (Jugendstil) façade. It was designed by Ernst Haiger and Henry Helbig in 1899–1900. The highly intricate scheme features decorative floral and mock-antique motifs.

Highly ornamental terracotta frieze on a window at the Akademie der Bildenden Künste

For hotels and restaurants in this region see pp262–5 and pp276–9

Schwabing

At the end of the 19th century Schwabing was well known as a bohemian district inhabited by writers and avant-garde artists. *Simplicissimus*, an anti-authoritarian satirical magazine, and the Elf Scharfrichter cabaret associated with it, were both located here. Many writers' cafés determined the atmosphere of the district. It had its heyday in the years preceding

Logo of Alter Simpl, a local cult café

World War I, when the writers Thomas Mann and Frank Wedekind and the artists Wassily Kandinsky and Paul Klee lived here. Paradoxically, after 1918, it became the favourite haunt of Adolf Hitler, who set up the offices of the *Völkischer Beobachter* newspaper here. After 1945 the district strove to revive its former glory with the help of local artists and students.

Art Nouveau window decoration *on the house at Leopoldstraße 77 is a fine example of the trend for geometrical Art Nouveau typical of houses in Schwabing.*

The suburbs of Munich *are seen here in a painting by Wassily Kandinsky. The Russian-born painter lived in Schwabing from 1902 to 1914, becoming a German citizen in 1927.*

Artists from Schwabing *formed the avant-garde Neue Künstlervereinigung in Munich in the early 1900s. This photograph was taken on the balcony of Kandinsky's house at No. 36 Ainmillerstraße. It shows, from left to right: Maria and Franz Marc; Bernhard Koehler, Kandinsky (seated), Heinrich Campendonk and Thomas von Hartmann. In 1911 the Der Blaue Reiter group was established in Munich, with Kandinsky at the forefront.*

This front door *decoration on the Jugendstilhaus in Ainmillerstraße shows Art Nouveau asymmetry and symbolism. It reflects local artistic bohemian culture, in which the legendary Countess Reventlow, who propounded a free, erotic lifestyle, was a leading figure.*

Englischer Garten

The Englischer Garten (English Garden) is so named because it is naturalistically laid out, in the manner of English landscaped grounds. One of Europe's largest city parks, it came into existence thanks to the vision of Sir Benjamin Thompson, an American officer on whom the Elector Karl Theodor bestowed the title Count von

Bas-relief on the Rumford Memorial

Rumford. As Bavaria's Minister of War, he ordered that the swampy terrain around the Isar be developed for military use. It became a municipal park, with many landscaped features designed by Rumford, Reinhold von Werneck and Friedrich Ludwig von Sckell, in 1789. Today the park is a valued green area for the people of Munich.

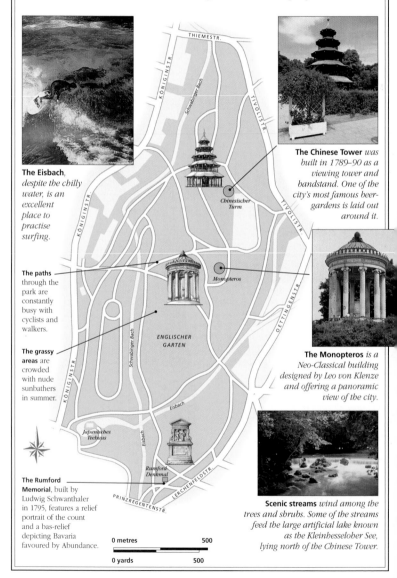

The Eisbach, *despite the chilly water, is an excellent place to practise surfing.*

The Chinese Tower *was built in 1789–90 as a viewing tower and bandstand. One of the city's most famous beer-gardens is laid out around it.*

The paths through the park are constantly busy with cyclists and walkers.

The grassy areas are crowded with nude sunbathers in summer.

The Monopteros *is a Neo-Classical building designed by Leo von Klenze and offering a panoramic view of the city.*

The Rumford Memorial, built by Ludwig Schwanthaler in 1795, features a relief portrait of the count and a bas-relief depicting Bavaria favoured by Abundance.

Scenic streams *wind among the trees and shrubs. Some of the streams feed the large artificial lake known as the Kleinhesseloher See, lying north of the Chinese Tower.*

| 0 metres | 500 |
| 0 yards | 500 |

Archäologische Staatssammlung ⓫

Archaeological Museum

Lerchenfeldstr. 2. **Map** 4 E1.
Tel 21 12 402. 🚋 17. 🚌 100.
☐ 9:30am–5pm Tue–Sun. ♿

The Archaeological Museum, at the southern end of the Englischer Garten, is a modern glass and steel construction consisting of six blocks arranged in chequerboard formation. Formerly known as the Museum of Prehistory, it is one of the largest regional museums of archaeology in Germany.

The collections date back to the foundation of the Bavarian Academy of Sciences in 1759. The exhibits, which span a period of time from as early as 100,000 BC to AD 800, are chronologically presented in three separate sections: Pre-historic, Roman and Early Medieval.

A Celtic staff, probably for use in rituals

Implements and jewellery, coins and religious artifacts illustrate the history of human settlement in Bavaria. There is a rich collection of Roman exhibits, including bronze masks from Eining, the Straubing Treasure and many mosaics from Roman baths. A popular attraction is the mummified body of a 16th-century woman that was discovered in marshland.

Schack-Galerie ⓬

Prinzregentenstr. 9. **Map** 4 E1.
Tel 23 80 52 24. 🚌 100. 🚋 17.
☐ 10am–6pm Wed–Sun. 📷

This interesting collection of 19th-century paintings was formed by Friedrich von Schack (1815–94), a wealthy baron from Mecklenburg. As well as an art collector, he was a man of letters, a translator and a traveller. In 1857 Schack bought a palace near the Propyläen, which he used to house his ever-growing art collection. Von Schack's main interest lay in contemporary

Munich painters, and he often sponsored young artists who had not yet gained due recognition. Under the terms of his will, von Schack's art collection was bequeathed to the Emperor Wilhelm II, who then decided to give the collection a home in Munich, commissioning a building especially for it. Designed by Max Littman and completed in 1910, the building has a Neo-Classical façade and is similar to the Berlin castle of the collection's founder, who is praised in an inscription on the façade.

In 1939 the Schack-Galerie was merged with the Bavarian State Art Collection. In 17 halls, it presents German painting from the late Romantic period. Among the 270 paintings are works by Moritz von Schwind, including Turnip-counter and King Olch, Arnold Böcklin's Villa by the Sea and Triton and the Nereids, and Anselm Feuerbach's Portrait of a Roman Woman and Paolo and Francesca. Also of interest are the paintings by Karl Spitzweg, Franz von Lenbach and Hans von Marées, and copies of Old Master paintings made by young artists sponsored by von Schack.

Façade of the Schack-Galerie, based on von Schack's Berlin castle

Bayerisches Nationalmuseum ⓭

See pp108–109.

Poster for an exhibition at the Haus der Kunst

Haus der Kunst ⓮

Art House

Prinzregentenstr. 1. **Map** 4 D1. *Tel* 21 12 70. ☐ 10am–8pm daily (until 10pm Thu). ♿

At the end of World War II, the palatial Haus der Kunst housed the finest collection of modern art in the country. Built between 1933 and 1937, the Neo-Classical building is the work of architect Paul Ludwig Troost; Adolf Hitler laid the foundation stone and the building became the model for the nascent National Socialist architecture.

The museum, known as the House of German Art under the Nazi regime, opened its doors in July 1937 with a display of propaganda art, proclaimed by the Nazis as "truly German". This was followed by "The Exhibition of Degenerate Art", opened in the Hofgarten Arcades, now the German Theatre Museum *(see p85)*. Several of the masterpieces were denigrated and ridiculed by the public during the opening. The "Great German Art Exhibition", housed here, displayed the work of officially approved artists.

In 2002 the National Collection of Modern and Contemporary Arts moved into the Pinakothek der Moderne *(see pp116–7)*. Today, while housing no permanent collections of its own, the museum showcases regular temporary exhibitions of the world's major contemporary artists.

Bayerisches Nationalmuseum ⓭

A 16th-century suit of armour

In architectural terms, the Bavarian National Museum was intended to embody the idea of a 19th-century artistic shrine. It was built by Gabriel von Seidl in 1894–5, and features a mixture of styles that expresses the richness and variety of the collections within. The decoration of the interior was devised with the exhibits in mind. The nucleus of the collection is that of the Wittelsbachs, which Maximilian II donated to the country in 1855. One of Germany's largest history museums, its collections span Classical antiquity to the 19th century.

Model of Munich
Commissioned by Albrecht V, this wooden model was made by Jacob Sandtner in 1570.

First floor

Bauernstube (Farmhouse Parlour)
These pieces of traditional furniture were made by Anton Perthaler of Lower Bavaria in the late 18th century.

Ground floor

★ Judith with the Head of Holofernes
This alabaster figure was made by Conrad Meit in 1515, with the figure of Judith being depicted as a nude.

Main entrance

★ Christmas Crib
This 18th-century Neapolitan crib forms part of the largest and most important collection of its kind in the world.

Basement

Harpsichord
This harpsichord in the Musical Instruments Hall was made in Paris in 1754 by Jean Henri Hemsch.

VISITORS' CHECKLIST

Prinzregentenstr. 3. **Map** 4 E1. **Tel** 211 24 01. **U** Lehel. 17. 100. ○ 10am–5pm Tue–Wed & Fri–Sun, 10am–8pm Thu. ⚌ ⚌ ♿ by arrangement. **www. bayerisches-nationalmuseum.de**

★ St Mary Magdalene
This statue of the saint borne by angels was made by Tilman Riemenschneider in 1490–92 for an altarpiece.

MUSEUM GUIDE
The collections are laid out on three floors connected by grand staircases. The basement contains a collection of Christmas cribs and a section devoted to folk art. Painting, sculpture and crafts up to the 18th century are exhibited on the ground floor. The upper floor contains collections of musical instruments, porcelain and Biedermeier art.

STAR EXHIBITS

- ★ Christmas Crib
- ★ Judith with the Head of Holofernes
- ★ St Mary Magdalene

Gothic Hall
Laid out like a church, the hall contains religious art and tombstones of around 1500, including paintings by Jan Polack.

Romanesque Sculpture
Sculpture and architectural details dating from the first half of the 13th century and originating from the Wessobrunn Benedictine monastery fill this sculpture hall.

KEY

- ☐ Folk art
- ☐ Cribs
- ☐ Late 16th-century art
- ☐ 17th- and 18th-century art
- ☐ Thematic exhibition, including musical instruments and porcelain
- ☐ Non-exhibition space

THE MUSEUMS DISTRICT

A competition for an architectural design to embellish the area along the Royal Route between the Residenz and Schloss Nymphenburg was announced in 1807. The winning design was one jointly produced by Friedrich Ludwig von Sckell and Karl von Fischer, although it was later modified by Leo von Klenze.

Coat of arms on the façade of the Palaeontology Museum

The axis of this area, known as the Maxvorstadt, is Briennerstraße.

Maximilian I Joseph and Ludwig I dreamed of turning Munich into a city of the arts, commissioning the Alte Pinakothek and Neue Pinakothek, and grand buildings on Königsplatz. The 19th-century painter Franz von Lenbach had an imposing villa (now an art gallery) built on the square. The omnipresence of art here is underscored by the district's many private galleries, antique shops and bookstores.

SIGHTS AT A GLANCE

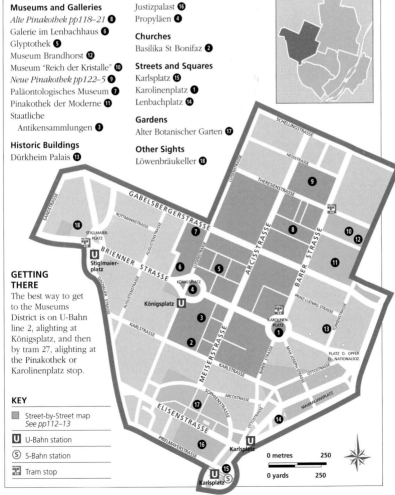

GETTING THERE

The best way to get to the Museums District is on U-Bahn line 2, alighting at Königsplatz, and then by tram 27, alighting at the Pinakothek or Karolinenplatz stop.

KEY

- Street-by-Street map See pp112–13
- **U** U-Bahn station
- **S** S-Bahn station
- Tram stop

0 metres   250
0 yards   250

◁ Fountain in the beautiful front garden of the Lenbachhaus

Street-by-Street: Around Königsplatz

Several days are needed for a thorough exploration of this part of the city. The many museums here contain world-class art – from prehistoric to modern. On Königsplatz, Greek and Roman sculpture can be seen in the Glyptothek, and Classical and other antiquities in the Antiken-sammlungen. The Alte Pinakothek, Neue Pinakothek and Pinakothek der Moderne nearby contain some of the richest collections of European painting in the world. The Lenbachhaus is renowned for works by the Blaue Reiter group. Those interested in natural history will enjoy the Palaeontology Museum.

A Cupid in the garden of the Lenbachhaus

Paläontologisches Museum
One of the most impressive exhibits in the museum is the cast of a mammoth skeleton from the early Tertiary period **7**

Galerie im Lenbachhaus
The Lenbachhaus interior sets in its context the bourgeois lifestyle of Franz von Lenbach, the famous late 19th-century portraitist. Closed for renovation until 2012.

Propyläen
The frieze decorating the side towers of the Propyläen, with motifs and scenes from the Greek War of Independence, is by Ludwig Schwanthaler **4**

Staatliche Antikensammlungen
Among the museum's treasures is a collection of antique art and artifacts **3**

Basilika St Bonifaz
This church contains the tomb of Ludwig I **2**

★ **Glyptothek**
The Glyptothek's Ionic colonnade with pediment is flanked by statues of great artistic figures from Classical antiquity: Hephaestus, Prometheus, Daedalus, Phidias, Pericles and Emperor Hadrian **5**

★ Neue Pinakothek

After viewing this modern museum's impressive collection of paintings ranging from 1780 to 1910, visitors can relax on the terrace, with its pools of water **9**

LOCATOR MAP
See Street Finder map 1

★ Alte Pinakothek

Giovanni Battista Tiepolo's painting The Adoration of the Magi *is one of the most important 18th-century works of Viennese art* **8**

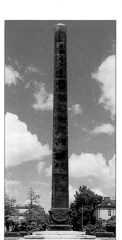

Karolinenplatz

In the centre of this square, which was named in honour of Karolina, mother of Ludwig I, stands a large obelisk commemorating the 30,000 Bavarian soldiers in Napoleon's army who died during his Russian campaign **1**

Old Town

| 0 metres | 100 |
| 0 yards | 100 |

KEY

– – – Suggested route

STAR SIGHTS

★ Alte Pinakothek

★ Glyptothek

★ Neue Pinakothek

The Amerikahaus on Karolinenplatz

Karolinenplatz ❶

Map 1 C5, 3 A1. 🚋 27.

Maximilian I Joseph, who continued the development of Munich that was begun by his predecessor Karl Theodor, focused his attention on the area around Briennerstraße. The Royal Route connecting the Residenz with Schloss Nymphenburg was opened up, and it became the focal point of the development of this suburb, which was named Maxvorstadt in the king's honour.

In 1809–12 a square was built at the junction of Briennerstraße and Barerstraße. This was Karolinenplatz, the first star junction in Munich. Designed by Karl von Fischer, it was modelled on the Place de l'Étoile in Paris. In the centre of the square stands a bronze obelisk 29 m (95 ft) high, designed by Leo von Klenze and cast from Turkish guns captured at the Battle of Navarino and commemorates the 30,000 Bavarian soldiers who died during Napoleon's Russian campaign of 1812.

On the northwestern side of the Karolinenplatz is the Anthropologische Staatssammlung, the only anthropological collection of its kind in Germany, with a curious assortment of skulls. On the western side is the Amerikahaus, an American cultural centre, built in 1955–7.

Basilika St Bonifaz ❷
Basilica of St Boniface

Karlstr. 34. **Map** 3 A1, 5 A1.
◯ 8am–8pm daily. 🚋 27.

The Basilica of St Boniface, which was commissioned by Ludwig I, functioned as the parish church of the Maxvorstadt but was later dedicated to the Benedictine monks who moved to Munich. The church, which takes the form of an early Christian basilica, was built in 1835–48 by Georg Friedrich Ziebland.

Behind the portico, which is supported by Ionic columns, are three arched doorways. The central one is flanked by statues of St Peter and St Boniface, and the arch is crowned by a portrait of the architect himself – a rare occurrence – in medieval dress. The location of the church and monastery at the rear of the Kunstausstellungsgebäude (now the Antikensammlung) illustrates contemporary ideas about architecture, in which religion was to be linked with art and science, as represented by the Benedictine order.

The basilica, which was built after the destruction brought by the Franco-

Central section of the façade of the Basilika St Bonifaz

Prussian War, carries no memory of the original double-aisled church, which had colourful paintings and an open-beam roof supported on 66 monolithic columns. Of its furnishings, the white marble tomb of Ludwig I survives, with the tombstone of his wife Theresa behind it.

Staatliche Antikensammlungen ❸
The National Collection of Antiquities

Königsplatz 1. **Map** 1 B5. **Tel** 59 98 88 30. Ⓤ Königsplatz. 🚋 27. ◯ 10am–5pm Tue–Sun (to 8pm Wed). 📷

In 1838 Ludwig I, temporarily at loggerheads with the court architect Leo von Klenze, commissioned Georg Friedrich Ziebland to design the southern side of the Königsplatz. The king wished for an exhibition hall that would adjoin the Benedictine monastery and Basilica of St Boniface at the rear. The building, completed in 1848, was modelled on the design of a late Classical Greek temple, its proportions differing from those of the

Greek kylix (drinking vessel), Staatliche Antikensammlung

Glyptothek on the opposite side of the square. Over the large colonnaded portico is a tympanum containing a figure of Bavaria as patroness of art and industry. From 1898 to 1916 the hall housed the gallery of the Munich Secession (Art Nouveau movement), after which it was taken over by the Neue Staatsgalerie. Since 1967 it has housed the National Collection of Antiquities.

This impressive collection includes an important assemblage of Greek and Etruscan vases, plus fine pottery and glass, bronze and terracotta figures and jewellery. The core of the collection was donated by Ludwig I, who was a passionate collector and an ardent admirer of the ancient world.

Propyläen ❹

Map 1 B5. 🅄 *Königsplatz.*

From 1815, Ludwig I and Leo von Klenze planned the layout of the Royal Square, or Königsplatz, west of Karolinenplatz. The latter was laid out as an almost perfect square, with the Glyptothek and what is now the Antikensammlungen facing one another on opposite sides. To the west of the square was a gate built by Leo von Klenze in 1854–62, named the Propyläen.

According to the designs of the king and the architect, the buildings on three sides of the square would each represent one of the orders of architecture. The Propyläen would represent the Doric order, the Glyptothek the Ionic, and the exhibition hall the Corinthian.

The Propyläen was based on the Propylaeum in Athens, which consists of a central entrance way crowned by a grand tympanum and flanked by towers. Munich's Propyläen was intended to function as the western gate into the city, the Neo-Classical equivalent of the medieval Isar Gate. When, however, the city's development rendered it superfluous, Ludwig I and von Klenze emphasized the Hellenistic character of the Propyläen, turning it into a kind of monument to the Greek War of Liberation against Turkey (1821–9). In so doing they strove to underline the connection between Bavaria and the newly independent Greek state (Otto I Wittelsbach was its first ruler).

LEO VON KLENZE (1784–1864)

After Karl Friedrich Schinkel, Leo von Klenze is considered to be the most prominent representative of the Neo-Classical movement in 19th-century German architecture. In the reign of Ludwig I, his constant if fussy patron, von Klenze was responsible for the new face of Munich, designing such buildings as the Alte Pinakothek, the forum of the Königsplatz, the Residenz, the Ruhmeshalle and Ludwigstraße. He was responsible for planning Munich as the new Athens, as well as the Walhalla near Ratisbon, the Befreiungshalle in Kelheim and the New Hermitage in St Petersburg.

Bust of the architect crowned with laurel

Glyptothek ❺
Glyptoteca

Königsplatz 3. **Map** 1 B5. **Tel** 28 61 00. 🅄 *Königsplatz.* ⏰ 10am–5pm Tue–Sun (to 8pm Thu). 🖼

The idea of building a museum to house Greek and Roman sculpture originated in 1805, when Ludwig I, the future king, was on his first tour of Italy. In 1816 Leo von Klenze was assigned the task of designing a museum for his collection. It was named the Glyptothek, from the Greek word *glypte*, meaning "carved stone". It is regarded as von Klenze's finest Neo-Classical work.

The museum's hall contains the world's finest collection of antique sculpture. Prize exhibits include Archaic figures from the Temple of Aphaia on Aegina of 500 BC, the famous Barberini Faun of 220 BC and the Rondanini Alexander of 338 BC.

Galerie im Lenbachhaus ❻
Lenbachhaus Art Gallery

Luisenstr. 33. **Map** 1 B5. **Tel** 23 33 20 00. 🅄 *Königsplatz.* ⚫ for renovation until 2012. 🖼

The portraitist Franz von Lenbach (1836–1904) commissioned Gabriel von Seidl to build him a grand residence behind Königsplatz. Completed in 1891, the house and its garden are in the style of an Italian suburban villa, with Renaissance and Baroque elements.

In 1924 the property was bought by the municipality for use as an art gallery. The exhibition area contains galleries in which Munich painting from the Gothic to the Art Nouveau periods is displayed, the 19th and early 20th centuries being well represented with works by Karl Spitzweg, Wilhelm Leibl and Lovis Corinth. The museum is also renowned for its fine paintings by artists of the Blaue Reiter group, which was active in Munich from 1911 to 1914 *(see p215)*. In 1957 Gabriele Münter, Wassily Kandinsky's partner up to 1914, gave her collection of pictures from his defining Munich and Murnau period. The gallery is closed for renovation and scheduled to re-open in 2012. Works from the gallery can be seen at the Kunstbau space underneath Königsplatz U-Bahn station.

Propyläen, Leo von Klenze's grand city gate in the Neo-Classical style

Paläontologisches Museum ❼

Palaeontology Museum

Richard-Wagner-Str. 10. **Map** 1 B5.
Tel 21 80 66 30. Ⓤ Königsplatz.
◯ 8am–4pm Mon–Thu, 8am–2pm
Fri, 10am–4pm first Sun of the
month. ♿

Since 1950, the Bavarian
palaeontological collection
has occupied an eclectic
building dating from 1899–
1902. Built by Leonhard
Romeis as a crafts school,
there are decorative motifs in
the main entranceway. The
main hall is an arcade with a
glass roof, where skeletons of
large animals are exhibited.

The displays are divided
into various thematic groups.
Skeletons found in Bavaria
include a mastodon, woolly
rhinoceros and giant tortoise.
Fossilized palm trees show the
existence of a tropical climate
here in prehistoric times.

Alte Pinakothek ❽

See pp118–21.

Neue Pinakothek ❾

See pp122–5.

Museum "Reich der Kristalle" ❿

Mineralogy Museum

Theresienstr. 41 (entrance in Barer
Straße) **Map** 1 C5. **Tel** 21 80 43 12.
Ⓤ Theresienstr. 🚋 27. ◯ 1–5pm
Tue–Sat, 10am–5pm Sun. ♿

The exhibits here are part
of the great collection of the
Mineralogische Staat-
sammlung, which originated
with collections of rocks and
minerals found in the 18th
century. The museum owes
its valuable collection to Duke
Maximilian von Leuchtenberg,
who supervised mineral
extraction in Siberia. His
collection was added to that
of the Bavarian Academy of
Sciences in 1858.

The present museum is in a
modern building. Visitors can
enjoy colourful mineral formations from all over the world,
and study their structure.

Pinakothek der Moderne ⓫

The Pinakothek der Moderne opened in 2002 as
one of the world's largest museums of modern art. Its
vast collection contains works from the 20th and
21st centuries and is intended to complement the
Alte Pinakothek and the Neue Pinakothek nearby.
The museum houses outstanding artworks, from
Cubism (with works by Pablo Picasso and Georges
Braque), the Neue Sachlichkeit and paintings by
Giorgio De Chirico and Max Beckmann through
to Pop Art, Minimal Art, Photorealism and the Junge
Wilde movement of the 1980s. The gallery also
houses collections of drawings, installations,
design, photography and architecture.
The jewellery exhibition focuses on
international contemporary pieces.

★ **The Falling Man** (1915)
*This bronze cast of a naked youth by Wilhelm
Lehmbruck mirrors the artist's shocked feelings
about World War I. It was originally to form part
of a monument entitled* Suffering of Mankind.

Ground
Floor

Proust's Armchair (1978)
*Designed by Alessandro Mendini,
this piece is one of 60,000 objects
that illustrate the history of design.*

GALLERY GUIDE
*The collections are laid out over three floors.
The basement level is devoted to design, from
here stairs lead down to the Danner Rotunda. The
ground floor contains exhibition rooms for
architecture and works on paper. One of the
world's leading collections of painting, sculpture
and new media is located on the first floor.*

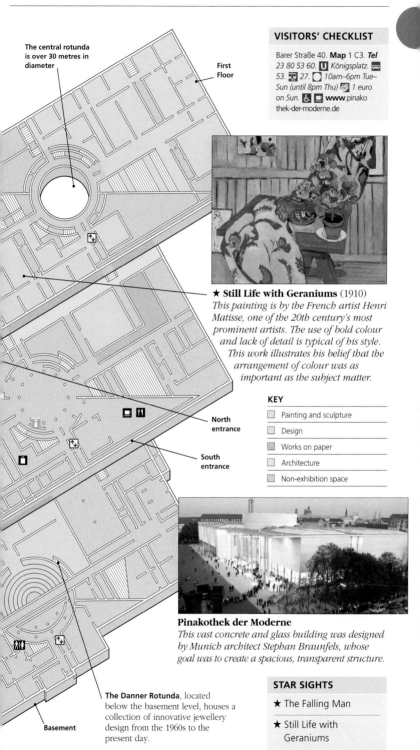

The central rotunda is over 30 metres in diameter

First Floor

VISITORS' CHECKLIST

Barer Straße 40. **Map** 1 C3. **Tel** 23 80 53 60. Ⓤ *Königsplatz.* 53. 27. ◯ *10am–6pm Tue–Sun (until 8pm Thu)* 1 euro on Sun. www.pinako thek-der-moderne.de

★ **Still Life with Geraniums** (1910)
This painting is by the French artist Henri Matisse, one of the 20th century's most prominent artists. The use of bold colour and lack of detail is typical of his style. This work illustrates his belief that the arrangement of colour was as important as the subject matter.

North entrance

South entrance

KEY

▢	Painting and sculpture
▢	Design
▢	Works on paper
▢	Architecture
▢	Non-exhibition space

Pinakothek der Moderne
This vast concrete and glass building was designed by Munich architect Stephan Braunfels, whose goal was to create a spacious, transparent structure.

The Danner Rotunda, located below the basement level, houses a collection of innovative jewellery design from the 1960s to the present day.

Basement

STAR SIGHTS

★ The Falling Man

★ Still Life with Geraniums

Alte Pinakothek **8**

The Alte Pinakothek, one of the world's most famous art galleries, opened in 1836. It is a building in the Italian Renaissance style, designed by Leo von Klenze. The history of its collections goes back to the Renaissance, when Wilhelm IV the Steadfast (ruled 1508–50) decided to adorn his residence with historic paintings. His successors were equally keen art collectors and, by the 18th century, an outstanding collection of 14th- to 18th-century paintings had been amassed.

St Luke Painting the Madonna (c.1484)
This painting by the Netherlandish artist Rogier van der Weyden is one of his most widely copied works.

★ **The Battle of Issus** (1529)
This famous painting by Albrecht Altdorfer depicts the decisive moment in Alexander the Great's victory over the Persians.

★ **Pietà** (c.1490)
The rich, contrasting colours, strong effects of light and shadow and homogeneous composition of this painting are typical of the later work of Sandro Botticelli.

Portrait of Karl V (1548)
This portrait of the emperor in Augsburg, once attributed to Titian, was in fact painted by Lambert Sustrio who worked in his studio.

Main entrance

KEY

☐	German painting
☐	Netherlandish painting
☐	Flemish painting
☐	Dutch painting
☐	Italian painting
☐	Spanish painting
☐	French painting
☐	Non-exhibition space
☐	Special exhibition space

STAR PAINTINGS

★ The Battle of Issus

★ The Deposition

★ Pietà

GALLERY GUIDE

The collections are laid out on two floors. The ground floor is occupied mainly by Flemish painting from the 16th and 17th centuries. On the first floor are works by German painters as well as Dutch, Netherlandish, Flemish, French, Italian and Spanish paintings.

Peasants Playing Cards (c.1625–49)
This is an expressive, semi-satirical scene from Flemish peasant life painted by Adriaen Brouwer.

VISITORS' CHECKLIST

Barer Straße 27. **Map** *1 C5.*
Tel *23 80 52 16.*
U *Königsplatz.* 🚌 *27.*
🕐 *10am–6pm Wed–Sun (until 8pm Tue).*
🎫 *Children under 14 free.* ♿
🖥 **www**.alte-pinakothek.de

★ **The Deposition** (c.1633)
In this dramatic painting, Rembrandt consciously challenges Rubens' idealised version of Christ's sacrifice by focusing on the pained expressions of the other figures in the composition.

Portrait of the Marquise de Pompadour (1756)
One of the finest French Rococo paintings by François Boucher.

Italian Baroque painting is represented by such masters as Tiepolo and Guido Reni.

First floor

Adoraton of the Magi (c.1502)
This scene by Hans Holbein the Elder forms part of an altarpiece from Kaisheim.

Land of Cockaigne (1567)
The Flemish artist Pieter Brueghel painted this visual satire on the mythical land of plenty, condemning gluttony and indolence.

Exploring the Alte Pinakothek

After World War II, the Alte Pinakothek was rebuilt by
Hans Döllgast. The entrance hall, ticket office, book-
shop and cafeteria are on the ground floor, as are the
section on German Gothic painting, the Breughel Room
and the temporary exhibitions gallery. The collections
on the first floor are grouped according to the great
national schools. The larger paintings are exhibited in
the main rooms, and smaller ones in the side galleries.

*The Abduction of the Daughters of
Leukippos (1618) by Rubens*

*Four Apostles (1526), a pair of
panels by Albrecht Dürer*

GERMAN PAINTING

The Alte Pinakothek is renowned for its important
collection of German late
Gothic and Renaissance art.
The section opens with a
collection of paintings by
the Cologne School, from
the Master of St Veronica
(c. 1420), to the fine altar of
St Bartholomew (1500–10),
which anticipates the Renaissance. Late 15th-century
painting is represented by
Michael Pacher's *Altar of the
Church Fathers*, with a bold
handling of perspective.
　The collection of paintings
by Albrecht Dürer documents
the development of his work
from a *Self-Portrait* of 1500 to
the *Four Apostles* of 1526.
Two paintings by Matthias
Grünewald show a strong
Renaissance influence, as
does the *Crucifixion* (1503)
by Lucas Cranach the Elder.
Albrecht Altdorfer of Regensburg, a painter of the Danube
School, is represented by his
Battle of Issus with its
pioneering use of landscape.
　Mannerism is exemplified
by the allegories by Hans
Baldung Grien and Hans von

Aachen's *Allegory of Truth*.
Painting of the 17th century
includes works by Adam
Elsheimer and Johann Liss.

NETHERLANDISH PAINTING

This school, which split into
the Flemish and Dutch
schools at the end of the 16th
century, is introduced by the
fine works of Rogier van der
Weyden, particularly his
Cologne Altarpiece with the
famous *Adoration of the Magi*.
　Hans Memling's *Seven Joys
of the Virgin* depicts scenes
from the life of Christ in an
extensive symbolic landscape.
A glimpse of the grotesque
world of Hieronymus Bosch
is given by a fragment of his
Last Judgement, while a
completely different climate
bathes Pieter Breughel's *Land
of Cockaigne*. An outstanding
example of the assimilation of
Italian Renaissance style is
Danae by Jan Grossaert.

FLEMISH PAINTING

The largest collection
of works by the great 17th-
century painter Peter Paul
Rubens can be seen here.
They range from the intimate
*Rubens and Isabella Brandt
in the Honeysuckle Bower*
(1609), painted to celebrate
the artist's marriage, to *The
Abduction of the Daughters of
Leukippos* and *The Battle of
the Amazons* in the High
Baroque style. Here also are
the large-scale *Last
Judgement, Fall of the Rebel
Angels* and *Women of the
Apocalypse*, as well as
sketches for the scenes from
the life of Marie de Medici.
　This section also includes
paintings by Rubens' pupils
Anthony van Dyck and Jacob
Jordaens, and the peasant
scenes of Adriaen Brouwer,
the most notable of which is
Peasants Playing Cards.

The Adoration of the Magi (c.1455) by Rogier van der Weyden

For hotels and restaurants in this region see pp262–5 and pp276–9

DUTCH PAINTING

The gallery's rich collection of 17th-century Dutch art represents the Golden Age of Dutch painting. It includes an outstanding series of Passion scenes by Rembrandt that were executed in the 1630s and are important examples of the Baroque style.

Outstanding among the wealth of portraits is a self-portrait by Carel Fabritius and the *Portrait of Willem van Heythuysen* by Frans Hals.

Landscape painting is represented by the work of Jacob van Ruisdael and by the townscapes and river scenes of Han van Goyen. Among the genre painters, Jan Steen, Gabriel Metsu and Gerard Terborch are particularly noteworthy names.

Portrait of Willem van Heythuysen (1625–30) by Frans Hals

ITALIAN PAINTING

Such is the comprehensive nature of the gallery's collection that it is possible to make a thorough study of Italian painting here. Most of the early works came to the gallery thanks to Ludwig I's infatuation with the art of this particular period.

Paintings of the 14th century include Giotto's *Last Supper*. Florentine art, which flowered a century later, is represented by the religious paintings of Fra Filippo Lippi and Dominico Ghirlandaio. Other highlights include

The Annunciation (c. 1473) by Antonello da Messina

Leonardo da Vinci's *Madonna and Child* (c. 1473), Perugino's *Vision of St Bernard* and works by Raphael, outstanding among which is the *Madonna dei Tempi* (1507).

The Venetian School is represented by Titian's *Crown of Thorns* and Tintoretto's series of battle scenes glorifying the Gonzaga family. Great works of the 18th century include the religious canvases of Tiepolo and the fascinating Venetian townscapes of both Canaletto and Francesco Guardi.

SPANISH PAINTING

Although it is smaller than other sections in the gallery, the collection of Spanish painting is no less interesting and includes works by the major masters of the Spanish School. The dramatic *Disrobing of Christ* by El Greco is one of three versions of this famous work. There are also paintings by Diego Velázquez, as well as the Mannerist scenes from the *Legend of St Catherine* by Francisco de Zurbarán, one of his finest works.

Also of interest are Murillo's paintings, in particular his genre scenes depicting street urchins in Seville. Other notable works include studio paintings by the lesser-known Claudio José Antonílez of about 1670.

FRENCH PAINTING

Despite their political connections with France, the Wittelsbachs did not collect French art on a large scale. The museum has three small paintings by Nicolas Poussin that, as early works, are not representative of his mature style. The work of Claude Lorrain is better documented, exhibits including his melancholic *Banishment of Hagar*.

By contrast, 18th-century French painting is well represented, most of the works having been acquired with the help of various banks. Noteworthy among them are paintings by Jean-Baptiste Pater and Nicolas Lancret, followers of Antoine Watteau, and Jean-Marc Nattier's excellent *Portrait of the Marquis of Baglion*. The work of François Boucher is generously represented, from the exquisite *Portrait of the Marquise de Pompadour* to his intimate study of the young Louise O'Murphy, mistress of Louis XV.

The eroticism of the Rococo age is illustrated by sketches by Jean-Honoré Fragonard, while Jean-Baptiste Greuze's moralistic *Grievance of Time* heralds the sentimentality of Neo-Classicism.

Disrobing of Christ (c. 1585) by El Greco

Neue Pinakothek ❾

The Neue Pinakothek, which contains 19th-century paintings displayed in a building designed by August von Volt, opened in 1853. From 1909 to 1914, under the curatorship of the art historian Hugo von Tschudi, the collection of academic paintings was extended in an avant-garde direction. The building itself was destroyed during World War II, and between 1976 and 1981 a new gallery, designed by Alexander von Branca, was constructed. Today the museum's exhibits consist primarily of German, French and English paintings dating from 1780 to 1910.

★ Italia and Germania
(1828) *This painting by Friedrich Overbeck looks back to the Renaissance.*

Heroic Landscape with Fishermen
(1818) *In this Romantic painting by Théodore Géricault, the Neo-Classical landscape is bathed in a romantic light.*

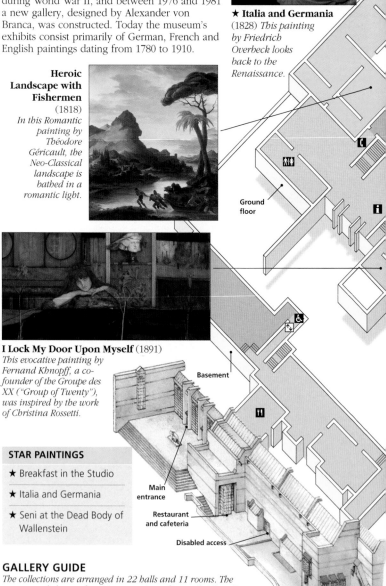

Ground floor

I Lock My Door Upon Myself (1891)
This evocative painting by Fernand Khnopff, a co-founder of the Groupe des XX ("Group of Twenty"), was inspired by the work of Christina Rossetti.

Basement

STAR PAINTINGS

- ★ Breakfast in the Studio
- ★ Italia and Germania
- ★ Seni at the Dead Body of Wallenstein

Main entrance

Restaurant and cafeteria

Disabled access

GALLERY GUIDE

The collections are arranged in 22 halls and 11 rooms. The recommended route for visitors, tracing a figure of eight, takes the collections in chronological order. The halls, of varying size, height and level, are arranged around two inner courtyards.

Portrait of the Marquesa de Caballero (1807)
In his role as court painter, Francisco de Goya executed many portraits of Spanish royalty and aristocracy such as this one.

VISITORS' CHECKLIST

Barer Str. 29 (entrance on Theresienstr.). **Map** 1 C4.
Tel *23 80 51 95.* Ⓤ *Königsplatz.*
🚋 *27.* ⚪ *10am–8pm Wed, 10am–5pm Thu–Mon.*
🎟 *1 euro on Sun.* 🚻 🖥 ♿
www.neue-pinakothek.de

★ Seni before the Corpse of Wallenstein (1855)
This illustration by Carl Theodor von Piloty of a scene from Schiller's famous play enjoyed enormous popularity during the 19th century.

Play of the Waves (1883)
Arnold Böcklin interpreted this mythological scene in a subtly erotic Neo-Baroque manner.

Still Life with Asparagus (c.1885/90)
The artist Karl Schuch remains underrated to this day. His painting of asparagus spears was influenced by the work of Édouard Manet.

KEY

☐	Neo-Classicism and Romanticism
☐	Nazarenes and Biedermeier
☐	Realism and late Romanticism
☐	History painting
☐	Böcklin, Marées and late Realism
☐	Impressionism
☐	Symbolism and Art Nouveau
☐	Temporary exhibitions
☐	Non-exhibition space

★ Breakfast in the Studio (1868)
This outstanding painting by Édouard Manet, with strongly contrasting dark and light tones, dates from the end of his pre-Expressionist period.

Exploring the Neue Pinakothek

The Neue Pinakothek is admirably designed for visitors.
The recommended route for viewing the collections
starts and ends in a large hall, and can easily be
extended or shortened. Glass roofs allow the rooms to
be illuminated by natural light. The varied rhythm of
the itinerary and the size and height of the rooms,
which are situated at different levels, keep the
experience interesting and full of stimulating variety.

**Church Ruins in the Forest (1831)
by Caspar David Friedrich**

NEO-CLASSICISM AND EARLY ROMANTICISM

The sculptures of Paris by
Antonio Canova and of
Adonis by Bertel Thorvaldsen
show these artists' different
approaches to Neo-Classicism.
Ascetic Neo-Classicism was
also shaped by Jacques-Louis
David with his *Portrait of the
Comtesse Sorcy de Thélusson*
(1790). Neo-Classical landscape painting is represented
by German painters including
Jacob Philipp Hackert.

Also on display is a series
of melancholy landscapes by
the German Romantic painter
Caspar David Friedrich. The
Dresden school of landscape
painters is represented by
Carl Gustav Carus and Johan
Christian Dahl, among others.
*Heroic Landscape with Fisher-
men* by Théodore Géricault
imbues the Neo-Classical
landscape with a Romantic
atmosphere. The paintings of
Eugène Delacroix, such as
Valentine Dying (c.1826) and
The Death of Ophelia (1838)
treat the Faustian and Shakes-
pearean themes so beloved
of the Romantic painters.

THE NAZARENES AND BIEDERMEIER

The gallery's body of
Nazarene paintings formed
the basis of its collection
when it first opened in 1853.
Italia and Germania, the
allegory by Friedrich
Overbeck in which the two
figures sit in a sisterly
embrace, expresses the artistic
relationship between the two
nations. Joseph Anton Koch's
paintings *Heroic Landscape
with Rainbow* (1812) and
*View of the Environs of
Olevano* (1830) combine
Romantic impulses with the
religious mood characteristic
of the Nazarenes.

Although they are artistic-
ally quite different, the genre
paintings of the Austrian artist
Ferdinand Waldmüller and
the fairy-tale cycles of Moritz
von Schwind (such as
Symphony) both express a
specific urban view of happi-
ness in line with the Biedermeier style's *Gemütlichkeit*
(domestic harmony).

REALISM AND LATE ROMANTICISM

In the early 20th century the
Neue Pinakothek started to
acquire French paintings of
the Realist school, whose

The Poor Poet (1839) by Carl Spitzweg

Don Quijote (1868) by
Honoré Daumier

origins date from about 1850.
The gallery's acquisitions
from that time include studies
by Camille Corot, notably
some of his Italian vignettes.
There is also a collection of
works by Gustave Courbet,
among which images of rocks
in landscapes predominate.
The contrast between
different paintings by the
caricaturist Honoré Daumier
is superb: while *Dramatist on
Stage* (1860) shows the world
of Parisian theatre, his in-
comparable *Don Quijote*
(1868) conveys the symbolic
character of the knight from
La Mancha. With his satirical
The Poor Poet (1839), Carl
Spitzweg created almost a cult
character in Germany.

HISTORY PAINTING

Historical subjects were a
favourite theme in the
19th century. This section
opens with Wilhelm von
Kaulbach's vast canvas *The
Destruction of Jerusalem*
(1846), in which the sacking
of the city by the
Emperor Titus is
given an allegorical
setting. Kaulbach
also painted canvases
showing the virtues
of Ludwig I, who
was a prominent
patron of the arts.
Historical painting
is represented to a
significant degree
by Carl Theodor
von Piloty, with

his famous *Seni before the Corpse of Wallenstein* (1855) and the much later *Thusnelda in the Triumphal Procession of Germanicus* (1873), a Neo-Baroque vision of what was seen as Germanic virtues.

BOCKLIN, MAREES AND LATE REALISM

After the unification of the German Empire in 1871, German art fragmented into various movements. Hans von Marées of the Rhineland sought new ways of treating Classical themes. The Neue Pinakothek houses his principal works, including the triptych *Hesperides II* (1884) and *Three Riders* (1887).

Anselm Feuerbach's superb handling of colour expresses a tragic interpretation of Classical themes, as in his *Medea* (1870), while Arnold Böcklin's world of Classical mythology is in harmony with Neo-Baroque trends (as in his *Play of the Waves*). Here also is a substantial collection of works by the Munich Realist Wilhelm Leibl, including *Portrait of Mrs Gedon* (1869), as well as paintings by Carl Schuch and Wilhelm Trübner.

Hesperides II (1884/87) by Hans von Marées

The Railway Cutting (1870). In the latter, a milestone in his artistic development, the artist shows for the first time his tendency to endow natural forms with geometric shapes. Edgar Degas' delightful *Woman Ironing* (1869) is accompanied by a number of his portraits and statuettes of dancers. The gallery also has paintings by Auguste Renoir, Camille Pissarro and Alfred Sisley.

German Impressionists are also well represented. On display are early works by Adolph von Menzel and paintings by Lovis Corinth, Max Slevogt and Max Liebermann, including his carefree *Boys on the Beach*. The room containing paintings by Paul Signac inaugurates the gallery's Post-Impressionist section. Paul Gauguin is represented by works from his Breton period as well as by *The Birth* (1896), a classic painting from his Tahitian period. Most notably, the Neue Pinakothek has a representative collection of works by Vincent van Gogh. Prominent among them are *Sunflowers* (1888) and two landscapes: *View of Arles* (1889) and *Plain at Auvers* (1890). All three paintings express the artist's delight in the beauty of the sun, the sky, flowers and crops.

Boys on the Beach (1898) by Max Liebermann

IMPRESSIONISM AND POST-IMPRESSIONISM

With regard to Impressionist painting, what the Neue Pinakothek lacks in quantity it makes up for in the importance of its collection. Mention should be made of masterpieces by Édouard Manet, such as *Barque at Argenteuil* (1874), Claude Monet's *Bridge at Argenteuil* (1874) and in particular of Paul Cézanne's

SYMBOLISM AND ART NOUVEAU

The interaction between the two artistic movements Symbolism and Art Nouveau is illustrated by *I Lock My Door Upon Myself* by Fernand Khnopff. James Ensor's expressive *Masks* and paintings by Edvard Munch and Maurice Denis can also be seen here.

Of equal interest are works by artists such as Pierre Bonnard and Édouard Vuillard who continued the Impressionist tradition. The erotic and eschatological themes typical of Symbolism can be seen in Egon Schiele's *Agony* (1902), for example. The *Portrait of Margarethe Stonborough-Wittgenstein* (1905) by Gustav Klimt comes at the end of the Neue Pinakothek's exhibits.

Sunflowers (1888) by Vincent van Gogh

Museum Brandhorst ⑫

Theresienstr. 35a. **Map** 1 C5.
Ⓤ *Königsplatz.* ◯ *10am–6pm Tue–Sun (until 8pm Thu).*
www.museum-brandhorst.de

Opened in spring 2009, Museum Brandhorst is home to the Brandhorst collection; an extensive and important collection of modern and contemporary art. Commissioned by the Bavarian government, the museum lies adjacent to the Pinakothek der Moderne.

Many of the leading art figures of the late 20th century – among them Joseph Beuys, Gerhard Richter and Damien Hirst – are shown here. With more than 60 works by abstract painter Cy Twombly, the gallery provides a retrospective of this artist's development. The museum building is impressive, with 23 different coloured panes of glass.

Triad of windows on the ground floor of Dürckheim Palais

Dürckheim Palais ⑬

Türkenstr. 4. **Map** 3 B1. 🚊 *27.*
⬤ *to the public.*

Built in 1843–4 for the chief-steward of the court, Count Georg Friedrich von Dürckheim-Montmartin, the palace was designed by Friedrich Jakob Kreuther. Up until 1909 the building housed the Prussian Embassy. Today it is used by Bayerische Landesbank. The modern building of the bank next door to the palace creates a strong sense of aesthetic dissonance.

The façade of the palace, with its distinctive brick and terracotta reliefs, makes reference to early Italian Renaissance architecture. The main entrance, which was originally centrally placed on the building, was moved to the right in 1912. The palace is a classic example of the transitional style of architecture that links the work of Friedrich von Gärtner and the Maximilian style.

Lenbachplatz ⑭

Map 3 A1. Ⓢ and Ⓤ *Karlsplatz/ Stachus.* 🚊 *16, 17, 18, 19, 20, 21, 27.*

This irregularly shaped square lies between Maximiliansplatz, the Alter Botanischer Garten and Karlsplatz. The buildings that line it are typical of the late 19th century. Standing in imposing groups and laid out in irregular fashion around the square, they create a set of contrasting perspectives.

On the west side stand the law courts (Justizpalast) and on the south side rises the bizarre outline of the Künstlerhaus. On the north side is the **Stock Exchange** (Börse). Built in 1868–98, it is an example of pompous Neo-Baroque, its splendour reflecting the power of the financial institution within. The neighbouring **Bernheimerhaus**, at No. 6, was built in 1889. In architectural terms, it was regarded as the ultimate residential building in Munich, a novelty at the time being the exposed iron structure of the ground floor and the huge picture windows.

On the east side of the square, bordering Maximiliansplatz, is

Allegorical statue on the Wittelsbacher Brunnen on Lenbachplatz

Munich's finest fountain, the **Wittelsbacher Brunnen**, built by Adolf von Hildebrand in 1893–5 to commemorate the completion of the city's new water-supply system. The fountain symbolizes both charity and the destructive power of water. It is dominated by two allegorical figures – a stone-throwing youth on a steed, and a woman seated on a bull holding a goblet.

Karlsplatz ⑮

Map 3 A1 (5 A2).
Ⓢ and Ⓤ *Karlsplatz/Stachus.*
🚊 *16, 17, 18, 19, 20, 21, 27.*

After the city's fortifications were blown up in 1791 on the orders of Karl Theodor, a vast square was laid out on the western side of the Old Town. It was named Karlsplatz in honour of the ruler, as was the gate called the **Karlstor**, which was preserved. The square also had a popular name – Stachus – which is still used today. It refers to the most popular inn in Munich, which since 1759 has stood on the southwest side of the square.

In 1899–1902 the architect Gabriel von Seidl added two semicircular wings, known as the Rondelbauten, to the Karlstor. These three-storey Neo-Baroque buildings, with two tower-shaped projections, have numerous shops in their ground-floor arcades. Another

People relaxing beside the fountains of Karlsplatz

architectural feature of the square is the mock-historic law courts (Justizpalast) on its northwest side.

The large fountain in the western part of the square is a favourite meeting place for the inhabitants of Munich and a resting place for tourists. In the 1970s the area beneath the square was converted into a major metropolitan hub and shopping centre.

Detail of the ornamental attic of the Justizpalast

Justizpalast 🔟
Law Courts

Elisenstr. 1a. (Karlsplatz) Priel-mayerstr. 7. **Map** 3 A1 (5 A2). **Tel** 55 97 01. Ⓢ and Ⓤ Karlsplatz/Stachus. 🚋 16, 17, 18, 19, 20, 21, 27.

On the northwest side of Karlsplatz stands one of the best-known late 19th-century landmarks in Munich. The law courts, built in 1891–98 by Friedrich von Thiersch, are an example of pure Neo-Baroque architecture, with discreet Neo-Mannerist elements.

The building's great novelty at the time was its vast steel and glass dome, which acted as a skylight. The interior – particularly the main hall and the main stairway, which are directly beneath the dome – has an extraordinary wealth of detail in its design.

North of the Justizpalast are the Neues Justizgebäude (New Law Courts). Built in 1906–08, also by Thiersch, they are in the Neo-Gothic style and have a clocktower and gables.

Alter Botanischer Garten 🔟
Old Botanical Garden

Map 3 A1 (5 A1). Between Elisen- and Sophienstr. Ⓢ and Ⓤ Karlsplatz/Stachus. 🚋 16, 17, 18, 19, 20, 21, 27.

Visitors to Munich who find themselves in need of respite from the bustle of the city centre will find a sanctuary in the Old Botanical Gardens north of the Justiz-palast. Laid out on a semi-circular plan in 1804–14, they were designed by Ludwig von Sckell, who was also respons-ible for the Englischer Garten.

The entrance to the gardens is through an early Neo-Classical gate built by Emanuel Joseph von Herigoyen in 1811 and bearing a Latin inscrip-tion by Goethe. In 1854 the greenhouse was demolished to make space for the Glas-palast. Modelled on London's Crystal Palace, it was built to house the First Industrial Exhibition. The Glaspalast burned down in 1931, destroying at the same time an exhibition of German Romantic painting.

In 1914 new botanical gardens were laid out in Nymphenburg, and the Old Botanical Gardens were converted into a muni-cipal park. A restaurant (today the Park Café) was built in 1935–7, as well as an exhibition hall designed by Oswald Bieber. The sculptor Josef Wackerle created the Neptune Fountain, which has a figure based on Michelangelo's David. The café garden, shaded by exotic trees, is an ideal place to relax and enjoy a cold beer.

The Neptune Fountain in the Old Botanical Garden

Löwenbräukeller 🔟

Stiglmaierplatz 2 /Nymphenburger-straße. **Map** 1 A5. **Tel** 52 60 21. Ⓤ Stiglmaierplatz. ◯ 10am–midnight daily.

Visitors entering the city from the west along Nymphenburgerstraße will see from afar the marble statue of the lion that crowns the Löwenbräukeller on Stigl-maierplatz. This famous Munich brewery has its own inn, which is large enough to hold 4,000 drinkers.

The picturesque brewery and inn were built in 1883 by Albert Schmidt and were refurbished by Friedrich von Thiersch at the turn of the 19th and 20th centuries. The sides of the octagonal tower are decorated alternately with the brewery's emblem – a white griffin – and the city's coat of arms. The tower rises above an arcaded entrance hall with a roof terrace. In summer drinkers are drawn to the beer garden shaded by large chestnut trees.

The building of the world-famous Löwenbräukeller

FURTHER AFIELD

Many of Munich's attractions lie outside the city centre and, thanks to a highly efficient transport system, they are easily reached. To the north, for instance, is the famous Olympiapark and the BMW factory's modern complex of buildings. To the west lies the Nymphenburg district, with its palace, park and botanical gardens. Southeast of the

Sculpture in the Nymphenburg gardens

Old Town is Theresienwiese, where the famous Oktoberfest is held, and unfailing attractions to the south are the Hellabrunn Zoo, in Thalkirchen, and the Bavaria Film Museum, in Geiselgasteig. To the east are some masterpieces of religious architecture – the great Mariä Himmelfahrtskirche in Ramersdorf, and Michaelskirche in Berg am Laim.

SIGHTS AT A GLANCE

Palaces and Historic Buildings
Asam-Schlössl ⑫
Blutenburg ⑯
Grünwald ⑪
Nymphenburg pp130–33 ❶

Museum
BMW-Museum ❹
Deutsches Museum
    Verkehrszentrum ⑬

Districts
Berg am Laim ❼

Ramersdorf ❽

Parks and Open Spaces
Botanischer Garten ❷
Olympiapark ❸
Theresienwiese ⑭
Tierpark Hellabrunn ❾

Others
Au ❻
Bavaria-Filmstadt ⑩
Hypo-Hochhaus ❺
Neue Messe München ⑮

KEY

▢	Central Munich
▢	Outskirts of Munich
▭	Motorway
▭	Major road
▭	Minor road
—	Railway line
🚉	Railway station

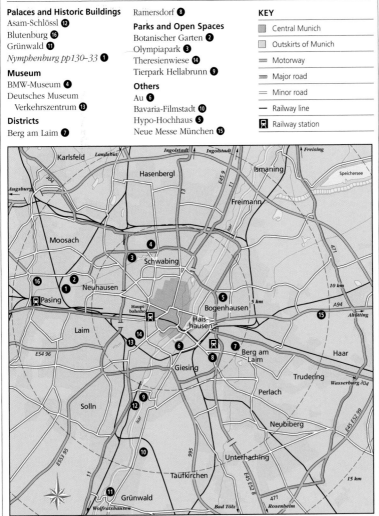

◁ **The Olympiapark, with the Olympiaturm, and the buildings of the BMW factory in the background**

Nymphenburg ❶

After the birth in 1679 of Maximilian Emanuel, the heir to the throne, his father, Duke Ferdinand Maria, presented his wife with a suburban palace. The queen named it Nymphenburg (Nymphs' Castle) and supervised the building work that ensued. Max Emanuel continued his mother's work, creating with architects Joseph Effner and Enrico Zucalli one of the finest palaces and gardens in Europe. Later, buildings were added around the courtyard fronting the palace. In the 1800s the formal French gardens were converted into a landscaped park incorporating the existing canals.

Porcelain parrot at the factory

★ **Amalienburg**

Built by François Cuvilliés, the Amalienburg was a small hunting lodge. Its circular hall was covered with fine shellwork, and the windows and mirrors created the illusion of great space.

Façade of the Palace

This stately palace, its broad façade, 600 m (1,968 ft) wide, broken up in typically Baroque style, is perfectly complemented by the geometric layout of the formal gardens.

★ **Marstallmuseum**

This museum contains coaches, carriages and sleighs that once belonged to Bavarian rulers, including Ludwig II's coronation coach, and portraits of his favourite horses.

The Porzellanmanufaktur has produced fine porcelain since 1761. The factory's chief designer was Franz Anton Bustelli.

Garden
The formal French garden at the rear of the palace, with an 18th-century canal, forms the main axis of the entire palace and its gardens.

VISITORS' CHECKLIST

Nymphenburg Tel *17 90 80.*
U *Rotkreuzplatz, then* 12.
12, 16, 17. 51.
1 Apr–15 Oct: 9am–6pm daily; 16 Oct–31 Mar: 10am–4pm daily.
www.schloesser.bayern.de
Museum Mensch und Natur
9am–5pm Tue–Fri (until 8pm Thu); 10am–6pm Sat, Sun & public hols.

Badenburg
The bathing hall and the first heated tiled pool are surrounded by a viewing gallery.

★ Pagodenburg
This pavilion was used for receiving visitors and for relaxation. The ground floor is covered with 2,000 Dutch Delft tiles depicting figures and landscapes.

The orangery was, at the time it was built, the first in Germany to be heated by hot water.

The Museum Mensch und Natur is dedicated to the structure of the earth and the workings of the human body.

STAR FEATURES

★ Amalienburg

★ Marstallmuseum

★ Pagodenburg

Magdalenenklause
This folly, built as a chapel in a grotto with hermits' cells, reflects the Baroque idea of withdrawal from courtly life into a world of peace and contemplation.

Schloss Nymphenburg

The oldest part of the palace is the central section, built in 1675 in the form of an Italianate villa. In 1702 Maximilian Emanuel commissioned the construction of side pavilions, which were connected to the villa by galleries. Soon after 1715, when Joseph Effner took charge of building work on the palace, the Steinerner Saal (Audience Hall) with stunningly lavish interior decoration was built, along with the other rooms in the wings, and the stables and orangery.

A staircase lantern

Italianate Villa
The façade of the oldest, 17th-century wing of the palace, facing the garden, is fronted by a double stairway supported on three arches.

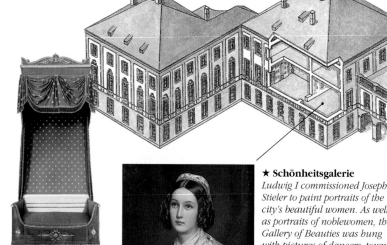

★ Schönheitsgalerie
Ludwig I commissioned Joseph Stieler to paint portraits of the city's beautiful women. As well as portraits of noblewomen, the Gallery of Beauties was hung with pictures of dancers, townswomen and "The Beauty of Munich", a tailor's daughter.

★ Royal Bed
The royal bedchamber in the south wing of the palace is decorated with fine paintings. and filled with mahogany furniture, including the Royal Bed, where Ludwig II was born.

Portrait of Karl Albrecht as Emperor Karl VII
This majestic portrait was produced in the studio of the court painter George de Marées in 1742. The pendant is the portrait of the Empress Maria Amalia, which hangs in the same room.

STAR FEATURES

★ Royal Bed

★ Schönheitsgalerie

★ Steinerner Saal

For hotels and restaurants in this region see pp262–5 and pp276–9

Paintings

The walls and ceilings of the palace halls are covered with colourful paintings framed with stuccowork. The finest is the ceiling of the Steinerner Saal, in which mythological scenes are shown in idyllic garden settings.

Lackkabinett

This corner cabinet with Chinese motifs is exquisitely decorated with black lacquer on wood panelling. The Chinese theme is reinforced by the Rococo painting of the ceiling.

Balustrades
decorated with vases line the stairways leading to the palace gardens.

Entrance

Vorzimmer

This anteroom in the north part of the palace is richly decorated in French Regency style. Paintings, stuccowork and wood carvings cover the walls, while the ceiling is decorated with Classical subjects.

★ Steinerner Saal

Upon entering the palace, visitors walk into a spacious hall with windows on either side decorated in a resplendent Rococo style.

Botanischer Garten ❷

Botanical Garden

Menzingerstr. 12. **Tel** 17 86 13 10.
🚋 17. ⬜ Feb, Mar & Oct: 9am–5pm;
Apr & Sep: 9am–6pm; May–Aug:
9am–7pm; Nov–Jan: 9am–4:30pm.
Greenhouses ⬜ 9am until half an
hour before the gardens close.

North of the gardens of
Schloss Nymphenburg, new
botanical gardens were laid

**The Botanical Garden with its
stunning variety of plants**

out in 1909–14.
Covering 0.22 sq km
(0.08 sq mile) and
containing over
14,000 species of
plants growing in
artistic arrangements,
this is one of the
finest botanical
gardens in Europe.

Entry to the garden
is through the
Botanical Institute,
which is fronted by
the colourful Schmuckhof
(Decorative Yard). Passing
through it visitors see a
section on ecology and
genetics, followed by a rose
garden and a plantation of
rhododendrons and protected
species, and of medicinal
plants and crops. There is
also an arboretum with rare
trees. Beyond this is a section
illustrating the vegetation of
meadows, plains, swamps and
sandy and arctic environments.

The impressive greenhouses
shelter tropical plants, cacti
and fruit trees, unusual
orchids and giant water lilies.

Vehicles displayed at the BMW-Museum

BMW-Museum ❹

Olympiapark 2. **Tel** 0180 211 88 22.
🇺 Olympiazentrum. ⬜ 9am–6pm
Tue–Fri, 10am–8pm Sat, Sun & public
hols. 📷 ♿ **BMW Welt** Olympiapark K1. ⬜ 9am–8pm daily.

In the early 1970s, the BMW
car manufacturing group
built a series of ostentatious
structures that went some
way to rival the architectural
development of the
neighbouring Olympiapark.

The designer in charge of
the concept, Karl Schanzer
of Vienna, used the idiom of

Olympiapark ❸

Munich's Olympic Park was built for the 20th
Olympic Games, which the city hosted in 1972.
The modern complex of sports facilities overlies
an area formerly used as drill grounds and
later as an airfield. The artificial lake is fed
by the Nymphenburg Canal and the hills
were made from the rubble removed
from the city after World War II. The
whole complex is dominated by the
Olympic Tower.

GEORG-BRAUCHLE-RING

Olympia-
stadion ①

Werner-von-
Linde-Halle

Tennis-
anlage

SPIRIDON-LOUIS-RING

Olympiahalle ②
The sweeping roofs,
designed by the
architect Günter
Behnisch, form a
canopy of steel
netting and acrylic
slabs supported
on masts up to 80m
(260 feet) high.

Olympiastadion ①
The main Olympic
stadium can hold
60,000 spectators.

architectural symbolism. He envisaged the 19-storey office building that dominates the complex as resembling the four cylinders of a car engine. The building, clad in silver aluminium, has a ground plan in the form of a clover leaf.

At the foot of the building, and counterbalancing its imposing structure, is what could be described as a shrine – the BMW-Museum. Built in concrete and taking the form of a bowl 41 m (135 ft) across, this window-less, silver-painted structure contains exhibits illustrating the history of the factory's production. A spiral ramp connects five platforms where the first cars, including the famous Dixi, are displayed, along with motorbikes, racing cars of the 1950s and 1960s, the modern BMW range and futuristic prototypes. There are also film and slide shows.

Nearby is BMW Welt in an impressive modern building, holding the world's largest permanent BMW exhibition.

Hypo-Hochhaus 5

Arabellastr. 12. **Tel** 3780.
U Richard-Strauss-Str.

Unlike many other major cities throughout the world, central Munich is not overshadowed by forests of skyscrapers housing the head-quarters of banks, tall buildings and hotels. Munich's modern urban agglomerations have been built outside the

Hypo-Hochhaus's silver-clad futuristic headquarters

Mittlerer Ring (ring road). One example of this is Arabella Park, a group of multifunctional exclusive residential developments, hotels and office buildings. The buildings of the Bayerische Hypo und Vereinsbank AG were built here in 1975–81 to designs by Walter and Bea Betz.

The architects achieved a unique effect. The 114-m (375-ft) skyscraper consists of three blocks of different sizes that are joined by gigantic rings supported by four cylindrical towers. The glazing and the silver panels covering the exterior of the buildings create an effect of levity and cool elegance.

It is worth walking round the building to experience the unusual metamorphosis of forms that is produced from different viewpoints. Despite its architectural significance, Hypovereinsbank's head-quarters is a typical example of the megalomania of major financial institutions today.

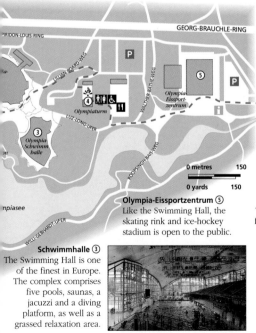

GEORG-BRAUCHLE-RING

SPIRIDON-LOUIS-RING

LILIAN-BOARD-WEG

WALTHER-RATHE-WEG

LUZ-LONG-UFER

Olympiaturm

Olympia-Schwimm-halle

ROOPSINGH-BAIS-WEG

Olympia-Eissport-zentrum

WILLI-GEBHARDT-UFER

| 0 metres | 150 |
| 0 yards | 150 |

TIPS FOR TOURISTS

Getting there:
U Olympiazentrum.
Start: Hans-Braun-Brücke.
Length of tour: 2 km (1.25 m).
Stopping-off places: at Olympiahalle and Olympiaturm.

Olympia-Eissportzentrum 5
Like the Swimming Hall, the skating rink and ice-hockey stadium is open to the public.

Olympiaturm 4
The Olympic Tower commands a fine view of the Olympic Hill, the lake and the stadium, where the Bayern München and TSV 1860 München soccer teams play.

Schwimmhalle 3
The Swimming Hall is one of the finest in Europe. The complex comprises five pools, saunas, a jacuzzi and a diving platform, as well as a grassed relaxation area.

KEY

-- Suggested route

☆ Viewpoint

P Parking

A performance at the puppet theatre in Au

Au **6**

Map 4 D5. 🚋 *25, 27.* 🚌 *52.*
🎪 *Auer Dult: Mariahilfplatz.*
Maidult: starts around 1 May;
Jakobidult: starts Sat after 25 Jul;
Herbstdult: starts third Sat. in Sep.
Otto Bille's Marionettenbühne *Tel*
15 02 168. ◯ *During performances.*

Up until the 15th century,
the district of Au was part of
the floodplain of the River
Isar, and it was only after the
river was controlled that
people started to settle here.
Au was incorporated into
Munich in 1854. Until the
early 20th century, the poorer
population of the city lived in
Au, and picturesque cottages
typical of old Munich can still
be seen there today.

Three times a year, for nine
days, Au is transformed into
a centre of games and entertainment. During Auer Dult,
stalls, shooting galleries and
merry-go-rounds are set up
on Mariahilfplatz. This local
event goes back to the 14th
century and is associated with
the fairs after St Jacob's Day.

The town square is
dominated by a Neo-Gothic
church. Built in 1831–9, it was
the first instance of the Gothic
revival in southern Germany.

The old puppet theatre,
known as **Otto Bille's
Marionettenbühne**, is a great
attraction for children.

Berg am Laim **7**

🚋 *19.* 🚌 *146.* **Michaelskirche**
Clemens-August Str. 9a.
◯ *8am–6pm daily.*

The name Berg am Laim
reflects its position: along
Harlbacher Bach is an elong-

ated hill *(Berg)*, from
which clay *(Lehm)*
was extracted.

By the beginning of
the 18th century, the
area had been taken
over by Clemens
Joseph, Bishop of
Cologne, who
founded the Brother-
hood of St Michael
here. His successor,
Clemens August,
ordered the construc-
tion of Michaelskirche.
For this he commissioned the
most prominent figures of his
time: the architect Johann
Michael Fischer, the
painter and stuccoist
Johann Baptist
Zimmermann and the
sculptor Johann Baptist
Straub. Work lasted
from 1737 to 1751 and
the result was one
of the finest
Rococo churches in
Germany.

While the twin-
towered façade is the
quintessence of late
Baroque style, the
interior has Rococo
furnishings and
paintings. The
painting of St Michael
overcoming Satan on the
high altar (1694) is
by Johann Andreas
Wolff, and the
figures of putti and
angels are ascribed
to Ignaz Günther. The pulpit,
crowned with a statue of
St Michael bearing the
Bavarian flag, is by Benedikt
Haßler. The dome and ceiling
are painted with scenes from
the life of St Michael.

**The pulpit in
Michaelskirche in Berg
am Laim**

In 1941–3 over 300 Jews from
Munich were rounded up by
the church and the monastery
before being deported to a
concentration camp. A modest
memorial is dedicated to them.

Ramersdorf **8**

Ⓤ *Karl-Preis-Platz and Innsbrucker
Ring.* **St Maria Ramersdorf**
Ramersdorfer Str. 6. ◯ *7:30am–7pm.*

Ramersdorf is one of
Munich's industrial centres.
In the midst of small
factories, garages and a close
network of streets is an oasis
of peace: the village church of
St Maria Ramersdorf. This
is one of the oldest
pilgrimage churches
in Bavaria.

Since the 14th century
processions of people
have made their way
here to worship a relic
of the Holy Cross that
is kept in a precious
monstrance. Since
1465 another object of
worship has been the
figure of the Madonna
Enthroned carved by
Erasmus Grasser.
While the exterior of
the church has retained its
Gothic character,
the interior is Bar-
oque. The Gothic
cloisters are deco-
rated with stucco-
work and have 17th-century
altars. The cemetery is worth
a visit, as is the Alter Wirt, an
inn dating from 1663 that was
frequented by pilgrims and
travellers on the road between Salzburg and Augsburg.

The Baroque interior of the pilgrimage church in Ramersdorf

Tierpark Hellabrunn ⑨

Munich's zoo was established in 1911. It has over 4,800 animals representing 480 species and covers an area of 3.6 sq km (1.38 sq miles). The species are arranged by continent and by their geographical occurrence. The design of the enclosures, which recreate natural environments, makes Hellabrunn one of the most beautiful zoos in the world. The zoo specializes in breeding animals that are under threat of extinction.

VISITORS' CHECKLIST

Tierparkstr. 30. **Tel** 62 50 80. Ⓤ Thalkirchen. 52. ◯ 8am–6pm daily (Oct–Mar: 9–5pm). ♿ 🍴 **www**.zoo-munich.de

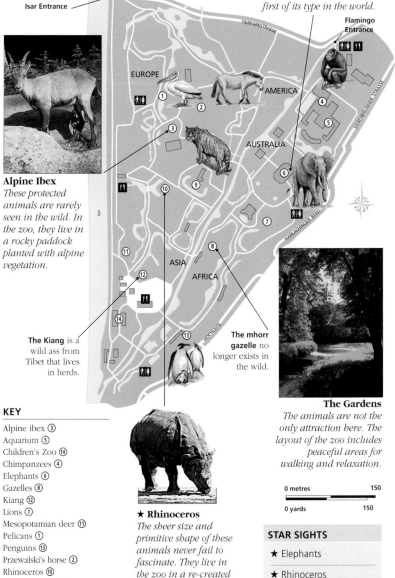

Isar Entrance

TIERPARKSTRASSE

Flamingo Entrance

SIEBENBRUNNER STRASSE

EUROPE

AMERICA

AUSTRALIA

HARLACHINGER BERG

ASIA

AFRICA

★ **Elephants**
The elephants live in a hall covered by a dome of reinforced concrete, the first of its type in the world.

Alpine Ibex
These protected animals are rarely seen in the wild. In the zoo, they live in a rocky paddock planted with alpine vegetation.

The Kiang *is a wild ass from Tibet that lives in herds.*

The mhorr gazelle *no longer exists in the wild.*

The Gardens
The animals are not the only attraction here. The layout of the zoo includes peaceful areas for walking and relaxation.

KEY

Alpine ibex ③
Aquarium ⑤
Children's Zoo ⑭
Chimpanzees ④
Elephants ⑥
Gazelles ⑧
Kiang ⑫
Lions ⑦
Mesopotamian deer ⑪
Pelicans ①
Penguins ⑬
Przewalski's horse ②
Rhinoceros ⑩
Siberian tigers ⑨

★ **Rhinoceros**
The sheer size and primitive shape of these animals never fail to fascinate. They live in the zoo in a re-created natural environment.

| 0 metres | 150 |
| 0 yards | 150 |

STAR SIGHTS

★ Elephants

★ Rhinoceros

The realistic reconstruction of the U-boat from the film *Das Boot*

Bavaria-Filmstadt ⑩

Geiselgasteig. Bavariafilmplatz 7.
***Tel** 64 99 20 00.* Ⓤ *Silberhornstr,
Wettersteinplatz (some distance away).*
🚋 *25.* Ⓢ *Rosenheimer Platz (some
distance away).* ⬜ *Mar–Oct: 9am–
4pm daily; Nov–Feb 10am–3pm daily.*
🎬 **Stuntshow:** *Mar–Dec: noon,
12:30pm, 3pm.* **Cinema:** *Apr–Oct:
9am–5pm daily; Nov–Mar: 10am–
4pm daily.* **www**.filmstadt.de

Commonly known as
Hollywood on the Isar,
Bavaria-Filmstadt is one of
Europe's major film studios.
Set up in 1919, they were
originally located in the
Stachus district. Among the
prominent people who have
worked here have been
directors such as Orson
Welles and Ingmar Bergman.
Every year scores of films for
the big screen and television
are made at the Filmstadt
("cinema city"), which
opened to the public in 1981.
The 90-minute tour of the
studios takes visitors on a
miniature railway and on foot,
through some fascinating film
sets. Entering the 57-m (187-ft)
reconstruction of the U-boat
used in the Oscar-winning
film *Das Boot* is an
unforgettable experience.
Another lasting impression is
made by the backdrops used
in the production of *Asterix
and Obelix*, set in the age of
the Romans and Gauls.
Other major attractions are
the heart-stopping exploits
of stuntmen. By arrangement,
groups of young people can
make their own films here,
directing, cutting and
watching the final results.

Grünwald ⑪

Grünwald Burg. Grünwald Zeillerstr.
3. ***Tel** 64 13 218.* 🚋 *25.* 🚌 *224,
271, 391.* ⬜ *10am–4:30pm
Wed–Sun.* 🎬 *31 Oct–mid-Mar.*

Grünwald, on the southern
outskirts of Munich, is one
of the city's most exclusive
villa suburbs. It is also
a good starting point for
walking and cycling tours.
The district's greatest
attraction is Burg Grünwald,

**Grünwald Burg's Gothic gatehouse,
set with coats of arms**

a well-preserved medieval
castle whose origins go back
to the 12th century. In 1270
the building came into the
possession of the Wittelsbachs. In the 15th century a
gatehouse was constructed:
its stepped gable is set with
11 coats of arms, those of
Bavaria at the apex and those
of Poland and Jerusalem
among the others further
down. From 1602 to 1857 the

castle accommodated a prison
and a gunpowder store.
The archaeological collections housed here illustrate
the history of the castle and
of Roman art in Bavaria.
There are lapidariums and
frescoes, a kiln and a reconstruction of a Roman kitchen.

Asam-Schlössl ⑫

Thalkirchen. Maria-Einsiedel-Str. 45.
Ⓤ *Thalkirchen.* 🚌 *135.*

In 1724 Cosmas Damian
Asam acquired a 17th-
century property in the Isar
valley. He intended to use it
as an out-of-town residence
and studio.
With the help of his brother
Egid Quirin Asam, Cosmas
Damian rebuilt the house that
he had bought, converting the
second floor into a spacious
studio lit by a huge semicircular window. The house
was named Maria Einsiedel in
honour of the Swiss pilgrimage church that the brothers
had decorated. The artist
covered the façade of his
new home with paintings. He
decorated the third floor
with a statue of Moses
bearing the Ten Command-
ments, and a painting of the
antique sculpture known as
The Borghese Fencer.
The building currently
houses a restaurant.

Deutsches Museum Verkehrszentrum ⑬

Theresienhöhe 14a. ***Tel** 500 806
762.* Ⓤ *Theresienwiese.*
⬜ *9am–5pm daily (to 8pm Thu).* 🎬
*1 Jan, Good Friday, 1 May, 1 Nov, 24,
25 & 31 Dec.* 🌐 **www**.verkehrs
zentrum.deutsches-museum.de

The historic exhibition halls
on Theresienhöhe house the
new transport section of the
Deutsches Museum. This
huge collection ranges from
the very first motorcar to the
ICE-Experimental train and
features interactive displays
that illustrate the past, present
and future of worldwide
travel and mobility.

Theresienwiese

Theresienwiese Ruhmeshalle-
Theresienhöhe Bavaria. *Tel 29 06 71.*
🕐 *Apr–15 Oct: 9am–6pm daily.*

The events that took place
in Munich on 17 October
1810 had far-reaching
consequences. This was the
day on which the marriage
of Theresa von Sachsen-
Hildburghausen and Ludwig
I, the future king, took place.
To mark the occasion, horse
races, a cattle fair and a folk
festival were held in meadows
outside the city. The folk
celebrations were repeated in
following years, and this
custom continued to grow
and eventually became the
Oktoberfest *(see p29)*, the
largest folk festival in the
world. The festival grounds
were named Theresienwiese
in honour of the bride.

The beer festival is not,
however, the only attraction
of Theresienwiese. On an
elevated ridge with a grand
stairway stands the Neo-
Classical Ruhmeshalle (Hall of
Fame), built by Leo von
Klenze in 1848–53. It is an
open hall fronted by 48
Ionian columns and containing the busts of 77 prominent
Bavarians. In front of the hall
stands a gigantic figure of
Bavaria as a Germanic god-
dess carrying a sword and an
oak wreath and accompanied
by a lion. This unusual work
by Leo von Klenze and
Ludwig Schwanthaler, which
stands 18m (59 ft) high, was
the first monumental cast iron
figure to be made. It predates
New York's Statue of Liberty
by some 30 years. Visitors can
view the city from a platform
in the figure's head.

The main entrance to the Neue Messe, with the flags of many nations

Neue Messe München ⓯

Am Messesee 2. Ⓤ *Messestadt-West, Messestadt-Ost.*

In 1992 the international
airport at Riem was closed
and the site, where building
work took place from 1995 to
1998, was transformed into a
huge exhibition area.

This was the Neue Messe
München, which came to
stand as an example of
modern functional yet
elegant architecture.
It was designed by
Bystrup, Bregenhoj &
Partners, architects
from Copenhagen,
the winners of the
international
competition that was
announced in 1991.

A sequence of 12
halls is arranged
along the Atrium, an
arterial axis 600 m
(1,968 ft) long. The
main entrance is
flanked by the
multifunctional ICM
(International
Congress Centre
Munich) building. The entire
covered area of 200,000 sq m
(50 acres) stands in front of a
large lake. Major international
events that are held in the

Neue Messe include an
information and
telecommunications fair, a
fashion show, a crafts show
and a mineralogy congress.

Blutenburg ⓰

Blutenburg. Ⓢ *Obermenzing (some
distance away).* 🚌 *75.* **Internationale Jugend-bibliothek** *Tel 89 12
110.* 🕐 *10am–4pm Mon–Fri.*

On a man-made island in
the River Würm stands
Blutenburg, a small
hunting lodge surround-
ed by greenery and
water. From 1425 the
lodge belonged to
the Wittelsbachs and
its residents included
Duke Albrecht III,
his son Sigismund,
the later Princess
Henriette Adelaide,
Theresa Kunigunde
Sobieska and
Maximilian I Joseph.
The lodge now
houses the **Inter-
nationale Jugend-
bibliothek**. Contain-
ing over 500,000
volumes in 110
languages, the library is the
largest collection of children's
and young people's literature
in the world and is under the
patronage of UNESCO.

The only original part of
the lodge that still stands is
St Sigismund's Chapel (1488),
built by the architects of
Munich's Frauenkirche. The
frescoes on its exterior walls
are among the few surviving
examples of late Gothic mural
painting. The interior of the
chapel, covered with intricate
rib vaulting, contains some
treasures of religious art,
including altarpieces of 1491
by Jan Polack and late Gothic
sculptures and stained glass.

**The doorway of
Blutenburg's
Gothic chapel**

The great statue of Bavaria fronting the Ruhmeshalle in Theresienwiese

SHOPPING IN MUNICH

Munich often claims to be Germany's richest and most sophisticated city and when it comes to shopping you are sure not to be disappointed. The key shopping areas are dotted around the centre of the city. You can conveniently walk around the pedestrianized central area, with numerous options for taking

Accessories from Slips

a break for lunch or a coffee. Not to be missed is the visual and gourmet treat of the Viktualienmarkt food market, the classic department store Ludwig Beck and some of the smaller speciality shops tucked away in side streets. In the less commercial shopping streets, shops tend to open late morning or in the afternoon only.

MAIN SHOPPING AREAS

Munich's key luxury shopping street is Maximilianstraße and those streets connected to it, Theatinerstraße, Brienner-straße and Residenzstraße. Here you will find all the top international brands and jewellery shops. For more affordable shops head to the central pedestrianized area between Kaufingerstraße, Neuhauserstraße and Marienplatz. Here you will find family shops, large chains, mid-market fashion, souvenirs and department stores. For less conventional areas with small specialist boutiques and local designers seek out the Glockenbach-viertel around Hans-Sachs Straße, or streets radiating out from Gärtnerplatz, home to the Art Nouveau State Theatre and relaxed cafés. Schwabing is the young Bohemian area with a variety of casualwear and jeanswear shops, plus fashion boutiques and plenty of laid-back bistros and coffee bars.

DEPARTMENT STORES AND SHOPPING CENTRES

The most famous department store in Munich is **Ludwig Beck**, which has a particularly impressive Christmas decorations department in December. **Galeria Kaufhof** is another large national department store chain offering several floors of goods. Shopping Centres (*Einkaufspassagen*) are also aplenty. **Fünf Höfe** (the five courtyards) is central and upmarket. It sits between Theatiner, Maffei, Kardinal-Faulhaber and Salvator streets and mixes shopping, art and culture with cafés including a great café/restaurant attached to the Kunsthalle Art Museum. Munich has three other large shopping centres. **Olympia-Einkaufszentrum** (OEZ) is vast with over 140 shops on two levels, **Perlacher Einkaufs-passage** (PEP) has over 110 shops and the **Riem Arcaden** is home to the largest branch of H&M, a huge Lego store, C&A and Ludwig Beck Fashion.

The exclusive shopping centre, Fünf Höfe

Pedestrianized shopping area in central Munich

FASHION

Munich has a wide variety of shops for clothes and accessories. For Munich-style chic try boutiques such as **Theresa** which has the best choice of designer fashion and accessories, **Slips** in Gärtnerplatz which offers the pick of top brands and **Off & Co** in Schwabing for fashion items for both men and women. Hohenzollern-straße in Schwabing is a good place to shop for youth-styled street fashion and trainers. For traditional Bavarian Loden costumes take a look in **Loden-Frey**.

CHILDREN'S SHOPS

Munich is a stylish and expensive city and parents love to dress their children accordingly. This means there are some good shopping opportunities for kids' clothing and toys, mainly in the department stores and C&A. A large central shop for

One of the city's regularly held flea markets

mother and baby is **Schlichting**, as well as **Thierchen Kindermode** for original handmade clothing. **Noemi & Friends** is a lovely kids' beauty salon-cum-accessories shop and is a haven for girls, big and little. **Die Puppenstube** is also good for old-fashioned toys and gifts.

FLEA MARKETS

Flea markets are popular, especially at the weekends. Most take place on Saturday, some every two weeks and most only from spring to late autumn. The key ones around Munich are **Zenith Flohmarkt** at Lilienthalallee, **Air Antik**

fleamarket at the airport between the terminals, every second Sunday in the month, and **Flohmarkt Riem**, the largest in Bavaria, at the trade show grounds.

FOOD SHOPPING

Viktualienmarkt *(see p64)* is a huge produce market, selling fruit, vegetables, spices, meat, poultry, fish, preserves and flowers. Open daily, it is a feast for all the senses and a permanent fixture. *Bio* is the German word for organic and Germans have always been enthusiastic about organic produce. **Basic Bio** is a good organic supermarket in the city centre. For a selection of gourmet treats head to

Dallmayr or **Käfer**, the city's top delicatessens, while butchers' shops sell the famous Bavarian white sausages.

CHRISTMAS MARKET

Munich holds a traditional Christmas market *(Christkindlmarkt)* from the first week of Advent until Christmas Eve. The market is a great tourist attraction and special trips are organized from all over Europe. Wooden stalls sell a huge variety of handcrafted decorations, in particular delicately carved wooden mangers and tree decorations, in addition to candles, ornaments, food and mulled wine *(see p33)*.

Christkindlmarkt, **Munich's Christmas market**

DIRECTORY

DEPARTMENT STORES AND SHOPPING CENTRES

Fünf Höfe
Theatinerstraße. **Map 2** B4. www.fuenfhoefe.de

Galeria Kaufhof
Kaufingerstraße 1–5. **Map 2** B4. *Tel (089) 231851.* www.galeria-kaufhof.de

Ludwig Beck
Marienplatz 11. **Map 2** B4. *Tel (089) 7236910.* www.ludwigbeck.de

Olympia Einkaufszentrum
Hanauerstraße 68. www.olympia-einkaufszentrum.de

Perlacher Einkaufspassage
Thomas Dehler Straße 12. www.einkaufscenter-neuperlach.de

Riem Arcaden
Willy-Brandt-Platz 5. www.riem-arcaden.de

FASHION

Loden-Frey
Maffeistraße 7. **Map 2** B4. www.loden-frey.com

Off & Co
Belgradstraße 5. www.offandco.com

Slips
Am Gärtnerplatz 2. www.slipsfashion.de

Theresa
Maffeistraße 3. **Map 2** B4. www.mytheresa.com

CHILDREN'S SHOPS

Die Puppenstube
Luisenstraße 68. *Tel (089) 2723267.*

Noemi & Friends
Marktstraße 13, Schwabing. www.noemiandfriends.de

Schlichting
Weinstraße 8. **Map 2** B4. www.schlichting.de

Thierchen Kindermode
Hans-Sachs-Straße 15. www.thierchen.net

FLEA MARKETS

Air Antik
Munich Airport Center. *Tel 0173 832 7877.* www.airantik.de

Flohmarkt Riem
Am Messeturm. *Tel (089) 960 51632.* www.flohmarkt-riem.com

Zenith Flohmarkt
Lilienthalallee. *Tel 0173 683 5152.* www. flohmarkt-freimann.de

FOOD SHOPPING

Basic Bio
Westenriederstraße 35. **Map 2** B4. *Tel (089) 242 0890.* www.basic-ag.de

Dallmayr
Dienerstraße 14–15. **Map 2** B4. www.dallmayr.de

Käfer
Prinzregentenstraße 73. www.feinkost-kaefer.de

Viktualienmarkt
Peteplatz-Frauenstraße. **Map 2** B4.

ENTERTAINMENT IN MUNICH

Munich is best known for the Oktoberfest, the Olympic grounds and Hofbräuhaus, but it also has an international reputation as a city of culture. There are 56 theatres, three large orchestras and one opera house. Munich has the rich and the powerful of its past to thank for creating and preserving its many splendid venues. This cultured metropolis on the Isar caters to all tastes, from traditional to modern, whether in theatre, music or film. There are several festivals during the year, as well as various sporting events, when the city attracts thousands of visitors from all over the world.

Bird from Munich Zoo

ENTERTAINMENT GUIDES AND TICKETS

Munich Found is the best events magazine and the **Munich Tourist Board** has comprehensive listings of events happening all over Munich. Also, check the Thursday edition of *Süddeutsche Zeitung* and the daily *Münchner Merkur*.

Tickets can be booked at box offices, by phone or in person. There are also two **Zentraler Kartenverkauf** ticket kiosks in the Marienplatz underground concourse, or use the **Abendzeitung Schalterhalle** (kiosk).

THEATRE, OPERA AND CLASSICAL MUSIC

State theatres are subsidized and tickets, therefore, are very reasonably priced. The Bavarian State Orchestra, Opera and Ballet all perform at the **Nationaltheater**. The **Deutsches Theater** offers musicals and shows, while the **Prinzregententheater** is home to the Bavarian State Opera and a concert hall. The

Art Nouveau **Staatstheater am Gärtnerplatz** presents opera, ballet, operetta, musicals and the Symphony Orchestra. **Gasteig Culture Center** is a world-class concert hall, home to the Munich Philharmonic Orchestra. The city also hosts an opera festival in July.

MUSIC AND DANCE

The **Pasinger Fabrik** offers a good programme of jazz, chansons and café theatre. There are numerous dance events and dance clubs. Big name artists, such as James Blunt, Massive Attack and The Rolling Stones, tend to perform at the **Circus Krone Bau**, **Zenith Kulturhalle**, **Olympiahalle** and the **Olympic Stadium**.

FILM

As the centre of the German film industry Munich offers 76 cinemas and a college for film and television. The **Bavarian Film Studios** offers tours of their studios daily at 1pm. The **Munich Film Festival** in

July boasts over 200 films on 15 screens, almost all of them German, European or world premieres.

FESTIVALS

Munich's most famous festival is the **Oktoberfest**. For the whole of September it takes over a dedicated fairground, Theresienwiese, with beer

Munich's world-famous Oktoberfest

tents, traditional Bavarian brass bands, people dressed in traditional Bavarian costume (*Trachten*), fairground rides and the famous iced gingerbread hearts, *Lebkuchen*. There is also the **Tollwood Festival** in July and December, which has music, food, a circus, performances in tents and a craft fair. Munich also celebrates the *Dult* on three occasions throughout the year. *Dult* is the old word for street fair or market and there are traditional stalls and merry-go-rounds all over the city. Carnival or *Fasching* is celebrated throughout Munich with parties, processions and dressing up, but it is not as important here as in other cities.

The imposing Nationaltheater on Max-Joseph-Platz

Munich's ultra-modern Allianz Arena

SPORT

Most Münchners love the outdoors. Many make regular trips to the not too distant Alps. Running, skiing, rollerblading, cycling, Nordic walking and football are all very popular. The English Garden in the city centre is a huge park where people rollerblade, cycle, run or go walking.

Munich has two football teams: FC Bayern Munich and TSV 1860 München, also known as "the Lions" because they are sponsored by the Löwenbräu Munich brewery which has a lion as its coat of arms. The **Allianz Arena** is the fantastic stadium built for the 2006 World Cup. It is an architectural marvel which lights up in various colours. For Bayern Munich merchandise head to the **FC Bayern Shop** in the Arena. The shop website gives details of other stores located at Central Station and the Hofbräuhaus.

Other key sporting events are the Bavarian International Tennis Championships (ATP tournament), the BMW International Golf Open and Munich Blade Night, on Monday evenings from April to September, when rollerbladers take over the streets. Runners will enjoy the Media Marathon and also the Münchner Stadtlauf (city run). A sport unique to Munich is surfing on the River Isar at the weirs.

KIDS' ENTERTAINMENT

Children will love Kids' Kingdom – **Kinderreich** – in the Deutsches Museum *(see pp94–97)*. The area is designated for children and has giant interactive water games, plus a real fire engine. Adults can only enter with their children. Several playgrounds can be found along the River Isar in the city centre, but the best is **Westpark Spielzone Ost Untersendling** which can be reached by the underground. The new **Sea Life Olympiapark** centre is also an excellent outing, as is the zoo at **Tierpark Hellabrunn**.

Close encounter at Sea Life Olympiapark, Munich

DIRECTORY

ENTERTAINMENT GUIDES AND TICKETS

Abendzeitung Schalterhalle
Sendlingerstr. 10. **Map 2** A5. **Tel** *(089) 267024.*

Munich Tourist Board
www.muenchen.de

Zentraler Kartenverkauf
Tel *0180 54 818181.*
www.muenchenticket.de

THEATRE, OPERA AND CLASSICAL MUSIC

Deutsches Theater
Schwanthalerstr. 13. **Map 1** E4. **Tel** *(089) 552 340.*

Gasteig Culture Center
Rosenheimerstr. 5.
Tel *(089) 480980.*

Nationaltheater
Max-Joseph-Platz. **Map 2** B4. **Tel** *(089) 21851920.*

Prinzregenten-theater
Prinzregentenstr. 12. **Map** 3 D3. **Tel** *(089) 21851920.*

Staatstheater am Gärtnerplatz
Gärtnerplatz 3.
Tel *(089) 202411.*

MUSIC AND DANCE

Circus Krone Bau
Marsstraße 43. **Map 1** E3. **Tel** *(089) 5458000.*
www.circus-krone.de

Olympiahalle and **Olympic Stadium**
Spiridon-Louis-Ring 21.
Tel *(089) 54 818181 (tickets).* www.
olympiapark-muenchen.de

Pasinger Fabrik
August-Exter-Str. 1.
(089) 82929079.

Zenith Kulturhalle
Lilienthalallee 29.
www.zenith-die-kulturhalle.de

FILM

Bavarian Film Studios
www.filmstadt.de

Munich Film Festival
www.filmfest-muenchen.de

FESTIVALS

Oktoberfest
www.oktoberfest.de

Tollwood Festival
www.tollwood.de

SPORT

Allianz Arena
www.allianz-arena.de

FC Bayern Shop
www.shop.fcbayern.de

KIDS' ENTERTAINMENT

Kinderreich
Deutsches Museum, Museumsinsel 1. **Tel** *(089) 21791.* www.deutsches-museum.de

Sea Life Olympiapark
Willi-Daume-Platz 1.
Tel *(089) 45 00 00.*
www.sealifeeurope.com

Tierpark Hellabrunn
Tierparkstr. 30. **Tel** *(089) 625 080.* www.zoo-munich.de

Westpark Spielzone Ost Untersendling
Pressburger Straße.

MUNICH STREET FINDER

Map references given for historic buildings and other sights throughout the chapter on Munich refer to the maps included in the following pages.

The key map below shows the area of Munich covered by the *Street Finder*. Buildings and monuments in pink are star sights that are covered in detail in the chapter; those in brown are sights and places that are

Bavaria on the Ruhmeshalle

worth seeing. Streets shown in yellow are closed to traffic.

The *Street Finder* maps include U-Bahn and S-Bahn stations as well as main car parks, hospitals, post offices, police stations, tourist information centres and taxi ranks in Munich. The word *Straße (Str.)* indicates a street, *Platz* a square, *Brücke* a bridge and *Bahnhof* a railway station.

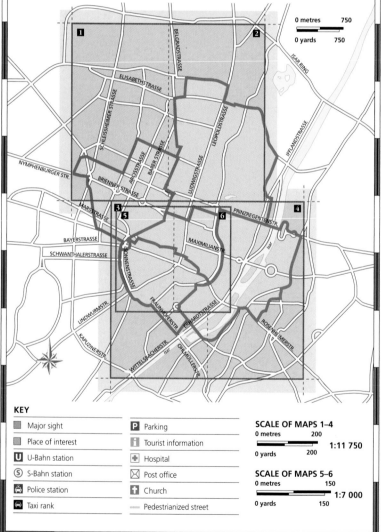

0 metres 750
0 yards 750

KEY

■ Major sight	🅿 Parking
■ Place of interest	ℹ Tourist information
Ⓤ U-Bahn station	✚ Hospital
Ⓢ S-Bahn station	⊠ Post office
🚓 Police station	✚ Church
🚕 Taxi rank	═ Pedestrianized street

SCALE OF MAPS 1–4
0 metres 200
0 yards 200
1:11 750

SCALE OF MAPS 5–6
0 metres 150
0 yards 150
1:7 000

Street Finder

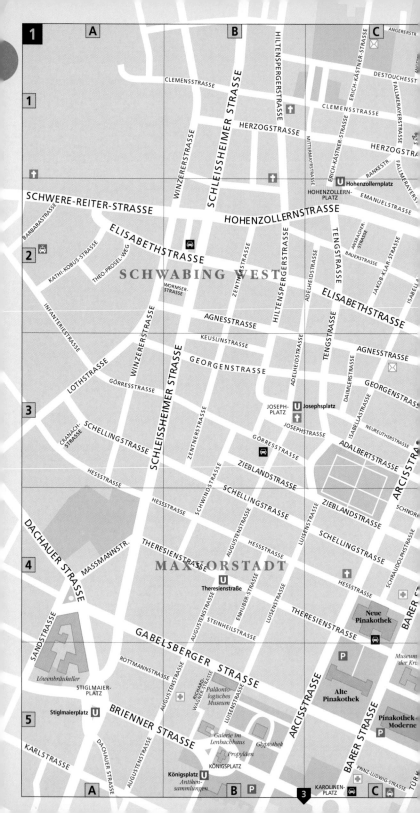

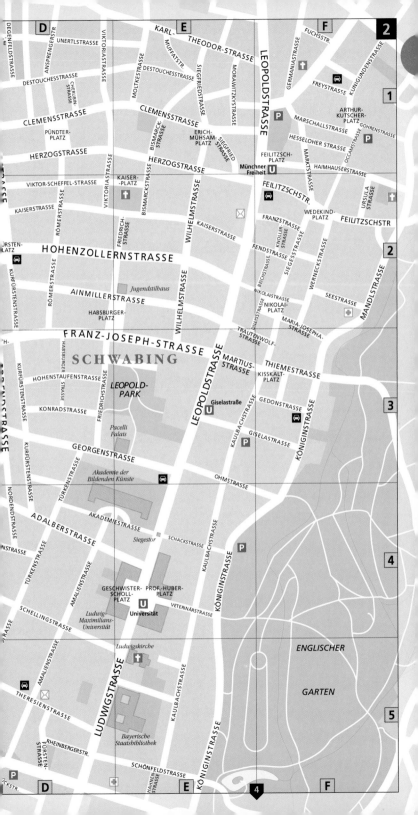

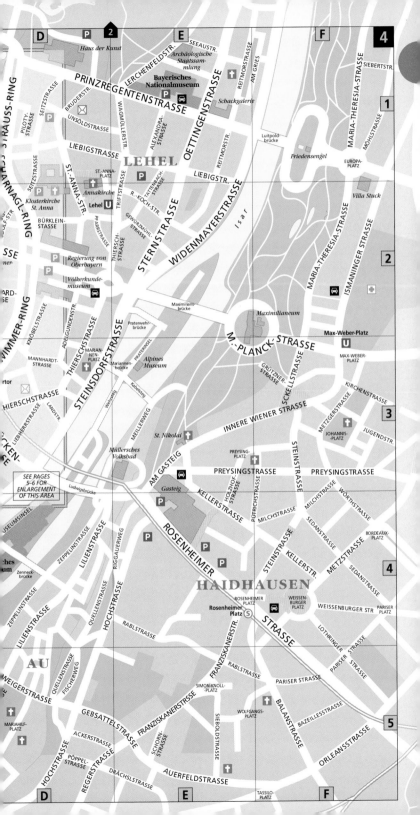

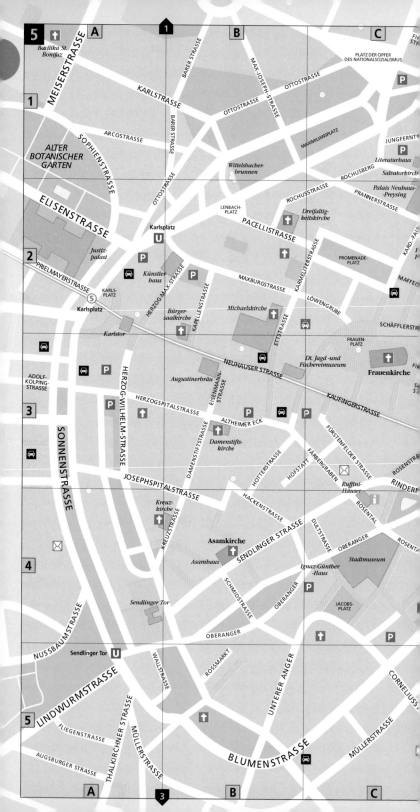

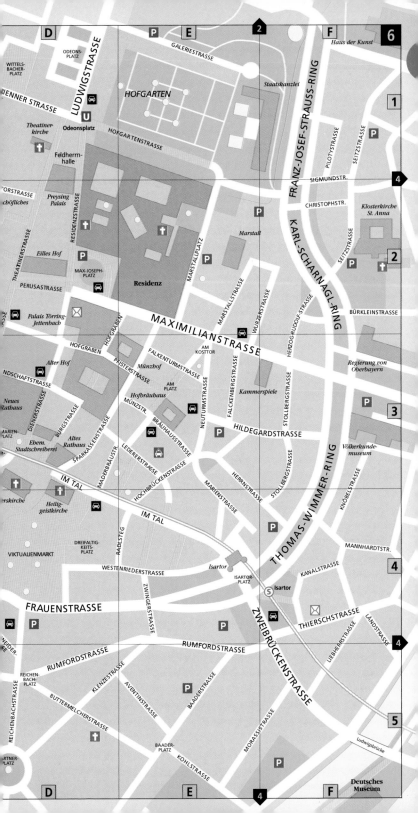

THE BAVARIAN ALPS AREA BY AREA

The Bavarian Alps at a Glance

The Bavarian Alps have much to offer tourists. Well endowed with ski lifts and shelters, the Alps offer ideal conditions for skiers, while the many lakes draw watersports enthusiasts and ice-skaters. The mountainous regions of the Bavarian Forest are a delight, both for their primeval natural surroundings and for the affordable prices to be found here. Many of the region's towns and villages contain buildings of great splendour and architectural importance.

Augsburg
Because of its many canals which are crossed by bridges, this town is known as the Venice of the North (see pp248–53).

Neuschwanstein
This castle is the embodiment of Ludwig II's idea of a romantic seat of power. It has a fantastical setting, and its design, particularly that of the towers, was the model for the Disneyland's fairy-tale castle (see pp230–31).

SOUTHERN SWABIA
Pages 238–55

THE ALLGÄU
Pages 222–37

UPPER BAVARIA (SOUTH
Pages 206–2

Ottobeuren
The Rococo stalls of this renowned Benedictine church are part of the overall decorative scheme (see p228).

Oberammergau
Like many others here, this house, built in 1775, is covered with Lüftlmalerei. Oberammergau is the centre of this type of trompe-l'oeil decoration (see p216).

0 km   30

0 miles   30

◁ Small parish church set in the Ramsau valley

Hallertau
This region is renowned for its hop plantations, which supply the country's brewing industry, so satisfying the Bavarians' demand for beer, their favourite drink (see p159).

Altmühl
Picturesquely set on a hill, Prunn Castle overlooks the River Altmühl with its wooden bridge – the oldest and longest in Europe (see p183).

UPPER BAVARIA (NORTH)
Pages 158–73

LOWER BAVARIA
Pages 174–93

UPPER BAVARIA (EAST)
Pages 194–205

Herrenchiemsee
Bavaria's largest palace, with the most extensive grounds, features sculpture created for Ludwig II (see p202).

Linderhof
The gardens surrounding Ludwig II's favourite palace were modelled on those of Versailles. The fountains and cascades add a magical dimension (see p200).

Schwarzeck
Schwarzeck is one of the many biking and skiing stations around Berchtesgaden, reached by a steep and winding road (see p200).

UPPER BAVARIA (NORTH)

onsisting of flat countryside traversed by the river valleys of the Danube and its tributaries the Isar, Ilm, Paar and Altmühl, this region of Upper Bavaria (Oberbayern) is not as varied as the south. However, it has plenty of historic monuments, as at Eichstätt and Freising, and architectural gems such as the palace at Schleißheim.

During the Jurassic period, 150 million years ago, a lagoon existed at the northern edges of this region. This became what is today the valley of the meandering River Altmühl, the location of the largest nature reserve in Germany. Many Jurassic fossils have been unearthed here, particularly in the area around Eichstätt.

More recent history concerns Dachau, a charming little town just 25 km (15.5 miles) northwest of Munich. Its name has become synonymous with one of the earliest concentration camps to be set up in Germany, in 1933. The camp is still surrounded by barbed wire and guard towers still stand. The site functions as a museum of the Nazis' cruel system of forced labour and extermination in which millions of victims of the Third Reich lost their lives. It is preserved as a memento and a warning to present and future generations.

The northern part of Upper Bavaria is mainly farmland. Extensive asparagus plantations stretch out around Schrobenhausen, while in a region of the Amper and Danube valleys, an area known as Hallertau, endless forest-like plantations indicate the large-scale production of the hops that are used in the brewing of beer, Bavarians' favourite drink. Hallertau forms part of the Hopfenstraße, or German Hop Trail. Along the way lies Ingolstadt, whose main claim to fame nowadays is the Audi car plant.

Here, too, are many fine historic buildings. The imposing outlines of castles tower over towns such as Beilngries, Eichstätt, Ingolstadt and Neuburg, on the northern fringes of this region. There is also a wealth of ecclesiastical buildings, the most prominent among which are the churches and abbeys at Scheyern, Indersdorf and Fürstenfeldbruck.

The imposing Baroque façade and formal gardens of the Neues Schloss in Schleißheim

◁ The town of Eichstätt, situated in the picturesque valley of the River Altmühl

Exploring Upper Bavaria (North)

Any exploration of the northern part of Upper Bavaria should take in the Baroque Neues Schloss at Schleißheim, the grandest building in the area, set in extensive parkland. Equally interesting is the town of Freising, with its fine cathedral and the Diözesanmuseum, which contains one of the most resplendent collections of religious art in Germany. Nature-lovers looking for particularly beautiful countryside should head for the Altmühltal or the region of Hallertau, where hop plantations stretch to the horizon.

GETTING AROUND

Several roads traverse northern Upper Bavaria. Motorways A9 and A93 lead to the north of Germany via Nuremberg and Regensburg. Motorway A8 leads west to Stuttgart, the A92 heads east to Lower Bavaria, and the A96 leads to the southwest. The S-Bahn local rail network and Deutsche Bahn national rail network provide links between towns. Franz-Josef-Strauß Airport, near Freising, provides air links with other cities in Germany and the rest of Europe.

SEE ALSO

- **Where to Stay** pp264–6.
- **Where to Eat** pp279–80.

The grand Baroque staircase of the Neues Schloss in Schleißheim

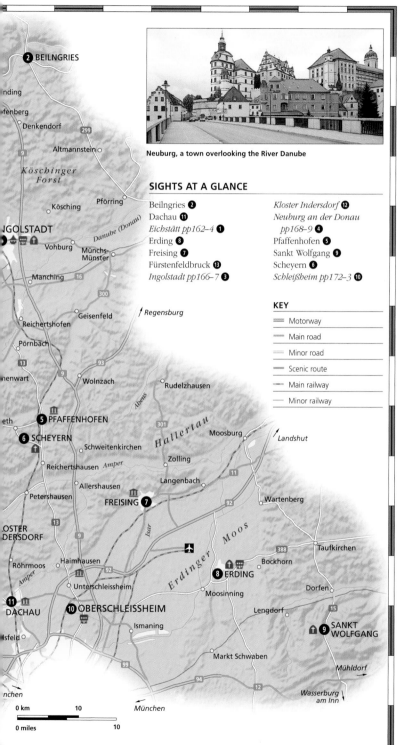

Neuburg, a town overlooking the River Danube

SIGHTS AT A GLANCE

KEY

▰▰▰	Motorway
▬▬	Main road
══	Minor road
▬▬	Scenic route
┿┿	Main railway
——	Minor railway

Map labels:

BEILNGRIES ❷
nding
fenberg
Denkendorf
Altmannstein
Köschinger Forst
Pförring
Kösching
IGOLSTADT
Vohburg
Münchs-Münster
Danube (Donau)
Manching
Regensburg
Reichertshofen
Geisenfeld
Pörnbach
nenwart
Wolnzach
Rudelzhausen
Abens
eth
PFAFFENHOFEN ❺
SCHEYERN ❻
Schweitenkirchen
Hallertau
Moosburg
Landshut
Zolling
Amper
Reichertshausen
Langenbach
Allershausen
Petershausen
FREISING ❼
Isar
Wartenberg
OSTER DERSDORF
Röhrmoos
Haimhausen
Erdinger Moos
Bockhorn
Taufkirchen
Petershausen
Amper
Unterschleissheim
ERDING ❽
DACHAU ⓫
OBERSCHLEISSHEIM ❿
Moosinning
Dorfen
Ismaning
Lengdorf
sfeld
SANKT WOLFGANG ❾
Markt Schwaben
Mühldorf
nchen
München
Wasserburg am Inn

0 km   10
0 miles   10

Eichstätt ●

Painting on a town house

Eichstätt, a see and centre of religious life since 741, is probably one of the prettiest towns in Bavaria. It stands in an exceptionally scenic location in the valley of the River Altmühl. The town's appearance was largely determined by 30 years of work by Maurizio Pedetti and Gabriel de Gabrieli, a prominent architect of the first half of the 18th century who was also active in Vienna. The town's unique atmosphere is further enhanced by the Catholic university and its students.

Tenement houses lining Marktplatz

⌁ Marktplatz

Marktplatz, north of the cathedral, is the focal point of the burghers' district. It is surrounded by the houses of prominent merchants, and these magnificent abodes alternate with modest craftsmen's houses. On the west side of the square stands the town hall, whose tower dates from 1444. The façade and upper part of the tower were built in 1823–4.

Eichstätt's other squares – Residenzplatz, Domplatz and Leonrodplatz – were also key elements in the urban planning of the town.

Residenzplatz is one of the finest squares in the whole of Germany. It lies south of the cathedral and has a trapezoid shape. The two-storey buildings that line the square were originally part of the chapterhouses that were designed by Gabriel de Gabrieli.

Domplatz, with the cathedral on its northeastern side, is laid out on the site of the former cemetery.

On Leonrodplatz stands the church and former Jesuit abbey, as well as the former cathedral deaconry.

⛪ Dom St Salvator und St Willibald

Domplatz.
Eichstätt's cathedral has a late Gothic nave and presbytery, the latter flanked by twin Romanesque towers. The Baroque façade was built by Gabriel de Gabrieli in 1716–18.

The Gothic cloisters on the south side of the cathedral adjoin the presbytery. The west wing of the cloisters contains a double-naved moratorium containing the Gothic tombs of priests, chaplains and benefactors of the cathedral. Distinctive among the many works of art to be seen in the

cathedral is the statue of St Willibald, who became the first bishop of Eichstätt in the 8th century. The statue, carved in the late Gothic style, was made in 1514 by Loy Hering. In 1745 Matthias Seybold built the two-sided Pappenheimer altar with a canopy to cover the statue of the saint and the tomb containing his relics. This altar is located on the elevated part at the west end of the cathedral.

♣ Fürstbischöfliche Residenz

Residenzplatz 1. ⬛ Apr–Oct: 11am, 3pm Mon–Thu, 11am Fri, 10:15am, 11am, 11:45am, 2pm, 2:45pm, 3:30pm Sat–Sun.
The former bishop's residence, which adjoins the cathedral on its southern side, was built in 1700–27 to a rectangular plan with a central courtyard. The interior is decorated with stuccowork and Rococo frescoes, and features a fine Rococo staircase and Hall of Mirrors, all dating from the 1700s. The Residenz houses the district administration.

The main staircase of the former bishop's residence

⛪ Schutzengelkirche

Ostenstr.
This former Jesuit church was built in 1617–20 under the direction of Hans Alberthal. Having suffered destruction in 1634, in the course of the Thirty Years' War, it was rebuilt in 1660. The interior was lavishly decorated by Franz Gabriel and Johann Rosner, among others, in the first half of the 18th century. To the south of the church

The magnificent tomb of St Willibald in the cathedral

**Romanesque rotunda in
the Kapuzinerkirche**

are the buildings of the
former Jesuit College, dating
from the 17th and 18th
centuries, with two courtyards
and cloisters. The college is
now used as a seminary.

🛉 Kloster Notre Dame du Sacré Coeur

Notre Dame 1. **Informations-
zentrum Naturpark Altmühltal**
Tel (08421) 98 760.
This convent was built for
a foundation established in
1711 for the education of
young girls. Work on the
convent began in 1712, and
on the church in 1719, both

to designs by the architect
Gabriel de Gabrieli.

The church has a central-
ized plan. The façade is
divided by huge pilasters and
decorated with a sculpture of
the Immaculate Conception
above the portal. Today,
the church and the convent
are the headquarters of
the information centre of
Altmühl Valley National Park.

🛉 Kapuzinerkirche Hl. Kreuz und zum Heiligen Grab

Kapuzinergasse 2.
This modest church of the
Capuchin monks was built
in 1623–5 and enlarged in
1905. To the south of the
nave stands an oval stone-
built Romanesque rotunda
crowned by an open
gallery and a dome
supported on tall, slender
columns. It was built in
1160 in imitation of the
Church of the Holy
Sepulchre in
Jerusalem.

🛉 Fürstbischöfliche Sommer Residenz

Ostenstr. 24.
The former bishop's summer
residence, also designed by
Gabriel de Gabrieli, dates
from 1735–7. The ground
and upper floors and narrow
side galleries now house the
offices of the Catholic university. The residence is set
in geometrically laid out
parkland that merges into
a landscaped park
descending in terraces
to the River
Altmühl.

The Baroque façade of the former bishop's summer residence

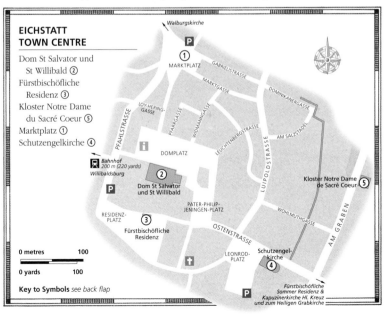

**EICHSTÄTT
TOWN CENTRE**

Dom St Salvator und
St Willibald ②
Fürstbischöfliche
Residenz ③
Kloster Notre Dame
du Sacré Coeur ⑤
Marktplatz ①
Schutzengelkirche ④

0 metres   100
0 yards   100

Key to Symbols *see back flap*

🔒 Walburgskirche

Westenstr.

This church was built on the spot where the relics of St Walburg were buried in 875. The present monastery dates from 1629–31. In the chapel behind the high altar is St Walburg's tomb, the church's most holy feature and the object of pilgrimages. The chapel, which contains numerous votive images placed there in gratitude to the saint, is decorated with intricate wrought-iron grilles. The altarpiece consists of Gothic carvings depicting St Walburg, his parents and his brother, St Willibald.

⚓ Willibaldsburg

Burgstr. 19. **Jura-Museum**
Tel (08421) 29 56, (08421) 47 30.
🔘 Apr–Sep: 9am–6pm, Tue–Sun;
Oct–Mar: 10am–4pm Tue–Sun. **Ur-und Frühgeschichtliches Museum**
Tel (08421) 89 450.
🔘 Apr–Sep: 9am–6pm Tue–Sun;
Oct–Mar: 10am–4pm Tue–Sun.

This castle, on a hill southwest of the town, overlooks the Altmühl river valley. It can be reached by car through a tunnel 63m (206 ft) long. The castle has an elongated design and is surrounded by 17th-century fortifications. From 1353 to 1725 it was the seat of bishops but was partly demolished in the 19th century. The present approaches to the castle were built in the first half of the 17th century. The castle walls contain the ruins of a residence built for Bishop Martin von Schaumberg (1560–90).

The western section of the hill is occupied by a three-winged building with central cloisters, and a main building with small towers. Both were built by Elias Holl, who was brought to Eichstätt by Bishop Konrad von Gemmingen in 1609. Together with Augsburg town hall, they are regarded as Germany's most important late Renaissance buildings.

The north wing houses the **Jura-Museum**, with a rich collection of fossils from the Jurassic period. The south wing contains the **Ur- und Frühgeschichtliches Museum** (Museum of Prehistory), with fascinating displays.

Beilngries ➋

Road map D2. 🏠 9,000. 🚌 🚊
ℹ️ Hauptstr. 14, (08461) 84 35.
www.beilngries.de

The best way to reach Beilngries is by road or boat from Kelheim along the scenic Altmühl valley. The town still has its defensive walls, which are set with nine towers and reinforced by a fosse (moat). Among the historic buildings on Haupt-

Romanesque tower, a vestige of the medieval castle outside Beilngries

straße is the late 16th-century house at No. 25, known as the **Kaiserbeckhaus**, which has a cantilevered upper storey supported on corbels.

The imposing Neo-Baroque **Stadtpfarrkirche** was built in 1912–13 to a design by Wilhelm Spannagl. The span of its vaulting and the ingenuity of its circular windows are impressive.

On a steep hill outside the town once stood a medieval castle, vestiges of which are two tall Romanesque **towers** flanking the gatehouse. In 1760–4 the castle was converted into the **Bishop's hunting lodge**. Its main decorative motifs are deer, which led to its being called Schloss Hirschberg ("Deer Mountain"). The Imperial Hall and the Knights' Hall are decorated with paintings by Michael Franz and have Rococo stuccowork. The palace chapel, built with material from the walls of the Romanesque castle chapel, was designed by Alexander von Brancas in the 1980s.

Ingolstadt ➌

See pp166–7.

Neuburg an der Donau ➍

See pp168–9.

FOSSILS FROM THE JURASSIC ERA

About 150 million years ago, the region of the Altmühl river valley in northern Upper Bavaria and southern Franconia lay beneath a shallow lagoon that was separated from the open Jurassic sea by a reef of corals and sponges.

Today collectors search quarries for fossils of ammonites, small crustaceans, insects and marine plants. For a modest sum impressive specimens can also be purchased from the quarry workers. A rich collection of fossils is on view in the Jura-Museum in Willibaldsburg castle in Eichstätt.

A fossil of *Archaeopteryx lithographica* in the Jura-Museum in Eichstätt

---

Pfaffenhofen ❺

Road map D3. 🏠 *21,600.*
🚌 🚃 🛈 *Hauptplatz 47, (08441)
49 15 11.* **www**.pfaffenhofen.de

The town, situated on
the River Ilm, lies at the
western extremity of the
hop-growing region. It
was once surrounded by
fortifications set with 17
towers and pierced by four
gates. Around the pleasant
square stands the Gothic
Johann Baptist Kirche and
a Neo-Gothic **town hall**. A
tall, square tower with a
steeple stands beside the
church presbytery. The
Mesnerhaus, a residential
house dating from 1786,
contains a **museum** with a
sizeable collection of art
dating from the 16th to
the 19th centuries.

**🏛 Museum im
Mesnerhaus**
Scheyerer Str. 5.
Tel (08441) 27 442 or
(08441) 3722.
⬜ *2pm–4pm on the first
Sun of every quarter
or by arrangement.*

**Soaring Gothic tower of Johann
Baptistkirche, Pfaffenhofen**

Scheyern ❻

Road map D3. 🏠 *4,200.* 🚌 🚃
in Pfaffenhofen. 🛈 *Ludwigstr. 2,
(08441) 80 640.*

Scheyern lies southwest of
Pfaffenhofen. In 1119, when
the seat of the Scheyern
family was converted into a
monastery, it was occupied
by monks of the Benedictine
order. After the first wave of

Façade of the Benedictine monastery in Scheyern

the dissolution of the
monasteries, the Benedictines
left but returned in 1837 at
the request of Ludwig I.

The triple-nave basilica
of **Mariä Himmelfahrt** was
remodelled in the Baroque
style in 1768–9, with
decorative mouldings by the
Wessobrunn stuccoists. The
Chapel of the Holy Cross
contains a Baroque altar with
a late Renaissance crucifix of
1600. The centrepiece of the
tabernacle is a Byzantine
relic of the True Cross,
which is kept in a magnificent
monstrance made by
Johann Georg in 1738.

Freising ❼

Road map D3. 🏠 *45,000.*
🚌 🚃 Ⓢ 🛈 *Marienplatz 7,
(08161) 54 122.* **www**.Freising.de

The seat of a bishopric from
720, the town was for
centuries the residence of the
bishops of Freising and
Munich. The hill on which the
cathedral stands is known as
Mons Doctus (Learned
Mount). The cathedral
dates from the mid-
13th century, with
the cloisters added
in the 15th century.
It was remodelled
in 1723–4 with
the involvement of
the Asam brothers
(see p68).

An outstanding
feature of the interior
is a Pietà of 1492 by
Erasmus Grasser and
Gothic stalls dating
from 1485–8. The
Romanesque crypt
contains a column
known as the

**Oriel window of
Freising town hall**

Bestiensäule, which is
decorated with carvings
symbolizing the fight against
evil. Beside the crypt is the
Maximiliankapelle, with
stuccowork and paintings
by Hans Georg Asam.

The late Gothic **cloisters**
feature paintings by Johann
Baptist Zimmermann of 1717
and tombstones dating from
the 15th to the 18th centuries.
The cloisters are linked to the
Gothic **Benediktuskapelle** of
1345, and a stunning Baroque
cathedral library designed by
François Cuvilliés.

The Gothic **Johannis-
kirche**, in front of the
cathedral, is linked to the
bishop's residence, which has
fine Renaissance cloisters. On
the cathedral hill is the
Diözesanmuseum, the largest
museum of religious art in
Germany.

In the town at the bottom
of the hill are the church or
St Peter und Paul, designed in
the early 18th century by
Giovanni Antonio Viscardi,
with paintings by Johann
Baptist Zimmermann, and
the late Gothic
Georgskirche, with
a Baroque tower,
as well as the Neo-
Renaissance **town
hall** of 1904–05.

On Weihenstephan
hill stands the world's
oldest **brewery**,
founded in 1040. The
Benedictine monas-
tery now houses
certain departments
of Munich's Technical
University.

🏛 Diözesanmuseum
Domberg 21. **Tel** (08161)
48 790. ⬜ *10am–5pm
Tue–Sun.*

Ingolstadt ❸

Fountain statue

Ludwig the Rich founded Bavaria's first university here in 1472. Initially a centre of humanism, it later became a focal point of the Counter-Reformation. In the 16th century Ingolstadt was the largest fortified town in southern Germany, and was defended by Swedish soldiers during the Thirty Years' War. It suffered severe bomb damage during World War II but was restored soon after. Today Ingolstadt is known principally for the Audi cars manufactured here and for its oil refinery. However, it has some noteworthy buildings.

Alte Anatomie, now the Deutsches Medizinhistorisches Museum

The Baroque interior of the Asamkirche Maria de Victoria

🏛 Museum Mobile

Audi Forum Ingolstadt, Ettingerstrasse. **Tel** (0800) 283 4444. ◯ 9am–6pm daily. 📷

With its "museum mobile", the Audi Forum is a delight for car enthusiasts. More than 80 Audi cars, motorbikes and bicycles are on display and the history of the automobile is documented in great detail.

⛪ Asamkirche Maria de Victoria

Neubaugasse. ◯ Jan–Feb: 1–4pm Tue–Sun (also 10am–noon Sun); Mar–Apr: 9am–noon, 1–5pm Tue–Sun (May–Oct: daily); Nov–Dec: 10am–noon, 1–4pm Tue–Sun. 📷

This hall was built in 1732–6 as the meeting place of the Marian students' association. The stuccowork is by Egid Quirin Asam, and the painting by his brother Cosmas Damian Asam, who exploited the various points of perspective as he covered the ceiling with extensive frescoes. The sacristy contains a famous monstrance of 1708 by the Augsburg goldsmith Johannes Zeckl, depicting the defeat of the Turks at the Battle of Lepanto in 1571.

⛩ Kreuztor and City Walls

The city walls, together with their semicircular towers, were built from 1362 to 1440. Of the four original city gates, only the western one, known as the Kreuztor, survives. It is considered to be one of the finest of its kind in Germany.

The Taschenturm, a tower with stepped gables, also survives. Of the fortification towers, built from 1539 to 1579 and demolished in 1800, only the ruins of casemates and bastions still stand today. Fortifications begun in 1823 are dotted around the town.

⛪ Liebfrauenmünster

Bergbräustr./Kreuzstr. 1.

This great 15th-century church with diagonally set twin towers is one of the largest Gothic brick buildings in Bavaria.

The high altar, completed in 1572, commemorates the centenary of the foundation of Ingolstadt's university. The altar, 9 m (30 ft) high, incorporates 91 paintings by Hans Mielich. Other features of the interior are the Renaissance stalls and pulpit, the Gothic and Renaissance stained glass, and the monument to Johannes Eck, Martin Luther's greatest opponent, who died in 1543.

⛩ Alte Anatomie

Anatomiestr. 18/20. **Deutsches Medizinhistorisches Museum Tel** (0841) 305 2860. ◯ 10am–noon & 2–5pm Tue–Sun. 📷

This fine Baroque building, completed in 1723, originally housed the university's Department of Medicine and is now home to a museum of medical history. The pleasant courtyard has a garden where medicinal herbs are grown.

The Gothic Kreuztor, Ingolstadt's western gate

♣ Neues Schloss

Paradeplatz 4. **Bayerisches Armeemuseum** *Tel* (0841) 93770. ◯ 8:45am–5pm Tue–Sun. ▨

The Neues Schloss (New Castle) was built in the first half of the 15th century. Set with corner towers, the two-storey castle has the appearance of an impregnable stronghold. A Renaissance gateway leads into the inner courtyard. Today the castle houses the **Bavarian Army Museum**, with displays of items captured in the wars against the Turks.

♣ Herzogskasten

Hallstr. 4.
This ancient castle, standing on the southwestern corner of the city walls, was built in 1255. The oldest secular

The Neo-Renaissance Altes Rathaus, with its elaborate gable

building in Ingolstadt, it was a ducal residence until it was superseded by the Neues Schloss, which was built in the 15th century. The castle then was converted into a

VISITORS' CHECKLIST

Road map D2. ∰ 117,000. ▦
▣ (0841) 93 41 825. ▮ *Altes Rathaus, Rathausplatz 4, (0841) 30 53 030.* **www**.ingolstadt-tourismus.de @ touristinformation @ingolstadt.de ▧ *Ingolstädter Bürgerfest (first weekend in Jul).*

granary. Rising two storeys high, it has a very tall roof with a Gothic stepped gable. It now houses a library.

▦ Altes Rathaus

Rathausplatz 2.
The elegant town hall was lavishly remodelled in the Neo-Renaissance style by Gabriel von Seidl in 1882–3. Its sculptural decoration was designed by Lorenz Gedon. The building incorporates a former residence.

⌂ Moritzkirche

Hieronymus Str. 3.
Begun in the mid-14th century and completed in 1489, the church is a Gothic basilica with a 14th–15th-century watchtower known as the Pfeifturm.

The hospital nearby, completed in 1434, served as the main university building from 1472 to 1800.

The Neues Schloss, an elegant and imposing residence

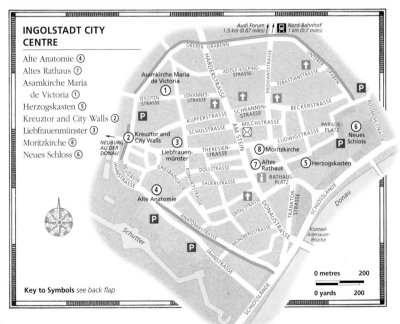

INGOLSTADT CITY CENTRE

Alte Anatomie ④
Altes Rathaus ⑦
Asamkirche Maria de Victoria ①
Herzogskasten ⑤
Kreuztor and City Walls ②
Liebfrauenmünster ③
Moritzkirche ⑧
Neues Schloss ⑥

Audi Forum 1.5 km (0.87 miles)
Nord-Bahnhof 1 km (0.7 miles)

OBERER GRABEN
HARDERSTRASSE
ADOLF-KOLPING-STRASSE
UNTERER GRABEN
PROVIANTSTRASSE
SEBASTIANSTRASSE
ROSSMÜHLSTRASSE

Asamkirche Maria de Victoria ①
JESUITEN-STRASSE
JOHANNES-STRASSE
BECKERSTRASSE
KUPFERSTRASSE
SCHRANNEN-STRASSE
MILCHSTRASSE
PARADE-PLATZ
Neues Schloss ⑥
SCHULSTRASSE
AM STEIN
LUDWIGSTRASSE

Kreuztor and City Walls ②
NEUBURG AU DER DONAU
THERESIEN-STRASSE
⑧ Moritzkirche
Liebfrauen-münster ③
GRIESBADGASSE
KONVIKTSTRASSE
DOLLSTRASSE
⑦ Altes Rathaus
⑤ Herzogskasten
SAUERSTRASSE
RATHAUS-PLATZ

JAHNSTRASSE
NEUGASSE
Alte Anatomie ④
ANATOMIESTRASSE
SPITALSTRASSE
DONAUSTRASSE
TRANKTOR-STRASSE
SCHLOSSLÄNDE
Donau
Konrad-Adenauer-Brücke

Schutter
JAHNSTRASSE
MÜNZBERGSTRASSE

SCHLOSSLÄNDE

0 metres 200
0 yards 200

Key to Symbols *see back flap*

Neuburg an der Donau ➍

Situated on the River Danube (Donau), Neuburg is considered to be one of Bavaria's most beautiful towns. The atmosphere from the time when it flourished as a ducal residence lives on in the streets and squares of the Obere Stadt (Upper Town). These are rivalled by the Obere Vorstadt, an early centre of the Counter-Reformation, which has an Ursuline con-vent as well as patricians' town houses and the palaces of the court elite. Along the Danube lies the Englischer Garten, a park traversed by the road to the 16th-century castle of the Wittelsbachs in nearby Grünau.

Oberes Tor, gateway to the Upper Town

🏰 Oberes Tor and Town Walls
In the 14th century Obere Stadt was enclosed by walls, towers and galleries. Considerable vestiges of the upper town remain, notably Oberes Tor, the main gate. It was rebuilt in 1530, when it was flanked by circular towers and topped with a Renaissance gable.

🏛 Peterskirche
Amalienstr. 40.
The church stands on the site of the oldest church in Neuburg, first mentioned in 1214. It was designed by Johann Serro of Graubünden and built in 1641–6. The triple-nave open interior is decorated with Baroque painting and stuccowork.

🏰 Amalienstraße
Of the many fine gabled houses that line this street, two are especially worthy of note. One is the Eyßhaus, the old post office, built in 1720 and located next to Weveldhaus, and the other the Court Pharmacy, first mentioned in 1713. Both have ornamental gables. Equally elegant are the 17th and 18th-century houses that can be seen in Herrenstraße.

🏛 Stadtmuseum Weveldhaus
Amalienstr. A19.
🕙 10am–6pm Tue–Sun.
The two-storey late Gothic Weveldhaus was built in the 16th century, and was redecorated in 1715 by Gabriel de Gabrieli, who added a fine Baroque portal. The building now houses a museum that contains many artifacts relating to the history of the town and the surrounding area.

🏰 Karlsplatz
There are few town squares in Bavaria more charming than Karlsplatz. Surrounded by trees, it has a Mariensäule (Column of the Virgin) and a fountain in the centre. The square is dominated by the façade of Hofkirche, which occupies its entire eastern side. The square boasts exquisite proportions and fine, elegant buildings.

Baroque doorway of the Weveldhaus on Amalienstraße

On the northern side of the square stands the Renaissance town hall of 1603–09. Its double exterior stairway leads to the grand entrance on the first floor. Beside it stands the Taxishaus (named after the von Thurn und Taxis family). It was completed in 1747 and its façade is decorated with elaborate poly-chrome stuccowork. Further on is the Zieglerhaus, with fine wrought-iron grilles and an elegant gate.

On the west side of the square is the pleasantly proportioned and decorated Lorihaus and the library building, its Rococo façade facing onto Amalienstraße. Built in 1731–2, it was furnished in 1802 with furniture from the Kaisheim monastery library.

Mariensäule on Karlsplatz

🏛 Hofkirche
Karlsplatz 10.
The former Hofkirche (Court Church) was founded by the Protestant rulers of Neuburg in reaction to the building of the Jesuit Michaelskirche in Munich. Work began in 1608 but was interrupted by the death of Philip Ludwig. In 1617 his Catholic successor brought the Jesuits to Neuburg and donated the church to them. It was completed in 1627.

The late Renaissance building, with a flat façade and a central octagonal domed tower, was decorated with fine stuccowork in 1616–18. The paintings by Peter Paul Rubens that once graced the altar are now in the Alte Pinakothek in Munich. Some particularly interesting features of the presbytery are the ducal loggia and the stairway to the crypt, the dukes' final resting place. A passage connects the church to the neighbouring castle.

Interior of Pfarrkirche Mariä Himmelfahrt

♗ Schloss

Residenzstr. 2. *Tel (08431) 64430.*
◯ *10am–5pmTue–Sun.* 🎟 **Schloss museum** ◯ *Apr–Sep: 9am–6pm Tue–Sun; Oct–Mar: 10am–4pm Tue–Sun.*
The history of Neuburg Castle goes back to Roman times, when the fort of Venaxamodorum stood here. It has been in the possession of the Wittelsbach family since the 13th century. The present-day castle was built in 1530–45 and was redecorated in the Renaissance style in 1667–70. It has a pentagonal outline and is set with two circular towers that look onto the Danube. The attractive Renaissance courtyard is surrounded by a double-tiered gallery. The west side of the courtyard has sgraffito decorations and two stone figures of dukes, probably dating from the second half of the 17th century. The west wing has a Renaissance chapel with galleries and ceiling frescoes painted by Hans Bockberger in 1543. These were plastered over in 1616, when Protestant fervour celebrated its triumph over Catholicism, but they were uncovered again in 1934–51.

An underground passage beneath Neuer Bau, the north wing, leads from the Danube to Obere Stadt. The Baroque grottoes are open to visitors.

VISITORS' CHECKLIST

Road map C2. 🚉 28,000. 🚉
ℹ️ *Ottheinrichplatz. A118, (08431) 55 240.*
www.neuburg-donau.de
@ tourismus@neuburg-donau.de
🎊 *Schlossfest (in odd years, Jun/Jul); Volksfest (Jul); Kartoffelwochen (Oct).*

♗ Former Jesuit College

Am Unteren Tor.
This 17th-century college building has a modest but imaginatively designed façade. On the third floor is the former assembly hall, which is renowned for its excellent acoustics.

Stone figures in the arcaded courtyard of the Schloss

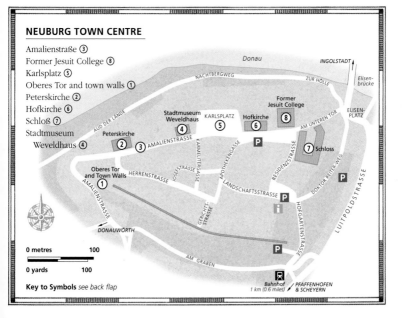

NEUBURG TOWN CENTRE

0 metres 100
0 yards 100

Key to Symbols *see back flap*

The Landshutertor in Erding, crowned by a Baroque dome

Erding ⑧

Road map D3. 🏠 *34,000.* 🚌 🚃 Ⓢ 🚹 *Landshuter Str. 1, (08122) 40 80.* **www**.erding.de

This town is bounded by the rivers Fehlbach and Sempt, which join in the south of the conurbation. The historic buildings are grouped along two intersecting axes: Landshuterstraße, which culminates in the elongated Schrannenplatz, and the streets of Lange Zeile.

At the west end of Schrannenplatz is the Gothic **Johanneskirche**, built in the late 14th to early 15th centuries. It has an unusual layout, with the presbytery facing the square. Outside the presbytery stands a tall, 10-storey **belfry**, its façade decorated with friezes and blind windows. Inside the church the most interesting feature is the larger-than-life figure of Christ on the Cross, carved by Hans Leinberger in about 1525.

On the opposite side of Landshuterstraße stands the Gothic town gate known as the **Landshutertor**, or Schöner Turm. Flanked by towers, its façade is divided by rows of arched blind windows and it is covered by a shingle-clad Baroque dome, making it one of the most outstanding town gates in southern Bavaria. At Landshuterstraße 1 is the former

residence of the counts of Preysing, dating from 1648, which is now the town hall. Opposite stands the Gothic **Hospital Church of the Holy Spirit**, while at No. 3 Schrannenplatz is the 14th-century **Frauenkirche**.

Sankt Wolfgang ⑨

Road map E4. 🏠 *4,400.* 🚌 🚃 *St Wolfgang. Hauptstr. 9, (08085) 18 80.* **www**.st.wolfgang-ob.de

The town is named in honour of St Wolfgang, the Bishop of Ratisbon (Regensburg), who was canonized in 1052. According to legend the saint, while on his way to Mondsee monastery, discovered a spring with miracle-working waters here.

In the early 15th century a **chapel** was built over the spring. **Wolfgangskirche** was built to the south of the chapel in 1430–77. This two-nave, web-vaulted church is an outstanding example of late Gothic Bavarian brick architecture. The foundations contain the Stone of St Wolfgang, a piece of red marble bearing what is said to be the saint's footprint. Substantial fragments of the original Gothic altar of about 1485 also remain. There is also a carving of St Wolfgang with St George and St Sigismund by Heinrich Helmschrot of Landshut (or his studio), and paintings of scenes from the life of St Mary.

Statue of St Wolfgang

In the elongated northern nave, and a few steps higher up, is the original **chapel** with the miracle-working spring, which attracts pilgrims. In the early 18th century it was decorated with fine stuccowork with acanthus motifs. The small figure of St Wolfgang that stands on the Rococo altar was made in 1470 and is said to have miraculous powers. Before the altar is a deep covered well. Visitors can lie down beside it and drink its curative water using a ladle.

The town hall is another interesting building. It was originally a presbytery, built by Johann Baptist Gunetzrhainer.

Oberschleißheim ⑩

Road map D3. 🏠 *12,000.* Ⓢ 🚹 *Freisinger Str. 15, (089) 315 61 30.* **www**.oberschleissheim.de

This town is best known for its three impressive **palaces** *(see pp172–3)*, set in the gardens of the Hofgarten. But also of interest is the **Flugwerft Schleißheim**, a museum located on one of the oldest aerodromes in Germany. Part of the Deutsches Museum, the museum is located in restored buildings dating from 1912–19, in a new exhibition hall and on the apron. Some 50 aircraft and helicopters are on display. There is also an exhibition illustrating the development of flight and of space flight.

🏛 **Flugwerft Schleißheim**
Effnerstr. 18. **Tel** *(089) 31 57 14 0.*
🕘 *9am–5pm daily.* 📷

Otto Lilienthal's aeroplane, built in 1894, Flugwerft Schleißheim

The gardens of the Renaissance castle in Dachau

Dachau **⑪**

Road map D4. 🏠 *42,000.* Ⓢ 🚆
🛈 *Konrad-Adenauer-Str. 1, (08131) 75 286 or 75 287.* **www.**dachau.info
📷 *Dachauer Volksfest (Aug).*

Set on a steep hill, this picturesque little town on the River Amper has a panoramic view of nearby Munich, although its name has become synonymous with the martyrdom of hundreds of thousands of people.

In 1933 the first Nazi **concentration camp** was set up here and it was in use up until 1945, during which time 30,000 prisoners perished here. The site of the camp was opened to the public as a place of remembrance in 1965.

One of the buildings contains the **KZ-Gedenkstätte Dachau**, a museum which documents the history of the concentration camps and the crimes against humanity that were committed here before and during World War II.

On the hill at the edge of the town, a **palace** was built on the site of a 15th-century castle as a summer residence for the Wittelsbachs. Of the original four wings constructed in 1558–77, only the southwest wing remains. The ceremonial hall on the first floor, which survives, was decorated in 1564–5 by Hans Wissreuter.

The focal point of the town is a triangular plaza on which the town hall and the church

stand. Hans Krumpper's late Renaissance **Jakobskirche** was built in 1624–5. It incorporates an earlier presbytery with a fine tower dating from about 1425 and extended in 1676–8 with the addition of a dome.

🏛 **KZ-Gedenkstätte Dachau (Museum)**
Alte Roemerstr. 75. **Tel** *(08131) 66 99 70.* ⭘ *9am–5pm Tue–Sun*

Kloster Indersdorf **⑫**

Road map C3.
🚌 Ⓢ 🚆 *Markt Indersdorf.*
🛈 *Markt Indersdorf, Marktplatz 1, (08136) 93 40.*
www.markt-indersdorf.de

This former Augustinian abbey built in the early 11th century stands on the north bank of the River Glonn. Vestiges of a 12th-century triple-nave Romanesque basilica with a twin-towered façade and Gothic remodelling are discernible in the later **Klosterkirche Mariae Himmelfahrt**. The latter was lavishly furnished during the 18th century. Franz Xavier Feichtmayr the Elder added the interior Rococo stuccowork in 1754–6, and the paintings of scenes from the life of St Augustine were executed by Matthäus Günther, assisted by Johann Georg Tiefenbrunner.

The extensive **abbey buildings** of 1694–1704, designed by Antonio Riva, are set around two courtyards south and east of the church.

Gate and guard tower of Dachau concentration camp

Gothic Madonna in Fürstenfeld-bruck's Baroque church

Fürstenfeldbruck **⑬**

Road map C4. 🏠 *33,000.* Ⓢ 🚆
🛈 *Hauptstr. 31, (08141) 280.*
www.fuerstenfeldbruck.de
📷 *Volks- und Heimatfest (Jun–Jul); Brucker Altstadtfest (Jul); Leonhardifahrt (Oct–Nov); Christkindlmarkt (Dec); Luzienhäuschen-schwimmen (13 Dec).*

The finest and most important building in the town is the former **Cistercian abbey**, situated on the way to Augsburg and built in 1263–90. Its establishment was funded by Ludwig II, the Severe, after the execution of his wife Maria of Brabant, who was unjustly accused of infidelity. In 1691–1754, remodelled by Giovanni Antonio Viscardi, it became one of the largest Baroque abbeys in Bavaria.

The monumental façade of **Mariae-Himmelfahrtskirche** conceals an interior of fine stuccowork by Pietro Francesco Appiani, vaulting lavishly painted by Cosmas Damian Asam and a high altar of 1760–62 designed by his brother Egid Quirin Asam.

The monastery, its interior decorated with stuccowork and painting in 1924, now houses a police college and museum. Many historic town houses line the main street. The old town hall, refurbished in 1866–8, features paintings dating from 1900.

On St Luke's Day, in memory of the flood of 1725, children float model houses illuminated with candles across the Amper, which flows through the town.

Schleißheim Palace

Mask on the Neues Schloss

Originally intended to rival the splendour of Versailles, the palace at Schleißheim was the architectural setting for the imperial ambitions of Maximilian Emanuel. The architect was Enrico Zucalli, and work started in 1701. It was then interrupted, but restarted in 1717 under the direction of Joseph Effner, who deviated from the original plans. The 330-m (1,082-ft) long Neues Schloss has an overpoweringly lavish interior, which was decorated by Cosmas Damian Asam and Johann Baptist Zimmermann. Today, as well as admiring the elaborate interior decoration, visitors can see the palace's outstanding gallery of Baroque painting.

Doors
The doors leading into the vestibule were carved by Ignaz Günther in 1736 and are counted among his masterpieces.

Altes Schloss
In the late 16th century Wilhelm V built himself a modest country seat. Under the direction of his son, Maximilian I, Heinrich Schön the Elder remodelled it in 1616–23, with mouldings and paintings by Peter Candid. It was rebuilt after World War II.

A gateway with clock tower built in about 1600 leads into the courtyard in front of the Altes Schloss.

★ Neues Schloss
The vestibule, decorated with fine stuccowork and frescoes, leads into a Rococo dining-room on one side and to a grand staircase on the other.

| 0 metres | 150 |
| 0 yards | 150 |

VISITORS' CHECKLIST

Road map D3. **Neues Schloss
and Schloss Lustheim**
Tel (089) 31 58 720.
☐ *Apr–Sep: 9am–6pm Tue–
Sun; Oct–Mar: 10am–4pm daily.*
Altes Schloss *Tel* (089) 31 55
272. ☑ **www**.schloesser.
bayern.de

★ Schloss Lustheim

*This small Baroque palace was built
as a love nest for Maximilian
Emanuel and his first wife. It
now houses a collection
of Meissen
porcelain.*

Canals
*Lustheim's
canals form the axis
of the park layout. In
front of Neues Schloss the
water flows into a basin with a
cascade and fountains.*

★ Park

*This is the only Baroque park
in Germany that has survived
in its original form. It is
characterized by canals and
pathways that mark out
geometrical patterns of greenery.*

MAXIMILIAN EMANUEL

In 1701 the Elector Maximilian
Emanuel ordered the extension
of Schleißheim and the rebuilding of Nymphenburg. Defeat
in the war against Austria
caused work to be temporarily
suspended, so that he did not
see its completion. Despite this
his patronage brought Bavaria
into the mainstream of the
high Baroque, giving the
Wittelsbach family a name for
splendour and prestige.

STAR SIGHTS

★ Neues Schloss

★ Park

★ Schloss Lustheim

LOWER BAVARIA

*L*ower Bavaria (Niederbayern), bordering Austria and the Czech Republic in the east, is both a distinct cultural entity and a separate administrative area. With a pristine natural environment, it is an oasis of peace, while its fine Baroque buildings leave an indelible impression on the visitor. With none of the bustle of big cities, towns like Landshut and Passau have retained an old-world flavour.

Lower Bavaria encompasses most of the Bayerischer Wald (Bavarian Forest), which includes a nature reserve and a national park. Increasing numbers of holiday-makers are appreciating the unspoiled natural environment here. As recently as the 1960s, out-of-the-way villages delighted visitors with their tumbledown thatched cottages. Today such sights are confined to the open-air museums of the Museumsdorf Bayerischer Wald and the Freilichtmuseum Finsterau.

The local people, known for their hospitality and friendliness, work in the region's forestry, tourist and glassware industries. Calm and restrained, they have a strong sense of their own worth. When Franz Xaver Krenkl, a Lower Bavarian, beat the royal carriage on its journey to Munich in his own cart, his comment was simply "Wer ko der ko" ("He who can, can").

From the Benedictine monastery at Weltenburg to the town of Kelheim the River Danube flows between high limestone cliffs overgrown with dense mixed foliage. On both sides of the river unique rock formations create fantastic shapes, and they have been named accordingly. Sailing along this stretch of the Danube is an unforgettable experience, as is the view down onto the river from the gallery around the Neo-Classical Liberation Hall in Kelheim. A canal completed in 1992 joins the Danube at Kelheim, providing a waterway link with the Rhine and the Main, using a stretch of the River Altmühl. This valley is as magical as that of the Danube.

Initiatives to industrialize Lower Bavaria have resulted in the construction of two modern factories in Dingolfing, where the famous BMW cars are produced.

Passau's beautiful Old Town, on the banks of the River Danube

◁ Baroque interior of the Benedictine Abbey library in Metten

Exploring Lower Bavaria

Landshut is the capital of Lower Bavaria. Every four years tourists come for the Landshut Wedding, a great historical spectacle held at the foot of Trausnitz castle *(see p31)*. Passau, at the confluence of the Danube, Inn and Ilz rivers, is equally picturesque. From here the "Asam Trail" begins, taking in the churches that the Asam brothers decorated in Aldersbach, Osterhofen, Straubing, Rohr and Weltenburg *(see p68)*. The piety of the local people can be seen in the many pilgrimage churches, the best known being at Bogenberg, known as the Mount Athos of Lower Bavaria, and Geiersberg, near Deggendorf.

Bavarian coat of arms on the town gate in Vilshofen

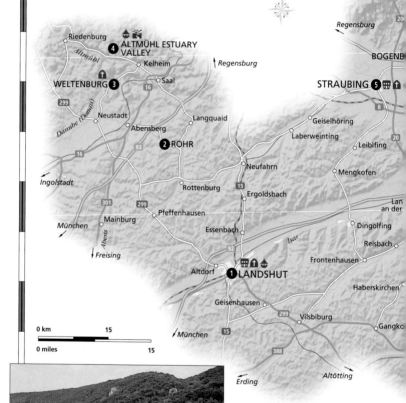

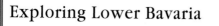

Barrage on the River Altmühl at Haidhof

GETTING AROUND

Lower Bavaria borders Austria and the Czech Republic. Three motorways pass through the region. The A92 links Landshut and Deggendorf, following the course of the River Isar, and the A3 links Regensburg and Passau, along the course of the River Danube. Regensburg can also be reached by A93. The railway network is sparse but there is a good bus service.

SIGHTS AT A GLANCE

KEY

━━ Motorway

── Main road

── Minor road

── Scenic route

┈┈ Main railway

── Minor railway

▬▬ International border

△ Summit

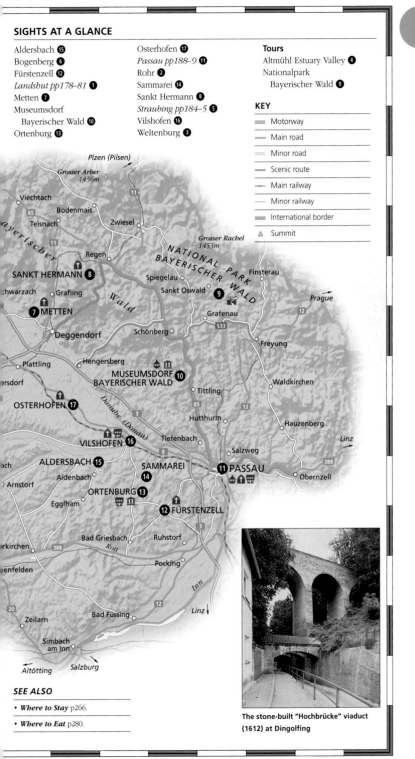

The stone-built "Hochbrücke" viaduct
(1612) at Dingolfing

SEE ALSO

• *Where to Stay* p266.

• *Where to Eat* p280.

Street-by-Street: Landshut ❶

Griffin on a house in the Schirmgasse

Landshut, the capital of Lower Bavaria, grew up around Trausnitz castle and flourished in the 14th and 15th centuries. In 1475 it was the scene of a grand and lavish wedding when Duke Georg of the House of Wittelsbach married the Polish Princess Jadwiga, daughter of Casimir Jagiellon. Wedding guests included the Emperor Frederick III and his son Maximilian. The event is commemorated today by a great spectacle, the Landshut Wedding *(see p31).*

★ Stadtresidenz
This palace, built for Duke Ludwig X in 1536–43, was the first Renaissance palace in Germany.

Emslander

Ländtor
The Gothic gateway leading into the city from the side on the River Isar is a vestige of the old city fortifications.

THEATERSTR.

HARNISCHGASSE

LÄNDGASSE

LÄNDGASSE

INNEREMÜNCHENER STR.

Burg
Trausnitz

Landschaftshaus
The Renaissance painting executed in 1599 on the walls of the house at Altstadt 28 is a good example of this kind of exterior decoration in Landshut.

STAR SIGHTS

★ Martinskirche

★ Stadtresidenz

★ Town Hall

★ Town Hall

The Gothic town hall has a fine Renaissance oriel window. The interior paintings and stained-glass windows on the theme of the Landshut Wedding date from 1860.

VISITORS' CHECKLIST

Road map E3. 👥 60,000. 🚆 Bahnhofplatz. 🛈 Altstadt 315, (0871) 92 2050. **www.** landshut.de 🚉 Landshuter Hochzeit (Landshut Wedding) (Jul, every four years; next in 2009), Landshuter Hofmusiktage (Jul, every 2 years; next in 2008), Landshuter Flohmarkt (May), Altstadtfest (Jul), Bartlmädult (Aug), Haferlmarkt (Sep).

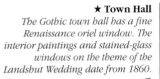

Grasbergerhaus

It was in this late Gothic house with stepped gables and street-level arcade that the betrothed Polish Princess Jadwiga stayed in 1475.

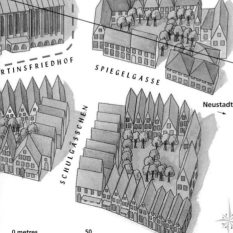

★ Martinskirche

The spacious interior of this triple-nave church, which took more than a hundred years to build (1389–1500), impresses with its height, its forest of columns and its fine vaulting.

ALTSTADT

STECKENGASSE

SCHIRMGASSE

KIRCHGASSE

...RTINSFRIEDHOF

SPIEGELGASSE

SCHULGÄSSCHEN

Neustadt

KEY

– – – Suggested route

0 metres 50

0 yards 50

Exploring Landshut

Landshut, like Munich, lies between a fork in the River Isar. It stretches out between Trausnitz castle, which is set on a vantage point, and the Cistercian abbey of Seligenthal. The central conurbation is concentrated around two wide parallel streets that function as squares lying on a north-south axis. They are known as Altstadt and Neustadt.

Landshut is perhaps the most quintessentially German of all Lower Bavarian towns. With its historic buildings spared damage during World War II, the town has retained the atmosphere of its earlier days of glory.

🔒 Jesuitenkirche
Spiegelgasse.

The Church of St Ignaz, located on the southern road leading out of Neustadt, was formerly part of a Jesuit monastery. Designed by the Jesuit architect Johannes Holl, it was built from 1613 to 1641. The interior features a fine Baroque high altar dating from 1663.

Side entrance to the Gothic Jodokkirche

🔒 Jodokkirche
Jodokgasse.

This Gothic triple-nave brick basilica, built in 1338–1450, was dedicated to St Jodok, the son of a Breton duke who lived in the 7th century and who became a pilgrim and hermit. In the mid-19th century the church was restored to its original Gothic appearance and was furnished in Baroque style.

Stone reliefs on the Gothic altar in Martinskirche

🔒 Martinskirche
Altstadt 219. **Tel** *(0871) 92 21 780.*
7:30am–6:30pm daily (to 5pm Oct–Mar; closed 1am–3pm Mon & Fri)

Three architects collaborated on the building of this Gothic church. One of them was Hans von Burghausen, whose tombstone, dated 1432, is built into its southern wall. At 131 m (430 ft) high, the brick church tower is the tallest in the world; the steeple was added in 1500. The tower commands a splendid view of the town and of the castle and its gardens. The interior of the church abounds in priceless Gothic furnishings.

🔒 Dominikanerkirche
Regierungsplatz.

The Church of St Blasien, part of the former Dominican monastery, was built in 1271–1384 in the form of a triple-nave Gothic basilica. The interior was remodelled in the Rococo style by Johann Baptist Zimmermann and decorated with lavish stucco-work. The Neo-Classical façade was added in 1805.

🔒 Spitalkirche
Heilige–Geist–Gasse.

The late Gothic Church of the Holy Spirit and the building of the former hospital located opposite stand on the south side of the road leading out of Altstadt. The triple-nave church was built by Hans von Burghausen in 1407–61.

The interior features fan vaulting and there is an ambulatory around the presbytery. On the northern side of the presbytery stands a large tower. The entrance to the church, in the west front, is a tall, ornamental portal fronted by a porch whose corners are set with low towers.

🏛 Stadtresidenz
Altstadt 79. **Tel** *(0871) 92 41 10.*
Apr–Sep: 9am–6pm Tue–Sun; Oct–Mar: 10am–4pm Tue–Sun.

This residence, in the Italian Renaissance style, consists of two adjacent buildings.

The Deutscher Bau, built in 1536–7, has a Neo-Classical façade dating from about 1780 on the side looking onto Altstadt. A museum of local history was laid out here in 1935.

The Italienischer Bau, built in 1537–43, has a fine arcaded courtyard. The building's façade, looking onto Länd-gasse, is decorated with a large cartouche bearing the coat of arms of Ludwig X of Bavaria, for whom it was built. Inside visitors can see the fine reception halls, which occupy two floors, and admire the beautiful Renaissance frescoes depicting mythological scenes.

Spitalkirche, on the road leading from Altstadt

Burg Trausnitz

This castle, whose history began in the year 1204, was the seat of the von Bayern-Landshut branch of the Wittelsbach family. It was extended in the 14th and 15th centuries, and was converted into a residence in 1568–79. In 1961 a fire destroyed the northwest wing, but painstaking restoration work has allowed it to re-open to visitors. The late Romanesque chapel and the original staircase were spared.

VISITORS' CHECKLIST

Burg Trausnitz 168.
Tel (0871) 92 41 10.
7 (to Kalcherstraße).
9am–5:30pm daily.
www.burgtrausnitz.de

★ **Narrentreppe**
The Fools' Staircase is decorated with lifesize figures from the Commedia dell'Arte painted in 1578 by Padovano. They commemorate the shows performed by an itinerant Italian theatre troupe for Wilhelm V.

St-Georgs-Rittersaal
The walls of this hall are hung with tapestries illustrating the exploits of Duke Otto Wittelsbach woven to designs by Peter Candid in Paris in 1618.

Arcaded courtyard

STAR SIGHT

★ Narrentreppe

Alte Dürnitz
This spacious two-nave hall is situated on the ground floor and features arches supported on palmate pillars.

The Castle
A steep flight of steps leads up to the castle and its gardens. The castle commands a fine view of the whole town and the valley of the River Isar.

Rohr ②

Road map D2. 🚃 🚆 *Abensberg.*
ℹ️ *Marienplatz 1, (08783) 96 080.*
Abbey Tel (08783) 96 000.
⭕ *6am–7pm daily.* 🎫 🎦
www.markt-rohr.de

This abbey dates from the
12th century. In the first
quarter of the 13th century,
when the church and **abbey**
were transferred to the
Benedictines, the buildings
were remodelled in the
Baroque style.
   Mariä Himmelfahrt is
renowned for its stuccowork
and the high altar of 1723 by
Egid Quirin Asam. The altar
was built in the form of a
theatrical stage with wings.
The sculptural group on the
altar depicts the Assumption
of the Virgin. It embodies the
idea of a *Theatrum Sacrum*
and is one of Asam's
masterpieces in this genre.

**The high altar of the church of
Mariä Himmelfahrt in Rohr**

Weltenburg ③

Road map D2. 🚃 🚆 *Kelheim.* ⛴️
Monastery Tel (09441) 20 40 or 20
41 36. ⭕ *mid-Mar–mid-Nov: 8am–
7pm:* ⭕ *mid-Nov–mid-Mar.* 🎫 🎦
www.klosterschenke-weltenburg.de

This Benedictine **monastery**
complex, dating from the
early 7th century, stands in a
picturesque setting on a
terrace beside the Danube.
   The Asam brothers added
to the complex the splendid
Baroque **Georgs- und
Martinskirche**, which was
completed in 1716. Cosmas
Damian was responsible for

A boat trip through the Danube Gorge from Weltenburg to Kelheim

the architectural designs and
the paintings, and Egid
Quirin Asam built the fine
high altar and the statue of St
George slaying the Dragon.
   There is a beer-garden in the
cloisters where visitors can
sample the monastery's beer.
Boat trips through the Danube
Gorge to Kelheim also depart
from a quay nearby.

Straubing ⑤

See pp180–81.

Bogenberg ⑥

Road map F2. 🏔️ *10,200.* 🚃
🚆 *Bogen.* ℹ️ *Bogen, Stadtplatz 56,
(09422) 50 50.* www.bogen.de

Rising above the small town
of Bogen, the Bogenberg,
or "Mount Athos" of Lower
Bavaria, was once a Celtic
sacred place. Since the Middle
Ages it has been a place of
pilgrimage. Standing on the
top is the Gothic **Hl. Kreuz
und Mariä Heimsuchung,**

**Angel and candles in the
pilgrimage church of Bogenberg**

which commands an excellent
view over the Danube valley.
   Pilgrims come here to
honour the miraculous statue
of the pregnant Virgin Mary,
dating from around 1400,
which is clothed in a
17th-century dress and
embroidered cloak. Dozens of
votive candles flicker in the
presbytery. According to an
ancient custom, at Pentecost
the strongest man from the
nearby village of Holzkirchen
brings to the church a great
candle – Die lange Stang – up
to 100 kg (220 lb) in weight
and 13 m (40 ft) long.

Metten ⑦

Road map F2. 🏔️ *4,200.* 🚃 🚆 ℹ️
Krankenhausstr. 22, (0991) 99 80 50.
www.markt-metten.de

The local **Benedictine
abbey** was founded in
about 766. In 1830, after it
had been appropriated as a
result of the dissolution of the
monasteries, it was returned
to its industrious owners.
   Michaelskirche, which has
been rebuilt several times
since its foundation in the
Romanesque period, was
remodelled in 1712–29.
The twin-towered façade
outlines two circular chapels.
The interior has paintings
and a high altar by Cosmas
Damian Asam.
   The most exquisite part of
the abbey is the library, built
in 1722–9 and decorated with
stuccowork by Franz Josef
Holzinger. It is one of the
finest library buildings in the
world. A remarkable pair of
Atlases support the low
vaulted ceiling.

Altmühl Estuary Valley ❹

The River Altmühl winds scenically from central Franconia, meandering through the northern part of Upper Bavaria and through Lower Bavaria before flowing into the Danube. The Altmühltal Naturpark, in the river valley, is one of the largest and finest nature parks in Germany. This tour takes visitors along the estuary, ending with the famous canal that connects the River Danube with the Main and the Rhine.

TIPS FOR HIKERS & DRIVERS

Length: About 20 km (12 miles).
Stopping-off places: There are cafés or bars at each of the places along the route. The larger towns have restaurants and some also offer accommodation.

Rosenburg ⑦
This castle is a centre for the breeding of birds of prey and contains a museum of falconry equipment. Displays with birds of prey, including eagles, are held here every day.

Schloß Prunn ⑤
This castle, looking as if it had grown from the rocks, houses a museum. The longest wooden bridge in Europe, over the Altmühl, is visible from the terrace.

Riedenburg ⑥
The local Crystals Museum is famous for having the world's largest cluster of rock crystal. It weighs 7.8 tonnes and comes from Arkansas in the United States.

Kelheimwinzer

Saal
REGENSBURG

INGOLSTADT

Essing ④
A narrow street leads to a delightful market square, while a medieval gate leads through to the wooden bridge (the longest in Europe) over the former course of the River Altmühl.

Randeck ③
A road running to the foot of the mountain leads to the ruins of an 11th-century castle, which was rebuilt several times, with the town of Essing at its feet.

Tropfsteinhöhle ②
These caves, off the road to Essing, were inhabited during the Stone Age. The temperature inside stays at a constant 9° C (48° C), regardless of external conditions.

Kelheim ①
The Independence Hall, built by Friedrich von Gärtner and Leo von Klenze in 1842–63, commemorates the defeat of Napoleon.

KEY

▬ Suggested route

═ Other road

0 km   10

0 miles   10

Straubing ❺

Standing on the south bank of the Danube in the fertile Gäuboden valley, Straubing pulsates with life. The medieval appearance of the Old Town has survived basically unchanged, bearing a faithful resemblance to the wooden model made in 1568 by Jakob Sandtner and now on view in the Bayerisches National-museum in Munich. A copy can be seen in the Gäubodenmuseum. Every year in August the town holds the Gäubodenvolksfest, a folk festival second in size only to Munich's Oktoberfest.

Gold mask in the Gäubodenmuseum

The Stadtturm (city tower) in the centre of the town square

🏛 Ludwigsplatz and Theresienplatz

The pedestrianized market square resembles a long, wide avenue cutting through the heart of the Old Town. It is pleasant to wander through the large garden between closely packed stalls and crates full of colourful flowers, fruit and vegetables, and admire the historic buildings. The **Stadtturm**, or tower, offers a sweeping panorama of the town, the Gäuboden and the Bavarian Forest. A Neo-Classical gate built in 1810 divides the market square into two, with **Ludwigsplatz** on the eastern side and **Theresienplatz** on the western.

Ludwigsplatz and Theresien-platz have two fountains dedi-cated to the town's patron saints, St Jacob (1644) and St Tiburtius (1685). On Theresien-platz stands a column built in 1709, featuring gilt figures of the Holy Trinity.

Opposite the town gates on the south side of the square is the two-storey **town hall**, its two wings enclosing a courtyard. The town hall was created in 1382, when two adjacent Gothic houses were conjoined behind a single façade. The stepped gable, however, dates from the 19th century.

🔒 Karmelitenkirche

Albrechtsgasse 20.
This spacious triple-nave Gothic church with a tower was partly remodelled in about 1700 by Wolfgang Dientzenhofer. The lavish

Baroque interior of Ursulinenkirche

17th and 18th-century furnishings successfully harmonize with the later Baroque decoration.

In the church is the tomb of Duke Albrecht II. His son, Albrecht III, secretly married Agnes Bernauer, who was the beautiful daughter of a barber from Augsburg. When he found out Albrecht II ordered the drowning of Agnes in the Danube in 1435. Every four years in June/July amateur actors re-create this historical tragedy in the Agnes-Bernauer-Festspiele.

🔒 Ursulinenkirche

Burggasse 9.
This church, which forms part of an Ursuline convent, was built and decorated by the Asam brothers in 1736–41. In their inspired collaboration, Egid Quirin Asam created the architectural design and Cosmas Damian Asam painted the frescoes and the altarpieces *(see p68)*.

♣ Herzogsschloss

Schlossplatz 2B. **Museum im Herzogsschloss**. *Tel (09421) 21 114.* ⬜ *10am–4pm Tue–Sun.* ⬛ *mid-Jan–mid-Mar.*
The castle, on the Danube, has an irregular plan and an inner courtyard. Its earliest parts date from the 14th century. The Bernauerturm on the southwestern corner is the turret from which Agnes Bernauer is said to have been thrown into the Danube. The museum is a branch of the Bayerisches Nationalmuseum.

🏛 Gäubodenmuseum

Fraunhoferstr. 9.
Tel (09421) 97 410. ⬜ *10am–4pm Tue–Sun.* ⬛
This local history museum was founded in 1845. Its most renowned exhibit is the Römerschatz, or Roman Treasure, which was discovered in 1950 and which caused a sensation among academics. It is the largest collection of Roman parade armour to have been found anywhere in the

View of the Herzogsschloss from the Danube

VISITORS' CHECKLIST

Road map E2. 🚊 *43,000.*
🚉 *Bahnhofplatz.* 🚌
ℹ️ *Theresienplatz 20, (09421)*
94 43 07. **Fax** *(09421) 94 41 03.*
www.straubing.de
@ tourismus@straubing.de
📅 *Internationales Jazz-Festival*
(July), Gäubodenvolksfest (Aug),
Agnes-Bernauer-Festspiele
(every four years, next in 2011).

former Roman Empire. The collection includes highly ornamental helmets with visors, shin-guards and metal masks for horses.

🏠 Kirche St Jakob- und St Tiburtius
Pfarrplatz 1a.
This is one of Bavaria's largest and most magnificent Gothic churches, begun in 1400 and not completed for almost a century. The forest of columns in the extraordinarily tall interior support 18th-century barrel vaulting.

The church has preserved its Gothic statues and paint-ings, including an image of the Mother of God ascribed to Hans Holbein, Baroque paintings and sculptures by the Asam Brothers, and

tombstones. The 15th-century stained-glass windows are the church's finest elements, giving the church interior a unique atmosphere.

Gothic stained-glass window in Jakobs- und Tiburtiuskirche

🏠 Kirche St Peter
Petersgasse. 50b.
Peterskirche, a Romanesque basilica dating from around 1200 whose steeples were enlarged in the 19th century, is one of the finest churches of its kind in Lower Bavaria. Among the interior features are a Romanesque Crucifix and a Gothic Pietà dating from about 1340.

The church cemetery is an interesting place to explore, as it is one of the oldest in Germany. It contains three Gothic chapels. One of them, the Bernauerkapelle, was built by Duke Ernst as penance for Agnes Bernauer's murder in 1435. Her symbolic tombstone can be seen within. The walls of the Totenkapelle, built in 1486, bear a cycle depicting the Dance of Death that was painted in 1763 by Felix Hölzl.

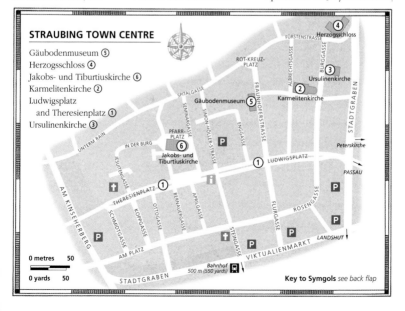

STRAUBING TOWN CENTRE

Gäubodenmuseum ⑤
Herzogsschloss ④
Jakobs- und Tiburtiuskirche ⑥
Karmelitenkirche ②
Ludwigsplatz
  and Theresienplatz ①
Ursulinenkirche ③

0 metres 50
0 yards 50

Key to Symgols *see back flap*

The chapel and church at Sankt Hermann

Sankt Hermann 8

Road map F2. Regen. *Bischofsmais, Hauptstr. 34 (09920) 94 04 44.* **www**.bischofsmais.de

Just outside Bischofsmais, on the site of the oldest hermitage in the Bavarian Forest, stands a group of three ecclesiastical buildings.

In about 1320 St Herman, a Benedictine monk from the Niederalteich monastery, lived here. His cult began in the 17th century, when pilgrimages were made to places that were associated with him.

The **Brunnenkapelle**, a small domed Baroque rotunda with a niche for the miracle-working spring, was built in 1611. **Hermannskirche**, a Baroque pilgrimage church, was built in 1653–4.

The **Einsiedeleikapelle** was added in 1690. It is a wooden chapel built in memory of the saint's hermitage. Its western part, the Hermannszelle (Herman's Cell), is full of wooden legs and crutches left here by pilgrims, in thanks for the miracle cures they received.

Museumsdorf Bayerischer Wald 10

Road map G2. *Tittling.* ***Tel*** *(08504) 84 82.* *week before Easter–Oct: 9am–5pm daily;* **Museum only** *Nov–Mar: 9am–4pm daily.* **www**.museumsdorf.com

Near Tittling, on the east side of the road from Grafenau to Passau, this open-air museum is one of the largest in Europe. Here over 140 buildings dating from the 18th and 19th centuries have been erected on a 200,000-sq m (50-acre) site. As well as traditional cottages with all their furnishings, visitors can see mills, forges, sawmills and also the oldest public school building in Germany.

Near the museum, in an **inn** dating from 1829, traditional Bavarian specialities are on offer. Visitors to the inn include prominent German figures, including the former chancellor Helmut Kohl and the writer Friedrich Dürrenmatt.

The museum is in the Dreiburgenland, so named after the three castles, **Saldenburg**, **Englburg** and **Fürstenstein**. They are well preserved but are not open to the public.

Passau 11

See pp188–191.

Fürstenzell 12

Road map G3. *7,500.* *Passau.* *Marienplatz 7, (08502) 80 228.* **www**.fuerstenzell.de

Founded in 1274, the **Cistercian abbey** here reached the height of its artistic development in the 18th century.

Marienkirche, built in 1738, was designed by Johann Michael Fischer, with stuccowork by Johann Baptist Modler and Johann Georg Funk and elaborate ceiling paintings by Johann Jakob Zeiller. The interior features Baroque and Rococo altars, the high altar by Johann Baptist Straub, and a fine Rococo pulpit. The Gothic tombs of the Cistercian abbots and the abbey's founders, which were transferred here from the medieval church, are also of interest.

The 19th-century inn at the Museumsdorf Bayerischer Wald

Marienkirche, Fürstenzell

The **monastery**, situated south of the church, was remodelled in 1674–87, and extended after 1770. The Festsaal (State Room), with frescoes of 1773 in the late Viennese Neo-Classical style, is outstanding.

The monastery library was decorated in about 1760. Together with the monastery library in the town of Metten nearby, it is the finest example of artistic patronage by the Cistercian order in Germany. The interior is lined with a gallery supported on alternating Tuscan columns and herms (head of Hermes on a stone pillar). The bookcases are decorated with Rococo putti, fencing figures and Atlases carved by Joseph Deutschmann.

Abbey
Tel *(08502) 91 100.* *mid-Feb–mid-Nov: 3pm Mon–Sat (only library and feast hall).* *compulsory.*

Nationalpark Bayerischer Wald ❾

This excursion leads through the Nationalpark Bayerischer Wald, established in 1970 and the first national park in Germany. It is an extensive hilly area of forests, woodland, swamps and meadows, picturesque lakes and interesting rock formations that combine to create unique landscapes inhabited by many species of birds and animals. The Hans-Eisenmann-Haus is the main information centre in the area.

Finsterau ③
The Freilichtmuseum Finsterau is not far from Finsterau, a village with overflowing window boxes, where there is a working smithy and a bakery selling fresh bread.

Hans-Eisenmann-Haus ④
A scenic forest road leads to the house. From here visitors can go to the Pflanzenfreigelände, a reserve with over 500 plant species, or take a trip to the Tierfreigelände, a reserve for wild animals.

NATIONALPARK

BAYERISCHER

WALD

ZWIESEL

REGEN

Kleine Ohe

Grafenau

PASSAU

85

85

533

Rischbach

12

12

PASSAU

St Oswald ⑤
The Waldgeschichtliches Museum illustrates the life and culture of the "forest people". The abbey and church of St Oswald were rebuilt in the Baroque style in 1876. The Brünnlkapelle stands beside a miracle-working spring.

TIPS FOR DRIVERS

Length of route: *50 km (31 miles).*
Stopping-off points: *There are bars and restaurants in Freyung, Finsterau, in the open-air museum and at Hans-Eisenmann-Haus.*

Freyung ①
Schloß Wolfstein contains a hunting and fishing museum. The Schramelhaus (at Abteistraße 6), with the Heimatmuseum, is also worth a visit.

Mauth ②
The village glassworks, the Glasbläserhof Mauth, are fascinating. Glass-blowers can be seen at work and visitors may try their hand at this difficult art.

| 0 km | 15 |
| 0 miles | 15 |

KEY

▭ Suggested route

═ Other road

Passau ⑪

Copy of a painting by Lucas Cranach

Passau is one of the oldest and most beautiful towns in Bavaria. Nestling in the hills at the confluence of three rivers, it is divided into three districts interconnected by 15 bridges. The Old Town lies on a peninsula between the Danube and the Inn, while Innstadt lies beside the Inn and Ilzstadt beside the Ilz. Passau's fine buildings give it its charm and magic, while the southern wind, felt both in the climate and the art, lends an Italian atmosphere.

Towers of the Dom St Stephan – Passau's great Baroque cathedral

🏯 Domplatz

In 1155 the cathedral chapter acquired a plot of land between the cathedral and the western section of the city walls with the aim of building on it chapterhouses arranged around a large square. What were the originally modest chapterhouses were later remodelled in a more ostentatious Baroque style.

Distinctive among them is the Lamberg Chapterhouse, at No. 6 Domplatz, on the west side of the square. Rebuilt in 1724, the chapterhouse is also known as **Lamberg Palace** for its magnificent façade, which is decorated with fine mouldings. The old chapterhouses at Nos. 4 and 5, known as the Barbarahof and Kanonikatshof Starzhausen, today accommodate the presbytery and the seminary.

The square itself features a monument to the Bavarian king, Maximilian I Joseph, and was created by Christian Gorhan the Younger in 1824.

🏛 Dom St Stephan

Domplatz 1.
The original cathedral, set on the highest point in the town, was destroyed in the Great Fire of 1662. It was rebuilt in 1668–77 by Carlo Lurago, who created the largest Baroque church north of the Alps, incorporating the surviving Gothic presbytery and transept into the new scheme.

The elegant towers can be seen from afar. The interior contains a stunning wealth of stuccowork and other ornamentation added in 1677–85 by Giovanni Battista Carlone, and paintings by Carpoforo Tencalla.

The burial chapels on the north side of the cathedral include the Gothic Herren-kapelle, which was built in about 1300 for the members of the cathedral chapter and which contains an enormous Romanesque Crucifix dating from about 1190.

Passau Cathedral is famous for its magnificent organ, one of the largest in the world. Occupying the Baroque organ loft, it was built in 1924–8 and refurbished in 1979–81. Organ recitals take place every day at noon from May to October.

♣ Neue Residenz

Residenzplatz 8. **Treasury and Diocesan Museum.** *Tel (0851) 393374.* ☐ *2 May–31 Oct: 10am–4pm Mon–Sat.* 📷
The new Bishop's residence, which occupies the south side of Residenzplatz, was built in 1713–30 to plans by Domenico d'Angeli and Antonio Beduzzi. It was refurbished in 1764–71 by Melchior Hefele of Vienna, with stuccowork by members of the local Modler family, the addition of a Neo-Classical façade and interior decoration in the late Baroque style.

The design and decoration of the vestibule and staircase are particularly successful. The reception rooms contain large collections of artifacts from the Diocesan Museum and Cathedral Treasury, some of which can also be seen in the cathedral.

The full splendour of the Dom St Stephan's Baroque interior

For hotels and restaurants in this region see p266 and p280

The pediment over the façade of the Neue Residenz

♣ Alte Residenz
Theresienstr. 18.

The Old Residence, whose buildings are crowded into a small area between the cathedral and a hillside, is an important landmark visible from the River Inn. The residence probably stands on the site of a bishopric mentioned in 1188. The medieval buildings have been remodelled over the ages, and their present uniform appearance dates from 1680.

The reception rooms were decorated in the 18th century, but soon afterwards the bishopric was moved to the New Residence. The buildings now house the Landgericht, or provincial court.

⚜ Residenzplatz
This square acquired its grand stately character in the Baroque period. Later, stuccowork façades were added to the houses that line it. Particularly noteworthy are the houses at No. 1, built in 1725–30, and No. 13, built in

about 1700. The Neo-Baroque fountain on the square was built by Jakob Bradl in 1906.

⛪ Michaelskirche
Michaeligasse 25.

In terms of architectural importance, the former Jesuit church is second only to Passau's cathedral. It was built and decorated in 1665–77 by members of the Carlone family. Its fine twin-towered façade makes it a

The Schaiblingsturm, part of Passau's medieval defences

VISITORS' CHECKLIST

Road map G3.
🚉 *50,000.*
🚌 🚆 ℹ️ *Rathausplatz 3,
(0851) 95 59 80.*
www.passau.de
🎭 *Maidult (May, every two years); Festspiele Europäische Wochen (Jun/Jul); Herbstdult (Sep).*

distinctive feature of the city's skyline. The lavish interior includes a high altar of 1712 by Christoph Tausch of Breslau, side altars of about 1677 and a pulpit and organ loft built in 1717–20.

The former Jesuit college, which was built in 1613–25, is now used as a high school. The courtyard that is enclosed on three sides by the wings of the building has been recently closed off on its northern side by a glazed passage. At the end of the east wing is a tall octagonal tower that once housed an observatory.

⚜ Schaiblingsturm
The 14th-century Schaiblings-turm, on the bank of the River Inn, is a vestige of the old city fortifications. In centuries gone by the tower protected the port on the important salt route.

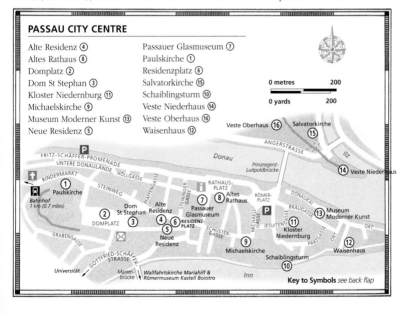

PASSAU CITY CENTRE

Alte Residenz ④
Altes Rathaus ⑧
Domplatz ②
Dom St Stephan ③
Kloster Niedernburg ⑪
Michaelskirche ⑨
Museum Moderner Kunst ⑬
Neue Residenz ⑤
Passauer Glasmuseum ⑦
Paulskirche ①
Residenzplatz ⑥
Salvatorkirche ⑮
Schaiblingsturm ⑩
Veste Niederhaus ⑭
Veste Oberhaus ⑯
Waisenhaus ⑫

0 metres 200
0 yards 200

Key to Symbols *see back flap*

The Veste Oberhaus and below it the Veste Niederhaus, overlooking the Danube

🏛 Waisenhaus

Innkai.

This former orphanage, a two-storey building with an inner quadrangle, was built in 1750–62 to a design by Michael Schneitmann. The north wing contains a chapel whose façade and interior feature fine stuccowork executed by Giovanni Martin Luraghi in 1753.

🔒 Kloster Niedernburg

Jesuitengasse.

Originally a Benedictine abbey, this was founded in about 740 on the site of the Roman Kastell Boiodurum. The present abbey church, which replaces an earlier one built in the early 11th century, is an example of an early Romanesque basilica with two towers and a transept. The presbytery was rebuilt in the Gothic style in the 15th century and the interior was redecorated in the Baroque style after it was damaged by fire in 1662 and 1680.

The south transept contains a Romanesque tombstone marking the tomb of the abbess, St Gisela, who was the sister of Emperor Henry II and widow of St Stephen, king of Hungary. In 1420 a sarcophagus with openwork sides was built over the tomb.

🔒 Salvatorkirche

Ferdinand-Wagner-Str.

Standing on the site of a synagogue, this former pilgrimage church, is associated with a pogrom in 1477 against the Jews, sparked off by their alleged sacrilege against the Host. On the west side the church is joined to the rock where the Veste Oberhaus stands. Before a tunnel was made between the upper and lower forts in 1762, the church was accessible only by boat. It is now used as a concert hall.

⛪ Veste Oberhaus and Veste Niederhaus

Oberhaus 125. **Oberhausmuseum Passau Tel** (0851) 49 33 512.
◻ 15 Mar–15 Nov: 9am–5pm Mon–Fri, 10am–6pm Sat–Sun and public hols; 16 Nov–6 Jan: 10am–4pm daily.
⬤ 24 & 31Dec. 🖼

Work on the imposing Oberhaus (Upper Castle) began in 1219, initiated by the bishop Ulrich II. It is set on a rocky outcrop known as St Georgsberg, on the bank of the Danube opposite the Old Town. The main castle consists of Gothic buildings and a chapel. The Niederhaus (Lower Castle) is connected to the Oberhaus by a gallery descending from the polygonal tower. Work

on the Niederhaus, on a spit of land between the rivers Inn and Ilz, began in 1250. Both castles, which have been extended and fortified over time, symbolize the power of the church over the town.

The Oberhaus now houses a historical museum. On the route to the Observatoriums-turm (observatory tower) is the Passauer Tölpel (Fool of Passau), a huge head with a mocking expression. This is the remains of a statue of St Stephen of about 1370 that fell from the cathedral during the Great Fire of 1662.

The Niederhaus, whose present apperance dates from about 1444, was the home of the painter Ferdinand von Wagner from 1890 to 1907. He filled the interior with antique furniture and his own paintings. A private residence, it is closed to visitors.

🏛 Altes Rathaus

Rathausplatz. **Tel** (0851) 39 60. ◻ Apr–6 Jan: 10am–4pm daily. 🖼

The Town Hall stands on the site of the former Fish Market alongside the Danube. By the annexation of houses standing between Schrottgasse and Markt-gasse, the town hall was constantly enlarged up until the 19th century. The original tower, which was demolished in 1811, was replaced in 1890–95 by a fine Neo-Gothic tower designed by Heinrich

The Altes Rathaus, with Neo-Gothic tower

von Schmidt. It is encircled by a gallery and has a steep sloped roof. Floodmarks on the façade show the high levels reached by the Danube at various times. Entering the building from the side facing Schrottgasse, visitors pass through a late Gothic carved portal of 1510.

The town hall's interior and three courtyards date from the 16th and 17th centuries. The halls, open to the public, contain historical paintings by Ferdinand von Wagner.

🏛 Passauer Glasmuseum

Am Rathausplatz. **Tel** (0851) 35 071. ⬜ 1pm–5pm daily. 📷

Housed in the former Wilder Mann hotel, Passau's museum of glass contains over 30,000 pieces of decorative and household glassware from the 18th to the 20th centuries.

The large collection of Czech glassware and the glass made in the workshops of the Bavarian Forest are particularly remarkable. There is also an interesting section on Art Nouveau glass.

Captivated by the museum's exhibits, the writer Friedrich Dürrenmatt called it "the most beautiful glass museum in the whole world".

Art Nouveau vase in the Glasmuseum

🔒 Paulskirche

Rindermarkt.

The parish church of St Paul was built in 1663–78 on the site of a medieval church that was destroyed by the Great Fire of 1622. The stuccowork in the interior was executed as recently as 1909. The façade's tall, picturesque tower, rising over the Rindermarkt, is a prominent Passau landmark.

🏛 Museum Moderner Kunst

Bräugasse 17. **Tel** (0851) 38 38 790. ⬜ 10am–6pm Tue–Sun. 🔴 24, 25, 31 Dec. 📷

Located in one of the old town's most beautiful houses, Passau's Museum of Modern Art exhibits art from the 20th and 21st centuries. There are regular international exhibitions of different modern artists.

🎓 Universität

Innpromenade, Innstr., Augustinergasse.

In 1972 the buildings of the former **Augustinian monastery**, founded in about 1070 and turned into barracks in 1803, were converted into a newly founded university. Further buildings were added to the side of the monastery facing the river. These are joined by the **Geisteswissenschaften I** building, constructed in 1976–81 to a design by Werner Fauser. This reinforced concrete structure is rendered in red plaster and combines regional architectural elements with modern spatial concepts.

The **Nikolakirche**, today a seminary, still has its original Romanesque crypt, although the entire building was re-modelled in the Gothic style in 1348 and again in the Baroque style in 1716–17. The church furniture was moved to the parish church in Vilshofen in 1803.

🔒 Wallfahrtskirche Mariahilf

Mariahilfstiege.

This pilgrimage church, set on the hill known as Mariahilfsberg, dominates the River Inn and Passau's Innstadt district. It commands a fine view of the city and the Dreiflüsseeck – the confluence of the three rivers.

The Capuchin church and monastery, completed in about 1630, are reached by a covered flight of 321 steps. The object of pilgrimage is a copy

Picturesque houses on the banks of the Danube

of a painting of the Madonna and Child by Lucas Cranach the Elder which has been venerated since 1622 (see p188). The original painting was acquired from a gallery in Dresden by Leopold, Bishop of Passau in 1611. In 1650 the painting was moved to the Jacobskirche in Innsbruck, where it remains to this day.

The strikingly austere interior of Wallfahrtskirche Mariahilf features a silver eternal lamp made by Lucas Lang and presented by the Emperor Leopold I in 1676 on the occasion of his marriage in Passau.

🏛 Römermuseum Kastell Boiotro

Lederergasse 43.

Tel (0851) 34 769. ⬜ 10am–4pm Tue–Sun. 🔴 mid-Nov–Feb. 📷

This Roman fort was built in about AD 280. From then until 400 it was used by Roman soldiers, and in about 460 St Severinus built his cell in the ruins. Excavated in 1974, the ruins together with the finds unearthed here are open to visitors.

The imposing buildings of the Wallfahrtskirche Mariahilf

Ortenburg ❶

Road map F3. 🏃 7,000.
🚌 🚊 *Vilshofen or Passau.*
ℹ️ *Marktplatz 11, (08542) 16 421.*
www.ortenburg.de

This Renaissance **palace**,
which is set on a ridge,
was built in about 1567 on
the site of a medieval castle
belonging to the Bavarian
von Krailburg-Ortenburg
family. Joachim, one of the
family members, brought
the Reformation to the town
in 1563, and ever since then
Ortenburg has been a
Protestant enclave within
Catholic, Counter-Reformation
Lower Bavaria.

The palace is today in
private ownership, but it
contains a museum that is
open to the public. Visitors
can also see such features as
a fine late Renaissance
panelled ceiling dating from
around 1600 in the castle
chapel, the remnants of
trompe-l'oeil frescoes on the
wall of the Knights' Hall and
a torture chamber. The well
outside the palace, which
descends to a depth of 55 m
(180 ft), supplied the
townspeople with water up
until 1927.

The presbytery of the late
Gothic **church**, which has
been a Protestant church
since 1563, contains the
splendid tombs of the owners
of Ortenburg in the 16th and
17th centuries.

🏛 **Schlossmuseum
Ortenburg**
Tel (08542) 12 00. ⏺ Apr–Oct:
10am–5pm Tue–Sun

The chapel in Sammarei's church,
bedecked with votive images

Sammarei ❶

Road map F3. 🏃 200.
🚌 🚊 *Vilshofen or Passau.*
ℹ️ *Ortenburg, Marktplatz 11,
(08542) 16 421.* **www**.sammarei.de

Sammarei has one of the
most remarkable pilgrimage
churches in the whole of
southern Germany.

An old wooden **chapel**
miraculously survived the fire
that destroyed the neigh-
bouring house of Cistercian
monks from Aldersbach. The
chapel was subsequently
enclosed within the late
Renaissance church of **Mariä
Himmelfahrt**, occupying part
of the presbytery. The
construction of this stone-
built church was supervised
by Isaak Bader the Elder, a
court architect from Munich,
and work began in 1629.
While the church was
completed in 1631, the
interior decoration was not
finished until 1650. The

ambulatory that was created
between the walls of the
chapel and the presbytery
of the church are completely
covered with Baroque votive
images, as are the walls of
the chapel itself.

The chapel is separated
from the nave by a fine high
altar of 1645, which acts as a
kind of iconostasis.

The chapel's late Rococo
altar contains the miraculous
image that is venerated by
pilgrims to the church. It is a
copy of the original *Madonna
and Child* ascribed to Hans
Holbein the Elder in the
church of Jakobs- und
Tiburtiuskirche in Straubing.

Baroque façade of the Mariä
Himmelfahrt church, Aldersbach

Aldersbach ❶

Road map F3. 🏃 4,100. 🚌 🚊
Vilshofen. ℹ️ *Klosterplatz 1, (08543)
96 100.* **www**.aldersbach.de

Work on the **Cistercian
monastery** in the town
began at the end of the 17th
century. It was remodelled
by Domenic Madzin in the
first half of the 18th century,
when it became the church of
Mariä Himmelfahrt.

The interior, which is lit by
large windows, is decorated
with exquisite paintings and
stuccowork executed by
Egid and Cosmas Damian
Asam in 1718–20, the first
time that the brothers had
collaborated on a project
(see p68). Among the most
outstanding features are the
choir borne by angels in wide
flowing garments, and the
trompe-l'oeil paintings on the
ceiling over the nave.

The high altar, dating from
1723, is Matthias Götz'
masterpiece. The pulpit, of
1748, and the stalls, of 1762,
are by Joseph Deutschmann.

Courtyard of the Renaissance palace in Ortenburg

Vilshofen ⑯

Road map F3. 🏛 *16,500.*
🚃 ℹ️ *Stadtplatz 27, (08541) 20 81 12.* **www**.vilshofen.de

Founded in 1206 where the Vils, Wolfach and Pfudrach meet the Danube, Vilshofen centres around Stadtplatz. This long street is lined with colourful houses that were built after the great fire that destroyed the town in 1794.

The parish church of **St Johannes der Täufer**, built in the late 14th century, with two naves, was rebuilt in 1803–04. Its fine Baroque decoration was executed in the 18th century, and was originally intended for the Nikolakirche in Passau. The decoration was later transferred to this church.

Another notable feature of the town is the late Gothic **Barbarakirche**, built in the second half of the 15th century, and the **Mariähilfs-kirche**, a former pilgrimage church built in 1611 by Antonio Riva. The Mariähilfs-kirche is decorated with stuccowork and frescoes executed by northern Italian artists, among whom was Giovanni Petro Camuzzi.

The **gate tower** was built in 1643–7. It was designed by Bartholomäus Viscardi in the Mannerist style and has greyish-white tones and an onion dome. It has come to symbolize the town.

The high altar at the Asambasilika in Osterhofen

The most prominent building in Vilshofen is the **Benedictine abbey** of Schweiklberg, designed by Michael Kurz and built in 1909–11. The church has two Art Nouveau steeples.

The gate tower at the end of the Straßenmarkt in Vilshofen

Osterhofen ⑰

Road map F2. 🏛 *11,600.*
🚃 🚃 *Altenmarkt.*
ℹ️ *Stadtplatz 13, (09932) 40 30.*
www.osterhofen.de

This small Bavarian town, whose history goes back almost six centuries, boasts a jewel of Baroque architecture, the **Asambasilika**.

The church was built in 1726 on the site of a medieval Premonstratensian church. Its appearance is the result of a collaboration between the architect Michael Fischer and the Asam brothers. While its exterior is somewhat austere, with the façade merging with a wing of the monastery, the decorative scheme of the interior is phenomenal.

The unusual shape of the single-nave interior is created by its oval side chapels and serpentine walls. The architecture, painting and stuccowork, fused into a single entity, are highly distinctive, both as an ensemble and as individual elements. While the extensive ceiling frescoes by Cosmas Damian Asam create an illusion of extensive space, Egid Quirin Asam's stucco-work blurs the boundaries between reality and illusion. Absorbing the exquisite artistry and admiring the artists' skill can take some time *(see p68)*.

The Asambasilika made a profound impression on Pope John Paul II, who visited Osterhofen during his pilgrimage to Germany in 1980.

THE BAVARIAN FOREST

The area between the Danube, Regen and Chamb and the Czech border is covered by the largest woodland in Europe. Once Bavaria's most destitute region, it now draws tourists with its stunning scenery and low prices. The region is renowned for its locally made glass and crystal, its hiking trails and skiing areas. The heart of the Bavarian Forest is the densely wooded National Park Reserve.

A historic Alpine house in the open-air museum at Finsterau

UPPER BAVARIA (EAST)

Lying between the rivers Inn and Salzach, this region is very popular with tourists, who flock here for the breathtaking natural scenery. The steep, snow-covered Alpine slopes, the lush green vegetation of the valleys and the large lakes, such as the Chiemsee and Königssee, all have a magical atmosphere.

Alexander Humboldt, the famous geographer and explorer, named Berchtesgaden one of the most beautiful places in the world, alongside Naples, Constantinople and Salzburg.

The region is equally appreciated today. The Berchtesgaden National Park, which includes the Königssee and Watzmann, Germany's second-highest peak of 2,713 m (8,900 ft), covers an area of about 210 sq km (80 sq miles) and was established in the southeast of the region in 1978.

The region has more to offer than breathtaking scenery. The Romans discovered health springs here, and the spa of Bad Reichenhall attracts visitors from all over the country. The groundwater contains up to 25 per cent salt, which is extracted in saltworks throughout the region. One of the oldest working saltworks, in use since 1517, is in Berchtesgaden. Here visitors can see excellently preserved tunnels and can cross a 100-m (328-ft) underground lake on a raft.

Many previous rulers of Bavaria felt a special attraction for this area, and Hitler's "Eagle's Nest" residence was located on Mt Kehlstein. A silver urn in a chapel in Altötting contains the hearts of 21 Bavarian kings. The town also attracts many pilgrims, who come to the church with the figure of the Black Madonna, which is famed for its reputed miracle-working powers.

The region is dotted with fine historic buildings. The little churches of Maria Gern and St Bartholomä have a delightful charm. Burghausen boasts the world's longest castle, and one of the islands in Chiemsee wa chosen by Ludwig II for yet anoth of his magnificent residences.

The Kapellplatz in Altötting in winter

◁ Statues outside Herrenchiemsee Palace, Ludwig II's residence on Herreninsel in Ch.

Exploring Upper Bavaria (East)

The town of Rosenheim on the River Inn could be regarded as the capital of this region. Although not well endowed with historic features, it is well worth a visit in late summer, when the local beer festival takes place. While it vies with Munich's Oktoberfest, it has a much more authentic, local atmosphere. There are historic towns on the rivers Inn, Wasserburg and Rott, the latter containing the grave of the Christian Democrat leader Franz-Josef Strauß. The towns in the Salzach and Traun valleys are also worth exploring. The towns of Tittmoning and Laufen, with their captivating southern atmosphere, are very underrated.

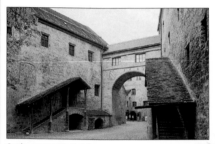

Castle courtyard in Burghausen

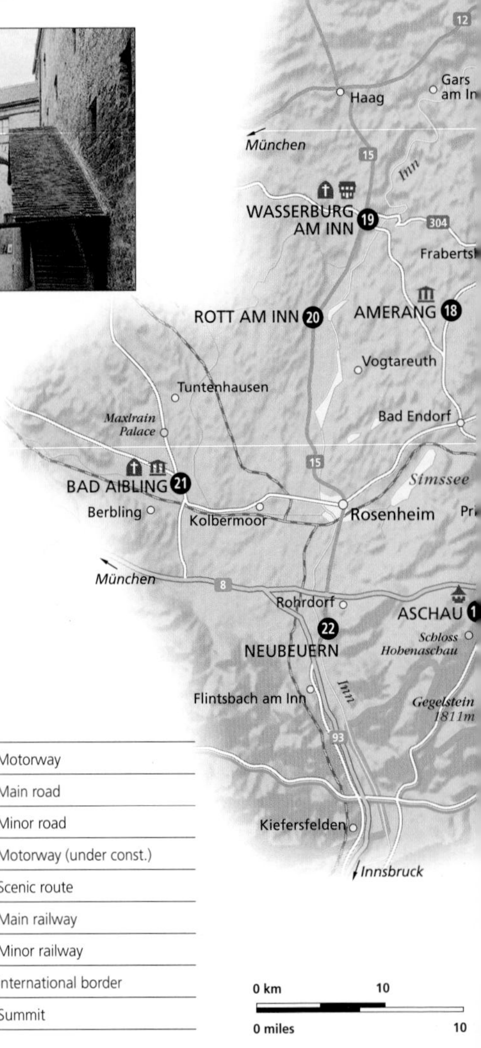

Buchbach
Landshut
Haag
Gars am In
München
Inn
WASSERBURG AM INN 19
Frabertsh
ROTT AM INN 20
AMERANG 18
Vogtareuth
Tuntenhausen
Bad Endorf
Maxlrain Palace
BAD AIBLING 21
Simssee
Berbling
Kolbermoor
Rosenheim
München
Rohrdorf
ASCHAU 1
22
NEUBEUERN
Schloss Hohenaschau
Flintsbach am Inn
Gegelstein 1811m
Kiefersfelden
Innsbruck
KEY
Motorway
Main road
Minor road
Motorway (under const.)
Scenic route
Main railway
Minor railway
International border
Summit
0 km 10
0 miles 10

SIGHTS AT A GLANCE

- Altötting 1
- Amerang 18
- Anger 5
- Aschau 13
- Bad Aibling 21
- Bad Reichenhall 6
- Berchtesgaden 8
- Burghausen 2
- Herrenchiemsee 14
- Kloster Seeon 17
- Königssee 9
- Laufen 4
- laria Gern 7
- eubeuern 22
- msau 10
- im Winkl 12
- am Inn 20
- olding 11
- an der Traun 16
- ning 3
- burg am Inn 19

n

Chiemsee 15

ap symbols *see back flap*

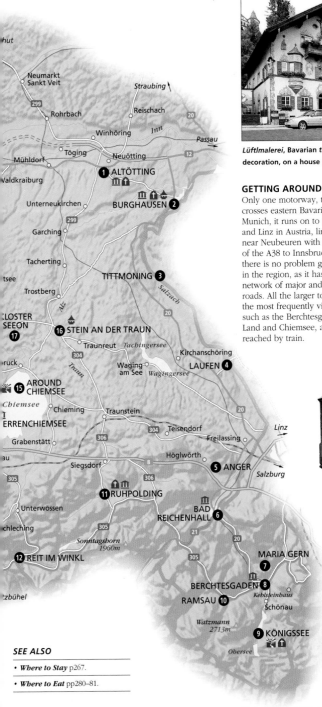

hut

Neumarkt
Sankt Veit

Straubing

299

Rohrbach   Reischach

Winhöring   20

Inn   Passau

Töging   Neuötting   12

Mühldorf

Valdkraiburg   **1** ALTÖTTING
                    🏛 ⓘ

Unterneukirchen   🏛 ⓘ ⛪
                    BURGHAUSEN **2**

299

Garching

Tacherting

TITTMONING **3**

tsee   *Salzach*

Trostberg   20

Alz

KLOSTER
SEEON   🏛 STEIN AN DER TRAUN
17   **16**

ruck   Traunreut *Tachingersee*

304   Kirchanschöring
          Waging
          am See *Wagingersee*   LAUFEN **4**

🌲 **15**
AROUND
CHIEMSEE

Chiemsee   Chieming

I   Traunstein

ERRENCHIEMSEE

Grabenstätt   304   Teisendorf   Linz

au   306   Freilassing

          Siegsdorf   Höglwörth   20

305   8

          306   **5** ANGER

Unterwössen   ⛪ 🏛   Salzburg

          11 RUHPOLDING

chleching   BAD
          🏛
          REICHENHALL **6**

305   21

Sonntagshorn   20
1960m

          305   MARIA GERN

12 REIT IM WINKL   **7**

zbühel   🏛
          BERCHTESGADEN **8**
          RAMSAU **10**   *Kehlsteinhaus*
                    Schönau

          Watzmann
          2713m
          9 KÖNIGSSEE
                    🌲 ⓘ
          Obersee

Lüftlmalerei, Bavarian *trompe-l'oeil*
decoration, on a house in Neubeuren

GETTING AROUND

Only one motorway, the A8,
crosses eastern Bavaria. From
Munich, it runs on to Salzburg
and Linz in Austria, linking up
near Neubeuren with a section
of the A38 to Innsbruck. However,
there is no problem getting around
in the region, as it has a good
network of major and minor
roads. All the larger towns and
the most frequently visited areas,
such as the Berchtesgadener
Land and Chiemsee, are easily
reached by train.

The Martersäule
in Bernau

SEE ALSO

Burghausen Castle, the longest castle in Europe

Altötting ●

Road map F4. 👥 12,500. 🚉
ℹ️ Kapellplatz 2a, (08671) 50 62
19/38. **www**.altoetting.de

This town, established in
the 8th century, is one of the
earliest Christian sites in
Europe. It is also the earliest
place of pilgrimage in
Bavaria, and is called the
Heart of Bavaria by some.
Every year about half a
million pilgrims come here
to pay their respects to the
Black Madonna. This early
13th-century statue is kept in
the **Heilige Kapelle** (Holy
Chapel) which stands in the
centre of a large square. The
chapel, with a Carolingian
apse and a Gothic nave, is
surrounded by an ambulatory
whose walls are covered with
votive images. Pilgrims
holding crosses inch up to it
on their knees. Pope John
Paul II paid a visit to the
shrine during his pilgrimage
to Germany in 1980.

The treasury of the late
Gothic **Stiftskirche** contains
valuable votive offerings from
the Holy Chapel. The most

highly prized of these is the
Goldenes Rössl (Golden
Steed) of 1404, a masterpiece
of French goldwork. The
crypt contains the mortal
remains of Johann Tilly, the
renowned military leader in
the Thirty Years' War.

Another feature of interest
is the **panorama** re-creating
the view from the hill of
Golgotha in Jerusalem. It is
located in a building dating
from 1902–03, and was
made by Gebhard
Fugel and Joseph
Krieger.

🏛 Panorama
Gebhard–Fugel–Weg 10.
Tel (08671) 69 34.
🕐 Mar–Oct: 9am–6pm
daily; Nov–Feb:
11am–2pm Sat–Sun. 🖼

Environs
Two km (1.5 miles)
north, on the River
Inn, is **Neuötting**.
Notable buildings
here include the Gothic
Nikolauskirche, designed by
Hans von Burghausen, and
the late Gothic Annakirche
completed in 1515.

Burghausen ●

Road map F4. 👥 19,000.
🚉 ℹ️ Stadtplatz 112, (08677) 887
140/141. **www**.burghausen.de
🎷 Jazz Festival (May); Historisches
Burgfest (Jul).

Situated on the River
Salzach, which forms
the border with Austria,
Burghausen is famous for
having the longest
castle in Europe.
With its six
courtyards, the
castle stretches
some 1,030 m
(3,380 ft) along a
ridge between the
river and Wöhrsee.
The castle was built
in 1025 and rebuilt
in 1490. The main
castle (Hauptburg)
contains several
museums,

Angel in Burghausen's
Schutzengelkirche including a local
history museum and
a photographic
museum. In the rooms that
are open to the public,
German paintings and
furniture are on display.

The Old Town, between the
castle and the river, has an
old-world atmosphere. The
market square is surrounded
by what are Burghausen's
finest buildings: the Gothic
Jakobskirche, with a
Baroque tower, the **town
hall**, the mid-16th-century
**old Bavarian government
building**, with a Renaissance
courtyard, the **Schutzengelkirche** of 1731–46, and many
historic houses. On the south
side of the square is the Jesuit
Josefskirche of about 1629
and the **Marienbrunnen**, a
mid-17th-century fountain.

Arcade on the the market square in Neuötting

Tittmoning ❸

Road map F4. 🏠 6,000.
🚌 🚃 Laufen, Burghausen.
ℹ️ Stadtplatz 1, (08683) 70 07 10.
www.tittmoning.de

The entrance to this little town on the River Salzach is through a gate in the town walls. The market square is lined with colourful houses with bay windows and wood carvings. Among them is the tall **town hall**, its tower and façade dating from 1711–12. The hill above the town, the summit crowned by a 13th-century **castle**, gives a fine view of the surrounding countryside and the Alps. The **Maria Ponlach** pilgrimage chapel of 1617 is reached by a road round the castle that follows a ravine overlooking the River Ponlach.

Iron bridge at Laufen, crossing over the border with Austria

Laufen ❹

Road map F4. 🏠 6,000.
🚃 ℹ️ Im Schlossrondel 2,
(08682) 18 10. **www**.stadtlaufen.de

Set on a bend in the River Salzach, this town has a southern, almost Italian feel. It was originally a Roman settlement, and flourished during the Middle Ages. Entry into the town is through two medieval **gates**. The streets are lined with arcaded houses with oriels and concave roofs typical of the region.

The 14th-century **parish church** is the oldest single-nave Gothic church in southern Germany. With its

Column of St Mary in Anger's main square

huge roof and late 12th-century Romanesque tower, it dominates the town.

North of the church is the **Dechantshof**, the old arch-bishop's castle, which contains plaques from the church. Its staircase is decorated with the portraits of bishops. The four-winged **castle**, with an inner court-yard, was built in 1606–08 by Vincenzo Scamozzi.

Anger ❺

Road map F5. 🏠 4,300. 🚌 🚃
ℹ️ Dorfplatz 4, (08656) 98 89 22.
www.anger.de

Ludwig I deemed Anger the prettiest village in Bavaria. Much of its charm has been eroded by the arrival of a motorway and commercial development, but it still has a delightfully situated late Gothic **church**. The large square, which is lined with interesting houses, has a col-umn with the statue of St Mary in the centre.

Environs

Two km (1.5 miles) to the north is **Höglwörth**, a tiny former Augustine abbey built in the 12th century on an island in a lake covered with water lilies.

Bad Reichenhall ❻

Road map F5. 🏠 16,500. 🚃
ℹ️ Wittelsbacherstr. 15, (08651) 60
60. **www**.bad-reichenhall.de

The town has been known for its salt since Celtic and Roman times, and in the mid-19th century it became an important spa. Noteworthy

buildings include the **Zenokirche,** a former Augustinian monastery dating from the first half of the 12th century. Although it was remodelled after the Gothic period, it retains its original Romanesque portal, which features two lions supporting the columns.

The former **jail** in the large spa park is now used as an inhalations room. In the **Alte Saline**, the old saltworks, which date from 1836–51, Ludwig I ordered a salt **museum** to be built. The exhibits include old salt-making equipment. The saltworks' marble enclosures date from 1524–36 and, together with an underground passage, were designed by the sculptor Erasmus Grasser.

🏛 **Alte Saline mit Salz-museum**
An der salinenstr.
Tel (08651) 70 02 146. 🕐 May–Oct:
10am–11:30am and 2–4pm daily;
Nov–Apr: 2–4pm Tue–Fri and the
first Sunday in the month.

The former jail in Bad Reichenhall's spa park

Maria Gern church seen against snowy Alpine peaks

Maria Gern ❼

Road map F5. 🚌 🚏 *Berchtesga-den*. 🛈 *Berchtesgaden, Königsseer Str. 2, (08652) 96 70.*

This pilgrimage church is in a serene and picturesque setting among woodland pastures. Built in 1708–10, its pink pilasters on the exterior make a pleasing contrast with the white walls and the steep polygonal roofs harmonize with the Baroque onion dome of the tower.

The interior is decorated with stuccowork by Joseph Schmidt. The walls of the presbytery are hung with votive images spanning the 12th to the 20th centuries, and the altar has a beautiful wooden carving of the Madonna by Wolfgang Huber before which the faithful pray for forgiveness.

The **Ölbergkapelle** below the church dates from 1710.

Berchtesgaden ❽

Road map F5. 🏘 *25,000.* 🚌 🚏 🛈 *Maximilianstraße 9, (08652) 94 45 300.* **www.**berchtesgadener-land.com

The area known as Berchtesgadener Land enjoys an excellent climate. The town is set in beautiful Alpine scenery on the River Ache at the foot of the Watzmann, which at 2,713 m (8,900 ft) is Germany's second highest peak.

The town is an ideal base for hikes throughout the region but with its old-world charm it also has plenty to offer. Here are houses with walls decorated with *Lüftlmalerei (see p213).* One of them, the **Gasthof zum Hirschen**, an inn dating from about 1600, has paintings depicting monkeys parodying human vices. Another interesting building is the Gothic **Franciscan church**, while a major attraction is the nearby saltworks – the **Salzbergwerk und Salzmuseum**. A little way from the town is the **Kehlsteinhaus**, also known as Hitler's Eagle's Nest *(see p201).* An interesting excursion follows the scenic **Roßfeld Panoramastraße**, which winds its way along hairpin bends to a height of 1600 m (5,249 ft).

The **Königliches Schloss**, formerly an Augustinian monastery and now owned by the Wittelsbach family, contains a museum with an interesting collection of furniture, paintings and

Gothic woodcarving. The adjoining **church** was remodelled in the Gothic style, although it retains its original Romanesque portal. The façade with its rose window and two towers were added in 1864–8. The Roman-esque cloisters, unusual in southern Germany, date from the 12th century.

🏛 **Salzbergwerk und Salzmuseum**
Bergwerkstr. 83. **Tel** *(08652) 60 020.* ⏰ *May–Oct: 9am–5pm daily; Nov–Apr: 11:30am–3pm daily.*

🏛 **Königliches Schloss**
Schlossplatz 2. **Tel** *(08652) 94 79 80.* ⏰ *16 May–15 Oct: 10am–noon & 2–4pm Sun–Fri; 16 Oct–15 May: 11am–2pm Mon–Fri.* 🎟 *11am & 2pm.*

A jetty on Königssee

Königssee ❾

Road map F5. 🛈 *Berchtesgaden, Franziskanerplatz 7, (08652) 64 343.* **www.**nationalpark-berchtes gaden.de

With its crystal-clear water and fjord-like setting between mountain ridges, Königssee is Bavaria's loveliest lake. The area also forms part of a national park.

The electric-powered boats that are used on the 8-km (5-mile) lake take visitors to the pilgrimage church of **St Bartholomä**, built in about 1700 and set on a peninsula below the eastern escarpment of the Watzmann. Nearby is a well-frequented inn. The boat trip offers views of awesome rock formations, enchanting little spots, waterfalls and echoing cliffs that throw back the sound of the boat's horn. The trip goes all the way to the northern end of Königs-see, from where **Obersee** can be reached on foot.

The town of Berchtesgaden, nestling in an Alpine valley

The main street in Reit im Winkl, a popular tourist resort

Ramsau ❿

Road map F5. 🚶 *1,900.* 🚌 🚉
Berchtesgaden. 🛈 *Im Tal 2, (08657)
98 89 20.* **www**.ramsau.de

This resort town, nestling
amid wooded mountain
slopes, has one of the most
photographed churches in
the world – the **Pfarrkirche
St Sebastian**, dating from
1512. Its picturesque
cemetery, which was laid
out in 1658, contains
tombstones spanning the
17th to the 20th centuries.
The church is scenically
situated above a stream,
and stands out wonderfully
against the magnificent
backdrop of the Reiteralpe.

Ruhpolding ⓫

Road map E5. 🚶 *6,400.* 🚌 🚉
🛈 *Hauptstr. 60, (08663) 88 060.*
www.ruhpolding.de

Ruhpolding attracts a high
volume of tourists. It is overlooked by **Georgskirche**, built
in 1738–54 with highly decorated altars and a pulpit
dating from the same period.
The right-hand altar features a
small Romanesque figure of
the Virgin Enthroned, with
large almond-shaped eyes,
dating from about 1200.
Above the church is the
old **cemetery**, which has
a Baroque chapel and
tomb-stones dating from
the 18th and 19th centuries.
The old Renaissance
hunting lodge houses the
Heimatmuseum, which has a
collection of furniture, glass
and jewellery spanning the
17th to the 19th centuries. Also
on display in the museum is a
collection of fossils and
interesting minerals that
were found in the sur-
rounding mountains.
Among the displays at
the **Museum für Bäuer-
liche und Sakrale
Kunst** (Museum of
Folk and Religious
Art) is a fine collection
of church ornaments,
as well as royal jewels
and crowns.

**The Madonna
of Ruhpolding**

🏛 **Heimatmuseum**
Schlossstr. 2. **Tel** *(08663) 41 230.*
⬜ *10am–noon Tue–Fri.* ⬛ *Nov–
Dec.*

🏛 **Museum für Bäuerliche
und Sakrale Kunst**
Roman Friesingerstr. 1. **Tel** *(08663)
5078.* ⬜ *9:30am–noon & 2–4pm
Tue–Sat, 9:30am–noon Sun.* ⬛ *25
Oct–25 Dec.*

Reit im Winkl ⓬

Road map E5. 🚶 *3,000.* 🚌 🚉
Marquartstein. 🛈 *Dorfstraße 38,
(08640) 80 027.*
www.reit-im-winkl.de

This small town, at an
altitude of almost 700 m
(2296 ft), may not have any
buildings of historic interest,
but it is still a very popular
tourist resort. Picturesquely
set in the middle of the forest,
with its colourful storybook
houses and narrow streets,
it is easy to see why the place
is so appealing. Many people
come here, especially in
winter, as the area has the
best snow cover in the
Bavarian Alps.
The town is also filled
with visitors in
summer, especially
hikers using it as a
base for day trips into
the surrounding area
or even into the
whole Berchtes-
gadener Land. The
road to Ruhpolding,
about 24 km (15 miles) in
length, is exceptionally scenic. Forming part of the
Alpine Route, it winds among
lakes which, when seen from
above, resemble a necklace of
green beads strung on either
side of the road that traverses
spectacularly beautiful
mountain scenery.

KEHLSTEINHAUS – "THE EAGLE'S NEST"

Set on the summit of Kehlstein, this stone building
resembling a mountain shelter is known as the Adlerhorst
(Eagle's Nest). It was given to Hitler by Martin Bormann on
behalf of the Nazi Party in 1939 and became the Führer's
favourite residence. The building was attached to the
summer residence built in
1933 and is situated on the
slopes of Obersalzberg. The
approach to Kehlsteinhaus
is a masterpiece of
engineering. First, a road
with stunning views passes
through five tunnels, after
which there is an elevator
whose shaft is cut into the
rock. The last stage of the
trip is a ride up in a high-
speed elevator, which is
taken by the thousands of
tourists who come here.

Hitler's famous "Eagle's Nest"

Road leading towards the Alps near Aschau

Aschau ⑬

Road map E5. 🏔 *6,000.*
🚌 🚉 ℹ *Kampenwandstr. 38.*
Tel *(08052) 90 49 37.*
www.aschau.de

In the centre of this small town, set against fine mountain backdrops, stands a twin-towered **church**. Originally built in the Gothic style, it was rebuilt in the Baroque period and in the early 18th century was decorated with stuccowork and paintings of scenes of the life of St Mary. Beside the church is the small **Kreuz-kapelle**, built in the mid-18th century, while opposite, at Kirchplatz 1, is an old **inn**, built in 1680 and today named the Post Hotel.

Environs
From Aschau a road leads south towards **Schloss Hohen-aschau**, which, set on a height, is visible from a distance. This mighty 12th-century fortress was decorated in the Baroque style in the 17th century, although its medieval walls and keep survive. The reception hall on the second floor was decorated in 1682–4 with Baroque mouldings.

⚜ **Schloss Hohenaschau**
Tel *(08052) 90 49 37.*
Museum ☐ *May–Sep: 9:30am–noon Tue–Fri; Apr & Oct: 9:30am–noon Thu.*
Guided tours ☐ *Apr & Oct: 9:30am, 10:30am, 11:30am Thu; May–Sep: 9:30am, 10:30am, 11:30am Tue–Fri.* 🎟 🎫

Herrenchiemsee ⑭

Road map E4. 🚉 *to Stock.* ⛴
www.herren-chiemsee.de

Herreninsel, the largest island in Chiemsee, has been settled since prehistoric times. Thanks to Ludwig II, it is among the region's main tourist attractions. The king aimed to build a huge palace set in a vast park filled with statues, fountains and a canal along its axis. It was to be the Versailles of Bavaria.

The **Schloss Herren-chiemsee**, based on Louis XIV's great Palace of Versailles, was built to satisfy Ludwig II's absolutist leanings. Built in 1878–86, it was to outdo all previous royal palaces, but it was never finished.

Ludwig II spent a mere nine days in it, and at the time of his death only 20 of the 70 rooms that were planned for the three wings were ready. They show an astonishing lavishness and splendour. Particularly spectacular are the Große Spiegelgalerie (Hall of Mirrors), and the Chambre

Fountain at Schloss Herrenchiemsee

de Parade. The palace also houses a **museum** dedicated to Ludwig II

There are also the remains of a church and an August-inian monastery on the island. These are known collectively as **Altes Schloss**.

🏛 **Schloss Herrenchiemsee, König-Ludwig II-Museum and Altes Schloss**
Tel *(08051) 68870.* 🎟 *Apr–mid-Oct: 9am–6pm daily; mid-Oct–Mar: 10am–4:15pm daily.* 🎫

The medieval castle of Höhlenburg, Stein an der Traun

Stein an der Traun ⑯

Road map E4. 🚌 🚉
ℹ *Rathausplatz 3, Traunreut, (08669) 85 70.* **www**.traunreut.de

One of Upper Bavaria's most distinctive buildings is **Höhlenburg**, a castle set 50 m (160 ft) above the River Traun. It forms part of a system of three castles. Torch in hand, visitors pass through a series of caves and tunnels. This is said to be the home of the fearful Heinz von Stein, a legendary giant knight who abducted girls. Casemates lead between the medieval upper castle, the lower castle and the new castle, which dates from the 15th century and was rebuilt in the Neo-Gothic style in 1885–9.

⚜ **Höhlenburg**
Tel *(08621) 25 01.*
🎟 *Apr–third Sun in Oct: 2pm Tue–Sun; mid-Jul–mid-Sep: 4pm Tue–Sun.* 🎫

Around Chiemsee ⑮

Chiemsee, also known as the Bavarian Sea, covers an area of 80 sq km (30 sq miles) and reaches a depth of 73 m (240 ft). Bavaria's largest lake, it is a favourite place for holiday-makers, and its shores are dotted with towns and holiday villages. The Alpine scenery, the watersports facilities and some fascinating buildings are the main attractions here.

Seebruck ⑥
This little town, whose history goes back to Roman times, is today a watersports centre with a large marina.

Frauenchiemsee ⑤
The Benedictine monastery on this island has a Romanesque church with a distinctive onion dome.

Herrenchiemsee ④
This is a favourite destination for visitors, who come to Ludwig II's grand unfinished palace.

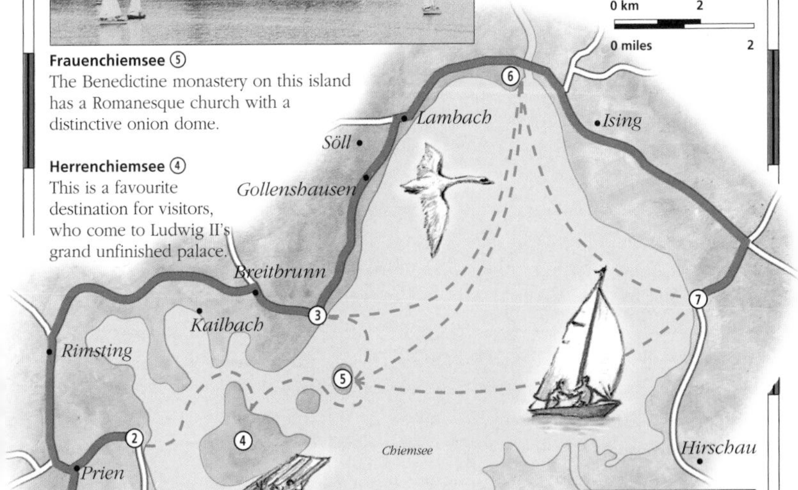

Lambach

Söll

Ising

Gollenshausen

Breitbrunn

Kailbach

Rimsting

Prien

Harras

Hirschau

Chiemsee

E52

Bernau

Gstadt ③
From this town there is a pleasant view of Frauenchiemsee, which can be reached by boat from here. An interesting sight is Peters- und Paulskirche, decorated in the Baroque style in about 1720.

Urschalling ①
The 12th-century Jakobskirche has some fine mural paintings dating from the 13th and 14th centuries.

Chieming ⑦
Attractions here are the beach, with a 7-km (4-mile) long promenade and houses with Lüftl-malerei *(see p212)* and lavish floral displays.

Stock ②
The Bockerl, a steam railway over 100 years old, provides a link between Stock and Prien. There are also boats to the lake's other islands and towns.

TIPS FOR TOURISTS

Length of route: *about 65 km (40 miles).*
Stopping-off places: *There are many cafés and restaurants in all the small towns round Chiemsee.*

KEY

▬ Suggested route
═ Other route
-- Ferry route

0 km 2
0 miles 2

Kloster Seeon, the Benedictine monastery, set on a promontory on Klostersee

Kloster Seeon ⑰

Road map E4. 🚌 🚊 *Obing.*
🛈 *Obing Kultur- und Bildungs-
zentrum, Klosterweg 1 (08624) 89
70.* **www**.kloster-seeon.de

On the edge of Klostersee
stands **Kloster Seeon**,
a monastery that was taken
over by Benedictine monks.
The original Romanesque
church was built in stages in
the 11th and 12th centuries.
Remodelled by Konrad
Pürkhel, it acquired its Gothic
appearance in 1433–8. The
ceiling was decorated by
Salzburg painters in 1539.
   St Barbara's Chapel
contains the magnificent tomb
of Aribo I dating from about
1400 and ascribed to the Salzburg sculptor Hans Heider.
   South of the church is a
monastery with a cloistered
courtyard of 1428–33, which
has Gothic tombstones.

Amerang ⑱

Road map E4. 🏚 *2,500.*
🚌 🚊 🛈 *Bahnhofstr. 3, (08075)
91 970.* **www**.amerang.de

The Renaissance **palace** in
this small town was built by
several Italian architects,
prominent among whom
were members of the Scaligeri
family of Verona. Its large
cloistered courtyard is a
venue for open-air concerts.
There is also a museum.
   At the other end of the
town is the **Bauernhaus-
museum** (open-air museum)
with farmhouses, a bakery, a
mill and a forge. The **EFA-
Automobil-Museum** (Museum
of German Automobile History) has 220 cars dating from
1886 to the present.

🏛 **Schloss Amerang** 🔲 *Easter–
15 Sep.* **Tel** *(08075) 91 920.* 📷 *on the
hour 11am–4pm Fri–Sun & public hols.*
🏛 **Bauernhausmuseum**
Hopfgarten 2. **Tel** *(08075) 91 50 90.*
🔲 *28 Mar–8 Nov: 9am–6pm Tue–Sun.*
🏛 **EFA-Automobil-Museum**
Wasserburgerstr. 38. **Tel** *(08075) 81
41.* 🔲 *Apr–Oct: 10–6pm Tue–
Sun; Nov–Mar: only Sun & pub hols.*

Amerang's Renaissance palace,
designed by the Scaligeri family

Wasserburg
am Inn ⑲

Road map E4. 🏚 *11,000.*
🚌 🚊 🛈 *Marienplatz 2, (08071)
10 522.* **www**.wasserburg.de

Wasserburg is set on a
promontory on a bend in
the Inn, and is one of the
best-preserved historic
towns on the river. The
best view of it is from the
bridge across the Inn.
   The bridge leads to a
picturesque Gothic **gate** which in
turn leads into
Bruck-gasse. At No.
25 in this lane is the
Mauthaus, the ducal
customs office,
dating from about
1400, with stepped
gables and three

Renaissance oriel windows,
which were added in 1539.
   The street leads to Marienplatz, which is lined with
houses. Among them is the
Kernhaus, which once
belonged to the patrician
Kern family. The façade
features decorative mouldings
by Johann Baptist Zimmer-
mann. Opposite stands the
Gothic **town hall**, which
occupies two buildings with
stepped gables. The
Frauenkirche was built in
1368 and is attached to the
watchtower.
   The large **Jakobskirche**
was begun in the early
15th century by Jans von
Burghausen. The **castle**, with
its covered staircase, can be
reached from the church.
Remaining parts of the castle
include the residential wing,
which was converted into
a granary during the
Renaissance, and a 15th-
century chapel. The streets
of the town are lined with
old houses with typical
gateways, courtyards, oriel
windows and arcades.

The Gothic façade of Wasserburg's town hall

Rott am Inn ⓴

Road map E4. 🏘 *3,500.* 🚌 🚉
ℹ *Kaiserhof 3.* **Tel** *(08039) 90 680.*
www.rottinn.de

The former Benedictine church of **Sts Marinus und Anianus** was rebuilt in 1759–63 to plans by Johann Michael Fischer, preserving the 12th-century Romanesque tower. The church has one of the finest Rococo interiors, decorated by the greatest artists of the time: the stuccoist Jakob Rauch, the fresco-painter Matthäus Günther and the sculptor Ignaz Günther. The church has undergone extensive restoration work and is open to the public.

Franz-Josef Strauß, the former leader of Bavaria's ruling conservative party, is buried in the cemetery of the church, which is regularly visited by members of his CSU party.

The town square in Rott am Inn

Bad Aibling ⓴

Road map D4. 🏘 *17,000.*
🚌 🚉 ℹ *Wilhelm-Leibl-Platz 3,*
(08061) 90 800.
www.bad-aibling.de

Bad Aibling is known for its mud baths, which were in use as far back as Roman times. However, it was only in the mid-19th century that it acquired its present status as a spa town.

There is much of architectural interest here. On a hill stands the church of **Mariä Himmelfahrt**, built in the late Gothic style but later remodelled in the Rococo style by Abraham Millauer to plans by Johann Michael Fischer. **Sebastianskirche** was built on the site of a 16th-century votive chapel after the plague epidemic of 1634, which decimated the local population.

After a series of fires that destroyed most of the town only a few houses survived. One is the 17th-century house at Kirchzeile 13 (today the **Hotel Ratskeller**), which has painted exterior walls and three oriel windows. The **Heimatmuseum** is also worth a visit.

🏛 **Heimatmuseum**
Wilhelm-Leibl-Platz.
Tel *(08061) 87 24.*
⭕ *by arrangement.*

Environs
Some 6 km (4 miles) northwest of Bad Aibling is **Berbling**, with an authentic Bavarian village atmosphere. The charming Rococo church, the old houses, the barns, the maypole and the fields that stretch right up to the houses are quintessentially Bavarian. The painter Wilhelm Leibl once stayed here, while he was living in Bad Aibling from 1882 to 1889.

The Renaissance **Maxlrain Palace** lies on the other side of Bad Aibling, 4 km (2.5 miles) to the southwest. It was built in 1580–88 and has a steeply pitched roof and four onion-domed towers. At the neighbouring 18th-century inn, beer from the palace brewery is served.

Neubeuern ⓴

Road map E5. 🏘 *4,000.*
🚌 🚉 *Raubling or Rohrdorf.*
ℹ *Marktplatz 4.* **Tel** *(08035) 21 65.*
www.neubeuern.de

This small town situated in the valley of the River Inn is held to be one of the prettiest in Bavaria, if not in the whole of Germany. It owes its present appearance to Gabriel von Seidl, who rebuilt the town and the medieval castle after two devastating fires in 1883 and 1893. Today it is often used by film-makers. With its **town gates, houses** and **church**, all of which are covered with *trompe-l'oeil* paintings, it possesses everything that a director needs to re-create an old-style Bavarian town.

Oriel window in Neubeuern

Above the houses, decked with greenery and colourful window boxes, towers the **castle** with its tall keep, built in the local historical style in 1904–08. On fine days there is a good view of the Alps from the castle terraces.

Environs
Some 4 km (2.5 miles) to the southwest is **Samerberg**. From its peak there is a panoramic view of the town of Rosenheim, Simssee and the surrounding area. It is worth taking a roundabout route via the delightful village of **Rohrdorf** to reach the summit.

The Renaissance Maxlrain Palace near Bad Aibling

UPPER BAVARIA
(SOUTH)

Upper Bavaria's southern region looks as if it belongs in the pages of a tourist brochure. It is a region of mountains, lakes and splendid buildings, with plenty to offer holiday-makers, including many opportunities for sporting activities. It borders the River Inn to the east and the Lech to the west. To the south it adjoins the Alps.

The Werdenfelser Land, the southernmost region of the Bavarian Alps, stretches from Murnau to Garmisch-Partenkirchen. Its name comes from that of the now ruined Werden castle, which once defended the surrounding area. The backdrop of this fine sub-Alpine landscape is made up of the imposing Karwendel, Wetterstein and Ammergauer mountain ranges.

The small towns and villages of the region are the essence of Bavaria. The houses are covered with *Lüftlmalerei (see p212),* and have wooden balconies that overflow with geraniums and other flowers.

From the pastures you can hear the sound of yodelling, also known as *Almschroa,* which can only be heard in the Bavarian Alps. The traditional costume of the local Bavarians is widely worn *(see p29),* and not just for show but as everyday wear.

Between the rivers Ammer and Lech, from Wessobrunn to near Steingaden, is the Pfaffenwinkel, or Clerics' Corner, which was given its name in jest in the 18th century because of the proliferation of abbeys, churches and chapels here. The finest among them is the church Wieskirche, known as the Lord God's Ballroom.

The largest town in the region is Landsberg, whose historic buildings and inviting small streets, alleys and squares make it a very interesting place to explore. The most famous and most visited town in the region is Garmisch-Partenkirchen, where the 1936 Winter Olympics took place.

Traditional festivals and holidays are celebrated enthusiastically in the towns and villages. The best are the painted carts parade and the St Leonard's Day horseback pilgrimage to Mount Calvary in Bad Tölz.

Satellite receivers outside a historic church in Raisting

◁ Moorings for yachts on Ammersee, one of the region's beautiful lakes

Exploring Upper Bavaria (South)

This region is Munich's natural recreation ground. The journey south to Garmisch-Partenkirchen, the area's largest winter sports and hiking centre, takes less than an hour and a fast suburban train connects the Bavarian capital with the Starnberger See and Ammersee. These lakes, together with the Wesslinger See, Wörthsee and Pilsensee, make up the Fünfseenland (Land of Five Lakes) and are also known as Munich's Baths. Rafting expeditions down the Isar start at Wolfratshausen.

SEE ALSO

• **Where to Stay** pp267–8.

• **Where to Eat** pp281–2.

SIGHTS AT A GLANCE

KEY

▬▬	Motorway
▬	Main road
═	Minor road
—	Scenic route
—	Main railway
—	Minor railway
▬▬	International border
△	Summit

The ornate interior of the Welfen-münster church in Steingaden

Sculpture in the gardens of Ludwig II's palace at Linderhof

GETTING AROUND

The southern region of Upper Bavaria is easily reached. The A8, A95 and A96 motorways from Munich lead to the region. The larger towns all have rail links, and those nearer Munich can be reached on the S-Bahn railway. The smaller towns, particularly those in the foothills of the Alps, are all served by convenient bus routes.

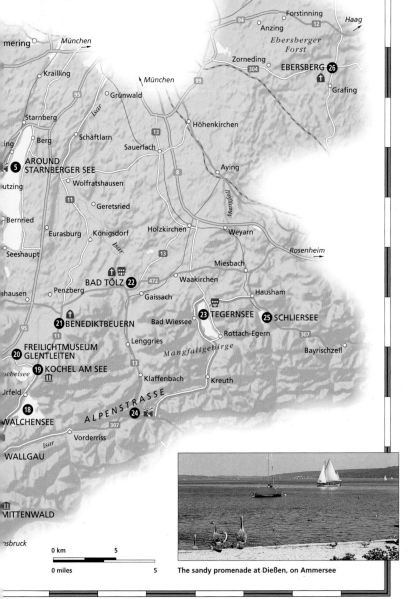

The sandy promenade at Dießen, on Ammersee

0 km   5

0 miles   5

Landsberg am Lech ●

Coat of arms on the Bayertor

Landsberg, which rises in terraces up the steep banks of the River Lech, is well worth more than a brief visit. Enclosed by walls set with towers and pierced by gateways, it largely retains its medieval character. The steep narrow streets, the hidden alleys, the market square and the steep-roofed houses create a special atmosphere. Landsberg was also the place where Adolf Hitler was jailed after his abortive putsch, during which time he wrote *Mein Kampf.*

Gothic bas-relief on the church of Mariä Himmelfahrt

The lavishly decorated stuccowork façade of the Rathaus

Exploring Landsberg

With its many streets, alleyways and squares boasting fine architecture and historic houses, Landsberg is a lovely place to explore on foot. There are delightful little corners, such as the Hexenviertel, Seelberg and Blattergasse. The Hintere Salzgasse is a particularly striking alley with rows of mid-18th-century single-storey cottages with large, steeply pitched roofs.

⊞ Rathaus

Hauptplatz 152.
Tel *(08191) 12 82 68.*
◯ *May–Oct: 10am–noon, 2–5pm at weekends and public holidays.*
The Rathaus, or town hall, stands on the west side of the square. The façade and rooms on the second floor have fine mouldings executed by Dominikus Zimmermann in

1718–20. Outside the Rathaus is the Marienbrunnen, a fountain with a statue of the Madonna, dating from 1783.

⊞ Lechwehr

This weir was built in the 14th century at the point where the Mühlbach stream branches off from the River Lech. Over the centuries, the weir has been repeatedly washed away by floods and rebuilt. The cascades are scenically set against the backdrop of the Old Town.

⛪ Klosterkirche der Dominikanerinnen Hl. Dreifaltigkeit

Peter Dörfler Str. 🖼
The church, with its uniform Rococo decoration, was built in 1764–6. It stands in the same street as the Dominican convent, whose façade was painted with murals in about 1765. This entire group of buildings was the last work that Dominikus Zimmermann executed before his death.

The Bayertor, one of the finest town gates in Bavaria

⊞ Bayertor and Town Walls

◯ *May–Oct: 10am–noon, 2–5pm daily.*
One of the best-known gateways in Bavaria is Landsberg's colourful Bayertor. Built in 1425, it has a 36-m (118-ft) high crenellated tower whose interior contains a stone sculpture of the Crucifixion and armorial cartouches.

The other surviving gates are the Mannerist Sandauertor, dating from 1625–30, the Bäckertor of about 1430, and the Färbertor, built in the later 15th century. The Sandauertor is crowned by the tall, circular Luginsland tower, which functioned as a watchtower during the Middle Ages.

Except for those on the west side, the medieval town walls have been preserved almost in their entirety. The earliest parts, built in the 13th century, can be seen on Vordere Mühlgasse and Hintere Salzgasse. The Schmalzturm, or Schöner Turm, dates from the 13th century. The most recent section of the walls was built in the early 15th century.

⛪ Hl. Kreuzkirche and Neues Stadtmuseum

Von-Helfenstein-Gasse 426.
Neues Stadtmuseum. ***Tel*** *(08191) 94 23 26.* ◯ *2pm–5pm Tue–Sun.* ● *Feb–Mar.* 🖼
The Hl. Kreuzkirche was built in 1752–4 to a plan by Ignaz Merani, replacing the previous building of 1580. It was the first Jesuit church in southern Germany. Set high up on a slope overlooking the town, it has a flat façade flanked by belfries with Baroque roofs. The ceiling is decorated with two trompe-l'oeil paintings by Thomas Scheffler, a pupil

of the Asam brothers. The paintings create the striking illusion of the Holy Cross falling from above. Monastery buildings stand beside the church. Prominent among them are the former Jesuit college's Renaissance cloisters, dating from 1576–1609.

Opposite the church, a little further down the hill, is the former Jesuit college, built in 1688–92 in a refined but pleasingly simple style. Since 1989 the building has housed the local history museum.

The Neues Stadtmuseum and, in the background, Hl. Kreuzkirche

Mariä Himmelfahrt

Georg-Hellmar-Platz.

The church, built in 1458–88 and retaining its Romanesque tower, was given its present Baroque appearance in about 1700. The windows of the presbytery have late Gothic stained glass, although this is unfortunately obscured by the high altar.

Also in the presbytery, in the Altar of the Rosary made by Dominikus Zimmermann in 1721, is a Gothic figure of the Madonna and Child, an outstanding work executed by Hans Multscher of Ulm in about 1440.

Johanniskirche

Vorderer Anger.

Built by Dominikus Zimmermann in 1750–52, this church has an oval plan, four semicircular external corner niches and a separate circular presbytery. Zimmermann, working with Johannes Luidl, was also responsible for the decoration of the interior, which features a magnificent high altar.

VISITORS' CHECKLIST

Road map C4. 25,000.
Bahnhof-Platz.
Bahnhof-Platz.
Hauptplatz 152, (08191) 12 82 46. **www**.landsberg.de info @landsberg.de Ruethenfest (Jul, every four years, the next will be held in 2011).

Mutterturm

Von–Kühlmann–Str. 2. **Herkomer Museum**. **Tel** (08191) 94 23 28. 2–5pm Tue–Sun. Feb–Mar.

The Mother Tower, built in 1884–7 on the side of the river opposite the town, was the summer residence and studio of Hubert von Herkomer, the painter and dramatist, who died in 1914. Dedicated to his mother (hence the name), the house was built in the style of a Norman castle keep and stands 30 m (98 ft) high.

The museum in the tower contains objects from the artist's studio as well as a selection of his drawings, etchings and paintings.

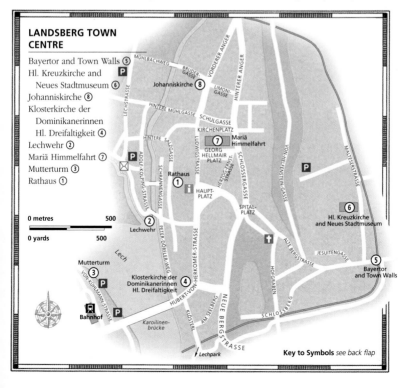

LANDSBERG TOWN CENTRE

Bayertor and Town Walls ⑤
Hl. Kreuzkirche and Neues Stadtmuseum ⑥
Johanniskirche ⑧
Klosterkirche der Dominikanerinnen Hl. Dreifaltigkeit ④
Lechwehr ②
Mariä Himmelfahrt ⑦
Mutterturm ③
Rathaus ①

0 metres   500
0 yards   500

Johanniskirche ⑧
Mariä Himmelfahrt ⑦
Rathaus ①
HAUPT-PLATZ
Lechwehr ②
SPITAL-PLATZ
Mutterturm ③
Klosterkirche der Dominikanerinnen Hl. Dreifaltigkeit ④
Bahnhof
Karolinen-brücke
Hl. Kreuzkirche and Neues Stadtmuseum ⑥
Bayertor and Town Walls ⑤
Lechpark

Key to Symbols see back flap

Yacht jetty at Dießen on Ammersee

Dießen ❷

Road map C4. 🏠 10,000. 🚌 🚆
ℹ️ Schützenstr. 9, (08807) 10 48.
www.tourist-info-diessen.de

This small fishing town is located on Ammersee, Bavaria's third-largest lake. The area is very popular with people from nearby Munich. Although large numbers of tourists come here, their presence is not especially noticeable. It is pleasant to walk along the lakeside promenade, and especially to visit one of the homely restaurants and to sample Ammersee's speciality, the salmon-like *Renken*.

A few old houses survive here, including the oldest wooden **peasant cottage** in Upper Bavaria, dating from 1491. The most exquisite historic building is the early Rococo **Marienmünster**, a church built for the Augustinian monastery in 1732–9 to a design by Johann Michael Fischer. The fine ceiling paintings, executed by Johann Georg Bergmüller in 1736, depict the saints and blessed members of the von Andechs family. The side altars feature depictions of St Sebastian by the Venetian painter Giovanni Battista Tiepolo and of St Stefan by Battista Pittoni.

Andechs ❸

Road map C4. 🏠 1,400. 🚌
🚆 Herrsching. ℹ️ Andechser Str. 16, (08152) 93 250.
www.gemeinde-andechs.de

Andechs is home to the oldest **church** in Germany. The main part of the building dates from 1420. The church was remodelled in the Baroque style in 1669–1751. The stuccowork and painting are the work of Johann Baptist Zimmermann.

The church attracts some 200,000 pilgrims every year. Because of its situation almost 180 m (590 ft) above the level of Ammersee, together with the Rococo decoration of its late Gothic church, the Benedictine monastery draws large numbers of visitors.

Another reason for the monastery's popularity with visitors is the strong beer that is brewed here. It is served at the monastery's inn and on the terrace, from which there is a breathtaking view over the lake.

The Rococo interior of the church in Wessobrunn

Wessobrunn ❹

Road map C4. 🏠 1,700. 🚌 🚆
Weilheim. ℹ️ Zöpfstr. 1, (08809) 313.

The exterior of the former Benedictine abbey here conceals a fine courtyard, lavish stuccowork in the **monastery** and Rococo decoration in the **church**, which was built in 1757–9. Of the original Romanesque buildings, all that remain are the defence tower and the Crucifix in the church. The stuccowork and trompe-l'oeil painting in the cloisters and on the monastery staircase were executed by the workshop of Johann Schmuzer in 1680–96.

It was here in 814 that the *Wessobrunner Gebet* was written. It describes the Creation and is the oldest surviving document in the German language. It is today preserved in the Bayerischen Staatsbibliothek in Munich (*see p65*).

LÜFTLMALEREI

Lüftlmalerei is the style of painting that is widely seen on houses in Upper Bavaria and the Allgäu, particularly in the Alpine and sub-Alpine areas. Dating from the 17th century, it was derived from Italia *trompe l'oeil* painting. A famous exponent of *Lüftlmalerei* was Franz Seraph Zwinck (1748–92), who lived in Oberammergau in a house called Zum Lüftl. It was probably after his house that this style of painting was named.

Lüftlmalerei in Berchtesgaden

Around Starnberger See ⑤

It was in Starnberger See, near the town of Berg, that Ludwig II, much loved by the Bavarians, drowned in 1886. Like many of Munich's elite, he owned a summer palace on the lake. This scenic region has long enjoyed great popularity. The wealthy citizens of Munich build fine residences here, while those of more modest means come for weekend breaks.

Starnberg ①
Linked to Munich by a railway since 1854, Starnberg boasts luxury villas and has a large marina.

Possenhofen ⑨
Royal visitors to this palace have included Elisabeth, future consort of Franz Joseph of Austria, and Sofia, Ludwig II's betrothed.

Feldafing ⑧
From 1855 to 1863 Ludwig II stayed in a romantic palace on nearby Roseninsel with his cousin Elisabeth (known as Sissi), the future empress of Austria.

FÜRSTENFELDBRUCK ◄ MÜNCHEN

Berg ②
The spot where Ludwig II met his death is marked by a Neo-Romanesque chapel built on the lakeshore in 1896–1900.

Assenhausen ③
In an extensive park stands Bismarck's Tower, built in 1896–9 in honour of the German Chancellor.

Tutzing ⑦
A monumental horseshoe-shaped palace surrounded by a landscaped park is currently the home of an evangelical academy.

WEILHEIM

Starnberger See

Bernried ⑥
The Gothic Martinskirche was remodelled in the Baroque style in 1658 by the architect and stuccoist Kasper Feichtmayr.

| 0 km | 2 |
| 0 miles | 2 |

WEILHEIM

Ammerland ④
The palace here, built in 1683–5, was presented by Ludwig I to the German poet and painter Franz Graf von Pocci in 1841.

PENZBERG

TIPS FOR TOURISTS

Length: about 46 km (28 miles).
Stopping-off places: There are many restaurants and cafés in every town on the route. Overnight accommodation is available, although it may be harder to obtain in summer.

Seeshaupt ⑤
This bustling resort, with a marina and elegant lakeside promenade, is very popular with watersports enthusiasts.

KEY

▬ Suggested route

── Other road

Hohen-peißenberg **6**

Road map C5. 🚶 *4,000.*
🚌 🚆 *Peißenberg or Peiting.*
ℹ️ *Blumenstr. 2, (08805) 92 1010.*
www.hohenpeissenberg.de

The mountain known as Hoher Peißenberg rises east of the town of Peißenberg. The summit, at a height of 988 m (3,241 ft) above sea level, is reached by a scenic winding road and offers an extensive panorama of Upper Bavaria, from Ammersee and Starnberger See to the Alps.

On the summit stands the **Gnadenkapelle**, built in the late Gothic period and remodelled in the Baroque style, the church of **Mariä Himmelfahrt**, built in 1616–19, and a former **chapter-house** of 1619. The chapel contains a miracle-working image of the Madonna Enthroned dating from 1460–80 and brought here from Schongau in 1514.

Schongau **7**

Road map C5. 🚶 *12,000.* 🚌 🚆
ℹ️ *Münzstr. 1–3, (08861) 21 41 81.*
www.schongau.de

Schongau is picturesquely located on the river Lech and surrounded by idyllic fields and pastures. The town is enclosed by almost completely preserved **town walls** with wooden walkways and

towers. They were built in the 14th century and later reinforced in the 17th century. The main street in Schongau is the wide Münzenstraße, which is lined with shops and restaurants.

One of the town's finest buildings is the church of **Mariä Himmelfahrt**, which was built by Dominikus Zimmermann in 1751–3 on the site of a Gothic church. Also of interest is the former **castle** of the Wittelsbachs, dating from the 15th century and refurbished in 1771–2, and the late Gothic **Ballenhaus**, whose ground floor with open-beamed ceiling houses the town hall. The **Stadt-museum Schongau**, a local history museum, is to be found in **Erasmuskirche**, a former hospital church, established in the 15th century and rebuilt in the 17th century.

Michaelskirche font, Altenstadt

🏛 Stadtmuseum Schongau
Christophstr. 55.
Tel (08861) 20 602. ⏰ *2–5pm Wed, Sat, Sun & public hols.*

Environs
Some 3 km (2 miles) north is **Altenstadt**, which boasts **Michaels-kirche**, the finest surviving monumental Romanesque basilica in Upper Bavaria. Dating from about 1200, it is surrounded by a wall. It is decorated with Gothic frescoes and contains the Great God of Altenstadt, a crucifix 3 m (10 ft) tall, and a carved Romanesque font.

Romanesque cloisters of the abbey in Steingaden

Steingaden **8**

Road map C5. 🚶 *2,900.* 🚌
🚆 *Peiting.* ℹ️ *Krankenhausstr. 1, (08862) 200.* www.steingaden.de

This town has a well-preserved Romanesque **Pfarrkirche St Johannes der Täufer**, built in the second half of the 12th century and partially rebuilt in the 15th century. It is a columned basilica with a triple apse and twin towers above the west front. The interior was decorated with Rococo mouldings and paintings in 1771–4.

In 1147 the Premonstratensians built an **abbey** here, of which the western cloisters, dating from the early 13th century, survive. The architect Dominikus Zimmermann was buried in the Romanesque chapel of St John in 1766.

Wieskirche **9**

Road map C5. 🚶 *2,800.* 🚌 🚆
Füssen or Peiting. ℹ️ *Krankenhausstr. 1, Steingaden, (08862) 200.*
🎵 *Abendkonzerte, Festlicher Sommer in der Wies (May–Sep).*

The attractive pilgrimage church of **Zum Gegeißelten Heiland**, nestling in the sub-Alpine scenery, is not only the most resplendent example of South German Rococo, but probably the finest Rococo church in the world. UNESCO

Green pastures and a country track near Schongau

listed it as a World Heritage Site in 1983.

In 1738, the figure of Christ in a small chapel in the fields southwest of the present church is said to have wept genuine tears, and soon afterwards pilgrims began to flock to the site of the miracle. In 1743–4 the Premonstratensian abbot of Steingaden commissioned Dominikus Zimmermann to design a church here.

Built in 1754 and decorated in 1765, the church represents the work of Dominikus and Johann Baptist Zimmermann at its peak. The nave is built to an oval plan and the ceiling is supported by eight pairs of columns. There is an elongated presbytery. The entire building displays an extraordinary fusion of painting, woodcarving and stuccowork and an almost mesmerising interplay of colour and light. The many windows, in fantastic and varied shapes, enliven the exterior and illuminate the interior. Not surprisingly, the church has been called the Lord God's Ballroom.

Murnau ⑩

Road map C5. 🏃 *11,300.* 🚌 🚉
ℹ️ *Kohlgruber Str. 1, (08841) 61 410.* www.murnau.de

Murnau is situated on an elevation between two lakes, Staffelsee and Riegsee, north of the marsh known as the Murnauer Moos, on what was once the Roman road to Augsburg. During World War II an officers' prisoner-

Rococo interior of the church in Wies, a World Heritage Site

of-war camp existed here. Today Murnau is famous for its breweries.

The **Nikolauskirche** is an interesting building. It was designed by Enrico Zucalli and was completed in 1734, after 17 years' work. The small Baroque **Mariahilf-Kirche** stands on Marktstraße, the main street, which commands a view of the Alps to the south.

There are numerous inns and guesthouses, a Neo-Gothic **town hall**, houses with oriel windows and decorative signboards, and narrow, winding alleys which give the town a unique charm. The **monument to Ludwig II**, on Kohlgruber Straße, was erected in 1894 and is the earliest monument to be dedicated to the king.

The finest building in Murnau is the Art Nouveau **Münter-Haus**, where the artist Wassily Kandinsky lived from 1909 to 1914 with his student and lifetime companion Gabriele Münter. Today it houses a

museum dedicated to the famous painter couple, along with works by other members of the Blaue Reiter group.

🏛 **Münter-Haus**
Kottmüllerallee 6.
Tel (08841) 62 88 80.
⏰ *2–5pm Tue–Sun.*

DER BLAUE REITER

Cover of the first issue of *Der Blaue Reiter*

Wassily Kandinsky and Franz Marc produced the first issue of *Der Blaue Reiter* in 1911. The journal is now considered one of the most significant manifestos of 20th-century art. The contributors were artists whose aim was to renew art, while retaining their stylistic individuality. They included Paul Klee, Alexej Jawlensky, August Macke and Gabriele Münter. The Blaue Reiter group marked the beginning of lyrical abstract painting.

A colourful flower stall on Untermarkt in Murnau

The Baroque basilica of the Benedictine abbey at Ettal, set in an Alpine valley

Oberammergau ⑪

Road map C5. 🏘 *5,000.* 🚌 🚊
ℹ️ *Eugen-Papst-Str. 9a, (08822) 922
740.* **www**.*oberammergau.de*
🎭 *Passionspiele (Easter, every
ten years, the next in 2010).*

Oberammergau is one of
the best-known towns in
Upper Bavaria. Its renown
rests on its **painted houses**,
and it is the centre of the
colourful style of *trompe-l'oeil*
house-painting known as
Lüftlmalerei, which is typical
of the region *(see p212)*.

The town also has an
international reputation for its
Passion play, which has been
performed here at Easter ever
since 1633, when an epidemic
of the plague finally passed.
Originally an open-air event,
the play has been performed
in a purpose-built theatre
since 1930.

The spectacle, which last
for six hours, is performed by
1,400 amateur actors, all of
whom must be local people
or their family members. The
play attracts an audience from
all over the world.

The Hotel Alte Post in Oberammergau

Ettal ⑫

Road map C5. 🏘 *1,000.*
🚌 🚊 *Oberammergau.*
ℹ️ *Ammergauer Str. 8, (08822)
35 34.* **www**.*ettal.de*

Set in a scenic Alpine valley,
this Benedictine **abbey** was
founded by Ludwig IV
in 1330. In 1710, when the
church was remodelled in
the Baroque style to plans
by Enrico Zucalli, a Gothic
rotunda was added. The two-
storey façade that Zucalli
intended was not
completed until the
early 20th century.

The impressive
interior decoration
is in a pure Rococo
style, crowned by the
large dome that is
visible from afar.
The paintings were
executed in
1748–50 by
Johann Jakob Zeiller
and the stuccowork,
one of the great achievements
of its time, is by Johann
Georg Üblher and Franz
Xaver Schmuzer. The high

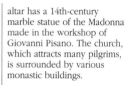

**Vase in the
Linderhof park**

altar has a 14th-century
marble statue of the Madonna
made in the workshop of
Giovanni Pisano. The church,
which attracts many pilgrims,
is surrounded by various
monastic buildings.

Linderhof ⑬

Road map C5. 🏘 *5,000.*
🚌 🚊 *Oberammergau.* **Palace**
Tel *(08822) 92 030.* ◯ *Apr–15 Oct:
9am–6pm daily; 16 Oct–Mar: 10am–
4pm daily.* 🎫 📷
Park ◯ *Apr–mid-Oct.*
www.*linderhof.de*

Of all Ludwig II's
many fairy-tale
residences, the **palace**
at Linderhof best
shows his great fond-
ness for France and
his regard for the
Bourbons and Louis
XIV. The smallest
of Ludwig II's castles
and the one he
visited most often, it was built
by Georg von Dollmann in
1874–8 and is surrounded by
an extensive **park**. The
extravagant luxury of the
interior decoration is based
on French Baroque style.
Although it was intended as a
private residence, the palace
still has an ornate royal
audience chamber. The
other rooms in the palace,
including the Tapestry Room
and Hall of Mirrors, are no
less extravagantly decorated.

The palace is surrounded
by French-style formal
gardens and by Italianate

terraced gardens with cascades, which in turn are surrounded by landscaped grounds. There is an artificial **grotto** dating from 1876–7 with a lake, a stage and a throne with colourful lighting that brings to mind the Venus Grotto in Wagner's opera *Tannhäuser*. Ludwig II would take rides on the lake in a conch-shaped boat.

Another attraction of the park surrounding the palace is the **Moorish kiosk**, made by Karl von Dibitsch in 1850 and purchased by the king in 1876. Inside it is a lavish Peacock Throne. Just as resplendent is the **Moroccan House** of 1878–9, which was installed here in 1989.

A house with Lüftlmalerei decoration in Garmisch-Partenkirchen

Visitors admiring Ludwig II's palace at Linderhof

Garmisch-Partenkirchen ⓮

Road map C5. 🏔 28,000.
🚌 🚉 🛈 *Richard-Strauss-Platz 2, (08821) 18 07 00.* **www.** garmisch-partenkirchen.de

Two villages, Garmisch and Partenkirchen, separated by the rivers Loisach and Partnach, were conjoined one year before the 1936 Winter Olympics. Thus came into being one of the best-known winter sports centres in Germany, with a convenient motorway link to Munich. The Alpine Ski World Championships were held here in 1978.

Garmisch, the older of the two villages, is mentioned as early as the 9th century. Partenkirchen, which until the 1930s retained its rural character, is 300 years younger. Both parts of the town have many houses with characteristically painted façades, some old and others quite modern.

The finest churches here include **St Anton**, in Partenkirchen, a pilgrimage church dating from the first half of the 18th century, with *trompe-l'oeil* painting by Johann Holzer. There are also two **churches** in Garmisch dedicated to St Martin. One is medieval, with Gothic frescoes in the interior, and the other is Baroque, with stuccowork executed by Josef Schmuzer in 1730–33 and paintings by Matthäus Günther of 1733.

The **Olympic stadium** in the south part of Partenkirchen was built in 1934. As well as having ski-jumps, it is decorated with larger-than-life sculptures that are typical of Fascist art.

Environs
A road south of Partenkirchen leads to the scenic **Partnach river gorge** (Partnach-klamm).

Further along, an uphill walk of several hours leads to Ludwig II's hunting lodge in Schachen, just below the summit of Dreitorspitze. Built in 1870 in imitation of a Swiss chalet, the lodge has an ornate Oriental-style interior. The king celebrated his birthdays in the lodge, and also came here on hunting trips.

Eibsee ⓯

Road map C5. 🚌 🚉 *Garmisch-Partenkirchen.*

The greenish-blue waters of this lake, surrounded by wooded mountain slopes, lie 974 m (3,195 ft) above sea level. The scenic paths along its shores lead to secluded jetties for yachts and boats.

A regatta, with processions of yachts and great firework displays, takes place here every summer. Above the lake towers **Zugspitze**, which at 2,963 m (9,717 ft) is the highest peak in the German Alps. The summit can be reached by cablecar or an old funicular train, which passes through many tunnels.

Eibsee, the lake at the foot of Zugspitze

Mittenwald, a town on a former trade route at the foot of the Alps

Mittenwald 16

Road map C5. 🏚 *8,400.* 🚌
🚆 **ℹ** *Dammkarstr. 3, (08823)
33 981.* **www**.mittenwald.de

Situated at the foot of the
Karwendel mountain range,
this small town stands on
what was once the main trade
route between Verona and
Augsburg. Up until the Thirty
Years' War, its wealth was
founded on trade but from
the 17th century its mainstay
was craftsmanship,
particularly violin-making.

The beginnings of the local
violin-making trade can be
traced back to the 17th
century and Matthäus Klotz
(1653–1743), a pupil of the
famous Nicolo Amati. A violin
school was founded in 1853,
and in 1930 the **Geigenbau-
und Heimatmuseum** (Museum
of Violin-Making) was
established in the house
where Klotz was born.
Kirche St Peter und Paul
was built in 1738–40 by Josef
Schmuzer. The late Gothic
presbytery survives, and the
tower was completed in 1746.
The Lüftlmalerei on the
façade is an outstanding
example of this type of
decoration *(see p212)*. It is by
Matthias Günther, who also
executed the paintings inside
the church. The monument to
Matthäus Klotz that stands
outside the church was
designed by Ferdinand Miller
in 1890.

Mittenwald is now widely
known as a tourist resort, and
is especially popular with
winter sports enthusiasts.

🏛 **Geigenbau- und Heimat-
museum**
Ballenhausgasse 3.
Tel (08823) 25 11. ◯ *10am–
5pm Tue–Sun (11am–4pm Jan, mid-
Mar–mid-May & mid-Oct–Nov).*

Wallgau 17

Road map C5. 🏚 *1,400.* 🚌
🚆 *Mittenwald.* **ℹ** *Mitten-
walderstr. 8, (08825) 92 50 50.*
www.wallgau.de

This delightful village has
small wooden **cottages** built
in the 17th and 18th centuries
with Lüftlmalerei *(see p212)*
by Franz Kainer dating from
the 1770s. Most of the
cottages have been thoroughly
modernized and now function
as hotels, spanning a range of
categories.

The town is popular with
the smart Munich set, who
come to play golf on the fine
local courses, which are set
in breathtaking scenery. The
Gasthaus zur Post is
renowned as the place where
Heinrich Heine stayed in 1828
on his journey to Italy.

One of the many fine golf courses
around the town of Wallgau

Walchensee 18

Road map C5. 🏚 *1,000.* 🚌 🚆
Kochel am See. **ℹ** *Ringstr.1,
(08858) 411.***www**.walchensee.de

This lake, which lies in an
attractive green valley, is
swept by strong winds, and
is therefore very popular
with windsurfers.

The small **church** near the
lake was built in 1633 and
refurbished in 1712–14.

Environs
In the nearby town of
Zwergern stands the
picturesque Margarethen-
kirche, which was built in the
14th century and remodelled

FRANZ MARC
1880–1916

Heavenly Horses, one of Marc's
best-known paintings

The Munich-born painter
Franz Marc began his
artistic career under the
influence of the Impres-
sionists and of Wassily
Kandinsky, with whom
he set up the group Der
Blaue Reiter *(see p215)*.
Marc adopted Paul
Delaunay's pure palette
of Symbolist colours and
the crystalline forms of
the Italian Futurists. His
paintings of humans and
animals show them in
harmony with their
surroundings. Marc enjoyed
painting from nature
outdoors and was often
visited in his home by
followers of the movement.
He was killed in 1916 at
the Battle of Verdun at
the age of 36.

---

in the Baroque style in 1670. Beside it stands a monastery known as the Klösterl. Built in 1686–9, it has striking white walls and a tall, steeply pitched roof.

Near **Urfeld**, hidden in the woods, stands a small bust of the great 19th-century German writer Johann Wolfgang von Goethe, who stayed in the town when he set off on his famous Italian travels in 1786.

The extensive cloisters of the monastery at Benediktbeuern

museum of his paintings and the works of other artists of the group Der Blaue Reiter (*see p215*).

🏛 Franz-Marc-Museum
Franz-Marc-Parc 8–10. **Tel** (08851) 924880. ⬜ 10am–6pm Tue–Sun & public hols (until 5pm Nov–Mar). ◼ 24 & 31 Dec. 🖼

Environs:
Above Kochelsee is **Walchensee hydro-electric power station**. It was built in 1918–24 to a design by Oskar von Miller, who aimed to electrify the Bavarian rail network and to supply electricity to the whole country. Walchensee power station is still one of the largest in Germany today.

Walchensee hydroelectric power station above Kochelsee

Kochel am See ⓫

Road map C5. 🏠 4,200. 🚌 🚉 🛈 Kalmbachstr. 11, (08851) 338. www.kochel.de

Kochel is a popular resort on Kochelsee. The local church, **Michaelskirche**, was built in 1688–90, probably by Kaspar Feichtmayr. The frescoes and stuccowork were added in about 1730.

Two famous figures are associated with Kochel. One is the blacksmith who became the hero of the Bavarian uprising against Austria in 1705 – a statue of him was erected in 1900. The other is the painter Franz Marc (*see p218*). The house in which he lived is now a

Freilichtmuseum Glentleiten ⓬

Road map C5. 🚌 🚉 Kochel am See, Murnau. 🛈 (08851) 18 50. ⬜ Apr–Nov: 9am–6pm Tue–Sun. 🖼

The largest skansen (open-air museum) in Upper Bavaria opened near Großweil in 1976. It re-creates the atmosphere of a traditional Bavarian village, with cottages and workshops. The interiors show the way villagers once lived. The surrounding fields and meadows are cultivated in the traditional way. Cows, horses, sheep and goats graze nearby.

Benediktbeuern ㉑

Road map C5. 🏠 3,500. 🚌 🚉 🛈 Prälatenstr. 3, (08857) 248. www.benediktbeuern.de

The holiday resort of Benediktbeuern, at the foot of the Bekedikenwand mountains, is known for its former Benedictine **monastery**. Founded in 739 as part of the see established by St Boniface, it was one of the first missionary monasteries that he founded in Bavaria.

Work on the present late Baroque **church**, which stands on the site of a Romanesque church, began in 1682 under the direction of Kaspar Feichtmayr of Wessobrunn. The interior features some fine stucco-work strongly influenced by Italian art. The vaulting over the nave and the side chapels was painted by Hans Georg Asam, father of the renowned Asam brothers, in 1683–7. The monumental altar, built to resemble a triumphal arch, is made out of three different kinds of marble.

By the presbytery, which is fronted by towers, stands the two-storey **Anastasiakapelle**. It was built in 1750–53 by Johann Michael Fischer and has an oval floor plan. The decoration, by Johann Michael Feichtmayr and Johann Jakob Zeiller, is a masterpiece of Bavarian Rococo style.

Also worth visiting are the **monastery buildings**, now owned by Silesians. Dating from 1669–1732, they are arranged around two court-yards. The Alter Festsaal (Old Banqueting Hall), the Kurfürstensaal (Assembly Hall) and the former library, now a refectory, are particularly worth seeing.

Wooden figure of a fisherman in the lakeside resort of Kochel am See

Bad Tölz ㉒

Road map D5. 🏔 *17,000.*
🚉 🚌 *Max-Höfler-Platz. 11, (08 041)*
78 670. **www**.bad-toelz.de
🎭 *Leonhardifahrt (6 Nov).*

Until quite recent times, the inhabitants of Bad Tölz, on the River Isar, made their living through a combination of trade, logging and making and selling their famous painted furniture. When iodine-rich springs were discovered here in 1846, the village became a health spa. To exploit the local mineral water, a water park at

Leonhardiritte (painted cart), Bad Tölz

Alpamare, one of the largest in Germany, was built, and transport links, saunas and solariums were installed.

The character of the old town has been well preserved around **Marktstrasse**, which leads down to the Isar. Many of the houses, dating from the 17th to the 19th centuries, have characteristic trompe-l'oeil wall paintings and stuccowork, and distinctive overhanging eaves.

The **church** on Kalvarien-berg, one of the most famous in Bavaria, was begun in 1726 and completed at the end of the 19th century. Particularly impressive is the **Holy Staircase** inside the church. At the festival of St Leonhard, patron saint of horses and cattle, a horseback procession ascends Kalvarienberg and is then blessed. Proces-sions with horses and painted carts, or Leonhardiritte, take place in the town, too.

Tegernsee ㉓

Road map D5. 🏔 *4,200.* 🚌
🚉 *Tegernsee.* 🛈 *Hauptstr. 2,*
(08022) 18 01 40.
www.tegernsee.de

For the inhabitants of Munich, Tegernsee, within easy reach of the bustling capital, is an upper-class recreation ground.

The first settlement to be founded in the valley was the Benedictine **monastery** near Tegernsee, established in the 8th century. The monastery became an important centre of culture, and in the 11th century the Romanesque stained-glass windows made here were renowned. Examples can be seen in Augsburg cathedral. In 1823–4 Leo von Klenze converted the monastery into a summer residence for Maximilian I Joseph. Von Klenze also designed a new façade for the monastery church, built by Enrico Zucalli in the Baroque style.

Alpenstraße ㉔

In 1927, plans were made for a panoramic road that was to pass through the most beautiful parts of the German Alps. The route alternates between the High Alps and the foothills lying between Bodensee and Königssee. It traverses the most scenic areas, allowing travellers to admire Lower Bavaria's stunning scenery. Particularly impressive are the winding sections of the route, such as those around Hindelang and Bayrischzell, which offer breathtaking views.

Jochstraße ②
The scenic road that winds round Hindelang, at altitudes varying as much as 300m (985 ft) along a 7-km (4-mile) long route, offers views of Ostrachtal.

KEY

▬▬	Suggested route
═══	Other road
▬▬	Scenic route

Immenstadt ①
This picturesque little town, which has some fine historic buildings, is situated near the lake, Alpsee.

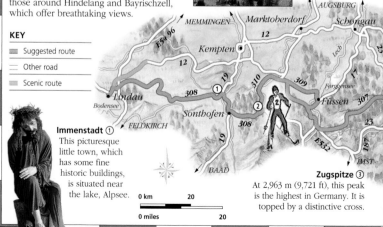

AUGSBURG

MEMMINGEN   Marktoberdorf   Schongau

Kempten

Lindau   308

Bodensee   Sonthofen

FELDKIRCH

Füssen

Forggensee

BAAD

IMST

0 km   20

0 miles   20

Zugspitze ③
At 2,963 m (9,721 ft), this peak is the highest in Germany. It is topped by a distinctive cross.

The town of Schliersee seen from the lake

Schliersee ㉕

Road map D5. 🏠 7,000.
🚊 🚌 Bahnhofstr. 11, (08026)
60 650. **www**.schliersee.de

Situated east of Tegernsee
and known as its "younger
brother", Schliersee offers
visitors much peace and quiet
and makes for a popular
escape in the summer. The
houses on the northern lakeshore all have balconies laden
with window boxes.
   The local **church of
St Sixtus** has frescoes and
stuccowork executed by
Johann Baptist Zimmermann
in 1714. The church also has a

distinctive figure of
God the Father with
Christ ascribed to
Erasmus Grasser,
and a Madonna
ascribed to Jan Polack.
The interesting **Heimat-
museum** (local history
museum) is housed in
an 18th-century hut.

🏛 **Heimatmuseum**
Lautererstr.
Tel (08026) 23 29. ◻ May–Sep:
4–6pm Tue–Fri, 10am–noon Sat;
Oct: 10–noon Sat–Sun.

Ebersberg ㉖

Road map D4. 🏠 9,000. 🚊
🚌 Marienplatz 1, (08092) 82 55 29.
www.ebersberg.de

This little town lies at the
southern end of Germany's
largest expanse of forest. Of
the Augustinian monastery
that was founded here in 934
all that remains is the
Sebastianskirche, built in

1217–31 and remodelled in
1472–1504 in the Gothic style.
Notable among the tombs,
which span the 14th to the
16th centuries, is that of the
couple who founded the
church. It features a model of
the church made by Wolfgang
Leb in 1501. On Marienplatz,
along with Baroque and Neo-
Classical houses, is the **monastery inn**, now the town hall.

**Doorway of Sebastianskirche in
Ebersberg, with gilded figures**

Bayrischzell ④
In this famous health
resort beneath the
Wendelstein moun-
tains, the first Alpine
folklore association
was founded, in 1883.
Traditional Bavarian
dress is still worn
here today.

Berchtesgaden ⑥
   This architect-
urally rich town,
   at the foot of
Watzmann, is the
hub of the tourist
area known as
Berchtesgadener
Land.

MUNICH · REGENSBURG · Chiemsee · 304 · Traunstein · CHAM
ICH · Bad Tölz · 472 · E52 8 · E52 8 · 20 · LINZ · Salzburg
au · 307 · ④ · 305 · E 55
Walchensee · 181 · 305 · ⑥
Isar · ⑤ · SPITTAL
BRUCK · Königssee

TIPS FOR DRIVERS

Length of route: About
450 km (280 miles).
Stopping-off places: The route
takes in Bavaria's best-known
places, where restaurants and
accommodation are plentiful.

Hintersee ⑤
The forest covering
the foothills around this
lake east of Ramsau –
one of the many lakes in
Berchtesgadener Land –
is known as the Zauber-
wald (Magic Forest).

THE ALLGÄU

The Allgäu is the part of Swabian Bavaria lying between the Landsberg-Memmingen motorway and the Allgäu Alps. In the east it borders the Lech valley, and in the west Baden-Württemberg, into which it protrudes as far as Bodensee (Lake Constance). The Allgäu is one of the least industrialized regions of Bavaria. Its main sources of wealth are cattle farming, dairy processing and tourism.

This verdant, hilly region, set against the backdrop of the sheer, craggy peaks of the Alps, attracts holiday-makers from Europe all year round. The gentle climate, the unspoiled scenery, the villages and towns with their historic buildings, and the excellent terrain for various sports makes this a suitable area for the developing tourist trade. The lush meadows and pastures are grazed by the characteristic brown Allgäu cows. The region's dairy produce is famous throughout the country and Germany's largest dairy processing plant is located in Kimratshofen, near Kempten.

Traditions and customs are still very much alive in the region. Local folk costumes, which vary from one district or village to another, are donned not exclusively for special occasions but are worn as everyday clothing.

After World War II, the influx of migrants (many from Sudetenland) considerably altered the structure of the population. The former inhabitants of Gablonz (Jablonec), in the Czech Republic, settled near Kaufbeuren in Neugablonz, bringing with them their traditional trade of jewellery-making.

In the Allgäu Alps, world-class sports are practised. In Oberstdorf, which is famous for its huge ski-jump, there is also a figure-skating school for young men and women from all over the country. The Alpine rockfaces are suitable for both amateur and professional mountaineers, while the cliff-tops are ideal starting-places for colourful paragliders and hang gliders. Neuschwanstein, perhaps the most extravagant of Ludwig II's castles, attracts visitors from all over the world.

Rolling green countryside around Immenstadt

◁ Neuschwanstein, one of the best known of Ludwig II's castles

Exploring the Allgäu

The capital of the Allgäu is Kempten, a town with Roman origins. Memmingen also has many historic monuments, but these are not the region's main attraction. Tourists are drawn to the castles of Hohenschwangau and Neuschwanstein at the foot of the Alps, which are reached by the Romantische Straße (Romantic Road). Equally splendid are the Renaissance castles of the Fuggers in Babenhausen and Kirchheim, and Ottobeuren Abbey. The south of the Allgäu has breathtaking Alpine scenery, including the Breitach gorge and Sturmannshöhle, a cave with stalactites, near Oberstdorf. This town is renowned for the Four Ski Jumps Tournament.

SEE ALSO

- *Where to Stay* pp268–9.
- *Where to Eat* pp282–3.

The church in Wasserburg on Bodensee (Lake Constance)

Ulm

Heimertingen

🏯🏰 MEMMINGEN

MARIA 🏛 STEINBACH **18**

Grön

Legau

Kimratshofen

0 km   10
0 miles   10

Wangen

Isny

We

Friedrichshafen

12
32
Lindenberg

Simmerberg

Alpse

WASSERBURG **16** 🏯🏰 **15** LINDAU

Oberstaufen 308 IMMENST

Bodensee

Feldkirch   Dornbirn

Bregenzer wa

SIGHTS AT A GLANCE

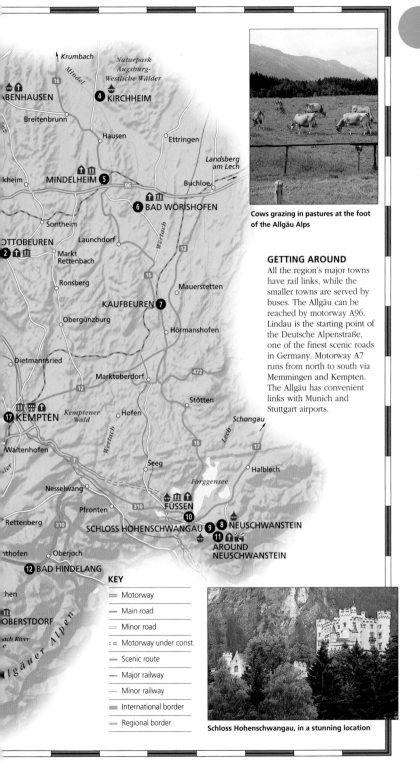

Krumbach

Naturpark
Augsburg-
Westliche Wälder

16

4 KIRCHHEIM

ABENHAUSEN

Breitenbrunn

Hausen

Ettringen

Landsberg
am Lech

kheim

MINDELHEIM 5

96

Buchloe

6 BAD WÖRISHOFEN

Cows grazing in pastures at the foot
of the Allgäu Alps

Sontheim

OTTOBEUREN

Launchdorf

2

Markt
Rettenbach

Ronsberg

Wertach

12

16

Mauerstetten

KAUFBEUREN 7

Obergünzburg

Hörmanshofen

Dietmannsried

Marktoberdorf

472

12

Stötten

Schongau

17 KEMPTEN

Kemptener
Wald

Hofen

Waltenhofen

Wertach

Lech

16

17

Seeg

Halblech

Nesselwang

Forggensee

Pfronten

310

FÜSSEN

10

Rettenberg

310

SCHLOSS HOHENSCHWANGAU 9 8 NEUSCHWANSTEIN

11

AROUND
NEUSCHWANSTEIN

nthofen

Oberjoch

12 BAD HINDELANG

OBERSTDORF

ach River
e

Allgäuer Alpen

GETTING AROUND

All the region's major towns
have rail links, while the
smaller towns are served by
buses. The Allgäu can be
reached by motorway A96.
Lindau is the starting point of
the Deutsche Alpenstraße,
one of the finest scenic roads
in Germany. Motorway A7
runs from north to south via
Memmingen and Kempten.
The Allgäu has convenient
links with Munich and
Stuttgart airports.

KEY

— Motorway

— Main road

— Minor road

=·= Motorway under const.

— Scenic route

— Major railway

— Minor railway

▬ International border

— Regional border

Schloss Hohenschwangau, in a stunning location

Memmingen ❶

Memmingen, a town known as the gateway to the Allgäu, was founded in the 12th century. It stands on the site of an Alemani settlement, on the course of an old Roman road. In 1438 Memmingen became a Free Imperial City, in 1522 it accepted the Reformation, and in 1803 it became part of Bavaria.

Memmingen has retained all the characteristics of a large trading centre. Various residential and artisans' districts have developed both within and outside the town walls. The wide streets often functioned as cargo-handling areas. The mainly timber-framed houses that line them have preserved their Gothic character.

The rich Gothic carvings on the stalls in Martinskirche

The façade of the town hall, with decorative Rococo stuccowork

🏛 Rathaus
Marktplatz 1.

Originally built in 1488, the Gothic town hall was remodelled and enlarged in the 16th century. Its current appearance dates from 1589, the Rococo stuccowork was added later to the façade in 1765. This elegant Renaissance building has a projecting central axis with oriel windows on the lower storeys culminating in a polygonal tower, and the wings are flanked by side towers.

🏛 Steuerhaus
Marktplatz 16.

The former customs house was built in 1495 to an elongated rectangular plan. It opens on to Marktplatz with an arcade of 20 arches. The second floor and the shaped gables were added in 1708. The painting on the façade dates from 1906–09. The building currently houses various municipal offices.

♣ Hermansbau
Zangmeisterstr. 8. **Stadtmuseum und Heimatmuseum Freudenthal** *Tel (08331) 85 01 34.* ◯ *May–Oct: 10am–noon and 2–4pm Tue–Fri, Sun and public holidays.* 📷

This late Baroque patrician palace with an arcaded courtyard was built in 1766 for Benedikt Freiherr von Herman. The façade is lavishly decorated with stuccowork, and the central section has a gable with an armorial cartouche.

🏛 Martinskirche
Zangmeisterstr. 13. *Tel (08331) 85 69 20.* ◯ *Easter Sun–Apr & Oct: 10am–4pm daily (till 5pm May–Sep).*

The Protestant Martinskirche was built in the 15th century, replacing a Romanesque basilica. This late Gothic church has a quadrilateral tower with a later steeple.

The interior has notable wall paintings dating from the 15th and 16th centuries. The most interesting feature of the interior, however, is the presbytery stalls, made by craftsmen from Memmingen in 1501–07. The decorative carvings, with lifelike portraits of the founders, are among the most outstanding examples of late Gothic Swabian art.

🏛 Westertor and Town Walls

The walls of the old town were completed before 1181. The outer walls were added in the 13th–15th centuries. In the 19th century they were partially demolished, but significant fragments with bastions and walkways have been preserved.

The most noteworthy gate is Westertor, which was rebuilt in 1648 to replace Elias Holl's town gates, and Kemptentor, built in 1383 and topped by a tall brick tower.

🏛 Antonierhaus
Martin-Luther-Platz 1. **Strigel- and Antoniter-Museum** *Tel (08331) 85 02 45.* ◯ *10am–noon and 2pm–4pm Tue–Sat, 10am–4pm Sun & public holidays.* 📷

This former Antonine monastery and hospital, oldest established by the order, was built in 1383. It stands on the site of an earlier castle.

The four-winged building has internal cloisters with external staircases. Painstakingly rebuilt, since 1996 they have housed a library as well as a café and cultural institutions.

Decorative armorial cartouche on the façade of the Steuerhaus

⚓ Fuggerbau

Schweizerberg 8.
The house of the Fugger
family *(see p252)* was built in
1581–91 for Jakob Fugger. It
is a monumental four-winged
building with two square
stairwells rising from the
corners of the courtyards.

🔒 Frauenkirche

Frauenkirchplatz 4. *Tel (08331) 22 53.*
This three-nave basilica was
originally a Romanesque
building. It was enlarged at
the end of the 14th century,
and was remodelled in 1456.
From 1565 to 1806 the church
was shared by Catholics and
Protestants.

The late Gothic paintings
on the walls and ceiling were
uncovered in 1893. Their state
of preservation and wide
thematic range make them
among the most significant
in southern Germany.

♨ Siebendächerhaus

Gerberplatz 7.
The "House with Seven
Roofs", built in 1601, was
specially designed for drying

hides. Destroyed in April
1945 and painstakingly
rebuilt, it is one of the town's
most distinctive buildings.

🎭 Theater

Theaterplatz 2. *Tel (08331) 94 95 16.*
The building on what is now
Theaterplatz was originally a
monastery's barn. Built in
1680, it became an arsenal
and then a theatre in 1803,
when the Neo-Classical
façade was added.

The distinctive Siebendächerhaus,
the "House with Seven Roofs"

VISITORS' CHECKLIST

Road map B4 👥 43,000. 🚌
🚉 *Bahnhofstr.* 🛈 *Marktplatz 3,
(08331) 85 01 72, 85 01 73.*
www.memmingen.de
@ info@memmingen.de
🎭 *Wallensteinspiel (Jul, every
4 years), Kinderfest and Fischertag
(Jul), Jahrmarkt (Oct),
Christkindlesmarkt (Dec).*

🔒 Kreuzherrenkirche

Hallhof 5. ⏰ *2–5pm Tue–Fri & Sun;
10am–12:30pm, 2–5pm Sat.*
This two-nave church with a
tall onion-domed clock tower
was built in 1480–84 in the
Gothic style. In 1709 the
interior was decorated with
lavish Baroque stuccowork
by Matthias Stiller and
paintings in the style of
Johann Baptist Zimmermann.
When the church was
deconsecrated in 1803, the
interior was horizontally
divided so as to make two
storeys. After World War II it
was restored and since 1947
it has served as an exhibition
gallery and concert hall.

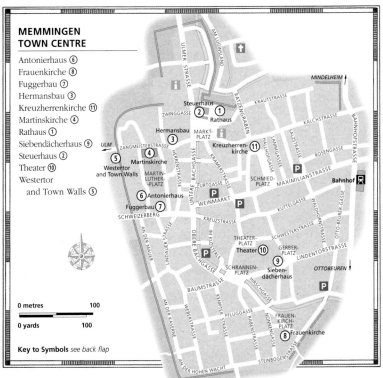

**MEMMINGEN
TOWN CENTRE**

0 metres   100

0 yards   100

Key to Symbols see back flap

The lavishly decorated interior of the abbey church at Ottobeuren

painters. The gallery forms part of the Bayerische Staatsgemäldesammlungen.

🏛 Klostermuseum Abtei Ottobeuren and Staatsgalerie Ottobeuren, Kaisersaal
Benediktiner. **Tel** *(08332) 79 80.*
⏱ *Palm Sunday–end-Oct: 10am–noon & 2–5pm daily; Nov– Mar: 2–5pm daily.*

Babenhausen ❸

Road map B4. 🏠 *5,600.*
🚌 🚉 **i** *Auf des Wies 12, (08333) 93 132.*
www.babenhausen-schwaben.de

The most prominent land-marks in this town are the castle and the parish church.

The **castle**, which is mentioned as early as 1237, became the property of the von Rechberg family after 1378. It was probably they who were responsible for the steep-roofed two-storey edifice built here in the 15th century and incorporated into the castle. In 1539 the castle passed into the hands of the Fuggers (*see p253*), who refurbished it in 1541, adding the west and south wings. In 1955 the **Fuggermuseum** was founded, with the family retaining ownership of the park surrounding the castle.

The **church**, which is connected to the castle, was rebuilt in the Baroque style in 1715–30. The interior contains Baroque altars and a pulpit, as well as the tombs of the Rechbergs and Fuggers.

🏛 Fuggermuseum
Tel *(08333) 29 31.* ⏱ *Apr–Nov: 10am–noon & 2–5pm Tue–Sat, 10am–noon & 1–6pm Sun.* 📷

Ottobeuren ❷

Road map B4. 🏠 *8,000.* 🚌
🚉 **i** *Marktplatz 14, (08332) 92 19 50.* **www**.ottobeuren.de

The Benedictine abbey in Ottobeuren, whose beginnings go back to the 8th century, is one of the finest Baroque monasteries in Germany. The abbey **Church of St Theodore and St Alexander**, rebuilt and refurbished on numerous occasions, received its present appearance in 1748–66, when it was remodelled by Johann Michael Fischer.

Nestling in wooded slopes overlooking the River Günz, this fine monumental building is a breathtaking sight. The lavish interior, in a uniform Rococo style, features four domes, the largest of which is 25 m (82 ft) high. The decoration and furnishings are by various artists, including Johann Michael Feichtmayr and Johann Jakob and Franz Anton Zeiller.

The **abbey**, to the west of the church, is known as "the Escorial of Swabia". Built to plans by Christoph Vogt in 1711–31, it is an imposing quadrilateral edifice with four cloisters.

Ottobeuren Abbey has been in the hands of Benedictine monks since its foundation. Today the Library, the Abbot's Chapel, the Theatre Hall and the Knights' Hall are open to visitors.

The **Klostermuseum** contains exhibits that include sculpture dating from the 12th to the 18th centuries, the works of artists who worked in Ottobeuren (on the church murals, for example), clocks and other artifacts.

The abbey's Kaisersaal is occupied by the **Staatsgalerie**, an interesting art gallery devoted to the works, mostly on religious themes, of Swabian Gothic

The castle and church in Babenhausen

Kirchheim ❹

Road map B4. ⚒ *1,500.*
🚌 🚆 *Mindelheim.*
ℹ *Marktplatz 6, (08266) 86 080.*
www.kirchheim-schwaben.de

The main attraction of this small town is the Renaissance **castle**, owned by the Fugger family since the mid-16th century. The famous Cedar Hall is decorated with wood-carvings on its ceiling and door, and on its window surrounds and chimneypieces.

The altar of **Peter- und Paulskirche** features a painting of the Holy Family ascribed to Domenichino and of the Assumption ascribed to Rubens. Also worth seeing is the tomb of Hans Fugger, who died in 1598. Made of white lime-stone, it was the work of Alexander Colin.

Knight statue, Kirchheim Castle

Part of the inlaid ceiling of the Cedar Hall at Kirchheim Castle

Mindelheim ❺

Road map B4. ⚒ *13,500.* 🚌
🚆 ℹ *Maximilianstr. 26, (08261) 99 15 20.* **www**.mindelheim.de
📅 *Frundsbergfest (every three years, the next in 2012).*

During the 15th and 16th centuries **Mindelburg**, built by Heinrich der Löwe in 1160, belonged to the Frundsberg family, as did the whole town. The castle was rebuilt in the late 15th to early 16th centuries and again in the late 19th century.

The town's two main streets, Maximilianstraße and Kornstraße, are lined with fine town houses. The former

Jesuit **Maria Verkündigungs-kirche**, built in 1625–6 and refurbished in 1721, has fine stuccowork and altars.

Stephanskirche, built in the early 18th century and rebuilt in the early 20th century, contains the tomb of Duke Ulrich von Teck and his two brides. In the former chapel of St Sylvester is the **Schwäbisches Turmuhrenmuseum**, displaying belfry clocks.

🏛 **Schwäbisches Turm-uhrenmuseum**
Hungerbachgasse 9.
Tel (08261) 69 64.
🕐 2–5pm Wed & the last Sun in the month.

Bad Wörishofen ❻

Road map B4. ⚒ *14,400.*
🚌 🚆 ℹ *Luitpold-Leusser-Platz. 2, (08247) 99 33 55/56.*
www.bad-woerishofen.de

This spa resort owes its existence to Duke Sebastian Kneipp. Among the 19th-century guest houses here are the **Sebastianeum** at Kneipp-straße 8 and the **Kneippianum** at Alfred-Baumgartenstraße 6. The **Justinakirche** and **Klosterkirche** both have decoration by Dominik and Johann Baptist Zimmermann.

🏛 **Sebastian-Kneipp-Museum**
Schulstr. **Tel** (08247) 39 56 13.
🕐 15 Jan–15 Nov: 3–6pm Tue–Sun.

Kaufbeuren ❼

Road map D4. ⚒ *44,000.*
🚌 🚆 ℹ *Kaiser-Max-Str. 1, (08341) 40 405.* **www**.kaufbeuren.de
📅 *Tänzelfest (Jul).*

With steep, winding narrow streets lined with colourful houses, the hilltop town of Kaufbeuren retains much of its medieval character.

The old town still has its fortifications, complete with walls and defensive towers, one of which is the Fünfknopf-turm, which was built in about 1420. After World War II, Neugablonz, a settlement for refugees from Sudeten-land, now part of the Czech Republic, was built here.

The Gothic Fünfknopfturm, part of Kaufbeuren's fortifications

---

SEBASTIAN KNEIPP (1821–1897)

Sebastian Kneipp, a parish priest from St Justin's Church in Bad Wörishofen, introduced a method of therapy involving five factors – water, movement, herbal treatment, diet and inner harmony – but above all cold baths, showers and exercise. In 1903 a monument to Duke Kneipp was erected in the street bearing his name. Portraits of the clergyman (painted in 1936) can be seen on the ceiling of Justinakirche, and the town's former Dominican monastery contains a museum dedicated to him. The local rose-gardens also grew a new variety of rose, the Kneipp Rose.

The Kneipp Monument in Bad Wörishofen

Schloss Neuschwanstein seen against its woodland backdrop

Neuschwanstein ⑧

Road map B5. ⛪
Neuschwansteinstr. 20,
Hohenschwangau, (08362) 93 08
30. **www**.neuschwanstein.com

Schloss Neuschwanstein, one
of Ludwig II's most renowned
castles, was built at enormous
expense from 1868 to 1892. It
received its present name
after the king's death in 1886.

The monumental castle,
based on Wartburg Castle in
Thuringia, was built to plans
by the theatre designer
Christian Jank, who expressed
the king's vision inspired by
Wagner's operas *Lohengrin*
and Tannhäuser. The interior
decoration was executed by
Julius Hoffmann in 1880.

The castle has a breath-
taking situation on an outcrop
of rock towering over a gorge
in the River Pöllat. There is a
particularly memorable view
from Marienbrücke, which
giddily spans the rushing
waters in the ravine below.

⛪ **Schloss Neuschwanstein**
◯ *Apr–Sep: 9am–6pm daily;*
Oct–Mar: 10am–4pm daily.
⬤ *1 Jan, 24, 25, 31 Dec.* ▨ ▨

Schloss Hohenschwangau ⑨

Road map B5. ⛪ *Alpseestr. 12,*
(08362) 93 08 30.
www.hohenschwangau.de

This 14th-century castle,
which was destroyed during
the Napoleonic Wars, was
acquired by Maximilian II, the
king of Bavaria, in 1832. The
restoration and rebuilding

work executed up to 1837
was primarily the work of
Domenico Quaglio.

A bulky building, set with
towers and painted yellow, it
is situated over a lake against
a picturesque backdrop of
Alpine scenery.

⛪ **Schloss Hohenschwangau**
◯ *Apr–Sep: 9am–6pm daily;*
Oct–Mar: 10am–4pm daily. ▨

Statue of the Madonna and Child
in St Mang-Kirche at Füssen

Füssen ⑩

Road map B5. ⛫ *16,450.*
⛪ *Kaiser-Maximilian-Platz 1, (08362)*
93 850. **www**.stadt-fuessen.de

The town's location in the
foothills of the Alps,
surrounded by lakes and
overlooking the River Lech,
together with its proximity to
Schloss Neuschwanstein and
Schloss Hohenschwangau,
ensure that it is always full
of tourists.

In Roman times Füssen
stood on the road connecting
northern Italy with Augsburg.
In 1313 it passed into the
hands of the bishops of

Augsburg, who made it their
summer residence. The
town's rapid growth was
interrupted by the Thirty
Years' War and a fire in 1713.
After the secularization of the
state and its incorporation
into Bavaria in 1803, Füssen
again enjoyed a period of
prosperity, thanks to the
interest the Bavarian
kings took in the region.

Füssen has many fine old
buildings. The medieval
castle has an arcaded façade
decorated with trompe-l'oeil
paintings executed in 1499.
Its halls now house the **Filial-**
galerie der Bayerischen
Staatsgemäldesammlungen
(art gallery).

The **Benedictine monas-**
tery, founded in the 9th
century, now houses the
Museum der Stadt Füssen, a
local history museum, where
a collection of locally made
lutes and violins is displayed.
Beside it is **St Mang-Kirche**,
built in 1720-21. The façade
of **Heilig-Geist-Spitalkirche**,
painted by Joseph Anton
Walch in 1749, is also of note.

🏛 **Museum der Stadt Füssen**
Lechhalde 3. **Tel** *(08362) 90 31 45.*
◯ *Apr–Oct: 11am–5pm Tue–Sun;*
Nov–Mar: 1–4pm Fri–Sun. ▨

🏛 **Filialgalerie der**
Bayerischen Staats-
gemäldesammlungen
Magnusplatz 10. **Tel** *(08362) 90*
31 45. ◯ *Apr–Oct: 11am–5pm*
Tue–Sun; Nov–Mar: 1–4pm
Fri–Sun. ▨

The painted façade of Heilig-Geist-
Spitalkirche in Füssen

Around Neuschwanstein ⓫

This tour, probably the most scenic in the whole of Bavaria, takes about a day, as it inevitably involves queueing for tickets at both the castles. They are reached from car parks at the foot of Schloss Hohenschwangau. An effortless way of reaching the giddy heights of Schloss Neuschwanstein is by horse-drawn chaise. Another memorable experience is a boat trip on Alpsee.

Kolomanskirche ①
This small, distinctive Baroque church of 1673–82 stands in isolation at the foot of Schwangauer Berge.

Tegelbergbahn ②
Recently discovered remains of Roman buildings can be seen from the lower station of this cable car, which runs to the summit of Tegelberg.

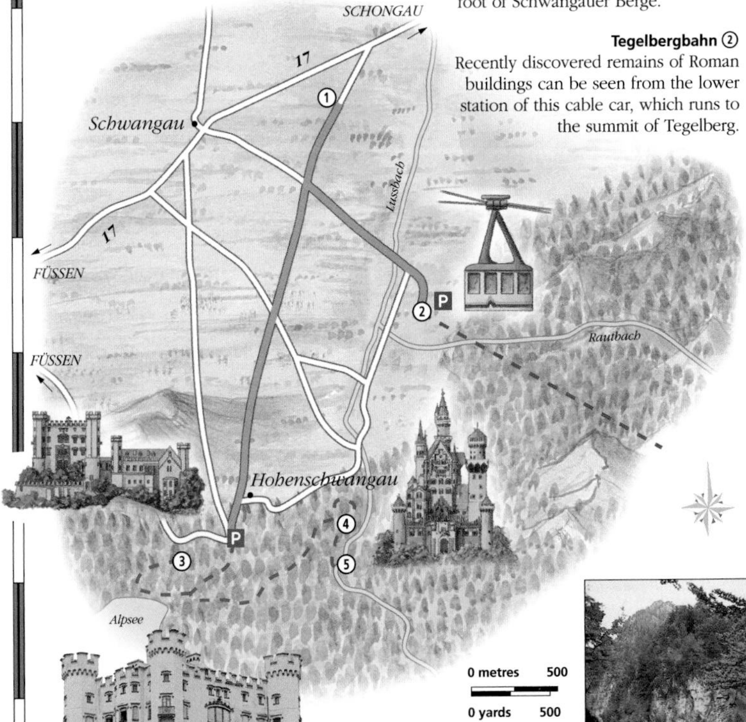

SCHONGAU

Schwangau

FÜSSEN

FÜSSEN

Hohenschwangau

Alpsee

Lussbach

Rautbach

| 0 metres | 500 |
| 0 yards | 500 |

Marienbrücke ⑤
The cast-iron bridge that spans the Pöllat gorge is constantly occupied by people fascinated by staring 90 m (300 ft) down into the giddy depths.

Schloss Hohenschwangau ③
Part of the richly furnished interior of this castle is open to visitors.

KEY

- Suggested route
- Suggested walk
- Other road
- Railway line
- P Parking

Neuschwanstein ④
The white silhouette of Ludwig II's castle, set with numerous turrets, has an almost surreal appearance when it is seen against the woodland backdrop, which changes colour through the seasons.

TIPS FOR VISITORS

Length of route: about 15 km (9 miles).
Stopping-off places: Meals and refreshments are available near Schloss Hohenschwangau and Schloss Neuschwanstein.

The Oberstdorf ski jumps, where the Four Ski Jumps Tournament is held

Bad Hindelang ⑫

Road map B5. 🏔 4,900. 🚍 🚉
Sonthofen. 🛈 *Am Bauernmarkt 1,
(08324) 89 20.*
www.hindelang.net

This health resort is set in beautiful woodland scenery in the Ostrach river valley. The town is best explored by walking down Marktstraße, starting from the Neo-Gothic **church**. The 17th-century **bishop's palace** opposite now houses the town hall. The beautifully restored houses are covered in colourful flowers in summer.

Lüftlmalerei on a hotel in Hindelang

Environs
About 1 km (0.6 mile) south of Hindelang is the spa resort of **Bad Oberdorf. Hinterstein**, 6 km (4 miles) further on, is popular with mountaineers. The road to **Oberjoch**, 6.5 km (4.5 miles) northeast, known as the Jochstraße, is the most tortuous section of the **Deutsche Alpenstraße**.

Oberstdorf ⑬

Road map B6. 🏔 12,000. 🚍 🚉
🛈 *Prinzregenten-Platz 1, (08322) 7000.* **www**.oberstdorf.de

The best-known health resort and holiday centre in the Allgäu, Oberstdorf, situated in the Iller river valley, is also renowned for its **ski jumps** on the slope of Schattenberg.

One event in the Four Ski Jumps Tournament is held here every year. The best-known ski jump in Oberstdorf is in the Stillach valley. It was the first large-scale ski jump (*Skiflugschanze*) in the world, and competitors can achieve distances of more than 170 m (550 ft). It was built in 1949–50 by the ski jumper and architect Heini Klopfer. The town itself, with its narrow streets and old houses, is extremely attractive. The **Heimatmuseum** has exhibits relating to local history, and includes the world's largest shoe.

🏛 Heimatmuseum
Oststr. 13. **Tel** (08322) 54 70.
🕐 10am–noon & 2–5:30pm
Tue–Sun & public hols.

Environs
The **Breitach river gorge**, 6 km (4 miles) west of Oberstdorf, is a major attraction. A vertiginous track winds for 2 km (1.25 mile) above the water that rushes between sheer cliffs rising to heights of 100 m (325 ft).

For the walk, a waterproof overgarment and sturdy hiking boots will be needed.

At the **Sturmannshöhle** cave outside **Fischen**, some 200 steps lead to a large cavern with impressive stalactites and stalagmites. The cave's galleries are connected by rushing underground streams that can be heard from the cave mouth.

Immenstadt ⑭

Road map B5. 🏔 14,000. 🚍
🚉 🛈 *Marienplatz 12, (08323) 91 41 76.* **www**.immenstadt.de
🎿 *Klausentreiben (5–6 Dec).*

It is best to approach Immenstadt from the north, as this route provides a fine view of Alpsee. The town has much to offer to watersports enthusiasts and mountaineers. It also contains many historic buildings. **Nikolauskirche** has been rebuilt several times since the Middle Ages. In 1602–20 a **palace** was built on the market square. One of its apartments has a stucco-work ceiling of about 1720 with hunting scenes and views of castles. The **town hall** was built in 1649 and the local history museum is in a **mill** dating from about 1451.

Environs
2 km (1.25 mile) north is **Bühl**, where Stephanskirche contains a chapel that was built as a replica of the Holy Sepulchre in Jerusalem. The nearby Maria Loretto Chapel with the Cottage of Our Lady of Loretto is made up of the Baroque choir of St Annakapelle.

Lindau ⑮

See pp234–5.

Sarcophagus in Nikolauskirche in Immenstadt

Wasserburg 16

Road map A5. 🏔 *2,900.*
🚌 🚉 ℹ *Lindenplatz 1, (08382)
88 74 74.* **www.**wasserburg-
bodensee.de

With a stunningly beautiful
location on the tip of a
promontory on Bodensee
(Lake Constance), Wasserburg
is a charming village of
flower-filled streets with
views of the lake and its
backdrop of hills. Its location
makes it a popular place for
sailing and other watersports.

The village's history dates
from the 8th century, then in
the 10th century a **castle** was
built here to resist Hungarian
invaders. The castle was
modernized in the 13th
century and rebuilt after a fire
in 1358. It is a three-winged
building with an irregular
plan. The east wing is a
vestige of the medieval
structure, while the south
wing dates from the 16th
century and the west wing
from the 18th century. It is
now a hotel.

Georgskirche is equally
historic. It was founded in the
8th century but was later
converted and together with
the cemetery wall was
incorporated into the town's
fortifications. Remnants of
these defences reach down to
the shores of the lake. The
present building is a late
Gothic fortified hall dating
from the second half of the
15th century.

The square tower, built in
1396–1403, was given its
onion dome in 1656. The
church is connected to a
two-storey presbytery.

The **Malhaus** (1597), once
a residence of the Fuggers
(see p252), now houses a
museum illustrating the
culture of the region and
also the fishing industry,
formerly Wasserburg's
main source of livelihood.

🏛 **Museum im Malhaus**
*Halbinselstr. 77. **Tel** (08382) 89
369.* ⏱ *Apr–Oct: 10:30am–
12:30pm Tue–Sun, 2:30–5pm
Wed, Sat & Sun.*

Georgskirche beside Bodensee
(Lake Constance) in Wasserburg

Kempten 17

See pp236–7.

Maria Steinbach 18

Road map A4. 🚌 🚉 *Leutkirch.*
ℹ *Markt Legau, Marktplatz 1,
(08330) 94 010.* **www.**legau.de

Maria Steinbach is famed
for its pilgrimage church,
Mariä Schmerzen, which is
a masterpiece of Rococo
architecture. Situated on
a hill in the idyllic rolling

The Rococo church in Maria Steinbach

landscape of the Iller river
valley, the church was built
in 1746–54 on the site of
earlier Romanesque and
Gothic shrines.

The building was inspired
by the works of Dominik
Zimmermann. The undulating
façades, with trompe-l'oeil
painting, conceal a dazzling
interior. The outstanding
mouldings and painting by
Franz Georg Hermann, the
stuccowork of the altars,
pulpit, stalls, confessionals
and organ loft combine to
produce a unified whole.

The figure of the Grieving
Madonna, which since 1730
has been renowned for its
miracle-working powers,
was an object of pilgrimage in
southern Germany during
the 18th century.

The group of **presbytery
buildings** set around a
courtyard west of the church
dates from the mid-18th
century. The **Wallfahrtsmuseum** contains a large
collection of votive gifts made
to the Madonna by pilgrims.

🏛 **Wallfahrtsmuseum**
*Kirchhof 4. **Tel** (08394) 92 40.*
⏱ *by appointment.*

Bodensee (Lake Constance) and the Alps seen from Wasserburg

Lindau

Fresco in Peterskirche

Lindau is the only town on Bodensee (Lake Constance) that is officially in Bavaria. The old part of the town, which stands on an island in the lake, is connected to the mainland by a railway and road bridge. Founded as a fishing settlement in Roman times, Lindau is an extremely pleasant town. It was granted the status of a city in the 13th century. It still retains its medieval plan, which is based around three long parallel streets.

Maximipanstraße, the main street in Lindau

🏛 Maximilianstraße

The town's main street, Maximilianstraße, is also its widest. Like the parallel streets of In der Grub and Ludwigstraße, it contains houses dating from the 15th to 19th centuries.

The small, compact houses with gables facing the street have windows that are often divided by columns, while the façades are broken up by oriels. The arcades and the old hoisting devices of the warehouses in the garrets bear witness to the town's character as a centre of trade.

🏛 Altes Rathaus

Bismarckplatz 4.
The old town hall, built in 1422–36, was remodelled several times during the 16th century, and again in 1724 and 1865. The programme of rebuilding that took place in 1885–7 was undertaken by Friedrich von Thiersch, who restored the stepped gable that had been removed in 1865 and reconstructed the exterior staircase. The façade was also painted by Joseph Widmann.

🏛 Neues Rathaus

Bismarckplatz 3.
The new town hall, built in 1706–17, was also remodelled by Friedrich von Thiersch in 1885. A two-storey building crowned by a tall shaped gable decorated with vases and obelisks, it now houses a cloth shop.

🏛 Haus zum Cavazzen

Marktplatz 6. **Städtisches Museum**
Tel (08382) 94 40 73.
◯ Easter–Oct: 11am–5pm Tue–Fri, Sun, 2–5pm Sat. 📷
This elegant patrician building is named after the de Cavazzo

family, in whose ownership it was from 1540 to 1617.

The present Baroque house was built for the von Seutter family in 1729–30. It has a tall mansard roof and the façade is covered with paintings of herms, atlantes, sphinxes and garlands of fruit. The house now accommodates the **Städtisches Museum** (local history museum), which contains an interesting collection of artisans' tools.

🔒 Stephanskirche

Marktplatz 8. **Tel** (08382) 33 44.
Originally a Catholic church, it became a Protestant church in 1528. The original 12th-century Romanesque building was refurbished several times during the 14th, 15th and 16th centuries. Its present-day form – a three-nave, barrel-vaulted basilica – dates from 1781–3, when it was remodelled.

🔒 Münster "unserer Lieben Frau"

Stiftsplatz 1. **Tel** (08382) 58 50.
The church originally belonged to the Benedictine monks who settled here in about 800. Vestiges of the pre-Romanesque church, which was built after 948, are preserved in the west wall. In about 1100 a Romanesque basilica with a transept and a west tower was built.

After the fire that devastated the town in 1728, the church was rebuilt to its Romanesque plan. The present airy Baroque church, lavishly decorated with mouldings and wall paintings, resulted from work carried out in 1748–55 under the direction of Johann Caspar Bagnato.

Baroque epitaph in the Haus zum Cavazzen

A lion and a lighthouse framing the harbour entrance against the Alps

VISITORS' CHECKLIST

Road map A5. 🏚 *25,000.*
🚌 *Tel (08382) 94 44 16.*
ℹ *Ludwigstr. 68, (08382)
26 00 30.*
www.Lindau.de;
www.prolindau.de
@ info@prolindau.de

🛥 The Harbour

The harbour that was built at the southern end of the island in 1811 was modernized in 1856. A marble Lion of Bavaria set on a pedestal 6 m (20 ft) high was added to the tip of the mole at the harbour entrance. A new lighthouse, 33 m (108 ft) high was built on the tip of the opposite mole. These two structures came to symbolize Lindau.

The promenade beside the harbour, where the former lighthouse, known as the **Mangturm**, stands, is popular with tourists. Built in about 1200, the old lighthouse has a projecting upper storey with a pointed steeple covered in 19th-century glazed tiles. It was originally part of the city's fortifications.

⛪ Peterskirche

Oberer Schrannenplatz 5/7.

This is the oldest church in the entire Bodensee region. The presbytery and eastern section date from about 1180. The western part was added in the late 15th century. The five-storey tower that stands near the apse, and that was originally in the Romanesque style, was rebuilt in 1425. The interior walls are decorated with frescoes dating from the 13th to 16th centuries. They include works ascribed to Hans Holbein the Elder. Since 1928 the church has functioned as a memorial to war heroes.

Beside the church stands the **Diebsturm** (Thieves' Tower), a circular watchtower built in 1370–80, which was used in conjunction with the Pulverturm (Powder Tower), Ludwigsbastion and Maximilianschanze (Maximilian's Redoubt).

The Mangturm, formerly a lighthouse and watchtower

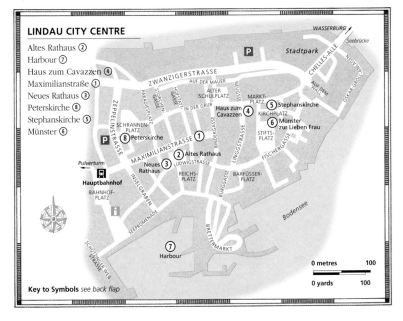

LINDAU CITY CENTRE

Altes Rathaus ②
Harbour ⑦
Haus zum Cavazzen ④
Maximilianstraße ①
Neues Rathaus ③
Peterskirche ⑧
Stephanskirche ⑤
Münster ⑥

WASSERBURG
Seebrücke
Stadtpark
CHELLES-ALLEE
ZWANZIGERSTRASSE
AUF DER MAUER
AUF DEM WALL
STOCKGASSE
HOFSTATTGASSE
PARADIEPLATZ
IN DER GRUB
ALTER SCHULPLATZ
SCHULPLATZ
ZEPPELINSTRASSE
MARKT-PLATZ
Haus zum Cavazzen ④
KIRCHPLATZ
⑤ Stephanskirche
BINDERGASSE
⑥ Münster zur Lieben Frau
STIFTS-PLATZ
OSKAR-GROLL
ANLAGEN
SCHRANNEN-PLATZ
⑧ Peterskirche
MAXIMILIANSTRASSE ①
② Altes Rathaus
Neues ③ LUDWIGSTRASSE
Rathaus
LINGGSTRASSE
FISCHERGASSE
Pulverturm
Hauptbahnhof
BAHNHOF-PLATZ
INSELGRABEN
REICHS-PLATZ
BURGGASSE
BARFÜSSER-PLATZ
Bodensee
SEEPROMENADE
BRETTERMARKT
⑦ Harbour
SCHÜTZINGER WEG
SCHÜTZINGER STRASSE

0 metres   100
0 yards   100

Key to Symbols *see back flap*

Kempten

Originally a Roman town, Kempten was divided into a monastic and a secular district in the Middle Ages. The monastic district was centred around a Benedictine abbey, and in 1712 the monks were granted city rights. The secular district of Burghalde, which grew at the foot of the hill, was a Free City of the Empire from 1289 and accepted the Reformation in 1527. In 1802 the two districts were combined into a single entity and incorporated into Bavaria. Today Kempten is the Allgäu's thriving capital.

Coat of arms on the town hall

The late Gothic façade of St Mang Kirche, with its tall tower

Façade of the town hall, featuring Kempten's coats of arms

🏛 Rathaus
Rathausplatz.
The late Gothic town hall, built in 1474, has a stepped gable crowned by a small tower. The wooden ceilings of the interior date from about 1460 and originally came from the house of the weavers' guild. Before the town hall stands a copy of a Mannerist fountain of 1601.

🏛 Rathausplatz
The square on which the town hall stands is lined with patrician palaces and merchants' and guildsmens' houses, which were either remodelled or newly built in the Baroque and Neo-Classical periods. The three-storey Londonerhof at No. 2 has a Rococo façade lavishly covered with stuccowork and featuring a Neo-Baroque doorway of 1899. The Hotel Fürstenhof at No. 8 was built in about 1600. The Ponickau-haus at Nos. 10 and 12 was

created in 1740 when two 16th-century houses were knocked together, the first floor being converted into a lavishly decorated Festsaal.

🔒 St Mang-Kirche
St.-Mang-Platz 6.
The original church dedicated to St Mang was built in 869. The present church dates from 1426–28, when it was built as the parish church of the Free Imperial City. In 1525 it became a Protestant church, and was remodelled as a three-nave basilica with a tall tower. It was most recently rebuilt in 1767–8, when the vaulting and late Rococo mouldings were added.

🏛 The Residence
Residenzplatz. **Prunkräume der Residenz** *Tel* (0831) 25 62 51.
🕐 Apr–Sep: 9am–4pm Tue–Sun; Oct: 10am–4pm Tue–Sun; Nov–Mar: 10am–4pm Sat. 📷
In 1651–74 a group of 11th-century buildings, which were destroyed in 1632, was replaced by a new Baroque monastery. It was also a

residence. The monastery consists of buildings grouped around two courtyards. The elegant apartments on the second floor, which were decorated in 1732–42, echo those of the Residenz in Munich (*see pp74–7*). The mouldings were executed by stuccoists from Wessobrunn, while the vaulting is by Franz Georg Hermann. The Throne Hall is one of the finest examples of Bavarian and Swabian Rococo interiors.

🏛 The Orangery
The garden once adjoined the Residence on its southern side. The orangery that was built here in 1780 now houses the municipal library.

🏛 Alpinmuseum and Alpenländische Galerie
Landwehrstr. 4. *Tel* (0831) 25 25 740. 🕐 10am–4pm Tue–Sun. 📷 mid-Nov–1 Mar. 📷
The Alpine Museum, in the Residence's former stables, is dedicated primarily to skiing and mountaineering, but also encompasses topography and the natural environment, and

One of the fine apartments in the Residence

poetry and painting relating to the mountains. There is also a gallery of regional art.

🔒 Lorenzkirche

Landwehrstr. 3.
The church is a three-nave basilica with two pairs of domed side chapels and an octagonal presbytery that is also crowned by a dome. This arrangement created two separate areas: one for the faithful and one for the friars. The interior is breathtaking. The stuccowork in the nave, aisles and presbytery was executed by Giovanni Zuccalli in 1660–70, and the ceilings were painted by Andreas Asper. A comparatively modest twin-towered façade is fronted by a grand staircase. To the east of the presbytery stands the Residence.

The prominent towers and dome of the Lorenzkirche

🏯 Kornhaus

Großer Kornhausplatz 1. **Allgäu-Museum** *Tel* (0831) 54 02 120.
⬜ 10am–4pm Tue–Sun.
This former grain warehouse was built in 1700. Today it houses a museum dedicated to the history, culture and art of the town and the region.

VISITORS' CHECKLIST

Road map B5. 🚊 *68,000.* 🚌
🚉 *Bahnhofplatz.* 🛈 *Rathausplatz 24, (0831) 25 25 237 or 19 433.* **www**.*kempten.de*
@ *touristinfo@kempten.de*
🎭 *Allgäuer Festwoche (Aug).*

🔒 Burghalde

Burgstr.
In 1488 a castle was built on a hill beside the River Iller, where a Roman fort once stood. The castle was incorporated into the town's fortifications and was then demolished in 1705. Part of the town walls, together with the northern tower and its wooden gatehouse of 1883 survive. Today, Burghalde is an open-air theatre with concerts and cinema. You can also walk round the town walls.

🏛 Archäologischer Park Cambodunum

Cambodunumweg 3.
Tel (0831) 79 731. ⬜ May–Oct: 10am–5pm Tue–Sun; Nov–Apr: 10am–4:30pm Tue–Sun. ⬤ Jan–Feb. 📷
Kempten was once the Roman settlement of Cambodunum. Excavations have uncovered a forum, a basilica and baths. The most impressive building was the basilica, which was as large as the present St Lorenz-Basilica.

Remains of Roman baths in the settlement of Cambodunum

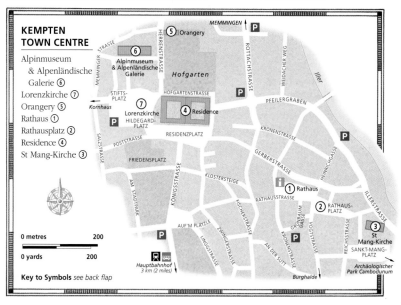

KEMPTEN TOWN CENTRE

Alpinmuseum & Alpenländische Galerie ⑥
Lorenzkirche ⑦
Orangery ⑤
Rathaus ①
Rathausplatz ②
Residence ④
St Mang-Kirche ③

0 metres 200
0 yards 200

Key to Symbols *see back flap*

NORTHERN SWABIA

Northern Swabia constitutes that part of historical Swabia that now belongs to Bavaria, hence its name – Bayerisches Schwaben (Bavarian Swabia). In terms of its politics and its culture as well as its scenery, it is the most diverse region of southern Bavaria. Its main attractions for tourists are its historic towns, notably Augsburg, the great Ries Basin and its scenic river valleys.

Throughout the course of history, this region was divided into numerous ducal and monastic possessions and Imperial Cities (Reichsstädte). This served to promote the development of art, which can be seen in the region's castles and palaces and particularly in its churches and monasteries. From 1803 Swabia formed part of Bavaria, and was subjected to assimilation. However, in this transitional area between the German states of Bavaria and Baden-Württemberg, significant differences in attitude, language and customs survive to this day among Swabians.

The historical need for differentiation, self-definition and individuality has made Swabia a country of small towns each with their own character and history. This is particularly apparent during local festivals.

The scenery is equally diverse and varied. The north consists of the rolling wooded hills of the western Schwäbische Alb massif. Beside them lies the Nördlinger Ries. This area, renowned for its microclimate and its rich soil, has been inhabited since Palaeolithic times.

The Danube cuts through the northern part of Swabian Bavaria. The extensive moors of the Donauried (the Danube valley) bear witness to frequent river flooding in the past. Lying almost parallel from south to north are the great moraine valleys of the Iller, the Günz and the Lech.

Augsburg, almost in the centre of the region and founded in Roman times, was an early centre of the Reformation and of goldsmiths. West of Augsburg is the Westliche Wälder, a vast forest reserve whose unspoiled scenery makes it popular with hikers.

A flower shop in Augsburg, with its displays spilling onto the pavement

◁ Golden Hall of the Town Hall in Augsburg

Exploring Northern Swabia

Northern Swabia's principal city is Augsburg. The third-largest city in Bavaria after Munich and Nuremberg, Augsburg demands several days' exploration, as it has much to offer of architectural interest. The city is also a useful starting point for various excursions. Within easy reach to the north are the Ries Basin, a huge crater nestling the town of Nördlingen, and the impressive Harburg Castle, as well as towns on the Danube such as Donauwörth, Dillingen and Günzburg. In the southwest are the castles belonging to the Fugger family. With their varied architecture and scenic settings, all of the region's towns have much to interest visitors.

Christ on a donkey, from the former Augustinian monastery at Wettenhausen

SIGHTS AT A GLANCE

GETTING AROUND

Two motorways run through Swabia. The A8, running along an east–west axis, connects Munich and Stuttgart via Augsburg and Günzburg. The A7 runs in a north–south direction, following the course of the River Iller. Parallel to it is the Romantische Straße (Romantic Route), which passes through towns such as Nördlingen, Harburg, Donauwörth and Augsburg. The good road network makes the other towns of the region easily accessible by car or by bus. The larger cities also have rail links. Situated near to Munich, Augsburg has its own airport.

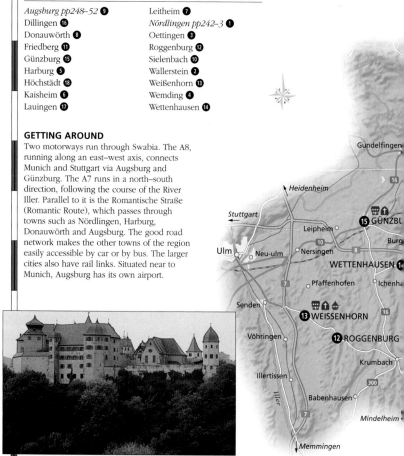

Harburg Castle in its picturesque location

SEE ALSO

• **Where to Stay** p269.

• **Where to Eat** p283.

KEY

═══ Motorway

──── Major road

──── Minor road

┄┄┄ Main railway

──── Minor railway

──── Regional border

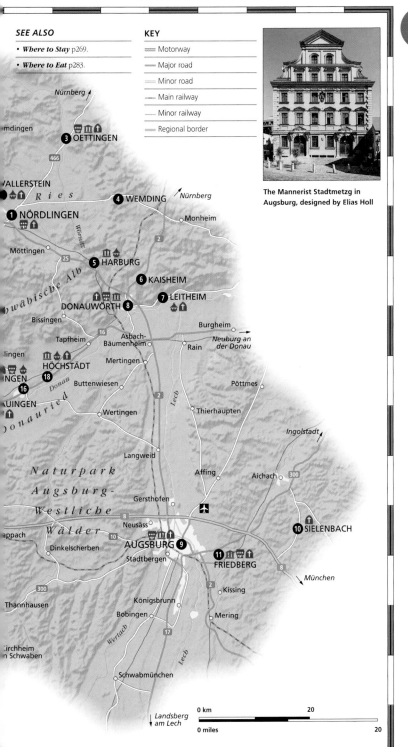

The Mannerist Stadtmetzg in Augsburg, designed by Elias Holl

Nürnberg

mdingen

3 OETTINGEN

466

WALLERSTEIN

Ries

4 WEMDING   Nürnberg

1 NÖRDLINGEN   Monheim

Möttingen

2

25

Wörnitz

5 HARBURG

Schwäbische Alb   **6** KAISHEIM

7 LEITHEIM

DONAUWÖRTH **8**

Bissingen

Burgheim

Tapfheim   Asbach-   Neuburg an
16   Bäumenheim   der Donau

lingen   Rain

Mertingen

18 HÖCHSTÄDT   *Donau*

NGEN

16   Buttenwiesen

Donauried   Pöttmes

Wertingen   *Lech*

Thierhaupten

Ingolstadt

Langweid

Naturpark   Affing   Aichach   300

Augsburg-

Westliche   Gersthofen

Wälder   Neusäss

ppach   8

Dinkelscherben   10   **10** SIELENBACH

AUGSBURG **9**

Stadtbergen   **11** FRIEDBERG

300   2   München

Thannhausen   Kissing   8

Königsbrunn

Bobingen   Mering

17

Wertach   *Lech*

Kirchheim
in Schwaben   Schwabmünchen

0 km   20

↓ Landsberg
am Lech   0 miles   20

Nördlingen ●

Coat of arms in Baldingerstraße

Nördlingen, encircled by defensive walls, is the "capital" of the Ries Basin and one of the most picturesque towns in Swabia. Several hours can be spent wandering along its streets and alleys, where the Gothic and the Renaissance periods have left their mark. In the 14th century the town almost doubled in size and was surrounded by walls. The streets that run from the five town gates merge on Marktplatz, at the heart of the town. A good time to visit is in July, when the Scharlachrennen, a horse race and parade dating back to the 15th century, is held.

Exploring Nördlingen

The most attractive aspect of Nördlingen is its houses, most of which are half-timbered, with colourful, cascading window boxes. Many of the houses are several storeys high, with attic storerooms. In the Gergerviertel, the tanners' quarter, the houses on the River Eger are well preserved. Two of the town's most interesting houses are that at Paradiesstraße 4, dating from 1350 and the town's oldest half-timbered house, and the 1678 Wintersches Haus at Braugasse 2, the best-preserved private house in Nördlingen.

Bas-relief of a fool on the town hall

🏛 Rathaus

Marktplatz 1.
The town hall was built in the 13th century and rebuilt after 1500, acquiring its present form at the beginning of the 17th century. Its most noteworthy feature is the external stone stairway, built by Wolfgang Waldberger. Beside the doors beneath the stairway is a bas-relief depicting a fool, with the ironic inscription "*Nun sind unser zwey*" ("Now it is the two of us") addressing the reader. The wall of the grand Federal Room on the second floor has a painting of the heroic feats of biblical Judith by Hans Schäufelein.

🔒 Georgskirche

Am Obstmarkt.
Georgskirche, built in 1427–1505, stands in the centre of the town. Like many other buildings in the region, it was built with suevite from the Ries Basin (*see p244*). The interior features finely carved late Gothic stalls and a pulpit, a sacrarium of 1522–5 and numerous epitaphs and tombs. The tower, 90 m (295 ft) high, known as the Daniel Tower, can be seen from far away. A flight of 331 stairs leads to the top. The effort of climbing them is rewarded by a panoramic view of the Ries Basin. For 300 years a night watchman has called from the top of the tower, sometimes every half hour. Today this occurs only between 10pm and midnight.

🏛 Tanzhaus

Marktplatz 15.
This Gothic half-timbered hall dating from 1442–4 was built for official dances and receptions. The ground floor contained bakers' shops, which is why the building was also known as the Brothaus (Bread House). On a console on the eastern façade stands a Gothic statue of 1513. Known as *The Last Knight*, it depicts Maximilian I as a knight in armour. Maximilian was a frequent visitor to Nördlingen, which he greatly admired.

The richly decorated Mannerist doorway of the Klösterle

🔒 Klösterle

Beim Klösterle 1.
The monastery church known as the Barfüßerkirche, built in 1422, was converted into a Renaissance-style grain warehouse by Wolfgang Waldberger in 1584–6. The southern façade has a fine doorway dating from 1586, crowned with the town's coat of arms and decorated with figures of tradesmen. Today the Klösterle houses a hotel.

🏛 Hohes Haus

Marktplatz 16.
This tall, nine-storey house, next to the Tanzhaus, is the oldest brick building in Nördlingen. It is mentioned as early as 1304 and was used as a warehouse.

Organ loft in the Gothic Georgskirche

Spital

Vordere Gerbergasse 1. **Stadt-museum Tel** (09081) 27 38 23 0.
☐ 1 Mar– 4 Nov: 1:30–4:30pm
Tue–Sun. 🏛 Eugene-Shoemaker-Platz 1. **Rieskrater-Museum
Tel** (09081) 27 38 220.
☐ 10am–noon, 1:30pm–4:30pm
Tue–Sun. 🏛

The town's former hospital complex is the largest in Germany. The buildings of the Spitalkrankenhaus and Holzhofstadel that form part of it have been converted into museums.

The **Stadtmuseum**, founded in 1960, has a collection of paintings on panel by late Gothic and Renaissance artists including Friedrich Herlin, Hans Schäufelein and Sebastian Daig, and a model of the Battle of Nördlingen of 1634 with 6,000 tin soldiers. The **Rieskrater-Museum** features among its exhibits Moon rocks donated by NASA.

Hallgebäude

Weinmarkt 1.

On the south side of the Wine Market stands a fine building of 1543 with four attic storeys. A corner has polygonal oriels, one of them decorated with a cartouche containing the civic coat of arms. The building

The domed Löpsinger Tor, one of Nördlingen's five town gates

was once used for storing wine and salt, for currency offices and the town weights.

Alte Schranne

Schrannenplatz.

This storehouse, built in 1602, has a total of five storeys, three of which are in the attic

VISITORS' CHECKLIST

Road map B2 🚍 21,000. 🚆
🛈 Marktplatz 2, (09081) 84 116.
www.noerdlingen.de
@ tourist-information@
noerdlingen.de
🎭 Stabenfest (second Mon in
May); Scharlachrennen (Jul).

area. The southern façade features a sundial and an Art Nouveau fountain is in the square before the building.

Löpsinger Tor and Town Walls

Stadtmauermuseum Tel (09081) 91 80. ☐ Apr–Oct: 10am–4:30pm Tue–Sun.

The walls encircling Nördlingen were begun in 1327. The walkway around the fortifications provides a variety of views over the town. The walls are pierced by five gates, 12 towers and a bastion. All the gates except the Baldinger Tor have towers. They are the Reimlinger Tor, the oldest and largest gate, on the road from Augsburg; the Berger Tor; the Löpsinger Tor, which houses the **Stadtmauermuseum**, whose domed circular tower dates from 1593–4, and the taller and narrower Deininger Tor.

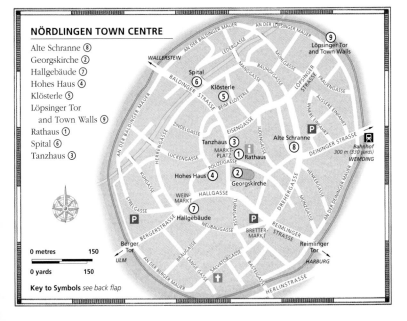

NÖRDLINGEN TOWN CENTRE

Alte Schranne ⑧
Georgskirche ②
Hallgebäude ⑦
Hohes Haus ④
Klösterle ⑤
Löpsinger Tor
   and Town Walls ⑨
Rathaus ①
Spital ⑥
Tanzhaus ③

0 metres   150

0 yards   150

Key to Symbols see back flap

Wallerstein ❷

Road map B2. 🏛 *3,200.* 🚍 🚉
ℹ️ *Weinstr. 19, (09081) 27 600.*
www.markt-wallerstein.de

Wallerstein is a small town at the foot of a hill on which stands a castle that commands a fine view of the Ries Basin. On the hilltop are the remains of 12th-century fortifications, which were destroyed in 1648, as well as a **ducal brewery** and restaurant.

The **Schloss Wallerstein** opposite the castle hill is surrounded by a park and contains a porcelain museum. **Albanskirche** was built in 1242 in the Gothic style. The **plague column** commemorates the Marseilles plague of 1722–25, has figures of saints and is crowned with figures of St Mary and the Holy Trinity.

Plague column in Wallerstein

> 🏰 **Schloss Wallerstein**
> Berg 78.
> ⭕ *9am–5pm Tue–Sun.* 📷

Oettingen ❸

Road map B2. 🏛 *5,200.*
🚍 🚉 ℹ️ *Schlossstr. 36, (09082) 70 90.* **www**.oettingen.de

This town, with an oval outline, was surrounded by a wall in the late 13th century. The town gates on the south side – the **Unteres Tor** and the **Königsturm**, which was built in the 16th century – still stands.

Schlossstraße, the main street, is lined with half-timbered town houses built between the 15th and 18th centuries. The 15th-century Gothic **town hall** contains the local history museum.

Despite their elegance, the **town houses** pale in comparison to **Residenzschloss**, the resplendent Baroque residence of the Dukes of Oettingen-Spielberg, built in 1679–83. To the west the palace looks out over landscaped gardens, which are peopled with statues of dwarfs and a Hercules of 1678 based on the statue on the fountain in Augsburg by Adriaen de Vries. The palace, whose interior is decorated with stuccowork and mural paintings, is now the **Staatliches Museum für Völkerkunde**. Visitors can see the apartments and reception rooms and admire the collections of 18th-century pewter, porcelain and faience. The palace courtyard is surrounded by outbuildings and has a fountain dating from 1720–28 in the centre.

The **Jakobskirche** which stands nearby was remodelled in the Baroque style after 1680 and decorated with stuccowork by Matthias Schmuzer the Younger. Inside is an interesting pulpit and baptismal font from the last quarter of the 17th century, and numerous tombstones and plaques from the 15th to 18th centuries.

> 🏛 **Staatliches Museum für Völkerkunde**
> Schlossstr. 1. **Tel** (09082) 39 10.
> ⭕ *11am–5pm Tue–Sun.* 📷

Wemding ❹

Road map B2. 🏛 *5,600.* 🚍
🚉 ℹ️ *Mangoldstr. 5, (09092) 96 90 35.* **www**.wemding.de

Set on the rim of the Ries Basin, this charming little town retains its medieval character. The main square, lined with Renaissance and Baroque houses with typically Bavarian decorated gables, has often been used as a location by filmmakers.

Prominent among these houses is the Renaissance **town hall** of 1551–2. On Wallfahrtstraße, near the gate tower, is a typical mid-16th-century house with a corner oriel, now the **Gasthaus zum Weißen Hahn** inn. The tower of **Emmeramskirche** dominates the skyline. The church dates from the 11th

Renaissance tombstone in Jakobskirche, Oettingen

RIES BASIN

This crater, 25 km (15 miles) across, was made when a meteorite hit the Earth 15 million years ago. The impact melted the rocks, creating suevite, or Swabian rock, which the local people used as a building material. NASA carried

Suevite on the edge of the Ries Basin

out scientific studies on the crater and used it for astronauts who were to be sent to the Moon. They later found rock identical to suevite on the Moon. A suevite moon rock donated by NASA can be seen in the Rieskrater-Museum *(see p243).*

---

century, but its current Baroque form is the result of rebuilding carried out in the 17th century.

It is worth taking a walk along the **defensive walls**, built in the first half of the 14th century and particularly well preserved on the north side of the town.

On the road leading out towards Oettingen the small pilgrimage chapel of **Maria Brünnlein** can be seen in the distance. The interior is decorated with Rococo mouldings and frescoes by Johann Baptist Zimmermann.

The Baroque palace and palace chapel at Leitheim

One of the courtyards in Harburg Castle

Harburg ❺

Road map B2. 🏠 5,900. 🚌 🚉
ℹ️ Schlossstr. 1, (09080) 96 99 24.
www.stadt-harburg-schwaben.de

The large **castle** was built by the Hohenstaufens before 1150. It was later acquired by the counts of Oettingen, and since 1731 has been in the possession of the Oettingen-Wallerstein family. It is one of the oldest, largest and best-preserved castles in southern Germany.

Dramatically situated on a high rocky hill overlooking the Wörmitz river valley, Harburg castle dominates the entire area. In the 14th and 15th centuries it was surrounded by walls set with towers. It has two entrance gates on the northwestern side, with a picturesque gatehouse dating from 1703. Within the walls stands

Michaelskirche, the castle church. At the bottom of the castle hill nestles the small town of Harburg. It is worth a visit for a walk around the charming and diminutive market square and along the winding streets, which have picturesque old houses.

🏛 **Burg Harburg**
Burgstr. 1. **Tel** (09080) 96 860.
⭕ three weeks before
Easter–Oct: 10am–5pm Tue–Sun.

Kaisheim ❻

Road map C2. 🏠 4,000. 🚌
🚉 ℹ️ Münsterplatz 5, (09099)
96 600. www.kaisheim.de

The extensive complex of the former Cistercian monastery consists of the 14th-century Gothic **Mariä Himmelfahrtskirche** as well as the monastery itself, which has two cloisters dating from 1716–21. The monastery was converted into a prison in the 19th century. The exquisite Kaisersaal (Imperial Hall), with ornate stuccowork, was completed in about 1720.

Notable features of the church include the Baroque organ loft of 1677, whose carvings are ascribed to Andreas Thamasch. In the nave is a sarcophagus of 1434 with a statue of the founder of the original Romanesque church, who died in 1142, showing him holding a model of the church in his hands.

Crest in the Kaisersaal, Kaisheim

Leitheim ❼

Road map C2. 🚌 🚉 Donauwörth.
ℹ️ Rathausgasse 1, Donauwörth,
(0906) 78 91 51.

Set high on a bank of the Danube, **Schloss Leitheim and a chapel** were built in 1685 to designs by Wölfl as a summer residence for Cistercian monks from the monastery at Kaisheim. For centuries the monks tended vineyards on the sunny slopes around the residence. Indeed, Leitheim was one of the centres of wine-making in the Danube region, and the quality of the wine produced here rivalled that of the Rhine wines.

The chapel was decorated in the late 17th century by artists from Wessobrunn. In the mid-18th century an additional storey and a mansard roof were added to the palace. The stuccowork and painting in the state rooms on the second floor are among the finest examples of Bavarian-Swabian Rococo.

After 1835 the palace passed into the hands of the Tucher von Simmeldorf family. The owners organize highly popular chamber concerts here.

♣ **Schloss Leitheim**
Schlossstr. 1. **Tel** (09097) 10 16.
⭕ May–Sep: by prior arrangement only.

Donauwörth ⑧

Road map C2. 👥 18,000. 🚌
📮 ℹ️ *Rathausgasse 1, (0906)
78 91 51.* **www**.donauwoerth.de
🎭 *Schwäbischwerder Kindertag
(first Sun in Jul), Reichsstraßenfest (Jul,
every two years, the next in 2011),
Donauwörther Kulturtage (Oct).*

Donauwörth is one of the
largest towns in Swabian
Bavaria. It is located at the
confluence of the Wörnitz
and the Danube, and its
development was shaped
largely by its position at the
point where major trade
routes crossed the Danube.

Reichsstraße, the main
street, is lined with colourful
gabled houses and is one of
the finest streets in southern
Germany. It stretches from **Zu
Unserer Lieben Frau**, the
church built in 1444–67 and
decorated with 15th- and
16th-century frescoes, to the
town hall, remodelled in the
Neo-Gothic style in 1854.

The west end of the town is
dominated by a former Bene-

ROMANTISCHE STRASSE

Information signpost at Neuschwanstein

The Romantic Route
follows the course of the
Roman Via Claudia.
Beginning in Franconian
Würzburg, it passes
through the towns of
Nördlingen, Donauwörth,
Augsburg, Landsberg,
Schongau, Steingaden and
Füssen, in southern
Bavaria, and ends at
Neuschwanstein, Ludwig
II's famous castle. The
best known and most
frequented of the tourist
routes in Germany, it is
particularly popular with
American and Japanese
tourists. Directions are
even given in Japanese.

The picturesque Reichsstraße in Donauwörth

dictine monastery, of which
the **Kreuzkirche**, built by
Josef Schmuzer in 1717–20,
formed a part.

Not to be missed is a walk
along the **town walls**, which
run parallel to an arm of the
Wörnitz. The **Riedertor**, one
of the two town gates, houses
a museum dedicated to the
town's history. Also worth
visiting are the **Heimatmuseum** of local history and
the **Käthe-Kruse-Puppen-
Museum**, with a collection of
dolls made by Käthe Kruse.

🏛 **Käthe-Kruse-Puppen-
Museum**
Pflegstr. 21a. **Tel** (0906) 78 91 70.
⬜ Apr and Oct: 2–5pm Tue–Sun;
May–Sep: 11am–5pm Tue–Sun; Nov–
Mar: 2–5pm Wed, Sat–Sun & public
hols; 25 Dec–6 Jan: 2–5pm daily.

🏛 **Heimatmuseum**
Hindenburgstr. 15.
Tel (0906) 78 91 70.
⬜ May–Oct: 2pm–5pm Tue–Sun;
Nov–Apr: 2pm–5pm Wed, Sat & Sun.

Augsburg ⑨

See pp248–53.

Sielenbach ⑩

Road map C3. 👥 1,500.
🚌 📮 *Weissenhorn.*
ℹ️ *Schweigstr. 16, (08258) 91 40.*
www.sielenbach.de

The pilgrimage church of
**Unserer Lieben Frau im Birn-
baum** (Mary in the Pear Tree)
is located at the southern end
of the town, which it

dominates. It is an exceptional
work of 17th-century
Bavarian architecture. It was
built in 1661–8 by Konstantin
Bader to a design by Jakob
von Kaltenthal, a Commander
of the Teutonic Knights. It
consists of five circular, semicircular and oval rooms. In
particular the towers and
onion domes are unique,
and are reminiscent of an
Eastern church.

The interior, which is lit
by large windows in the
shape of upright ovals and
decorated with stuccowork
by Matthias Schmuzer the
Younger, is far more unified.

The object of worship is a
late Gothic Pietà dating from
the early 16th century, to
which miraculous powers are
ascribed. It stands on the high
altar in a pear tree. The tree
and the name of the church
commemorate the miraculous
survival of the figure in 1632,
during the Thirty Years' War
when in the course of the
Swedish invasion the figure
survived thanks to its being
hidden in a pear tree.

Unserer Lieben Frau im Birnbaum, an Eastern-style church in Sielenbach

Friedberg ⑪

Road map C3. 👥 29,000. 🚌
📮 ℹ️ *Marienplatz 5, (0821) 60
02 611.* **www**.friedberg.de
🎭 *Friedberger Zeit (every three years
in Jul, the next in 2010).*

During the Middle Ages
this town was a fortress, its
purpose being to protect the
region from attacks by the
inhabitants of Augsburg. In
about 1490 defensive walls
set with semicircular towers

The Baroque town hall in Friedberg's main square

Elder and Johann Michael Feichtmayr. The silver antependium of the high altar was made by Johann Georg Herkomer of Augsburg. The altar in the south aisle contains a 15th-century group of figures of the Sorrowing Christ to which miraculous powers are ascribed. Votive images fill the aisles.

🏛 Museum der Stadt Friedberg im Schloss
Schlossstr. 21. **Tel** (0821) 600 21 48.
⏰ 2–6pm Tue–Fri, 11am–5pm Sat–Sun and public holidays.

were added. The medieval **castle** in the north of the town was destroyed during the Thirty Years' War and rebuilt in 1559. It now houses a local history museum, the **Museum der Stadt Friedberg**.

The streets are lined with outstanding houses dating from the 17th and 18th centuries. In the centre of the main square stands the **town hall**, built in 1673 and decorated in the style of Elias Holl. **Jakobskirche**, which has an unusual design, was built in 1871 in imitation of the Romanesque cathedral of St Zeno in Verona.

The finest building in Friedberg is **Herrgottsruh**, a pilgrimage church located in the east of the town. In the Middle Ages it was built as a rotunda resembling the Church of the Holy Sepulchre in Jerusalem. Fragments of the building were uncovered beneath the presbytery of the present church.

The latter, built in 1731–51 by Johann Benedikt Ettl, has a tall tower and imposing domed rotunda. The paintings in the presbytery and the dome are by Cosmas Damian Asam, while those in the nave are by Matthäus Günther. The Rococo mouldings are by Franz Xaver the

Roggenburg ⑫

Road map B3. 🚶 2,500.
🚌 🚉 Vohringen. Prälatenhof 2.
Tel (07300) 96 960.
www.roggenburg.de

The towers of the town's former Premonstratensian monastery can be seen from a distance and rightly suggest that this is an exceptional building. Despite its monumentality, the cavernous interior of **Mariä Himmelfahrtskirche**, which was built in the late 18th century, produces an impression of levity, and it is light even though the windows, which are concealed behind the columns, cannot be seen. The organ loft is one of the finest in Germany. However, the real rarities here are the two

Interior of the church in Roggenburg

reliquaries with painted images of the bodies of St Severinus and St Laurentius, in fine costume of the period. The monastery, built from 1732 to 1766, houses local government offices, although parts are open to the public.

Painting from Oberes Tor, one of Weißenhorn's town gates

Weißenhorn ⑬

Road map A3. 🚶 12,300.
🚌 🚉 Vohringen. Kirchplatz 2/4.
Tel (07309) 840.
www.weissenhorn.de

Neat, quaint and tidy, Weißenhorn is the quintessential small Swabian town. Its historic character is preserved virtually intact. The main thoroughfare is the Hauptstraße, running from a large, irregular square where the church and palace stand, to the **Unteres Tor** (Lower Gate). The 15th-century **Oberes Tor** (Upper Gate), flanked by circular towers, opens on to the square. Adjoining the gate is the former **weighhouse**, dating from the 16th century, and the **Neues Rathaus**, built in the 18th century, which together form a harmonious group.

The **Altes Schloss**, dating from 1460–70, and **Neues Schloss**, built by the Fuggers (*see p253*) in the 16th century, are interconnected. The dominant building in the town is **Mariä Himmelfahrtskirche**, built in 1864–71, one of the finest examples of the revivalist trend in Swabia's religious architecture.

Street-by-Street: Augsburg ❾

Goldsmith statue on the fountain

Bavaria's third-largest city, Augsburg has a population of a quarter of a million and is the main university town of Bavarian Swabia. Founded by the Emperor Augustus on the final stretch of the trans-Alpine Via Claudia, it was a bridgehead for Italian culture. It stands at the confluence of the rivers Lech and Wertach, and because of its system of canals it has been called the Venice of the North. Tourists are drawn by the city's history and magic. It is the city of the Protestant Confession of Augsburg and a centre of the goldsmith's art. It is also the birthplace of Bertolt Brecht, Rudolf Diesel and the ancestors of Mozart.

Period houses
on Steingasse were destroyed by World War II air raids in 1941, but were rebuilt in the 1960s.

Augustusbrunnen
This statue of the Emperor Augustus on the fountain on Rathausplatz is a copy. The original, cast in bronze in 1588, is in Augsburg's Town Hall.

★ Annakirche
The chapel of the Fugger family (1509–12) is an architectural jewel. It is the earliest Renaissance building in Germany.

★ Zeughaus
The old arsenal, which was begun in 1607 by Elias Holl, features a beautiful frontage built in the Mannerist style by Josef Heintz.

★ Maximilianmuseum
The museum, currently being renovated, is located in two of the city's finest patrician palaces, built in 1543–6. Exhibits include artifacts by local goldsmiths.

KEY

‑ ‑ ‑ Suggested route

The Perlachturm is a tower 70 m (230 ft) on the west front of Peterskirche. Its height was increased through the centuries, and in 1616 Elias Holl added the steeple.

VISITORS' CHECKLIST

Road map C3. 275,000.
5 km (3 miles) north.
Schiessgrabenstr. 14, (0821) 50 20 70. www.regio-augsburg.de
@ tourismus@regio-augsburg.de
Frühjahrsplärrer (week after Easter), Herbstplärrer (Aug/Sep), Friedensfest (8 Aug), Mozartsommer (Aug), Christkindlmarkt (Dec).

★ Rathaus
Built in 1615–20 by Elias Holl, Augsburg's town hall is the finest secular Mannerist building in Europe. The famous Golden Hall is on the second floor.

Merkurbrunnen
The sculpture on this fountain was cast by Wolfgang Neidhart in 1599 after a model by Adriaen de Vries. It is crowned by a statue of Mercury, god of trade.

Fuggerhäuser
The two adjacent palaces at Maximilianstraße 36 each have elegant, airy Renaissance courtyards.

Maximilianstraße
Augsburg's main street, with its two fountains, Mercury and Herkules, by Adriaen de Vries, is one of the finest in southern Germany.

St Ulrich- und St Afrakirche

Moritzkirche, a Gothic-Baroque church, was modernized several times over the centuries. Destroyed by bombing in 1944, it was rebuilt in 1946–51.

0 metres   50
0 yards   50

STAR SIGHTS

★ Annakirche

★ Maximilianmuseum

★ Rathaus

★ Zeughaus

Exploring Augsburg

Coat of arms on the town hall

Augsburg is known for its secular buildings. Although many of them were destroyed by air raids in 1944, they were rebuilt after World War II. The city's appearance was largely defined in the early 17th century by Elias Holl, the architect of many of the buildings here, most notably the Mannerist town hall. The surrounding countryside, with its forests and the Kuhsee, provides the inhabitants with ideal places for weekend outings.

The Gothic Dom St Maria

The entrance to the Baroque Residenz am Fronhof

🏛 Dom St Maria

Frauentorstr. 1.
The cathedral, whose origins go back to the 9th century, retains the twin towers on the west front that were built in 1150, and two Romanesque crypts. It was remodelled in the Gothic style in the 14th and 15th centuries.

Among the cathedral's many notable features is the world's oldest Romanesque stained-glass window, dating from 1140 and depicting figures of the Prophets. Its 11th-century Romanesque bronze doors, with scenes from the Old Testament, are now on display in the Diocesan Museum.

🏛 Residenz am Fronhof

Fronhof 10.
The former bishop's residence was given its present appearance in 1743–52. Since 1817 it has housed the government offices of Bavarian Swabia.

It was in the ornate Festsaal in the west wing that the Emperor Karl V received the historic Confession of Augsburg in 1530. The Hofgarten adjoining the residence contains a fountain and 18th-century gnomes.

🏛 Stadtmetzg

Metzgplatz 1.
This Mannerist building was built by Elias Holl in 1606–09 for the butchers' guild. A technological innovation of the time was routing one of the town's canals beneath the cellars of the Stadtmetzg so that they would be kept cool for the effective storage of perishable food.

🏛 Fountains

Augsburg is renowned for its beautiful fountains, of which there are more than 30. The most famous are the Mannerist Augustus, Mercury and Hercules fountains, made in the late 16th century to mark the city's 1,600th anniversary. The two latter, located on Maximilianstraße, were designed by Adriaen de Vries (although they are copies, the originals now being in the Maximilianmuseum). Also noteworthy are the Neptunbrunnen of 1536, the Georgsbrunnen of 1565, and the Art Nouveau Goldschmiedebrunnen of 1913.

⛪ Schaezlerpalais

Maximilianstr. 46. *Tel* (0821) 32 44 102. ◯ 10am–8pm Tue, 10am–5pm Wed–Sun. **Staatsgalerie** ◯ 10am–5pm Tue–Sun. 🖼
The palace, the finest Rococo building in Augsburg, was built in 1765–70. The famous Festsaal features fine stuccowork, paintings, carvings, chandeliers and candelabras.

The palace's art galleries – the Staatsgalerie and the Deutsche Barockgalerie – contain works by such masters as Dürer, Hans Holbein the Elder, van Dyck and Tiepolo.

TOWN HALL

This, Europe's largest and finest Mannerist town hall, was built by Elias Holl in 1615–20. The building's showpiece is the Golden Hall. Its exquisite ornate ceiling is attached to the roof beams by means of 27 chains.

Destroyed during air raids in 1944, the town hall was meticulously restored, and the ceiling of the Golden Hall was reconstructed in 1985 to comemmorate the 2,000th anniversary of the foundation of the city in 15 BC.

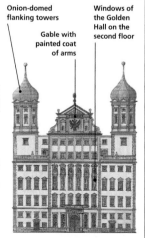

Onion-domed flanking towers

Gable with painted coat of arms

Windows of the Golden Hall on the second floor

♣ Fuggerhäuser
Maximilianstr. 36/38.

These two neighbouring early 16th-century Renaissance palaces of the Fugger family were rebuilt after being destroyed in 1944. The splendour of the original buildings with their inner courtyards can be seen in the arcaded marble Damenhof. The palace was inhabited by the family of Jakob II der Reiche Fugger and his descendant Anton.

♟ Zeughaus
Zeugplatz 6.

The arsenal, Elias Holl's first project and also one of his finest works, was built in 1607. The façade is decorated with a bronze sculpture by Hans Reichle depicting St Michael overcoming Satan.

♟ Annakirche
Im Annahof 2.

The former Carmelite church of St Anne, now Protestant, was built in the 14th century, at the same time as the monastery. It was rebuilt in the 15th century and the tower, designed by Elias Holl, was added in 1607. In the mid-18th century the interior was remodelled in the Rococo style. It contains one of the earliest organ lofts in Europe, dating from 1512.

An exceptional example of Renaissance art is the burial chapel of the Fuggers (1509–12), with epitaphs by Albrecht Dürer, a sculpted *Lamentation* by Hans Daucher, and figures of putti on the balustrade.

▥ Römisches Museum
Dominikanergasse 15.
Tel (0821) 32 44 131. ◻ *10am–8pm Tue, 10am–5pm Wed–Sun.*

The Roman Museum is housed in the former Dominican monastery, built in 1513–15. The two-naved hall, which is divided by a row of columns, was rebuilt in the Baroque style in 1716–24. The ceiling, which dates from that time, is decorated with religious stuccowork and paintings. The museum has interesting exhibits from

---

---

the Roman and as well as the early Medieval periods, including a gilded horse's head that once formed part of a Roman equestrian statue.

♟ St Ulrich- und St Afrakirche
Ulrichplatz 23.

Putto in the burial chapel in Annakirche

This late Gothic triple-nave basilica is the most recent in a succession of churches built for the Benedictine monastery that has stood here since about 1000, but that was dissolved in the early 19th century. Work on the basilica began in 1474 and continued for almost 140 years. Although two towers were planned, only the northern one was built, in 1594. Rising a height of 93 m (305 ft) high, it is visible from a great distance.

Baroque grille, St Ulrich- und St Afrakirche

The Mannerist furnishings were added in 1604–08. The exquisitely designed and crafted altar, pulpit, organ loft and stalls harmonize well with the late Gothic architecture of the interior. The nave and aisles are separated by a delicate grille of 1712.

♟ Rotes Tor and City Walls
The Rotes Tor (Red Gate) was built by Elias Holl in 1622, replacing the medieval gate. Leading in from the road that followed the old Roman Via Claudia, it was the main gate into the city. The Rotes Tor, together with the Wallanlage and the Heilig-Geist-Spital, are the finest group of buildings designed by Elias Holl.

Large sections of the city walls still stand to the north and east, as do the walls surrounding the Jakobervorstadt, with two bastions of about 1540, and the Gothic Jakobertor. There is a landing stage for canoes at the tower of the Oblatterwall bastion.

✡ Synagogue
Halderstr. 8. **Jüdisches Kulturmuseum** *Tel (0821) 51 36 58.* ◻ *9am–6pm Tue–Thu (to 8pm every 1st Wed of month), 9am–4pm Fri, 10am–5pm Sun.*

Built in 1913–17, the synagogue is one of the finest to be built in Europe at the time. The exquisite interior is crowned by a tall dome decorated in the Byzantine style. The Jüdisches Kulturmuseum (Jewish Culture Museum) is laid out in one of the wings of the synagogue.

The Fuggerei of Augsburg

Bell-pull on a house

Among Augsburg's main tourist attractions is one of the world's oldest public housing projects. It was established by Jakob II Fugger, "the Rich", together with his brothers, for the people of Augsburg who had fallen on hard times. Built by Thomas Krebs in 1514–23, it was called the Fuggerei in honour of its founder. Situated east of Rathausplatz, in the Jakobervorstadt, this walled "town within a town" has retained its medieval atmosphere. This can best be savoured outside the tourist season, when it is less crowded. The Fuggerei is entered through gates that bear the original dedication, the date 1519 and the Fuggers' armorials.

VISITORS' CHECKLIST

The settlement is located east of Maximilianstr. ☐ Apr–Oct: 8am–8pm daily; Nov–Mar: 9am–6pm daily. No vehicular access.
Fuggereimuseum, Mittlere Gasse 13. **Tel** (0821) 31 98 810.
☐ as above. 🖳 www.fugger.de

★ **Fuggereimuseum**
On view here is an apartment (bedroom and kitchen) furnished in the style of the period.

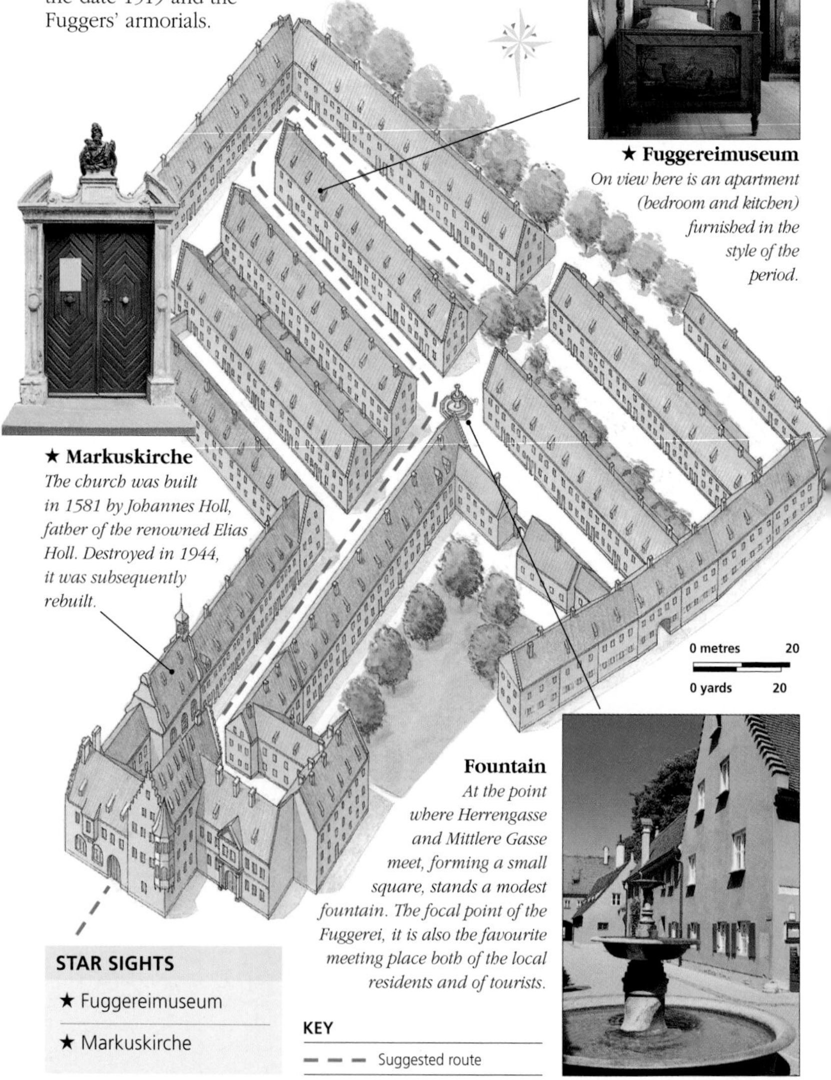

★ **Markuskirche**
The church was built in 1581 by Johannes Holl, father of the renowned Elias Holl. Destroyed in 1944, it was subsequently rebuilt.

0 metres   20
0 yards   20

Fountain
At the point where Herrengasse and Mittlere Gasse meet, forming a small square, stands a modest fountain. The focal point of the Fuggerei, it is also the favourite meeting place both of the local residents and of tourists.

STAR SIGHTS

★ Fuggereimuseum

★ Markuskirche

KEY

– – – Suggested route

Gardens at the rear of the houses in the Fuggerei

Exploring the Fuggerei

The estate originally comprised 53 buildings designed to house 106 families. Partly forming a continuous, symmetrical ensemble, they stand on an uneven plot of land and are surrounded by a wall with five gates.

The houses have modest façades and steep roofs with stepped gables. Each front door still has its bell-pull and iron handle, and the exterior walls still have sandstone plaques with the old house numbers inscribed on them.

The Fuggerei was badly damaged by the air raids of 1944. During the painstaking process of reconstruction, which was carried out in 1947–55 and was financed by the Fugger estate, 14 additional houses were built.

Today about 200 people live in the Fuggerei. All the houses have been modernized and have electricity, heating and other modern conveniences. The estate of the Fugger family decides who can live in the Fuggerei. Originally housing families with children, it has recently been designated for needy people, who must be Catholic and must have lived in Augsburg for at least two years. Residents pay a nominal annual rent equal to 1 Rhenish guilder (88 cents), in return for which they undertake to say a daily prayer for the founders. There is also supplement of €46 per month to finance communal services.

Herrengasse, the main street in the Fuggerei

An interesting feature of the Fuggerei is the fine late Gothic oriel of 1504–07 on the corner of the Seigniory House by the gate on Jakoberstraße. It was transferred from the bombed ruins of a house belonging to the Höchstetter family, contemporaries of the Fuggers. The **Seigniory House,** which was rebuilt after 1954, contains on its ground floor a Gothic chapel that was transferred here in 1962 from the ruined house of the Welsers.

Markuskirche, in Herrengasse, is decorated with a tall shaped gable and has an Angelus bell. It is furnished with items from various other churches. A *Crucifixion* by Jacopo Palma the Younger of about 1600 can be seen on the Mannerist high altar. Ulrich Fugger's epitaph, depicting the deceased wrapped in a shroud, was designed by Albrecht Dürer and made by Adolf Daucher in 1512–15.

The resident of the house at Mittlere Gasse 14 was Franz Mozart, great-grandfather of the composer Wolfgang Amadeus. He made himself unpopular with his clients by carrying out burials for the executioner, which was considered to be a disgraceful deed. As a result he lost business and became so impoverished that he had to go and live in the Fuggerei.

THE FUGGERS

The career of the Fuggers began in 1367, when Hans Fugger, a native of Graben, came to Augsburg. Jakob I (who died in 1459) founded the family of merchants and bankers that still exists today. His sons Ulrich, Georg and particularly Jakob II, "the Rich", acquired unheard-of wealth, ensuring a life of opulence for the entire family. Jakob II was banker to emperors, kings and popes. He funded the election of Karl V as German Emperor. He was also known as a patron of the arts, and thanks partly to him Renaissance art took root in Germany. He also founded social institutions. Once the owners of 100 villages, the Fuggers still own several castles in Bavaria.

Monument to Hans Jakob Fugger, Augsburg

Memorial plaque to Franz Mozart, one-time resident of the Fuggerei

The Imperial Hall of the former Augustine monastery in Wettenhausen

Wettenhausen ⑭

Road map B3. 🚌 🚊 *Günzburg.*
Abbey *Kammeltal, Dossenberger-
str. 46.* **Tel** *(08223) 40 040.*

Standing like a fortress, the
old Augustinian monastery in
Wettenhausen dominates the
surrounding landscape. **Mariä
Himmelfahrtskirche**,
originally a Romanesque
church, was rebuilt in the late
Gothic style in the early 16th
century and remodelled in the
Baroque style in 1670. The
frescoes, of about 1685, and
the highly decorative altars
and pulpit, dating from the
same period, create a unified
interior. The altar in the south
chapel features a fine late
Gothic Coronation of the
Virgin carved in 1524.

Part of the **abbey**, including
the Imperial Hall and the
cloistered courtyard, are open
to the public. The rooms in
the cloister are visible through
a decorative wrought-iron
grille. One of them contains
a figure of Christ seated on
a donkey made in 1456,
probably in the workshop
of Hans Multscher of Ulm.

Günzburg ⑮

Road map B3. 🏠 20,000. 🚌
🚊 🛈 *Schloßplatz 1, (08221)
200 444.* **www**.guenzburg.de

The origins of this sizeable
town at the confluence of the
rivers Günz and Danube go
back to Roman times. Much
of it has been pedestrianized,
and it invites leisurely strolls
through its attractive streets.

Münzgasse, lined with 17th-
and 18th-century houses with
projecting upper storeys, is
especially picturesque.

The main square, closed
off by the 14th-century
Unteres Tor (Lower Gate), is
surrounded by Baroque
houses with typically
Swabian gables. These
houses recall the days
when the town was
at its height. Notable
is **Brentanohaus** at
No. 8, built in 1747
with a tiled mansard
roof and Rococo
mouldings on its
elegant façade.

Beside the old
Franciscan monastery
stands the **Frauen-
kirche**, built in
1736–41 by
Dominikus Zimmermann.
Substantial fragments of the
15th-century town walls,
defensive towers and
gateways survive.

Houses in Münzgasse, one of
Günzburg's picturesque streets

Dillingen ⑯

Road map B3. 🏠 18,000.
🚌 🚊 🛈 *Königstr. 37,
(09071) 54 108, 54 109.*
www.dillingen-donau.de

For centuries Dillingen, the
spiritual capital of Swabia and
a town dubbed the "Rome of
Swabia", was the seat of the
bishops of Augs-burg and a
major university town. The
main street, König-straße,
lined with patrician town
houses, defines the town's
character. Königstraße leads
into Kardinal von
Waldburgstraße, on which the
elongated Baroque façade of
the **Jesuit University** rises.
It was built in 1688–9 to a
design by Michael Thumb
and visitors can admire
the Rococo Golden Hall
within. The former
college beside the
university has a fine
Baroque library,
which occupies
two floors and has
furnishings carved by
Georg Bschorer.

The highlight
of the town is the
formerly Jesuit
**Mariä Himmel-
fahrtskirche**, built in
the early 17th
century by Johann
Albertal. The early
Baroque archi-
tecture of the building and its
Rococo stuccowork, painting
and furnishings combine to
produce a splendid ensemble.
The high altar still has its
Theatrum Sacrum, where
the tradition of performing
Passion plays at Easter was
recently revived.

The early Rococo
Franciscan monastery and
church were designed by
Johann Georg Fischer. The
stately 13th-century **castle**,
which before the secularization of the state was the seat
of the capital and of the
bishops of Augsburg, has
preserved its defensive
character despite rebuilding
on numerous occasions over
the centuries. Fragments of
the town walls, set with
towers and pierced by the
Mitteltor (Middle Gate),
can still be seen today.

Lion outside the
castle in Dillingen

Roman ruins in Faimingen, a suburb of Lauingen

Lauingen ⑰

Road map B3. 🏘 10,500. 🚌
🚊 ℹ️ *Herzog-Georg-Str. 17, (09072) 99 80.*
www.lauingen.de

Set on a high bank over-looking the Danube, this town has largely preserved its medieval character. It has an oval outline and was once surrounded by walls, the surviving parts of which are a **gate** and two bastions.

The slender outlines of two tall towers that dominate the town can be seen from a distance. The more distinctive of the two is the former watchtower that stands in the main square. Exceptionally tall and narrow, it was built in 1457–78 together with the adjacent arcades containing market stalls, and was extended in 1571. It is known as the **Schimmelturm** (Grey Mare Tower) because of the image of the horse near the bottom, which has been renewed and repainted several times.

The **town hall**, built in 1782 to a Neo-Classical design by Lorenz J Quaglio, was erected on the orders of the Elector Karl Theodor despite strong opposition from the townspeople.

Martinskirche, the parish church built in 1515, is one of the last Gothic hall-churches to have been built in southern Germany. Its triple-nave interior with web vaulting is unparalleled in height and the walls and ceilings are decorated with frescoes painted in 1521.

Among the many tombs and epitaphs is a fine cenotaph that is the symbolic tomb of Elisabeth, wife of the Palatine, who died in 1563.

The tomb is surrounded by a wrought-iron grille and on it lies a white marble figure of the deceased supported by four lions. The tall free-standing **belfry** is, with the Schimmelturm, a defining feature of the town's skyline.

Environs
In the suburb of Faimingen, on the road to Günzburg, the remains of Roman buildings can be seen. The partially reconstructed **Temple of Apollo Grannus**, the Roman deity who also came to be worshipped by the Celts, bears witness to Lauingen's long history.

The Schimmelturm, the tallest tower in Lauingen

Höchstädt ⑱

Road map B3. 🏘 6,800. 🚌
🚊 ℹ️ *Herzog Philipp-Ludwig-Str. 10, (09074) 44 12.*
www.hoechstaedt.de

This little town on the banks of the Danube is flanked by its church and its castle. On the west side are the church and the town hall, on a square located between two streets that lead to the castle.

The late Gothic **Mariä Himmelfahrtskirche**, which was completed in about 1520, is decorated with frescoes in the same style, painted in 1520–30 and also with Mannerist frescoes in a contrasting florid style dating from about 1600.

The town's finest historic building is the turret-shaped Gothic sacristy, built in attractive sandstone in 1480–90. The Baroque altar was added in 1695.

The polygonal **chapel** beside the church was built in 1664. It features a deep niche containing a Pietà dating from the first quarter of the 18th century. Above the statue is a theatrical scene depicting Christ and the Apostles on the Mount of Olives. The scene, consisting of figures set against a painted background, was created by Johann Michael Fischer in 1760.

The **Heimatmuseum** has numerous collections of objects relating to local history, including a display of 9,000 tin soldiers re-creating the Battle of Höchstädt that took place in 1760.

On a hill overlooking the town stands the Renaissance **castle**, built in about 1589 to replace the medieval seat of Duke Philip Ludwig, the Palatine of Neuburg. Well restored, it is used as the museum's headquarters. The castle complex has an almost square plan with a central courtyard, four circular corner towers and a chapel in the west wing. The main entrance is a doorway flanked by pairs of columns, with coats of arms in the tympanum and a barrel-vaulted archway with coffered ceiling.

🏛 **Heimatmuseum**
Marktplatz 7. **Tel** (09074) 49 56.
⭕ Nov–Mar: 2pm–5pm first Sun in the month and by arrangement; Apr–Oct: 2–5pm every Sun.

The doorway of the castle in Höchstädt

TRAVELLERS' NEEDS

WHERE TO STAY

Munich and the Bavarian Alps are the most popular tourist destinations in Germany. The region offers a wide variety of hotels with different levels of service. Finding somewhere to stay, either in Munich itself or throughout the Bavarian Alps, presents no problem, whatever price and standard of accommodation are required. As well as luxury hotels, which are often converted

Logo of Munich's Eden-Wolff hotel

stately palaces or romantic castles, and international chains such as Marriott, Hilton or Sheraton, travellers in the Bavarian Alps have a choice of many small hotels and guesthouses. Accommodation, particularly in Munich, is harder to find during the Oktoberfest and when trade fairs take place in the city, and during festivals and public holidays, when tourist resorts become more crowded.

The Kempinski Hotel Vier Jahreszeiten in Munich *(see p263)*

FINDING ACCOMMODATION

In towns and cities hotels are usually located in or near the historic centre or near tourist attractions. When choosing somewhere to stay it is advisable to ensure that it is not on or near a noisy street, or near a night-spot or a church, as the ringing of church bells can awaken the deepest sleeper.

If you decide on a hotel in central Munich, you may need to enquire about parking facilities. Organizations such as the **Bayerischer Tourismusverband** can be a great help here. If you choose a hotel further away from the centre, make sure that it is near public transport links. Most hotels, including de luxe hotels, are located on the periphery of the Old Town and in Schwabing. There are also hotels around Munich's

main railway station, although these are not of the highest standard. Hotels belonging to major groups such as Marriott and Sheraton can be found near main highways.

THE RANGE OF HOTELS

Many hotels are marked with stars indicating the quality (and therefore the cost) of the accommodation

and services that they provide. Top-class hotels usually have their own high-quality restaurants, as well as banqueting suites, swimming pool, gyms, saunas and laundry facilities. Those outside cities may also have tennis courts and golf links.

There is also a network of more modern bed-and-breakfast hotels that offer fewer supplementary services. On motorways and major roads, you can find motels or *Rasthäuser*, which are basically restaurants with single-night accommodation.

In tourist towns a common type of accommodation is *Halbpension* (half-board lodgings), where a hot meal is offered in addition to breakfast, or *Vollpension*, (lodging with full board).

All hotels and other types of accommodation are extremely clean. Toilet and bathroom facilities, even when shared, are of a high standard. Regardless of the category of the establishment, guests are often offered many extras.

Guests checking into a small hotel

The bar in the Königshof hotel in Munich *(see p264)*

HOTEL PRICES

Hotel prices vary greatly. A single room can range from €40–75 in a tourist-class hotel to €150 in a top-class hotel, and up to €360 in a luxury establishment. Prices in Munich are naturally higher than those elsewhere, and at their highest during the Oktoberfest.

At holiday and spa resorts a three-tier price system operates – high season, mid-season and low season. Prices at high season can be double those of low season.

Many hotels offer reductions at weekends and even if you turn up without having made a reservation, you may be able to negotiate a discount. If you are planning a longer stay, you may also be able to negotiate a discount, especially at times of year when business is slack.

HOW TO BOOK

Hotel accommodation can be booked direct by telephone, letter or fax, as well as by e-mail or through the Internet. Travellers already in Bavaria can obtain brochures and lists of addresses at tourist offices and health resort offices *(Kurverwaltung)*.

When making a reservation, you will need to confirm the method of payment. An advance payment or

credit card details will sometimes be requested. Those who make their reservation well in advance will usually receive written confirmation, often with a bank deposit form attached for the advance payment. Some hotels offer insurance against cancellation due to unforeseen circumstances.

On arrival guests are asked to complete a registration form and may be requested to show their passport. Full payment is made when checking out and, especially in the case of small provincial hotels, it is always worth making sure in advance that cards or travellers' cheques are accepted. In health spas an additional charge known as a *Kurtaxe* is payable. In top-class and luxury hotels,

The ornate courtyard of the Opera hotel in Munich *(see p263)*

tips are expected for additional services. It is also customary, even in more modest hotels, to leave a few Euros for the chambermaid.

DISABLED TRAVELLERS

An increasing number of hotels and youth hostels cater for disabled travellers. Most have ramp access and a few rooms with bathrooms and toilets adapted for use by disabled people. Facilities are, however, likely to be better in hotels of a higher standard than in budget hotels.

Handicapped-Reisen Deutschland is a guide that lists hotels in Germany with facilities for disabled people. Information can also be obtained from BAGH and CBF *(see p261)*.

Tables on the terrace restaurant at the Parkhotel in Donauwörth

TRAVELLING WITH CHILDREN

Travelling with children in the Bavarian Alps should not present any problems. Most hotels will provide an additional bed or cot, often at no extra charge. Many hotels have children's corners – play areas equipped with children's furniture as well as games and toys – and some of the better hotels have babysitting facilities. If a child is sick, the hotel's reception will call a paediatrician.

Standard equipment in every restaurant includes a high chair for toddlers, while menus almost always include the option of smaller portions for children.

Tourist resorts offer special programmes of supervised activities for children.

Alpenrose guesthouse, Alpsee *(see p231)*

ROOMS IN PRIVATE HOUSES

Bed-and-breakfast accommodation is not widespread in cities. However, in popular tourist areas and most smaller towns, you will often come across houses with a sign saying *"Zimmer"* (rooms). The sign will be accompanied by another saying either *"frei"* (vacancies) or *"belegt"* (no vacancies).

Prices for such rooms are relatively low – from €10 per person. Other benefits are a homely atmosphere and a lavish breakfast. Toilets and bathrooms are usually shared, but the rooms have wash-basins and telephones.

HOLIDAY APARTMENTS

For visitors spending their holiday in one particular place, holiday apartments *(Ferienwohnung)* are the best and cheapest type of accommodation. They are available in all holiday resorts, and brochures can be obtained at tourist information centres.

The size, standard and price of the apartments vary. Most have a kitchen, plus a television, vacuum cleaner, iron, bookshelves and cupboard with glasses and tablecloths.

Holiday apartments are found mainly in private houses and apartment blocks, and in some larger hotels. They are rented for at least a week. The tenant is responsible for the cleaning, and pays an additional charge for final cleaning *(Endreinigung)*.

AGROTOURISM

Staying on a farm *(Bauernhof)* is a popular and inexpensive way of spending a holiday. It is particularly suitable for families with children. Rooms in large farmhouses or separate apartments are provided, and they range in standard from modest to luxurious.

Guests have the opportunity to help with the daily work on the farm, and children can feed the animals. Another advantage is the delicious food, with fresh dairy products, that is served to guests staying on the farm.

Another type of holiday is a riding holiday. Guests stay on horse or pony farms *(Reiterhöfe* and *Ponyhöfe)*, and go horse-riding or pony-trekking.

YOUTH HOSTELS

Almost every sizeable town in Bavaria has a youth hostel *(Jugendherberge)*. Youth hostels are divided into four categories according to their location and the standard of accommodation they offer. Many are relatively comfortable, although there is always the possibility that the only beds available will be in a dormitory. Toilets and bathrooms are usually communal. Almost all youth hostels have dining rooms where breakfast and hot meals are served. Many hostels have their own sports facilities. The cost of accommodation is about €12 per night. In popular tourist resorts early booking is recommended. Information can be obtained from the **Landesverband Bayern des DJH**.

Bavarian youth hostels are open to members of the IYHF, people up to the age of 26 and families with children who have family membership. The age limit does not apply to people in charge of youth groups. Besides youth hostels, young tourists in Germany can also use student hotels and unaffiliated shelters.

Logo of the German Youth Hostel Association

MOUNTAIN SHELTERS

Mountain shelters offering food, rest and sometimes accommodation to skiers and hikers are to be found in many places in the Bavarian Alps. The German Alpine Association (**Deutscher Alpenverein**) alone has some 100 shelters. Members may use them at a discount and have priority in renting accommodation. As well as individual rooms, the shelters also have bunk beds in communal rooms.

Shelters are usually open during the summer months, from May to October or from June to September. Shelters near skiing pistes and along the most popular hiking trails are also open in winter.

A mountain shelter for hikers and skiers near Zugspitze

CAMPING

Southern Bavaria's many camp sites are usually situated in picturesque locations and are ideal for peaceful holidays. Although they vary in size and standard, most have good toilet and washing facilities, and may also have a shop and a café. Many also offer cultural programmes.

Most camp sites are open from April to October, although some are also suitable for use in winter.

GASTHÖFE

For travellers looking for unpretentious accommo-dation, the roadside inns known as *Gasthöfe* that are found throughout Bavaria are an attractive and con-venient option. The sign *"Gasthof"* will probably be accompanied by another saying *"Zimmer"* (rooms).

Prices are very affordable – usually between €20 and €35 for a double room.

A well-kept *Gasthof*, one of the many roadside inns in Bavaria

Drinking beer and eating simple homemade fare is one of the greatest pleasures of staying in a *Gasthof*.

SPA RESORTS

The bracing mountain air, as well as the many mineral springs and curative mud found in the region of the Bavarian Alps, have led to the growth of large numbers of spa resorts. Most can be identified by the word *"Bad"* (bath) before the name of the town.

In these resorts, a spa tax *(Kurtaxe)* is added to the charge of the room. This small additional charge also gives a reduction on the entry charge to many cultural and sporting events, and various kinds of therapy on offer.

Bavarian spas specialize mostly in respiratory and circulatory disorders and rheumatic ailments. Visitors to the spas have at their disposal excellent rest and recupera-tion facilities, with doctors and convalescence specialists to monitor their health.

DIRECTORY

INFORMATION ON ACCOMMODATION & RESERVATIONS

Bayern Tourismus Marketing Gmbh
Leopoldstr. 146, Munich.
Tel (089) 21 23 97 0.

Tourismusamt München
Neues Rathaus,
Marienplatz.
Tel (089) 23 39 65 00.
Fax (089) 23 33 02 33.
⏰ 10am–8pm Mon–Fri,
10am–4pm Sat. Haupt-bahnhof, Bahnhofplatz 2.
⏰ 9:30am–6:30pm
Mon–Sat, 10am–6pm Sun.
www.muenchen-tourist.de

BED & BREAKFAST

Bed & Breakfast Mitwohnzentrale
Schulstr. 31, Munich.
Tel (089) 16 88 781.
Fax (089) 16 88 791.

City Mitwohnzentrale
Lämmerstr. 6,
Munich.
Tel (089) 19 430.
Fax (089) 59 45 64.

AGROTOURISM

"Urlaub auf dem Bauernhof"
Kaiser-Ludwig-Platz 2,
Munich.
Tel (089) 544 799 950.
www.bauernhof-urlaub.com

YOUTH HOSTELS

DJH-Gästehaus
Miesingstr. 4,
Munich.
Tel (089) 72 36 550/560.
Fax (089) 72 42 567.

DJH München
Wendl-Dietrich-Str. 20,
Munich.
Tel (089) 13 11 56.
Fax (089) 16 78 745.

Haus International
Elisabethstr. 87, Munich.
Map 1 A1.
Tel (089) 12 00 60.
Fax (089) 12 00 66 30.

Landesverband Bayern des DJH
Mauerkircherstr. 5, Munich.
Tel (089) 92 20 980.
www.djh.de

MOUNTAIN SHELTERS

Deutscher Alpenverein (DAV)
Von-Kahr-Str. 2–4, Munich.
Tel (089) 14 00 30.

CAMPING SITES

ADAC- Camping-Referat
Am Westpark 8, Munich.
Tel (089) 76 760.

Deutscher Camping Club
Mandlstr. 28, Munich.
Map 2 F2.
Tel (089) 38 01 420.

Langwieder See
Eschenrieder Str. 119,
Munich.
Tel (089) 86 41 566.

München-Obermenzing
Lochhausener Str. 59.
Tel (089) 81 12 235.

München-Tahlkirchen
Zentralländstraße 49.
Tel (089) 72 31 707.

DISABLED TRAVELLERS

Bundesarbeits gemenschaft Hilfe für Behinderte (BAGH)
Kirchfeldstr. 149, Düsseldorf.
Tel (0211) 31 00 60.

Club Behinderter und ihrer Freunde (CBF)
Eupener Str. 5, Mainz.
Tel (06131) 22 55 14.
Johann-Fichte Str 12.
Munich.
Tel (089) 35 68 808.

Choosing a Hotel

The hotels in this guide have been selected across a wide price range for their good value, facilities and location. Hotels are listed by region, starting with Munich and its environs, followed by the rest of the Bavarian Alps. Under each town or city, hotels are listed in alphabetical order within each price category.

PRICE CATEGORIES
Price categories for a standard double room per night including breakfast, service and tax

€ under 80 euros
€€ 81–130 euros
€€€ 130–180 euros
€€€€ 180–250 euros
€€€€€ over 250 euros

MUNICH

OLD TOWN SOUTH Deutsche Eiche   €€
Reichenbachstrasse 13, 80469 **Tel** *089 2311660* **Fax** *089 23116698* **Rooms** *26*   **Map** *3 C3*

A stylish hotel right in the heart of the arty Glockenbach quarter. Rooms are comfortable and there is a traditional bar-bistro downstairs plus a sauna. A favourite with young trendy guests and gay couples. Close to the food market, good shops and tram and metro links. **www.deutsche-eiche.com**

OLD TOWN SOUTH Daniel   €€€
Sonnenstrasse 5, 80331 **Tel** *089 548240* **Fax** *089 553420* **Rooms** *81*   **Map** *3 A2*

A standard modern city hotel with corporate-style decor and friendly staff. Some rooms are air conditioned and there is wireless Internet access. The hotel is located above the Eldorado cinema and is close to shops and transport links. Prices rise drastically during trade fair weeks and Oktoberfest. **www.hotel-daniel.de**

OLD TOWN SOUTH Hotel am Viktualienmarkt   €€€
Utzschneiderstrasse 14, 80469 **Tel** *089 23110 90* **Fax** *089 23110955* **Rooms** *27*   **Map** *3 B3*

A basic but comfortable hotel in a central location next to the famous fruit and vegetable market, Viktualienmarkt. Rooms are modern with contemporary photos, floral or striped fabric furnishings and plenty of green. The hotel owns its own café a few doors down. **www.hotel-am-viktualienmarkt.de**

OLD TOWN SOUTH Schlicker   €€€
Tal 8, 80331 **Tel** *089 2428870* **Fax** *089 296059* **Rooms** *69*   **Map** *3 C2*

This traditional hotel has been run by the same family for five generations. Rooms are tastefully decorated with classic furnishings. There is no parking or restaurant but the hotel is just a short distance from Marienplatz and is close to shops, bars, cafés and restaurants. Wireless Internet access. **www.hotel-schlicker.de**

OLD TOWN SOUTH Asam Hotel   €€€€
Josephspitalstrasse 3, 80331 **Tel** *089 2309700* **Fax** *089 23097097* **Rooms** *24*   **Map** *3 A2*

Popular with fashion, media and music stars, Asam Hotel offers good service and a certain level of style. Rooms have marble bathrooms and wireless Internet access. Choose from international cuisine in the hotel's own Speisekammer restaurant, cocktails in the bar or explore the area's nightlife. **www.hotel-asam.de**

OLD TOWN SOUTH Cortiina   €€€€
Ledererstrasse 8, 80331 **Tel** *089 2422490* **Fax** *089 242249100* **Rooms** *35*   **Map** *3 C2*

A favourite with the fashionable set, this hotel has a cool bar, oak panelling and floors in the rooms, and is located right in the heart of the city. Services include babysitting, wireless Internet connection and complimentary daily newspapers. You may be forgiven for thinking the hotel lobby is an art gallery. **www.cortiina.com**

OLD TOWN SOUTH Torbräu   €€€€
Tal 41, 80331 **Tel** *089 242340* **Fax** *089 24234235* **Rooms** *92*   **Map** *3 C3*

Housed in a historic building dating to 1490, this hotel is one of the city's oldest. The four star hotel is traditional in style and offers a lovely Italian restaurant, a café serving brunch, no-smoking rooms and wireless Internet access. Room prices increase during the Oktoberfest. **www.torbraeu.de**

OLD TOWN NORTH Concorde   €€€
Heernstrasse 38-40, 80539 **Tel** *089 224515* **Fax** *089 2283282* **Rooms** *71*   **Map** *4 D2*

Owned by the Tulip Inn chain, this hotel has a corporate look and feel but manages, nonetheless, to retain a warm family-run atmosphere. Parking is available for a modest fee, complimentary newspapers are provided and reception is open 24 hours. Quiet location near the opera and theatres. **www.concorde-muenchen.de**

OLD TOWN NORTH Platzl   €€€€
Sparkassenstrasse 10, 80331 **Tel** *089 237030* **Fax** *089 23703800* **Rooms** *167*   **Map** *3 C2*

Just a few minutes by foot from Marienplatz, this hotel is surrounded by some of Munich's oldest buildings. The hotel is popular with visitors who love its traditional Bavarian style. Old wooden furniture, painted façades and excellent service, as well as a restaurant and inn. Look out for the huge blue and white flags flying outside. **www.platzl.de**

Key to Symbols *see back cover flap*

OLD TOWN NORTH Bayerischer Hof

€€€€€

Promenadeplatz 2–6, 80333 **Tel** *089 21200* **Fax** *089 2120906* **Rooms** *395*

Map 3 B2

A large luxurious affair boasting an impressive list of famous guests from royalty to Hollywood stars. The rooms are elegant in a country-house style. Wonderful spa, three restaurants *(see p277)* and a cool bar. With a central location, this hotel is near the best shops, museums, opera house, theatres and restaurants. **www.bayerischerhof.de**

OLD TOWN NORTH Kempinski Hotel Vier Jahreszeiten

€€€€€

Maximilianstrasse 17, 80539 **Tel** *089 21250* **Fax** *089 21252000* **Rooms** *308*

Map 3 C2

Built for King Maximilian II in 1858, this hotel enjoys a prime location among the designer shops on Maximilianstrasse. A stunning entrance hall in rich gold and reds sets the tone. The service is excellent, as is the gastronomy and bars. The pool and wellness floor was completely revamped in 2006. **www.kempinski-vierjahreszeiten.de**

OLD TOWN NORTH Mandarin Oriental

€€€€€

Neuturmstrasse 1, 80331 **Tel** *089 290980* **Fax** *089 222539* **Rooms** *73*

Map 3 C2

This luxury Munich property offers spacious rooms, marble bathrooms and panoramic views of the city from the rooftop terrace's heated swimming pool. Dine in the fine Michelin-starred Mark's restaurant or alfresco on the terrace *(see p277)*. Central location just off the designer shopping mile. **www.mandarinoriental.com/munich**

AROUND THE ISAR Adria

€€

Liebigstrasse 8a, 80538 **Tel** *089 2421170* **Fax** *089 242117999* **Rooms** *45*

Map 4 D1

The Adria sits in a nice residential area of the city, a short distance from the museums on Prinzregentenstrasse. The decor here is modern, arty and minimal and the rooms have spacious bathrooms. Large breakfast buffet. Close to the Chinese Tower in the English Garden. **www.adria-muenchen.de**

AROUND THE ISAR Advokat

€€€

Baaderstrasse 1, 80469 **Tel** *089 216310* **Fax** *089 2163190* **Rooms** *50*

Map 3 B/C4

Advokat is the designer, sister hotel of the Admiral. The elegant decor is complimented with paintings, flowers and sculptures. There is a small roof terrace, and the lobby is a retro 60s style. Located cose to the trendy boutiques and great cafés of this arty quarter. **www.hotel-advokat.de**

AROUND THE ISAR Domus

€€€

St Anna Strasse 31, 80538 **Tel** *089 2177730* **Fax** *089 2285359* **Rooms** *67*

Map 4 D1

This hotel offers a quiet place to stay near the lovely St Anna Church. The rooms are standard, elegant and classic, some with small balconies. Amenities include Internet connection and an Italian restaurant. Domus is a short walk from the English Garden and designer shops on Maximilianstrasse. Ask for special weekend rates. **www.domus-hotel.de**

AROUND THE ISAR Splendid-Dollmann

€€€

Thierschstrasse 49, 80538 **Tel** *089 238080* **Fax** *089 23808365* **Rooms** *36*

Map 4 D3

Expect a traditional, charming and quietly located hotel in the old quarter of Lehel. Splendid has a fine English town-house feel with elegant rooms boasting antique furniture. There is also a restaurant, bar, library and babysitting service. Close to Munich's top address for designer shops, museums and the parliament. **www.hotel-splendid-dollmann.de**

AROUND THE ISAR Admiral

€€€€

Kohlstrasse 9, 80469 **Tel** *089 216350* **Fax** *089 293674* **Rooms** *33*

Map 3 C3/4

Just around the corner from the Deutsches Museum, this small four-star hotel enjoys a tranquil location not far from the river. Traditional in style with a garden and bar for evening drinks. Some rooms have balconies overlooking the garden. Good buffet breakfast with homemade jams. Caters for families. **www.hotel-admiral.de**

AROUND THE ISAR Hotel Ritzi

€€€€

Maria-Theresa-Strasse 2a, 81675 **Tel** *089 414240890* **Fax** *089 4142408950* **Rooms** *25*

Map 4 F1/2

The rooms here are all individual, decorated in bold colours with a global traveller feel. Themes include African inspired, Zen oriental, rich Baroque, white Regency or warm Moroccan themes. There is a wonderful Mediterranean all-day restaurant and a cosy Art Deco lounge and bar. **www.hotel-ritzi.de**

AROUND THE ISAR Opera

€€€€

St.-Anna-Strasse 10, 80538 **Tel** *089 2104940* **Fax** *089 21049477* **Rooms** *25*

Map 4 D1

Tucked in a side street close to a stretch of designer shops, this smart, upmarket townhouse has a beautiful façade and Italian Renaissance courtyard. Enjoy peace and quiet in the lovely inner courtyard or try some of the French, German or Italian specialities in the fine restaurant, Gandl *(see p277)*. **www.hotel-opera.de**

AROUND THE ISAR Hilton Munich City

€€€€€

Rosenheimerstrasse 15, 81667 **Tel** *089 48040* **Fax** *089 48044804* **Rooms** *480*

Map 4 E4

A modern, corporate hotel with excellent service and facilities. The high price reflects the busier trade fair weeks and Oktoberfest. Other rates are available. Suitable for business travellers and families alike and close to good transport links and the Gasteig cultural centre. **www.hilton.com**

UNIVERSITY DISTRICT Carolin

　　€

Kaulbachstrasse 42, 80538 **Tel** *089 345757* **Fax** *089 334451* **Rooms** *6*

Map 2 E4

Frau Mohr runs her little guesthouse on the first floor of a house of apartments. The guesthouse has just six rooms and is quiet, comfortable and familiar. Located next to the English Garden, with a handy bakery, newsagents and other shops nearby. Good restaurants and metro are also close. Cash payments only. **www.pension-carolin.com**

UNIVERSITY DISTRICT Am Siegestor

€€

Akademiestrasse 5, 80799 **Tel** *089 399550* **Fax** *089 343050* **Rooms** *20*

Map 2 D/E4

The lift in this hotel is one of Munich's oldest hotel lifts, dating back to the late 1800s. The rooms here are simple but adequate and the hotel provides easy access to the nearby art galleries and English Garden. It is also close to the lively Schwabing scene with good shops, bars and restaurants. **www.siegestor.com**

UNIVERSITY DISTRICT Hauser

€€

Schellingstrasse 11, 80799 **Tel** *089 2866750* **Fax** *089 28667599* **Rooms** *34*

Map 2 D4

This mid-range family-run hotel is owned by the Minotel chain and is right in the heart of the University district with good tram and bus connections. The hotel is located above a café-bar and offers cycle hire, a sauna and steam bath. There is a tiny courtyard outside. **www.hotel-hauser.de**

UNIVERSITY DISTRICT Cosmopolitan Hotel

€€€

Hohenzollernstrasse 5, 80801 **Tel** *089 383810* **Fax** *089 38381111* **Rooms** *71*

Map 1 B2

A contemporary hotel in a quiet street in the fashionable Schwabing district. The rooms boast Ligne Rost furniture and there is a pleasant terrace where breakfast is served in warmer weather. Short walk to the English Garden, Munich's lovely central park. Good transport connections. **www.geisel-privathotels.de**

MUSEUMS DISTRICT Theresia-Regina

€

Luisenstrasse 51, 80333 **Tel** *089 521250* **Fax** *089 5420633* **Rooms** *28*

Map 1 B4

This basic hotel is located just a short walk from the Neue Pinakothek art museum. There are plenty of cafés, bars and restaurants in the area and it is close to public transport. The price, which increases during trade fairs and Oktoberfest, reflects a slightly old-fashioned feel. Reception only until 9pm. Parking available. **www.hoteltheresia.de**

MUSEUMS DISTRICT Dorint Novotel

€€

Hochstrasse 11, 81669 **Tel** *089 661070* **Fax** *089 66107999* **Rooms** *305*

Map 4 E4

A contemporary four-star hotel with simple, sleek decor. The welcoming breakfast room has large floral photographic graphics. There is also a spacious pool and relaxation room plus fitness area. Central location and suitable for families. From here you can walk to Marienplatz, the cultural centre Gasteig or museums. **www.novotel.com**

MUSEUMS DISTRICT Savoy

€€

Amalienstrasse 25, 80333 **Tel** *089 287870* **Fax** *089 280161* **Rooms** *74*

Map 2 D5

One of the hotels in the Renner group, the Savoy is a small town hotel that sits above the Odeon Bar & Lounge. The hotel offers a basic service, but is conveniently located close to Munich's art museums, shops, restaurants and bars, and is a short walk to tram and bus links. **www.leonardo-hotels.com**

MUSEUMS DISTRICT Stefanie

€€

Türkenstrasse 35, 80779 **Tel** *089 2881400* **Fax** *089 28814049* **Rooms** *32*

Map 2 D4

Housed in a 1920s building, the Stefanie could do with some modernisation. However, the location is convenient for the student area of Schwabing as well as for theatres and galleries. Good transport links to other sights, airport and station. Soundproof windows and good breakfast. **www.hotel-stefanie.de**

MUSEUMS DISTRICT Hotel Königshof

€€€€€

Karlsplatz 25, 80335 **Tel** *089 551360* **Fax** *089 55136113* **Rooms** *87*

Map 3 A2

A renowned hotel offering five-star luxury in a central location. The decor is elegant, the service first class and the hotel boasts internationally acclaimed cuisine in its Michelin-starred restaurant *(see p278)*. Facilities include a fitness, sauna and wellbeing area. Children are welcome. **www.geisel-privathotels.de**

FURTHER AFIELD Gästehaus Englischer Garten

€€

Liebergesellstrasse 8, 80802 **Tel** *089 3839410* **Fax** *089 38394133* **Rooms** *25*

A cosy family-run guesthouse in a quiet residential area of Munich. Rooms are pleasant if a little small and there are longer-stay apartments available which have balconies and are more spacious. Once a watermill, the now listed building has a lovely garden where breakfast is served. **www.hotelenglischergarten.de**

FURTHER AFIELD Golden Leaf Altmünchen

€€

Mariahilfplatz 4, 81541 **Tel** *089 458440* **Fax** *089 45844400* **Rooms** *31*

Map 4 D5

With its own Bavarian tavern with a beer garden and stream, this rustic-style hotel oozes typical Bavarian charm. Facilities are good and include wireless Internet access, no-smoking rooms and non-allergic bedding. Quiet location and lavish buffet breakfast. **www.golden-leaf-hotel.de**

FURTHER AFIELD Hotel am Nockherberg

€€

Nockherstrasse 38a, 81541 **Tel** *089 6230010* **Fax** *089 62300129* **Rooms** *38*

What this hotel lacks in stylish design and celebrity clientele it makes up for in convenient location, being close to the River Isar, Deutsches Museum and Gasteig cultural centre. Modern, small and clean with basic decor. Rooms are simple but comfortable and adequate. **www.nockherberg.de**

FURTHER AFIELD Jedermann

€€

Bayerstrasse 95, 80335 **Tel** *089 543240* **Fax** *089 54324111* **Rooms** *55*

Map 5 A2

A clean and comfortable family-run hotel offering good services including free Internet access; transport tickets can also be purchased at reception. Despite the hotel's location on the a main road, the rooms are quiet and family rooms are available on request. Good breakfasts. **www.hotel-jedermann.de**

Key to Price Guide *see p262* **Key to Symbols** *see back cover flap*

FURTHER AFIELD Kriemhild

Guntherstrasse 16, 80639 **Tel** *089 1711170* **Fax** *089 17111755* **Rooms** *18*

For a more peaceful residential setting head out to this family-run hotel near Schloss Nymphenburg. Trams run into the centre in 10 minutes and there is a beautiful park a short walk away. A pleasant hotel with a small breakfast balcony in summer. Suitable for families. Local shops nearby. **www.kriemhild.de**

FURTHER AFIELD Eden Hotel Wolff

Arnulfstrasse 4, 80335 **Tel** *089 551150* **Fax** *089 55115555* **Rooms** *210*

Located directly opposite the main station's side entrance, this elegant four-star hotel offers well appointed modern rooms with wireless Internet access, a cosy bar, a spa oasis and a roof terrace. It also has a Bavarian restaurant. Ask for special packages and reduced rates. **www.ehw.de**

FURTHER AFIELD Insel Mühle

Von-Kahr-Strasse 87, 80999 **Tel** *089 81010* **Fax** *089 8120571* **Rooms** *38*

A romantic hotel housed in an old mill and surrounded by beautiful gardens that extend down to a small river. Rooms have country-style decor and are simple and comfortable. There is also an excellent restaurant, beer garden, wine cellar and bar. **www.insel-muehle.com**

FURTHER AFIELD Olympic

Hans-Sachs-Strasse 4, 80469 **Tel** *089 231890* **Fax** *089 23189199* **Rooms** *38*   **Map** *3 B4*

A small, stylish hotel that is favoured by artists, photographers and fashion designers. The decor is modern Italian with an art gallery lobby. Most rooms look out onto an inner courtyard. Peaceful atmosphere and friendly. Close to great boutiques and cafes and in the heart of a creative area. **www.hotel-olympic.de**

FURTHER AFIELD Anna

Schützenstrasse 1, 80335 **Tel** *089 599940* **Fax** *089 59994333* **Rooms** *56*   **Map** *3 A2*

A design-orientated hotel in the heart of Munich, ten minutes walking distance from Marienplatz. The hotel boasts a café, bar and restaurant, as well as a lounge area with pillars, chandelier and purple sofas. The restaurant serves modern innovative cuisine with Euro-Asian inspiration. **www.geisel-privathotels.de**

FURTHER AFIELD Das Palace

Trogerstrasse 21, 81675 **Tel** *089 419710* **Fax** *089 41971819* **Rooms** *74*

This rather noble hotel has become a haven for culture lovers and artists. It has a lovely garden, a roof garden and a smart restaurant. Guests are treated to mineral water and fruit on arrival and rooms have non-allergic bed linen. Facilities include a hotel bar, sauna, massage and fitness area. Children welcome. **www.muenchenpalace.de**

FURTHER AFIELD Hotel Excelsior

Schützenstrasse 11, 80335 **Tel** *089 551370* **Fax** *089 55137121* **Rooms** *114*   **Map** *3 A2*

An elegant, traditional-style four-star hotel in a convenient central location. The hotel's wine restaurant, Geisel's Vinothek, prides itself on an excellent choice of top Italian wines. Guests of the Excelsior can use facilities in its partner hotel, the Königshof. **www.geisel-privathotels.de**

FURTHER AFIELD Maritim

Goethestrasse 7, 80336 **Tel** *089 552350* **Fax** *089 55235900* **Rooms** *347*

A large hotel catering for conferences and business people. The hotel has two restaurants, a piano bar, sauna and steam bath. The large indoor pool has panoramic views from the top floor. Good central location for shopping and not far from the main station. Also handy for the famous Oktoberfest fairground. **www.maritim.de**

UPPER BAVARIA (NORTH)

DACHAU Fische

Bahnhofstrasse 4, 85221 **Tel** *08131 78205* **Fax** *08131 78508* **Rooms** *26*   **Road Map** *D4*

A clean, modern hotel with airy rooms, located opposite the station and five minutes from the old town. The hotel also has a Loefflers bar with a stage, so as a busy evening venue it may not suit those looking for a quiet hotel in a residential area. Laptop connection in room. **www.hotel-fischer-dachau.de**

DACHAU Zieglerbräu

Konrad-Adenauer-Strasse 8, 85221 **Tel** *08131 454396* **Fax** *08131 45439898* **Rooms** *12*   **Road Map** *D4*

In the middle of Dachau's old town, the Zieglerbräu has undergone a pleasant transformation. Major renovation has brought it into the 21st century and the rooms are bright, comfortable and modern. As well as beer from its own brewery, the hotel offers guests typical Bavarian and international food. Romantic suite available. **www.zieglerbraeu.com**

EICHSTÄTT Adler Hotel

Marktplatz 22–24, 85072 **Tel** *08421 6767* **Fax** *08421 8283* **Rooms** *28*   **Road Map** *C2*

The Adler is housed in a listed building, giving the hotel a traditional feel. The rooms are simply-furnished, clean and comfortable – the double studios overlook the Baroque market square to the front and the town wall to the rear. Ample breakfast buffet with organic and wholegrain products. **www.adler-eichstaett.de**

FREISING Bayerischer Hof

Untere Hauptstrasse 3, 85354 **Tel** *08161 538300* **Fax** *08161 538339* **Rooms** *70*   **Road Map** *D3*

Housed in a former brewery in the old town centre, this hotel has a traditional feel with a typically Bavarian restaurant serving good food. Rooms are clean, comfortable and compact and the hotel is close to shops and restaurants as well as being within easy reach of Munich airport.

FREISING Isar Hotel

Isarstrasse 4, 85356 **Tel** *08161 8650* **Fax** *08161 865555* **Rooms** *56*   **Road Map** *D3*

A family-owned hotel situated on the river Isar close to the old town of Freising. German rustic-style wooden decor, convivial bar and restaurant specialising in Asian food. There is a wireless Internet connection in the lobby, bikes are available for hire and there is a sauna, massage and beauty spa. **www.isarhotel.de**

INGOLSTADT Ara Hotel

Schollstrasse 10a, 85055 **Tel** *0841 95430* **Fax** *0841 9543444* **Rooms** *95*   **Road Map** *D2*

The family-run three star Ara Hotel is located near the centre of Ingolstadt. This is a large crimson-coloured hotel in a contemporary building with outdoor sun terrace and compact comfortable rooms. No-smoking rooms and rooms with wheelchair access are available. The Italian restaurant La Tosca is light and spacious. **www.hotel-ara.de**

NEUBURG Neuwirt

Färberstrasse 88, 86633 **Tel** *08431 2078* **Fax** *08431 38643* **Rooms** *40*   **Road Map** *C2*

A traditional and typically Bavarian small hotel with a familiar local feel. It has a Stube tavern and spacious beer garden that is partly undercover. The adequate rooms are simply decorated with rustic charm. Enjoy the freshly brewed beer from the in-house brewery, Juliusbräu, dating back to 1828. **www.neuwirt-neuburg.de**

LOWER BAVARIA

DEGGENDORF NH Parkhotel

Edlmaierstrasse 4, 94469 **Tel** *0991 34460* **Fax** *0991 3446423* **Rooms** *125*   **Road Map** *F2*

Located close to the River Danube promenade and the old town, this large modern hotel boasts a gym, sauna, solarium and jacuzzi, plus a good restaurant. 24-hour room service and wireless Internet access add to the facilities. There is also a garden terrace and bikes for use. **www.nh-hotels.com**

LANDSHUT Romantik Hotel Fürstenhof

Stethaimer Strasse 3, 84034 **Tel** *0871 92550* **Fax** *0871 925544* **Rooms** *24*   **Road Map** *E3*

Set in a beautiful Art Nouveau villa near the centre of gothic Landshut, this elegant hotel boasts a Michelin-starred restaurant that uses fresh local produce *(see p280)*. Other amenities include a sauna, wireless Internet connection and a peaceful garden. Hiking, golfing and riding are available in the area. **www.romantikhotels.com/landshut**

PASSAU Passauer Wolf

Rindermarkt 6–8, 94032 **Tel** *0851 931510* **Fax** *0851 9315150* **Rooms** *41*   **Road Map** *G3*

The hotel is located in the old town of Passau, next to the pedestrian precinct and on the banks of the Danube. Choose between rooms with a view over the river, the old town, or the courtyard. No-smoking rooms are also available. Bar and roof terrace and within easy walking distance of sights. **www.hotel-passauer-wolf.de**

PASSAU Residenz

Fritz-Schäffer-Promenade, 94032 **Tel** *0851 989020* **Fax** *0851 98902200* **Rooms** *51*   **Road Map** *G3*

Boasting a fabulous river setting with great views of the castle and the Danube, the Residenz is housed in a 15th-century historic building. Rooms have views over the Danube or the old town. The town square is close-by as are boats for taking trips down the Danube. Lovely terrace. **www.residenz-passau.de**

PASSAU Hotel Weisser Hase

Heiliggeistgasse 1, 94032 **Tel** *0851 92110* **Fax** *0851 9211100* **Rooms** *108*   **Road Map** *G3*

Situated in the heart of the city, the Weisser Hase combines 16th century charm with elegance and modern comforts. The hotel's Ludwigsstube is a Bavarian-style restaurant and serves Bavarian and international cuisine. No-smoking rooms are available. **www.weisser-hase.de**

STRAUBING Römerhof Hotel

Ittlinger Strasse 136, 94315 **Tel** *09421 99820* **Fax** *09421 998229* **Rooms** *26*   **Road Map** *E2*

What this hotel lacks in style, it makes up for in its convenient location. This is a good base for tours of the region or visits to the Bayerischer Wald. Most rooms have Internet access. No-smoking rooms are also available. Clean, comfortable and friendly. **www.roemerhof-straubing.de**

STRAUBING Asam

Wittelsbacher Höhe 1, 94315 **Tel** *09421 788680* **Fax** *09421 788688* **Rooms** *37*   **Road Map** *E2*

This four-star hotel is housed in a listed building with an old façade, but is a haven of modern luxury inside. The design and architecture are contemporary and stylish and a harmonious, elegant stay with good facilities is guaranteed. Enjoy the wellness area with steam baths and Finnish sauna, or massage and beauty treatments. **www.hotelasam.de**

Key to Price Guide *see p262*

UPPER BAVARIA (EAST)

ALTÖTTING Zur Post
🔲 🍴 ♨ 🛗 €€

Kapellplatz 2, 84503 Tel 08671 5040 Fax 08671 6214 Rooms 93 **Road Map** F4

Rich in tradition, archdukes, sovereigns and bishops have lodged in this hotel, located in the heart of a charming small town on one of Germany's oldest squares. The rooms are clasically elegant with fine wooden furniture. There are several restaurants, as well as a pool with sauna and steam bath. **www.zurpostaltoetting.de**

ASCHAU Residenz Heinz Winkler
🔲 🍴 ♨ 🛗 €€€

Kirchplatz 1, 83229 Tel 08052 17990 Fax 08052 179966 Rooms 33 **Road Map** E5

A culinary destination for real gourmands *(see p281)*. Masterchef Heinz Winkler took over the original Post Hotel here in 1989. The former medieval building now has luxurious rooms plus invigorating and rejuvenating spa treatments against a wonderful Alpine backdrop. Enjoy the terrace and garden. **www.residenz-heinz-winkler.de**

BAD REICHENHALL Axelmannstein
🔲 🍴 ♨ 🛠 🛗 🏢 €€€€

Salzburgerstrasse 2–6, 83435 Tel 08651 7770 Fax 08651 5932 Rooms 151 **Road Map** F5

Pamper yourself in this Steigenberger health and beauty hotel in the Bavarian Alps. As well as a wealth of beauty and massage treatments, the hotel has traditional first class service and facilities that include tennis, a putting green and excellent restaurant. Set in a beautiful park. **www.bad-reichenhall.steigenberger.de**

BERCHTESGADEN Alpenhotel Fischer
🔲 🍴 ♨ 🛠 🛗 €€

Königsseer Strasse 51, 83471 Tel 08652 9550 Fax 08652 955255 Rooms 54 **Road Map** F5

A pretty chalet-style hotel with balconies and fantastic Alpine views. Rooms have free wireless Internet access and are in a contemporary Alpine style. There is a cosy bar and lounge, as well as saunas, beauty and massage treatments, plus a good restaurant. Centrally located in Berchtesgaden, but quiet. **www.alpenhotel-fischer.de**

BURGHAUSEN Landhotel Reisingers Bayerische Alm
🍴 🛠 🛗 €€

Robert-Koch-Str. 211, 84489 Tel 08677 9820 Fax 08677 982200 Rooms 23 **Road Map** F4

A cosy, family-run hotel in Burghausen, overlooking the castle and old town. Amenities include wireless Internet access, free parking and non-allergic bedding. Enjoy excellent food in the hotel's beautiful beer garden, the menus are macrobiotic *(see p281)*, or sit under chestnut trees and take in the spectacular views. **www.bayerischealm.de**

REIT IM WINKL Unterwirt
🔲 🍴 ♨ 🛠 🛗 €€€

Kirchplatz 2, 83242 Tel 08640 8010 Fax 08640 801150 Rooms 71 **Road Map** E5

In the heart of the town is this elegant, rustic chalet with a frescoed façade. It has Alpine wooden furniture and an open fire and is located in a great skiing area. In summer take advantage of the many mountain walks, as well as indoor and outdoor pools. **www.unterwirt.de**

ROSENHEIM Panorama
🔲 🍴 🛠 €€

Brixstrasse 3, 83022 Tel 08031 3060 Fax 08031 306415 Rooms 89 **Road Map** E4

Centrally located in Rosenheim, the Panorama hotel has a variety of rooms to offer as well as two larger apartments. Pleasant decor and clean, comfy rooms, if not very contemporary. Take breakfast in the winter garden but dine elsewhere as the hotel restaurant is for groups or private parties. **www.panoramacityhotel.de**

WASSERBURG AM INN Paulanerstuben
🍴 🛠 €

Marienplatz 9, 83512 Tel 08071 39 03 Fax 08071 50474 Rooms 17 **Road Map** E4

The core of the building housing this hotel is Gothic, the façade is early Rococo. The right half of the building became a hotel in the early 1970s and makes for a pleasant stay. The rooms are basic but have good views and there is a restaurant and tavern at street level. **www.paulanerstuben-wasserburg.de**

UPPER BAVARIA (SOUTH)

BAD TÖLZ Jodquellenhof Alpamare
 €€€€

Ludwigstrasse 13–15, 83646 Tel 08041 5090 Fax 08041 509555 Rooms 90 **Road Map** D5

One for families and adventure lovers, this resort hotel is located at the Water Park Alpamare. Most rooms have balconies, and are housed in two villas that are well equipped and comfortable. Hotel guests have free entry to the water park. Beauty treatments also available. Five minutes walk to Bad Tölz town centre. **www.jodquellenhof.com**

BERG Seehotel Leoni
 €€€€

Assenbucher Strasse 44, 82335 Tel 08151 5060 Fax 08151 506140 Rooms 67 **Road Map** C4

A stylish modern building with an Italian flair. The rooms are in cool creams with contemporary art adorning the walls and there is a superb garden sitting directly on the Starnberg lake in Berg, 25km south of Munich. Good restaurant, views from the veranda and sun terraces, spa and pool. **www.seehotel-leoni.com**

DIESSEN Strandhotel
Jahnstrasse 10, 86911 **Tel** *08807 92220* **Fax** *08807 8958* **Rooms** *17* **Road Map** *C4*

This hotel enjoys a great location on lake Ammersee and makes for a good family base. The rooms are simple, functional and affordable and come in various categories. They all have a balcony or terrace. There is also a café with homemade cakes. Nearby are tennis, golf, swimming and watersports facilities. **www.diessen.net/strandhotel**

GARMISCH-PARTENKIRCHEN Hotel Bavaria
Partnachstrasse 51, 82467 **Tel** *08821 3466* **Fax** *08821 76466* **Rooms** *32* **Road Map** *C5*

A small, family-run hotel just out of the centre of Garmisch, offering guests an old fashioned charm and hospitality. Rooms are tastefully decorated and there is a wonderful garden – guests are permitted to fish in the river here. Swimming baths and fitness facilities are available not far from the hotel. **www.hotel-bavaria-garmisch.com**

GARMISCH-PARTENKIRCHEN Post-Hotel Partenkirchen
Ludwigstrasse 49, 82467 **Tel** *08821 93630* **Fax** *08821 93632222* **Rooms** *59* **Road Map** *C5*

The oldest building in the town, King Ludwig II once housed his generals here. The hotel is in traditional Bavarian style with antique wooden furniture and rich colours. The rooms are compact and cosy and there is a lovely terrace with mountain views. An elegant restaurant for formal meals, as well as good cakes in the café. **www.post-hotel.de**

KOCHEL AM SEE Grauer Bär
Mittenwalder Strasse 82, 82431 **Tel** *08851 92500* **Fax** *08851 925015* **Rooms** *26* **Road Map** *C5*

A lakeside hotel between Garmisch and Bad Tölz, the Grauer Bär offers comfortable, traditional-style accommodation surrounded by natural beauty. Whirlpools, sun terraces and beauty treatments are among the facilities. A wonderful place to relax and unwind or a good base for hiking. **www.grauer-baer.de**

LANDSBERG AM LECH Goggl Garni
Hubert von Herkomer Strasse 19–20, 86899 **Tel** *08191 3240* **Fax** *08191 324100* **Rooms** *60* **Road Map** *C4*

This is a pretty and traditional Bavarian house with some wonderful hand-painted furniture and four-poster beds in the suites. It dates back to 1667, is located in the heart of the old town and offers a good spa and wellness area. Comfortable beds and Internet access in the rooms. **www.hotelgoggl.de**

MURNAU Alpenhof Murnau
Ramsachstrasse 8, 82418 **Tel** *08841 4910* **Fax** *08841 491100* **Rooms** *60* **Road Map** *C5*

Alpenhof Murnau is a spa and luxury five-star chalet-style retreat, close to Oberammergau. It borders the Murnauer Moos nature reserve, overlooking the Alps and Staffel lake. An idyllic setting which inspired Kandinsky and Marc, among other artists. Enjoy the renowned cuisine in the Reiterzimmer restaurant. **www.alpenhof-murnau.com**

OBERAMMERGAU Turmwirt
Ettalerstrasse 2, 82487 **Tel** *08822 92600* **Fax** *08822 1437* **Rooms** *22* **Road Map** *C5*

In the same family for three generations, this small hotel is situated in the heart of Oberammergau, next to the church. It has a wooden reception in traditional Bavarian style with antique chests and rugs and a sun terrace with outdoor tables under chestnut trees. There is an à la carte restaurant and a café. **www.turmwirt.de**

THE ALLGÄU

FÜSSEN-HOPFEN AM SEE Alpenblick
Uferstrasse 10, 87629 **Tel** *08362 50570* **Fax** *08362 505773* **Rooms** *61* **Road Map** *B5*

Although cosy, guests come more for the stunning views across the lake and Alps than for the style of this hotel. This is a good place to relax and offers great opportunities for hiking, fishing and cycling. Hotel facilities include sauna, steam bath and solarium. The restaurant specializes in fish from the Hopfen lake *(see p282)*. **www.alpenblick.de**

FÜESSEN Treff Hotel Luitpoldpark
Luitpoldstraße, 87629 **Tel** *08362 9040* **Fax** *08362 904678* **Rooms** *131* **Road Map** *B5*

Housed in a majestic building in the heart of Füssen, this hotel boasts four restaurants *(see p282)* serving Bavarian cuisine, a fitness centre, massage, sauna and tanning salon. The decor is classic and modern and the surroundings – the Alps, lakes, King's Nook park – are superb. **www.luitpoldpark-hotel.de**

KEMPTEN Bayerischer Hof
Füssener Strasse 96, 87437 **Tel** *0831 57180* **Fax** *0831 5718100* **Rooms** *50* **Road Map** *B5*

The decor of this four-star hotel is an eclectic mix of styles from Mediterranean to Louis XIV. Rooms have views over the park or river and come with a complimentary bottle of mineral water and Internet access. There is also a Bavarian restaurant and beer garden plus a small exercise and relaxation area. **www.bayerischerhof-kempten.de**

LINDAU Bayerischer Hof
Seepromenade, 88131 **Tel** *08382 9150* **Fax** *08382 915591* **Rooms** *97* **Road Map** *A5*

Housed in a luxurious Neo-Classical building dating back to 1854, this hotel is located on the Lindau harbour front. The rooms and suites are spacious and light and the hotel has excellent fitness, sauna and well-being facilities. Enjoy the international cuisine in the restaurant *(see p283)* and the views from the bar. **www.bayerischerhof-lindau.de**

Key to Price Guide *see p262* **Key to Symbols** *see back cover flap*

LINDAU Reutemann Seegarten €€€

Seepromenade, 88131 **Tel** *08382 9150* **Fax** *08382 915591* **Rooms** *64* — **Road Map** *A5*

This hotel enjoys a lovely setting on the promenade of the pretty town of Lindau on Lake Constance. Rooms have balconies with views across the lake to the Austrian Alps. The hotel terrace and bar also boast good views. Fitness and well-being facilities are available at the Seegarten's sister hotel next door. **www.reutemann-lindau.de**

LINDAU Villino €€€€

Hoyerberg 34, 88131 **Tel** *08382 93450* **Fax** *08382 934512* **Rooms** *16* — **Road Map** *A5*

Located behind Lindau, in the bordering village of Hoyren on the Hoyerberg hill, is this idyllic country residence. Set in a beautiful garden, artistic culture and haute cuisine are paramount to the Villino. Used here are rich fabrics and decor, the cuisine is inspired by Asian-Italian fusion *(see p283)* and there is a terrace and spa. **www.villino.de**

OBERTSDORF Kappeler Haus €€

Am Seeler 2, 87561 **Tel** *08322 96860* **Fax** *08322 968613* **Rooms** *45* — **Road Map** *B6*

This three star chalet-style hotel in the Allgäu Alps is located in the heart of Obertsdorf, the southern most village in Germany. Expect mountain scenery, lots of wood and recently renovated rooms. Music recitals take place in the hotel and an in-house beautician is on hand to pamper guests. **www.kappeler-haus.de**

NORTHERN SWABIA

AUGSBURG Dom Hotel €€

Frauentorstrasse 8, 86152 **Tel** *0821 343930* **Fax** *0821 34393200* **Rooms** *52* — **Road Map** *C3*

Family owned for four generations, this historic hotel is located in a quiet street at the Bischofsmauer, the old town wall. Close to the cathedral and within walking distance of all the sights and local restaurants. There is a pool, sauna and fitness area and parking is available in the hotel's own garage. **www.domhotel-augsburg.de**

AUGSBURG Romantikhotel Augsburger Hof €€

Auf dem Kreuz 2, 86152 **Tel** *0821 343050* **Fax** *0827 3430555* **Rooms** *36* — **Road Map** *C3*

Located opposite Mozart's house in the centre of Augsburg, this newly-renovated hotel is located five minutes from the pedestrian zone. The contemporary rooms are decorated in a smart, rustic, country-house style. Regional Swabian food is served in the restaurant alongside a cosy and stylish café-bar. **www.augsburger-hof.de**

AUGSBURG Steigenberger Drei Mohren €€€

Maximilianstrasse 40, 86150 **Tel** *0821 50360* **Fax** *0827 157864* **Rooms** *105* — **Road Map** *C3*

This hotel, in the heart of the historic old town, is an excellent base for visiting the sights. Its well-appointed rooms house antiques and old paintings while its restaurant, Maximilian's, is one of the city's best. Comfort and excellent service. Short walk from the museum, theatre and palaces. **www.augsburg.steigenberger.de**

DILLINGEN Dillinger Hof €

Rudolf-Diesel-Strasse 8, 89407 **Tel** *09071 58740* **Fax** *09071 8323* **Rooms** *47* — **Road Map** *B3*

A contemporary hotel with pleasant rooms and a few design surprises including a glass lift and a tree in the breakfast room. The traditional restaurant serves local specialities for lunch and dinner under a vaulted ceiling. The basement boasts a large fitness room. This is a good place to stay for trips to local castles or Legoland. **www.dillingerhof.de**

DONAUWÖRTH Posthotel Traube €

Kapellstrasse 14, 86609 **Tel** *0906 706440* **Fax** *0906 23390* **Rooms** *40* — **Road Map** *C2*

This modern hotel boasts a historic past as the stopover for the post stage-coach. Located in the heart of the town, the Traube has a café, bar and restaurant, offering a variety of international and local cuisine, plus a beer garden for summer use. Sauna and massage facilities and friendly, English-speaking staff. **www.posthoteltraube.de**

HARBURG Zum Straußen €

Marktplatz 2, 86655 **Tel** *09080 1398* **Fax** *09080 4324* **Rooms** *15* — **Road Map** *B2*

Located in the market square, this small, family-run hotel is part of an inn with a traditional restaurant. Come for the typical Swabian hospitality and taste some of the local hearty dishes. The rooms are affordable and offer a good base for exploring the region. No-smoking rooms and parking available. **hotel-straussen@web.de**

NEU-ULM Römer Villa €€

Parkstrasse 1, 89231 **Tel** *0731 800040* **Fax** *0731 8000450* **Rooms** *23* — **Road Map** *B3*

This hotel is housed in an elegant, turreted building set back from the road on the edge of a park. It has a lofty vaulted reception, lounge with open fire, wine bar, high quality restaurant and a winter garden. The classic traditionally-furnished rooms come with a balcony or terrace. **www.roemer-villa.de**

NÖRDLINGEN Klösterle €€

Beim Klösterle 1, 86720 **Tel** *09081 87080* **Fax** *09081 8708100* **Rooms** *98* — **Road Map** *B2*

This former Franciscan monastery, with stepped gables, is stylish and modern on the inside with contemporary room decor, ambient lighting and comfortable furnishings. The restaurant serves up a good variety of international and regional dishes. There is a gym on the fourth floor. **www.nh-hotels.com**

WHERE TO EAT

Although the food that is normally served in the Bavarian Alps is rather basic fare, it is however always tasty and satisfying. Grilled knuckle of pork, sausage, dumplings and the indispensable litre mugs of beer are enjoyed everywhere from village inns to renowned Munich pubs. Consumed against a background of heated conversation, laughter and singing, they constitute a kind of culinary experience in themselves. The beer garden *(Biergarten)* is one of Bavaria's trademarks. The best-known beer gardens, usually attached to monastic breweries, are popular gathering places for local people and tourists alike.

However, those looking for a little more sophistication will find a variety of restaurants in towns and holiday resorts, where Italian, Turkish and Greek restaurants enjoy the greatest popularity.

Dallmayr restaurant and coffee house, Munich Old Town (see p277)

TYPES OF RESTAURANTS

The great variety of restaurants that can be found in the Bavarian Alps reflects the fact that the region is orientated towards tourism. Genuine Bavarian meals are served primarily in *Gasthaus*-type establishments. In central Munich and in tourist resorts, restaurants tend towards the kitsch, and some leave something to be desired. It is vastly preferable to eat in an inn frequented by local people, where prices are lower and where dishes, although they are served with less ceremony, usually taste much better. However, visitors should be prepared for a little local colour: some local inns are filled with cigarette smoke or may reverberate to the sound of loud conversations between drinkers who have over-indulged.

A good place eating place is usually the *Ratskeller*, a pub in the cellar of the town hall, where regional specialities are served. There are also wine bars *(Weinstuben)*, which in addition to fine wines also serve good food, although usually charging relatively high prices.

Other options for sampling good regional food along with local beer are the *Bierstuben* and *Bierkeller*, pubs usually belonging to a local brewery. They are often noisy, and seating is on long benches where you soon fall into conversation with your fellow-diners and drinkers.

Attractive features of Bavarian beer-drinking rituals are the gigantic beer tents *(Bierzelte)* that are put up during local holidays, as well as the charming little beer gardens *(Biergärten)*, where customers order their drinks from the bar. It is even permissible to bring your own food to some of them.

There are also Italian pizzerias, Greek tavernas, steak houses, and Chinese, Turkish and Balkan restaurants as well as the ubiquitous international fast-food outlets and snack bars.

At the other end of the scale, particularly in Munich, there are elegant, discerning restaurants with elevated standards of service, décor and cuisine, with high prices to match.

Exotic murals covering the walls of one of Munich's dining rooms

WHAT AND WHEN TO EAT

Breakfast is usually a hearty affair with various types of bread accompanied by cheese, sausages and marmalade. On Sundays brunch is served in

A sunny beer garden near the Viktualienmarkt, Munich

Formal dining at Königshof's gourmet restaurant *(see p278)*

most places until 2pm: this is a combination of breakfast and lunch, in the form of a Swedish buffet. During the lunch period (noon to 2pm) most establishments serve excellent salads or bowls of filling soup, while many restaurants offer a fixed-price menu. Restaurants start to fill up in the evenings between 6 and 7pm, although dinner is usually eaten after 8pm.

OPENING HOURS

Most cafeterias and fast-food chains open at 9am. Other establishments open at noon and usually close after the lunchtime period until about 6pm. Many restaurants close on one day of the week, known as *Ruhetag*. Beer gardens in towns usually close at 11pm. Most restaurants stay open right up until midnight or 1am.

MENU

Most restaurants post their menu, together with their prices, at the door. Attached to the main menu may be an additional sheet listing seasonal dishes, such as fresh mussels, or indicating the dish of the day, such as fresh fish, roast meat or homemade pies. Desserts and soft and alcoholic drinks are usually listed on a separate menu.

In many good restaurants the menu is written in German and English, and sometimes also in French. In cafés and less expensive restaurants, the menu may be handwritten, in which case staff may be able to help with a translation.

RESERVATIONS

Making a prior reservation is essential in all the best restaurants. In most good and medium-standard restaurants it is advisable to do so, particularly on a Friday or Saturday night or on public holidays. If you have not made a reservation, you may be asked to wait or to return later.

Many inns and restaurants in Bavaria have a *Stammtisch*, a table set aside for regular local people and groups at certain times on certain days.

PRICES AND TIPS

Prices charged in Bavarian restaurants are diverse, those in Munich's top restaurants being the highest. A meal consisting of roast meat with dumplings and salad served in a country inn is almost half the price that is charged in the most popular tourist areas.

The cost of a main course in an inn or restaurant ranges from €5–6 in the cheapest places to €13–18 in superior establishments. The average cost of a three-course meal

including salad and beer is about €25. This includes tax and service, but it is customary to leave a 10 per cent tip. If paying by card, this can be added to the bill.

VEGETARIAN FOOD

Vegetarian food has become increasingly popular in Germany in recent years. The number of vegetarian restaurants is increasing, and snack bars offering vegetarian meals are enjoying considerable popularity. More inns and restaurants now include meat-free meals on their main menus, while vegetarian pizzas are a standard item in Italian restaurants.

The Glöckl am Dom restaurant in Munich *(see p276)*

DISABLED VISITORS

Many inns and restaurants are unfortunately without access facilities for disabled people. Often doorways are too narrow for wheelchairs and tables are too closely placed, and there may be no specially adapted toilets. When making the reservation, it is advisable to enquire what the conditions are in a particular establishment.

The main room of the Munich Ratskeller

The Flavours of Munich & Bavaria

Bavarian cooking has a reputation for huge portions of hearty food, best enjoyed along with a beer. Sausages of all kinds, superb pork and beef, regional fish, and freshly baked breads and cakes are the standard fare for locals and visitors alike. But many restaurants now also prepare local and other German dishes with a lighter touch – indeed, Munich once spearheaded German *nouvelle cuisine*. While the city has lost its gourmet crown to the likes of Hamburg, Düsseldorf, and Berlin, the general standard of cooking in the Bavarian capital is still superb.

Harzer Roller and Emmenthaler cheeses

Giant pretzels, best eaten warm and soft from the oven

HEARTY BAVARIAN COOKING

Bavarian cooking developed in the countryside, where hard-working farmers needed high-carbohydrate food made using local, fresh produce – home-made bread, noodles and dumplings along with things like home-reared meat, farm-produced cheeses, and river fish such as carp.

In Munich, during its centuries as the seat of the Wittelsbach dynasty, these country influences were refined into a solidly bourgeois cuisine. To this day, the hearty, no-nonsense dishes of Bavaria are what the world considers to be German cuisine. Sweet *Weißwürstchen* (white veal sausages with a beer pretzel) are enjoyed in the morning, often with a beer. Dinner might be soup with liver dumplings, roast pork, *sauerkraut* and a pile of potato dumplings or noodles. Local produce is still held in high regard. Delicatessens abound in Munich, and markets are found throughout the region. Pride of place goes to the Viktualienmarkt, in the historic heart of town (*see p64*), where you can shop for, sample and eat authentic Bavarian cooking at the many food stalls.

Mehrkornbrötchen (mixed grain roll)   **Berliner Landbrot (mild rye bread)**

Laugenbrötchen (salty sourdough rolls)

Grau-Oder Mischbrot (wholewheat)

Semmel (milk-dough roll)

Selection of typical German loaves and bread rolls

BAVARIAN DISHES AND SPECIALITIES

Bavarian cooking is a great blend of filling dishes and tasty snacks or *brotzeit* ("bread time") between main meals. A typical *brotzeit* consists of any cold meat, such as smoked bacon or sausage, slices of roast pork or liver sausage, freshly sliced *radi* (radish) and some cheese, preferably Obatza, a creamy Camembert mousse. Main courses focus on pork, with the famous Schweinshaxe and Schweinsbraten (with beer gravy) leading the field. The Schweinshaxe in particular is a must-have in Munich. Both are eaten with potato dumplings – the famous Bavarian *knödel* – to absorb the rich gravy. Of course, none of these dishes would be complete without a nice, cold beer.

Pork salamis

Leberknödelsuppe *is a rich, clear beef broth in which little liver dumplings are lightly poached.*

Fresh vegetables on display at Munich's historic Viktualienmarkt

MUNICH'S GOURMET REVOLUTION

It may seem strange that a city of hearty and hefty cooking instigated a trend for low-fat gourmet German cuisine. At the forefront was Eckart Witzigmann (still Germany's most popular chef) who, inspired by French *nouvelle cuisine*, began to re-invent Bavarian and German dishes using unusual combinations of exquisite ingredients. Witzigmann's legendary Munich-based Aubergine was the first German restaurant to gain three Michelin stars. Munich's top restaurants still retain a reputation for innovative cooking. Recently, certain chic venues have also attracted the *bussi-bussi* (air kissing) crowd with Italian, Asian and Fusion cuisine, served in a stylish setting.

BAVARIAN BEER

Of the more than 1,250 breweries in Germany, many of the largest and most famous are in Munich, among them Löwenbräu, Augustiner, Paulaner and Hofbräu. Beer

Beer served in a traditional Munich *Biergarten* (beer garden)

is still brewed in strict accordance to the "Reinheitsgebot", a Bavarian decree of 1516 ordering that only malted barley, hops and water should be used. Today there many different kinds of beer available, from dark, strong Bock beer to lighter (in colour and alcohol) beers such as the famous Weizen or *Weißbier* (white beer).

Most beers on tap in Munich are served in a *mass*, a special 1-litre (2 pint) glass mug. For the more fainthearted, there is also a *halbe*, a half-litre mug.

The exuberant annual highlight of Munich's proud beer culture is the famous Oktoberfest (*see p29*).

WEISSWÜRSTE

There is no other dish from Bavaria as classic as a pair of Weisswürste. These delicious veal sausages are steamed and served hot with sweet, grainy mustard and a *Brezen* (beer pretzel). Traditionally, they should be eaten in the morning, as a second breakfast or a snack before lunch, but never at other times of the day; hence the old Munich saying that "the sausage should not hear the clocks sound noon". But even if it's early, a beer is the right accompaniment for Weisswürste. Some locals don't eat the sausages with a knife and fork, but simply suck out the meat from the Weisswürste's thin skin, an art called *auszuzeln* in Munich.

Tafelspitz, *poached beef brisket with vegetables, is usually served with red cabbage and horseradish.*

Schweinshaxe, *or roast pork knuckle, is a Bavarian classic. It is eaten with potato dumplings and sauerkraut.*

Dampfnudel *is a Bavarian yeasted dumpling cake that is soaked in a delicious vanilla-caramel sauce.*

Beer in Bavaria

Hop flower

Bavaria is famous the world over for its excellent beer, which is exported to over 140 countries. As part of their cultural tradition, Bavarians scrupulously observe the *Reinheitsgebot*, a law of 1516 according to which the only ingredients brewers may use are barley, hops and water. The Bavarians even made accession to the Weimar Republic in 1919 conditional on the acknowledgment of this law. The annual Oktoberfest is the high point of Bavaria's brewing tradition.

The Oktoberfest – a beer festival that is cheerfully celebrated by the Bavarians

The famous Löwenbräu beer

Logo of one of Bavaria's best-known breweries

A beer mat

BAVARIAN BREWERIES

In 1040 the monks of Weihenstephan monastery, which is now on the outskirts of modern Freising, were granted a licence to brew beer by the city's bishop. The brewery, which still produces beer to this day, is the oldest in the world. Fifty percent of all breweries in the European Union are located in Bavaria. Many Bavarian breweries have centuries of tradition behind them. The best-known are the main Munich breweries – Löwenbräu, Hofbräu, Paulanerbräu, Augustinerbräu, Spatenbräu and Hacker-Pschorrbräu.

Many smaller breweries can also be found throughout the region, usually with their own inns (*Wirtschaften*) or pubs with beer gardens. Many of them are the object of special "pilgrimages" made both by Bavarians and by tourists. The most highly esteemed of these inns include the Klosterbrauerei Andechs, the Weltenburg and Irsee breweries, which continue the time-honoured tradition of monastic brewing, and Schlossbrauerei Kaltenberg, which belongs to Duke Luitpold of Bavaria. The long-standing debate over who brews the best beer will, quite obviously, never be resolved.

TRADITIONAL DARK AND LIGHT BEERS

Until the 19th century, the only beer drunk in Bavaria was the sweeter dark beer (*Dunkel*). Some breweries continue to specialize in *Dunkel* today; the best known of these are the Weltenburg monastery brewery (which makes Barock Dunkel) and the Schlossbrauerei Kaltenberg (König Ludwig Dunkel).

In the 20th century dark beer was replaced by lighter lager-type beer (*Helles*), which is clear, a little more potent and with a less bitter taste. *Naturtrüb*, an unfiltered beer with an excellent taste, is slightly cloudy because of its yeast content.

Good beer is served cold and should have a thick head that does not settle quickly. It is served in a litre (2-pint) mug (*eine Maß*), as a half litre (1 pint) (*eine Halbe*) and more rarely as a quarter litre (half a pint) (*ein Kleines*). It tastes best when served from the barrel (as *Fassbier*). Beer served from a keg under pressure is sacrilege to a Bavarian. On hot days, people may drink *Radler*, which is *Helles* mixed with lemonade.

Berchtesgaden lager

König Ludwig dark beer

Paulanerbräu lager

MÄRZENBIER

Before the invention of refrigeration systems, beer was brewed in winter, when the heat would not disrupt the fermentation process. The last brewing was in March and the beer had a higher alcohol content, which helped to prevent it going off. If the brewers' stocks lasted until autumn, before the new season's beer was brewed the cellars were opened and a beer festival was held. The brewing of *Märzenbier* (March beer) continues to this day, even though modern technology has rendered the process obsolete.

At the big autumn beer festivals millions of litres of this strong-tasting light-brown beer are consumed. Beer brewed by the major Munich brewers specially for the Oktoberfest is called *Oktoberfestbier* or *Wiesenbier*. In the autumn it is on offer in many pubs and is sold bottled in shops.

The most widely used type of beer mug

Oktoberfestbier from the Paulanerbräu

BOCK AND DOPPELBOCK

This famous beer gets its name from the town of Einbeck in Lower Saxony. The word "Einbeck" was transmuted by the Bavarian brogue into "Oanbock", which was abbreviated to "Bock". *Bockbier* was first brewed by the court brewery (*Hofbräu*), founded in 1589. The Pauline monks were later renowned for making this type of beer. A more potent variety called *Doppelbock* was produced under the name Salvator. This beer, which the monks used to help them through the rigours of Lent, was brewed to celebrate 19 March, the feast day of St Joseph, the order's patron saint. To this day Joseftag marks the beginning of Munich's *Starkbierfest* (strong beer festival), which takes place in the Paulaner brewery's pub. Salvator inaugurated the production of several other *Doppelbock* beers. The beer is an amber colour and has a strong, slightly bitter taste and a 7 per cent alcohol content.

Salvator Doppelbock

Pretzels – an ideal snack to enjoy with beer

WEIZENBIER

This type of beer is extremely popular in southern Germany, particularly in summer as it is a very refreshing drink. During the brewing process, twice the amount of malted wheat is added to the malted barley, which is why it is known as *Weizenbier* (wheat beer).

Weizenbier has a 5 per cent alcohol content and is a *Vollbier* (full beer). To enhance the flavour it is often drunk with a sliver of lemon. There are many kinds of wheat beer: the light and dark *Weizen-Bockbier* and the yeasty *Hefeweizen* beer. The frothy *Weizen* is slowly poured into a glass which broadens at the top. Mixed with lemonade, it is called *Russ*.

Franziskaner Hefe-Weißbier

Paulanerbräu wheat beer

A beer garden is the best place to enjoy a glass of beer

WHERE TO DRINK

Beer, the Bavarian national drink, is also called "liquid nourishment". It is drunk anywhere and everywhere throughout the region – from the most exclusive restaurants down to the smallest food stalls. However, beer is best enjoyed in beer gardens or at the inns of breweries.

A certain amount of ceremony is attached to the drinking of beer: it is drunk sitting down, in large groups, with songs, laughter and flirting. Almost every town in Bavaria holds a beer festival at least once a year.

Choosing a Restaurant

The restaurants in this guide have been selected for their good value, exceptional food, or interesting location. These listings highlight some of the factors that may influence your choice, such as whether you can opt to eat outdoors or if the venue has a good wine list. Entries are listed alphabetically within each price category.

PRICE CATEGORIES
Price categories for a three-course meal for one with half a bottle of wine and including service and taxes:
€ under 30 euros
€€ 30–45 euros
€€€ 45–60 euros
€€€€ 60–90 euros
€€€€€ over 90 euros

MUNICH

OLD TOWN SOUTH Bratwurstherzl   €

Dreifaltigkeitsplatz 1, 80331 **Tel** *089 295113*   **Map** *3 C3*

A traditional tavern right behind the Viktualienmarkt food market serving a variety of *Bratwurst* sausage specialities, the best ones from Nürnberg. The *Bratwurst* come with potato salad, *sauerkraut* or creamed horseradish. There are also other hearty meat dishes on offer, some salads for the non-meat eaters and lots of beers.

OLD TOWN SOUTH Buxs   €

Frauenstrasse 9, 80469 **Tel** *089 2919550*   **Map** *3 C3*

This organic café-restaurant is a wonderful self-service vegetarian and vegan option. On offer are great lunch or inbetween light meals – pick from the warm and cold buffet bars then pay by weight at the till (cash only). Very healthy, tasty, colourful and fresh. Closed dinner; Sun.

OLD TOWN SOUTH Niederlassung   €

Buttermelcherstrasse 6, 80469 **Tel** *089 32600307*   **Map** *3 C3*

This cosy restaurant and bar with a lounge-style atmosphere is a hip nightspot for drinks and great food. The cuisine has a strong Asian influence with curries and soups, as well as good pasta. The fireplace, sofas and subdued lighting all make for an intimate atmosphere. Choose from a wide range of beers or try one of the many great cocktails.

OLD TOWN SOUTH Prinz Myshkin   €

Hackenstrasse 2, 80331 **Tel** *089 265596*   **Map** *3 B2*

Superb vegetarian restaurant with good quality cuisine. The Prinz has an arty atmosphere and a welcoming buzz. Popular for lunches and dinners alike, all the ingredients are fresh and the menu varies daily. A good alternative to Bavarian beer and wurst. Located in a side street off Sendlinger Strasse.

OLD TOWN SOUTH Yum   €

Utzschneiderstrasse 6, 80469 **Tel** *089 23230660*   **Map** *3 B3*

A fashionable and trendy Thai kitchen and bar with dark interior full of glamorous media types. Black walls, orchids and spotlit gilt buddhas provide the setting for wonderfully presented food. Sample authentic Thai curry with coconut sauce, stir fries and spicy fish soups. Great atmosphere.

OLD TOWN SOUTH Glockenspiel   €€

Marienplatz 28, 5th floor, 80331 **Tel** *089 264256*   **Map** *3 B2*

Tucked around the corner from the main town hall square, this great café-restaurant has a lovely terrace and views over the roof tops. Smart Parisian-style bistro with shuttered windows and warm coloured walls. Favourites include seafood on glass noodles, salmon on saffron spinach and good cakes.

OLD TOWN SOUTH Riva   €€

Tal 44, 80331 **Tel** *089 220240*   **Map** *3 C3*

Riva bar is a popular Italian pizzeria and espresso bar serving good food throughout the day. It appeals particularly to chic moneyed Müncheners who come here for lunch or drinks after work. Riva offers a taste of Italy without the kitsch decor and is well-located, a short walk from Marienplatz and metro stations.

OLD TOWN NORTH Glöckl am Dom   €

Frauenplatz 9, 80331 **Tel** *089 2919450*   **Map** *3 B2*

For a real taste of Bavaria come and tuck into some Nürnberger Bratwurst sausages, hearty noodle soups or ox fillet. There are also plenty of side dishes and salads. The restaurant has a pretty traditional flair with red geraniums in window boxes and tables out front in summer. Located on the cathedral square facing the vast Frauenkirche church.

OLD TOWN NORTH Zum Franziskaner   €

Residenzstrasse 9, Perusastrasse 5, 80331 **Tel** *089 2318120*   **Map** *3 C1*

A restaurant that is rich in tradition and one of the best places to head for typical Bavarian specials. The homemade white sausage here, *Weißwurst*, is famous in Munich. Also worth a try is the Bavarian meatloaf with mustard and the fillet of ox. Being the brewery restaurant, it is essential to sample the Franziskaner beer, originally brewed by monks.

Key to Symbols *see back cover flap*

OLD TOWN NORTH Dallmayr
€€

Dienerstrasse 14–15, 80331 **Tel** *089 2135100*   **Map** *3 C2*

Dallmayr is a Munich institution, famous for its coffee house and café. The elegant restaurant offers delicious treats such as zucchini flowers with lobster on a bed of ratatouille, plus a selection of superb wines. Popular with locals and tourists for its high level of service, patisserie and cuisine. Located behind Marienplatz.

OLD TOWN NORTH Kulisse
€€

Maximilianstrasse 26, 80539 **Tel** *089 294728*   **Map** *4 D2*

The theatre-restaurant of the Munich Kammerspiele remains a popular meeting place for theatregoers. There is a wide choice of food; from Asian-influenced dishes to Bavarian specialities and vegetarian dishes. The service is attentive and the outside tables are perfect for soaking up the atmosphere of Maximilianstrasse.

OLD TOWN NORTH Spatenhaus
€€

An der Oper, Residenzstrasse 12, 80333 **Tel** *089 2907060*   **Map** *3 C1*

This is part of the renowned Kuffler company and a classic place to sample traditional Bavarian cuisine. The first floor is more informal for hearty meals, the second more sophisticated with great views of the Opera House opposite. Specials include stuffed breast of veal or meatballs with homemade potato salad or a slow-baked cabbage roll.

OLD TOWN NORTH Austernkeller
€€€

Stollbergstrasse 11, 80539 **Tel** *089 298787*   **Map** *4 D2*

Well established with a great reputation for over 25 years, Munich's famous seafood restaurant specialises in oysters. The cuisine here is typically French using the fresh catch of the day. Be sure to ask for the daily specials. Also recommended are the scallops and French onion soup. Romantic and intimate feel with a central location.

OLD TOWN NORTH Dukatz
€€€

Salvatorplatz 1, 80331 **Tel** *089 2919600*   **Map** *3 B1*

Housed in Munich's Literaturhaus (House of Literature) Dukatz has won accolades for being good and priceworthy. The lofty cream and wooden bistro serves an excellent choice of light Mediterranean dishes with seasonal menus that change on a daily basis. Meat or fish with vegetables or salads in mouth-watering varieties.

OLD TOWN NORTH Ederer
€€€

Kardinal-Faulhaber-Strasse 10, 80333 **Tel** *089 24231310*   **Map** *3 B1*

This first-floor restaurant within the Fünf Höfe building offers sleek design, gourmet treats and excellent fish and seafood – try terrine of sardines and sweet peppers or pea soup and gambas, all fresh from the market. The cellar, furthermore, is stocked with over 500 great wines. Dine on the courtyard terrace in summer.

OLD TOWN NORTH Garden Restaurant
€€€

Promenadenplatz 2–6, 80333 **Tel** *089 2120993*   **Map** *3 B2*

This lovely roof garden restaurant is the elegant option within Munich's luxury hotel, Bayerischer Hof. The menu and decor are inspired by the southern Mediterranean. Try the grilled wild salmon, pan fried foie gras, orange and braised fennel ravioli, lamb or fish dishes. Fabulous views across the city rooftops.

OLD TOWN NORTH Mark's Restaurant Mandarin Oriental
€€€€

Neuturmstrasse 1, 80331 **Tel** *089 29098875*   **Map** *3 C2*

Mark's offers fine dining in sumptuous surroundings. There is a special monthly menu here and over 400 wines to choose from. Resident chef Mario Corti's lavish menu includes such dishes as white halibut in wild garlic and artichoke sauce, and medallion of beef fillet with green asparagus, risotto of morels and beurre blanc.

AROUND THE ISAR Gandl
€€

St.Anna-Platz 1, 80538 **Tel** *089 29162525*   **Map** *4 D1*

Gandl is the hotel restaurant of the attractive Opera Hotel (*see p263*), serving a light Italian cuisine at midday and a fine French cuisine in the evenings. Depending on the time of year you can eat by the open fire or on the lovely terrace. Excellent starters, steak, lamb, fish and duck dishes followed by French cheeses. Good selection of wines.

AROUND THE ISAR Königsquelle
€€

Baaderplatz 2, 80469 **Tel** *089 220071*   **Map** *3 C3*

A gem for whisky lovers who flock here for the whisky bar. The food ranges from simple to refined – the veal *Wiener Schnitzel* comes highly recommended. A warm friendly atmosphere with good reliable service. Good beer and wine as well as whisky. The restaurant is popular so book ahead.

AROUND THE ISAR Goa
€€€

Thierschstrasse 8, 80538 **Tel** *089 21111789*   **Map** *4 D2*

A good Indian restaurant near the Deutsches Museum and a short walk from Isartor metro station. On offer are a variety of Indian meals – chicken curries, lamb specials, kormas, koftas, marsalas and vegetarian specials. Cosy, small and friendly, it is popular for both lunches and dinners. Closed Sat lunch.

AROUND THE ISAR Nektar
€€€

Stubenvollstrasse 1, 81667 **Tel** *089 45911311*   **Map** *4 E3*

A contemporary, decadent experience awaits at Nektar. A supper club atmosphere where you eat several courses, with performances inbetween. Everything is white, optimizing the futuristic lighting, design, chilled music and video projections. Daily changing menus, good old-world wines and very popular, so book ahead. Closed Mon–Fri lunch.

AROUND THE ISAR Nero
 €€€

Rumfordstrasse 34, 80469 **Tel** *089 21019060* **Map** *3 C3*

This trendy but relaxed pizzeria serves the best thin, crispy, wood-oven baked pizzas in town. Also on offer are good antipasti, steaks and desserts. Begin with cocktails in the bar or on the upstairs sofas, then join others on the communal long wooden tables for your meal. Young clientele from the local arty neighbourhood.

UNIVERSITY DISTRICT Cohen's
 €

Theresienstrasse 31, 80333 **Tel** *089 2809545* **Map** *1 B4*

Popular with a younger crowd, this hip, laid-back location has a basic urban chic to it with old wooden pub chairs and red decor, surrounded by cream curtains. The menu is predominantly Jewish and Eastern European with plenty of stews. Affordable and frequented by students and artists.

UNIVERSITY DISTRICT Eisbach
 €

Marstallplatz 3, 80539 **Tel** *089 22801680* **Map** *3 C2*

A stylish restaurant located on the ground floor of an office block directly behind the Hofgarten and a short walk from Odeonsplatz. The menu offers a variety of soups, salads, and other contemporary Mediterranean-style dishes. Good for a long lunch or pre-theatre supper. Tables outside in a sunny courtyard during the warmer months.

UNIVERSITY DISTRICT Reitschule
€

Königinstrasse 34, 80802 **Tel** *089 3888760* **Map** *2 F4*

This restaurant has long been favoured by the chic set so expect to see fashionable diners. The setting is lovely, overlooking an indoor and outdoor riding school, and the interior elegant and bistro-like. Mediterranean and international cuisine and an affordable lunch menu that changes on a daily basis.

UNIVERSITY DISTRICT Kytaro
 €€

Königinstrasse 34, 80802 **Tel** *089 38887660* **Map** *2 F4*

A well known and popular Greek restaurant located under the Riding School café, next to the English Garden. Classic Greek dishes are served from meat kebabs to stuffed aubergines, specials are roast lamb and hot or cold *mezes*. The outdoor beer garden is used during the summer months.

UNIVERSITY DISTRICT Bistro Terrine
 €€€

Amalienstrasse 89, 80799 **Tel** *089 281780* **Map** *2 D4*

Bistro Terrine is Tantris' younger sister and specializes in delicious low-calorie dishes. Especially good are the lamb and fish dishes. The interior is light, bright and stylish with antique beaded lamps. There is also a lovely garden terrace for fine weather and children are welcome. Located in the lively student area of Schwabing.

MUSEUMS DISTRICT Sangeet
€€

Briennerstrasse 10, 80333 **Tel** *089 28674557* **Map** *3 C1*

Situated just off Odeonsplatz, this Indian restaurant seats up to 200 guests and boasts a smart interior and good service. All spices are carefully blended and dry-fried to ensure maximum flavour and dishes are cooked over an open fire or in a tandoor (charcoal oven). Closed lunch.

MUSEUMS DISTRICT Lenbach
€€€

Ottostrasse 6, 80333 **Tel** *089 5491300* **Map** *3 B1*

Lenbach is one of the city's best restaurants and is housed in a Renaissance building with interiors by Sir Terence Conran in the theme of the seven deadly sins. Specialities of the house include osso bucco of veal with chipolino and artichokes, and asparagus ravioli au gratin with raspberry and chervil. Choose from the three halls, bar, gallery or terrace.

MUSEUMS DISTRICT Königshof
 €€€€

Karlsplatz 25, 80335 **Tel** *089 551360* **Map** *3 A2*

This is a fine gourmet hotel restaurant with 1 Michelin star *(see p264)*. Chef Martin Fauster creates wonderful food such as medallion of venison with chanterelles and cabbage, fillet of sea bass with artichoke fond and ravioli, crème brûlée, and liquorice ice-cream with poached pear. A refined atmosphere and decor to match.

FURTHER AFIELD Vanilla Lounge
€

Leopoldstrasse 65, 80802 **Tel** *089 38666836* **Map** *4 F1*

In the heart of Schwabing, Munich's laid-back hip and arty district, you will find this modern café-bar-restaurant. Vanilla Lounge is trendy and comfortable with a club-like decor and changeable lights and colours. If you are in the neighbourhood, try this coffee bar-cum-lounge for relaxed and tasty dinners.

FURTHER AFIELD Al Pino
 €€

Franz-Hals-Strasse 3, 81479 **Tel** *089 799885*

This restaurant serves excellent Italian dishes mastered by chef Valerio Scopel. Portraits reminiscent of the Medicis line the walls but the decor is understated so as not to detract from the quality of the food. Try the red mullet on fennel puree, Zucchini flower ravioli in saffron butter and green apple mousse on cassis cream. Closed Sun lunch.

FURTHER AFIELD Ruffini
€€

Orffstrasse 22–24, 80637 **Tel** *089 161160*

With 25 years of experience behind it, Ruffini is a well-established address for good regional Italian cuisine. Try the Tuscan organic roast pork with rosemary potatoes or penne with Italian smoked sausage, tomatoes and paprika. Also popular as a bright, sleek café and patisserie. Guests come for the good Italian wine and food in the evenings.

FURTHER AFIELD Acetaia
Nymphenburgerstrasse 215, 80639 **Tel** *089 13929077*

This small, discreet and stylish restaurant has a small menu based entirely around balsamic vinegar. The cauliflower soup is sublime and homemade ravioli filled with ricotta cheese and mushrooms or pecorino, topped with a drop of 25-year-old balsamic vinegar from Modena, are unforgettable. Seats out front in summer.

FURTHER AFIELD Broeding
Schulstrasse 9, 80634 **Tel** *089 164238*

Broeding is a noble gastro restaurant and also an Austrian wine importer. The five course set menu changes daily (fish every first Wednesday of the month) and is complemented by top-quality wines. The restaurant was set up by a sommelier and chef who share a passion for excellent food and wine. Small but superb. Book well ahead.

FURTHER AFIELD Acquarello
Mühlbaurstrasse 36, 81677 **Tel** *089 4704848*

Fabulous, Michelin-starred Italian cuisine using fresh ingredients and special seasonings. Ask chef and owner Mario for his wine recommendations and try the tortelli of figs and foie gras, squab with red wine, walnut and parsley sauce followed by lemon ricotta tart. An unassuming place with typically Italian kitsch decor and excellent food.

FURTHER AFIELD Käfer Schänke
Prinzregentenstrasse 73, 81675 **Tel** *089 4168247*
Map *4 F1*

Michael Käfer's renowned gourmet restaurant attracts a mix of politicians, arty and business cosmopolitans. The small, intimate dining rooms are decorated in contemporary chic crossed with traditional Bavaria. Sit in the Hunting Room, Opera Room or open fire lounge. Excellent food and service.

FURTHER AFIELD Tantris
Johann-Fichte Strasse 7, 80805 **Tel** *089 3619590*

A classic establishment and renowned address in Munich for over 30 years. Designed in a 70s style, Tantris offers top class gourmet menus, a high standard of luxury and boasts two Michelin stars. Try the specials, the aubergine and sardine terrine with pesto or the lukewarm salmon in leek puree and brown butter. Booking essential.

UPPER BAVARIA (NORTH)

DACHAU Aurora
Rosswachstrasse 1, 85221 **Tel** *08131 51530*
Road Map *D4*

This small gourmet restaurant within the hotel Aurora on the edge of town offers a variety of regional dishes. Good meat dishes, from steak to lamb and venison. Sausages and sauerkraut also feature and there is a fixed-price gourmet menu. A garden terrace is used in summer and there is also a winter garden.

EICHSTÄTT Gasthof Krone
Domplatz 3, 85072 **Tel** *08421 4406*
Road Map *C2*

This long-established restaurant is located in the heart of Eichstätt, opposite the cathedral. The building itself dates from 1670. Bavarian cuisine is the speciality at this family-run guesthouse with local meat, fruits and vegetables featuring on the menu. The hearty portions ensure that you'll leave Gasthof Krone happily full.

FREISING Zur Alten Schießstätte
Dr.-v.-Daller-Strasse 1–3, 85356 **Tel** *08161 5320*
Road Map *D3*

Within the Dorint hotel in Freising, this restaurant has a good and well-deserved reputation for high-quality Bavarian cuisine. Just a stroll from the historic centre of the town, which is close to Munich's airport and 30 minutes from Munich city centre. It has a 470-year-old vaulted beer cellar and a beer garden under shady chestnut trees in summer.

HAINDLFING NEAR FREISING Gasthaus Landbrecht
Freisinger Straße 1, 85354 **Tel** *08167 8926*
Road Map *D3*

This small familiar restaurant is located in a quiet spot just north of Freising town. The à la carte menu offers a choice of regional gourmet specials and the meat, fish and vegetable dishes change with the season. Country touches include features such as wood panelling and traditional tiled stoves. Parking available. Closed Mon & Tue.

INGOLSTADT Hummel
Feldkirchener Strasse 69, 85055 **Tel** *0841 954530*
Road Map *D2*

A charming and friendly family-run hotel restaurant close to the old town. The contemporary decor adds to the relaxed feel. Open to non-hotel guests, the restaurant, which takes the owners' family name, serves both Italian and international cuisine, either à la carte or from fixed menus. Try the wonderful potato soup or smoked trout.

INGOLSTADT Restaurant im Stadttheate
Schlosslände 1, 85049 **Tel** *0841 935150*
Road Map *D2*

This restaurant is housed in a theatre which occupies a modern glass building with impressive views across the old town. The cosy dining room is bright and contemporary with two river terraces. The cuisine is both regional and international and the menus change daily. Good wines. Closed Sun dinner; Mon.

NEUBURG AN DER DONAU Zum Klosterbräu

€€

Kirchplatz 1, 86633 **Tel** *08431 67750* **Road Map** *C2*

A well-established restaurant now run by a young family and creative chef that specialises in quality Bavarian cuisine and Sunday roasts. Dine in the slightly more private Jakobsstube for a romantic meal, or in the cosy Gaststube. There is also a garden for fine weather dining alfresco.

LOWER BAVARIA

DEGGENDORF Grauer Hase

€€€

Untere Vorstadt 12, 94469 **Tel** *0991 371270* **Road Map** *F2*

Excellent fish and meat dishes are served in the so-called Grey Rabbit. This traditional establishment is run by a young innovative restauranteur and chef. The menu is given an exotic touch, updating classic dishes with a fruity or luxurious twist. Try the wonderful desserts such as *mille-feuilles* with apple and port. Rooms for groups or events.

GRAFENAU Säumerhof

€€

Steinberg 32, 94481 **Tel** *08552 408990* **Road Map** *G2*

Säumerhof is a friendly and welcoming restaurant in a small, three-star country hotel on the edge of town. This family-run business revolves around the kitchen. Hearty and rustic local specialities use ingredients fresh from nearby farms, rivers and forests. A typical Bavarian country experience. Closed Mon–Thu lunch; Fri–Sun.

LANDSHUT Fürstenhof
€€

Stethaimer Strasse 3, 84034 **Tel** *0871 92550* **Road Map** *E3*

This elegant restaurant in Art Nouveau dining rooms is the perfect romantic setting for a candlelit dinner. Run by masterchef André Greul, the Michelin-starred restaurant offers a wide range of gourmet food. Try the organic beef, venison, duck or char fish. Greul also has his own renowned cookery school.

LANDSHUT Schloss Schönbrunn
€€

Schönbrunn 1, 84036 **Tel** *0871 95220* **Road Map** *E3*

Situated just outside Landshut in a magnificent pale pink 17th-century Bavarian castle, this classic, vaulted hotel restaurant is the place to try some good old fashioned Bavarian cooking. The hearty meals in traditional style form the basis of the menu and international dishes are also served. Wonderful beer garden.

PASSAU Christophorous Stüberl
€€

Pfaffengasse 7, 94032 **Tel** *0851 7568090* **Road Map** *G3*

Located in a narrow old street in the heart of Passau, 'Stüberl' refers to an old tavern. This cosy cellar with lively atmosphere offers regional meat and fish dishes. The kingclip fish comes highly recommended as do the bison steaks. The restaurant also runs an on-line shop for Italian gourmet products.

PASSAU Heilig-Geist-Stift Stiftskeller

€€

Heiliggeistgasse 4, 94032 **Tel** *0851 2607* **Road Map** *G3*

This rustic restaurant and wine bar specializes in Bavarian food and has dark wood panelling throughout and old tiled stoves. Dinner is served in the Hunting Room or Bishop's Room, where coats of arms, hunting trophies and old prints adorn the walls. The freshwater fish, caught in three local rivers, the roast pork and the beef are recommended.

STRAUBING Seethaler

€

Theresienplatz 25, 94315 **Tel** *09421 93950* **Road Map** *E2*

A typical "Wirtshaus" inn, with excellent food and regional wines, as well as beer. The reliable and revered chef has been here for some years and uses only natural ingredients (no additives) and traditional regional recipes. The house dates back to 1462 as a brewery and inn. It is within a hotel situated in the central pedestrian zone of the town.

STRAUBING Bella Vista

€€

Krankenhausgasse 19, 94315 **Tel** *09421 89154* **Road Map** *E2*

For some typical Italian fare head to Bella Vista. Opened in 1996, the emphasis here is on great food and outstanding wines, hence the simple surroundings. Try the Sicilian swordfish, a house special. Tables are set up outside during the summer months.

UPPER BAVARIA (EAST)

ALTÖTTING Graminger Weissbräu

€

Graming 79, 84503 **Tel** *08671 96140* **Road Map** *F4*

This old brewery has a great beer garden under the shade of horse chestnut trees. Originally a farrier set up tables for his clients as they waited, then he brewed his own beer, and the rest is history. The restaurant has changed hands several times, but is now a family-run restaurant serving typical Bavarian specialities using locally grown produce.

ASCHAU IM CHIEMGAU Heinz Winkler
Kirchplatz 1, 83229 **Tel** *08052 17990* **Road Map** *E5*

Masterchef Heinz Winkler took over the original Post Hotel here in 1989 and has created a culinary destination for real gourmands *(see p267)*. Dine in Baroque palatial surroundings in the Venetian lounge or sit in the garden salon, winter garden or loggia terrace. Exceptional food and wine and a wonderful Alpine backdrop.

BAD REICHENHALL St Aegidi-Kelle
Poststrasse 20, 83435 **Tel** *08651 65333* **Road Map** *F5*

This 12th-century cellar restaurant is set in a historic house with lots of Gothic wooden furniture. Served up are light dishes with an Italian flair plus regional specialities. The food is simple and traditional and there is an excellent selection of wines. Wine recommendations that match the daily changing menu can be made.

BURGHAUSEN Bayerische Alm
Robert-Koch-Str. 211, 84489 **Tel** *08677 9820* **Road Map** *F4*

Guests come here not only for the exceptional Austrian and Mediterranean specialities, but also for the unrivalled views of Europe's longest castle with the Alps as a backdrop *(see p267)*. Dine outdoors in the beer garden or on the terraces in warm weather. Local produce is favoured, such as duck, lamb, venison and lake trout.

SEEON Klostergaststätte Seeon
Klosterweg 2, 83370 **Tel** *08624 8970* **Road Map** *E4*

This stunning restaurant within a former Benedictine monastery is set on an island peninsular jutting out into lake Chiemsee. Fish specialities and European dishes are the order of the day. Try the freshly caught pike-perch fillet from the lake. Peaceful and picturesque, with high vaulted ceilings, stone pillars, Gothic chairs and crisp white table linen.

TITTMONING Florianistube
Stadtplatz 44, 84529 **Tel** *08683 1032* **Road Map** *F4*

Located within the only hotel in Tittmoning's central square, this simple and charming restaurant with a country feel serves typical Bavarian dishes. The restaurant is run by a welcoming couple and during the summer months offers alfresco dining and drinks on the terrace. Closed Thu.

TRAUNSTEIN Schnitzlbaume
Taubenmarkt 11a–13, 83278 **Tel** *0861 986650* **Road Map** *E4*

Regional cuisine and typical local dishes with plenty of dumplings is what you can expect at the Schnitzlbaumer. The restaurant is housed in the brewery of the same name and is contemporary in style with open brickwork and leather sofas. Plenty of space and a young and lively clientele.

WAGING AM SEE Strandkurhaus
Am See 1, 83329 **Tel** *08681 47900* **Road Map** *F4*

A lakeside restaurant, most favourable in summer. As you would expect, lake specialities such as fresh fish are on the menu, as well as other traditional Bavarian dishes. All ingredients are organically and locally grown. Traditional fabrics and wooden rustic furniture in the dining room. In summer, enjoy the terrace and beer garden.

WASSERBURG AM INN Herrenhaus
Herrengasse 17, 83512 **Tel** *08071 5971170* **Road Map** *E4*

The daily changing menu at Herrenhaus serves up classic Bavarian, seasonal regional fare and even some French specials. Fish in mushroom sauce, salmon cooked in Riesling, grilled locally-farmed pork with roast potatoes, freshly caught pike or perch with Mediterranean vegetables. A smart dining room with wooden ceilings and stone walls.

UPPER BAVARIA (SOUTH)

ANDECHS Klosterhof Andechs
Bergstrasse 9, 82346 **Tel** *08152 93090* **Road Map** *C4*

The working monastery at Andechs provides ingredients and a great beer for the restaurant. Enjoy generous portions of traditional rustic meals such as knuckle of pork in the beer garden or more refined three-course meals in the restaurant. Great views across the valley from up on the hill.

BAD TÖLZ Altes Fährhaus
An der Isarlust 1, 83646 **Tel** *08041 6030* **Road Map** *D5*

This old ferry house has a lovely setting on the banks of the River Isar. The cuisine is regional, using freshly caught fish or game from the rivers and forests in the area. Specials include the fillet of venison in sloe sauce or grilled sole served with vegetables. Terrace with tables outside in summer.

BAYRISCHZELL Der Alpenhof
Osterhofen 1, 83735 **Tel** *08023 90650* **Road Map** *D5*

Located in an Alpine village close to Tegernsee lake and offering splendid Alpine views is this Michelin-starred restaurant. Fare includes Bavarian and international specials with fish, game, meat, vegetables and exquisite desserts. Elegant but comfortable surroundings.

FELDAFING Kaiserin Elisabeth

Tutzinger Strasse 2, 82340 **Tel** *08157 93090*

€€

Road Map *C4*

Part of the four star Kaiserin Elisabeth golf hotel on the banks of Starnberger See lake. Beautiful grounds surround the hotel, where the restaurant commands great views. Settle in to the elegant dining room or take drinks in the more casual Stüberl bar with its cosy open fire in winter. Good quality food and a good wine list to match.

GARMISCH-PARTENKIRCHEN Reindl's

Bahnhofstraße 15, 82467 **Tel** *08821 943870*

€

Road Map *C5*

This top restaurant in the Partenkirchner Hof Hotel boasts a long-standing tradition of fine cuisine and excellent service. The current chef presents a top notch Bavarian menu with a classic French leaning. From the marinated wild salmon to veal kidneys, rack of lamb or venison, expect great quality and some wonderful wines.

GARMISCH-PARTENKIRCHEN Best Western Hotel Obermühle

Mühlstraße 22, 82467 **Tel** *08821 7040*

€€

Road Map *C5*

The Mühlenstube restaurant in the Best Western Hotel Obermühle is a mere five minute stroll from the centre of Garmisch, and boasts magnificent views of the Zugspitz mountain and other Alpine peaks. The restaurant offers an international menu, as well as the Mill Wheel bar (Mühlradl), where you can feast on Bavarian specialities.

GARMISCH-PARTENKIRCHEN Grand Hotel Sonnenbichl

Burgstrasse 97, 82467 **Tel** *08821 7020*

€€€

Road Map *C5*

Set in fabulous Alpine scenery, the Grand Hotel Sonnenbichl's impressive Art Nouveau building offers magnificent views of the mountains. The hotel's fine gourmet restaurant, the *Blauer Salon* (Blue Salon), offers a variety of international dishes served in elegant surroundings. In warm weather guests can dine out on the terrace.

MITTENWALD Arnspitze

Innsbrucker Strasse 68, 82481 **Tel** *08823 2425*

€€

Road Map *C5*

The chef here manages to blend Bavarian-style dishes with a classic cuisine and some of his own innovative touches. The constantly changing menu uses the freshest seasonal ingredients. Try the duck liver pate with apple gelee or the delicious caramel chocolate cake with flambéed apricots. Good wines.

OBERAMMERGAU Böld

König-Ludwig-Strasse 10, 82427 **Tel** *08822 9120*

€€

Road Map *C5*

The restaurant in this classic chalet-style hotel offers traditional Bavarian hospitality. Expect a warm welcome, rustic but smart decor and good quality fare based on regional recipes and fresh local produce. Choose between the restaurant, bar and sun terrace and marvel at the spectacular views of the surrounding mountains.

TEGERNSEE Lieberhof

Neureuthstrasse 52, 83684 **Tel** *08022 4163*

€

Road Map *D5*

The Lieberhof is a chalet-style restaurant with several rooms decked out in wood in true Alpine style. Choose between three "Stube" – the cosy Pine Room, the Farmers' Room or the tiled Oven Room – and enjoy hearty Bavarian cuisine. Great views from the terrace in summer. Families are welcome.

THE ALLGÄU

FÜSSEN-HOPFEN AM SEE Alpenblick

Uferstrasse 10, 87629 **Tel** *08362 50570*

€

Road Map *B5*

The hotel Alpenblick's regional restaurant specializes in fish from the Hopfen lake and offers some stunning views across the lake and Alps *(see p268)*. Choose between the indoor restaurant, winter garden or large terrace. In addition to fish there are several *schnitzel* and *bratwurst* options on the menu.

FÜSSEN Treff Hotel Luitpoldpark

Luitpoldstraße 1, 87629 **Tel** *08362 9040*

€€€

Road Map *B5*

This magnificent hotel *(see p268)* offers various gastronomic treats, from the elegant restaurant Kurfürst von Bayern with its Bavarian specialities and international gourmet cuisine, to the cosy and traditional Lautenmacher Stube tavern, the Viennese café or even a Mexican restaurant. Peaceful surroundings and views of the Alps and lakes.

KEMPTEN Peterhof

Salzstrasse 1, 87435 **Tel** *0831 52440*

€€

Road Map *B5*

The Peterhof hotel is conveniently located in the heart of Kempten, next to the historical city centre and the pedestrian-zone. It has a smart, modern restaurant which serves a variety of Italian dishes to both residents and outside guests. Enjoy several light courses with Italian wine, rounded off by a great espresso.

LINDAU Alte Post

Fischergasse 3, 88131 **Tel** *08382 93460*

€

Road Map *A5*

This attractive, family-run restaurant was built in 1700 and offers diners a roof terrace, tables alfresco in the secluded square or indoor dining in a cosy room. Local fresh produce is created into a variety of simple to gourmet meals with a hint of tradition. Families with children welcome.

Key to Price Guide *see p276* **Key to Symbols** *see back cover flap*

LINDAU Bayerischer Hof

Seepromenade, 88131 **Tel** *08382 9150*   **Road Map** *A5*

For a classic grande dame style dining room, decked out in the finest swathes of rich fabrics, head to Hotel Bayerischer Hof's restaurant *(see p268)*. Excellent formal cuisine with a service to match. Located right on the promenade in Lindau's harbour with views across Lake Constance from the terrace in summer.

LINDAU Villino

Hoyerberg 34, 88131 **Tel** *08382 93450*   **Road Map** *A5*

Run by the young family Fischer, this restaurant offers a wonderfully warm atmosphere in an idyllic garden setting close to the lake. Villino's inspired dishes combine the cuisines of Asia and Italy and guests can dine on the peaceful terrace under the shade of the trees.

OBERSTDORF Exquisit

Prinzenstraße 17, 87561 **Tel** *08322 96330*   **Road Map** *B6*

This cosy, country-style Bavarian restaurant is set in an Alpine paradise with terraces overlooking sweeping lawns where guests dine in summer. The kitchen team provides a varied cuisine, from gourmet to low calorie, and the attentive waiting staff are friendly but unobtrusive.

NORTHERN SWABIA

AUGSBURG Magnolia Restaurant im Glaspalast

Beim Glaspalast 1, 86153 **Tel** *0821 3199999*   **Road Map** *C3*

Magnolia is housed in a listed industrial glass building, alongside original works of art. On offer is a refined, modern international menu that changes weekly. Try the tuna tartar with caviar crème fraiche and rocket, or provencale fillet of beef with foie gras. Fish dishes are equally impressive, as are much simpler creations. Wide choice of world wines.

AUGSBURG Ratskeller

Rathausplatz 2, 86150 **Tel** *0821 31988238*   **Road Map** *C3*

The cosy atmosphere of the traditional vaulted cellar of the Ratskeller is very inviting and ensures that guests will enjoy the dining experience here. Choose from hearty Bavarian dishes or snacks, light fish dishes or salads. The service is renowned for being very friendly. Live jazz is played every week on a Monday night.

AUGSBURG August

Frauentorstrasse 27, 86152 **Tel** *0821 35279*   **Road Map** *C3*

Expect a noble cuisine at August, but what makes it special is the complexity and artistry in the preparation and combinations. Several courses, painstakingly prepared using fresh seasonal vegetables, fish, seafood and game. Everything is incredibly light and has strong aromas as well as strong colours. Untypically delicate for Bavaria.

AUGSBURG Die Ecke

Elias-Holl-Platz 2, 86150 **Tel** *0821 510600*   **Road Map** *C3*

A fine Swabian-Bavarian restaurant in Augsburg famous for its innovative catfish dishes – try the baked catfish with horseradish on vegetables and rice with a Riesling sauce. Another house special is the roast lamb in Pommery and mustard crust on shallot sauce, beans and potato gratin. Also offers excellent wines.

DILLINGEN Storchennest

Demleitnerstrasse 6, Fristingen, 89407 **Tel** *09071 4569*   **Road Map** *B3*

Located in the heart of a little village on the outskirts of Dillingen is this country-style restaurant. The tiled stove in the centre of the restaurant warms it up on winter days and the great shady garden terrace provides ample room outdoors in warm weather. Choose between daily changing specials or a six course menu. Large choice of wines.

FRIEDBERG Herzog Ludwig

Bauernbräustrasse 15, 86316 **Tel** *0821 607127*   **Road Map** *C3*

International classics with an exotic twist are served up at Herzog Ludwig. Such delicacies include marinated tuna on a bed of Asian vegetables and couscous, Barbary duck in prune and balsamic sauce with rosemary polenta and Bavarian perch and thyme gnocchi. A welcoming place, run by a young couple and their team in the heart of the old town.

NEU-ULM Landhof Meinl

Marbacher Straße 4, 89233 **Tel** *0731 70520*   **Road Map** *A3*

Set in quiet country surroundings (part of the Silence hotel chain), this pleasant hotel restaurant has a rustic feel with a touch of modern elegance. The food here is influenced by the close lying Swabian Alb region. Try the lovely fresh salads with fish or chicken breast, or turkey in creamed pepper sauce with pan-fried potato *rösti*.

NÖRDLINGEN Meyers Keller

Marienhöhe 8, 86720 **Tel** *09081 4493*   **Road Map** *B2*

The emphasis here is on gourmet and high quality ingredients prepared with care and creativity. The owners offer seasonal specials of lamb, game or fish, and local produce as well as imported seafood is used. The restaurant is classic and elegant in style and has lovely garden tables. It also runs cookery courses around gourmet themes.

Pubs, Cafés and Bars in Munich

Munich abounds with bars, cafés, clubs and, of course, hugely popular pubs and beer gardens. There is something for every taste. Places where people go to drink coffee or beer, to have a snack or simply to socialize informally are mostly concentrated in the city centre and in Schwabing. Even in the more outlying districts an abundance of pleasant cafés and bars can be found. Many food shops also set aside a corner for eaters and drinkers.

PUBS AND BEER GARDENS

The features most typical of Munich, and seen everywhere in the city, are spacious pubs often fronted by gardens shaded by chestnut or linden trees. These pubs serve beer from the local breweries as well as generous helpings of good Bavarian food. Waitresses dressed in the traditional *Dirndl* wind their way among the tables and there is often an oompah band playing a repertoire of folk melodies.

Munich's most famous pub is the **Hofbräuhaus**, which today is filled with more American and Japanese tourists than local drinkers. Seated on wooden benches at large tables arranged in spacious rooms, garrulous crowds of guests enjoy their favourite drink as they sing along with and sway in time to the Bavarian music.

Almost equally renowned is the **Augustiner Gaststätte**, which also has a restaurant. The interior is decorated in late 19th-century style, and has a very pleasant courtyard surrounded by arcades, which induce the desire to linger for as long as possible.

Munich's next most famous pubs are the **Löwenbräu-keller** and the **Donisl**. In the latter, with its old-style furnishings, authentic Bavarian folk music is also played. The city's finest beer garden is the **Chinesischer Turm** in the Englischer Garten, where there are a total of 6,000 seats for its international clientele.

Many pubs and beer gardens allow drinkers to bring their own food. Beer is best served straight from the barrel. A popular type of beer is *Helles*, a light lager beer. Also widely drunk is *Radler*, beer to which lemonade is added *(see p274)*.

CAFES, BARS AND BISTROS

A great variety of different establishments come under the name of "café". They include traditional coffee shops, where people go for *Kaffee und Kuchen*, (coffee and cake), the coffee helping to wash down a large pastry or slice of cake. Two such coffee shops are the old-world **Café Kreutzkamm**, which moved here from Dresden after World War II (it is known for its chocolates, **Dresdner Stollen** and pyramidal cakes), and the **Café Luitpold**, which tempts with its equally excellent cakes and chocolates.

A real oasis of peace – a commodity highly valued by the citizens of Munich – is the **Café am Beethovenplatz**. Time passes more slowly here, and the gentle classical music seems to make the coffee smell and taste better than elsewhere. The atmosphere of the **Kaffeehaus Altschwabing** takes you back to the turn of the 19th and 20th centuries. Thomas Mann and other writers once enjoyed the strong coffee that is served here.

Another type of café is a place offering hot and cold food and a range of soft and alcoholic drinks. The atmosphere is more like that of a bar or bistro. These bar-type cafés are the centre of the social life of Munich. They range from somewhere to go to grab a sandwich or drop in for a coffee or beer, to pretentious places where high society meets. There are also gay and lesbian bars, such as **Café Glück** and **Iwan**, and bars for businessmen, as well as bars for connoisseurs of tobacco, wine or whisky and for pool players.

Many bars serve large and delicious breakfasts and lunches. Others specialize in ice cream. Many, including the **Roxy**, are open until late at night.

A feature once unique to Munich was Kunstpark Ost, an extensive leisure park near the Eastern Station. However, this is now in the process of closing. Some of its famous clubs, discos (such as the hugely popular Babylon) restaurants and bars (such as the much-frequented Bongo Bar) still exist or have moved to the Optimol Area.

TAKE-AWAYS (TAKE-OUTS)

Numerous booths and stalls selling take-away food are to be seen in the streets of Munich, particularly in the main shopping areas of the Old Town and Schwabing, as well as in pedestrian subways and at railway stations.

The traditional take-aways are those of the well-known international fast-food chains. There are also many take-away pizza, sausage, baguette and kebab houses. The **Nordsee** restaurant offers delicious freshly made sandwiches with herring, fried fish or crab salad, and the **Wienerwald** restaurants sell chicken cooked in every possible way.

There are also take-away stands in almost all butcher's shops, where pre-packaged lunch dishes in aluminium trays are sold. The food sold in Munich's most renowned delicatessens, the **Dallmayr** and **Käfer**, is excellent, although the prices can seem a little high *(see p287)*. A good alternative is the hot food stalls to be found in **Viktualienmarkt** *(see p64)*.

DIRECTORY

PUBS

Andechser am Dom
Weinstr. 7A.
Map 3 B2, 6 D3.
Tel 29 84 81.

Augustiner Gaststätte
Neuhauser Str. 27.
Map 3 A2, 5 B3.
Tel 23 18 32 57.

Augustiner-Keller
Arnulfstr. 52.
Tel 59 43 93.

Chinesischer Turm
Englischer Garten 3
Map 2 F4.
Tel 38 38 730.

Donisl
Weinstr. 1
Map 3 B2, 6 D3.
Tel 22 01 84.

Franziskaner Garten
Friedenspromenade 45.
Tel 43 00 996.

Grüntal
Grüntal 15.
Tel 99 84 110.

Hofbräuhaus
Am Platzl 9
Map 3 C2, 6 E3.
Tel 29 01 360.

Hofbräukeller
Innere Wiener Strasse 19.
Tel 45 99 250.

Kaisergarten
Kaiserstr. 34.
Tel 34 02 02 03.

Löwenbräukeller
Nymphenburgerstr. 2.
Tel 67 31 022.

Paulaner Bräuhaus
Kapuzinerplatz 5.
Tel 54 46 110.

Seehaus
Kleinhesselohe 3.
Tel 38 16 130.

Tassilogarten
Auerfeldstr. 18.
Tel 44 80 022.

Wintergarten
Elisabethplatz 4B
Map 2 D3.
Tel 27 37 31 34.

CAFES AND BARS

Atzinger
Schellingstr. 9
Map 2 D4.
Tel 28 28 80.

Café Altschwabing
Schellingstr. 56
Map 1 C4.
Tel 27 31 022.

Café am Beethovenplatz
Goethestr. 51.
Tel 54 40 43 48.

Café Glück
Palmstr. 4
Map 3 A5.
Tel 20 11 673.

Café Glyptothek
Königsplatz 3
Map 1 B5.
Tel 28 80 83 80.

Café im Lenbachhaus
Luisenstr. 33
Map 1 B5.
Tel 52 37 214.

Café Kreutzkamm
Maffeistr. 4
Map 3 B2.
Tel 99 35 570.

Café Luitpold
Brienner Str. 11
Map 6 D1.
Tel 24 28 750.

Café Munich
Leopoldstr. 9
Map 2 E3.
Tel 34 38 38.

Café Puck
Türkenstr. 33
Map 2 D4.
Tel 28 02 280.

Café Reitschule
Königinstr. 34.
Tel 38 88 760.

Café Schwabing
Belgradstr. 1
Map 2 D2.
Tel 30 88 856.

Café Wienerplatz
Innere Wienerstr. 48
Map 4 E3.
Tel 44 89 494.

Charivari
Türkenstr. 92
Map 2 D4.
Tel 28 28 32.

Cyclo Restaurant Bar
Theresienstr. 70
Map 1 C5.
Tel 28 80 83 90.

Engelsburg
Türkenstr. 51
Map 2 D4.
Tel 27 24 097.

Interview
Gärtnerplatz 1
Map 3 C3, 6 D5.
Tel 20 21 649.

Iwan
Hans-Sachs-Str. 20
Map 3 B4.
Tel 55 49 33.

Königsquelle
Baaderplatz 2
Map 3 C3, 6 E5.
Tel 22 00 71.

Kaokao
Tulbeckstr. 9.
Tel 50 54 00.

Mauz
Leopoldstr. 20
Map 2 E3.
Tel 38 32 99 47.

Münchner Freiheit
Münchner Freiheit 20.
Tel 33 00 79 90.

Niederlassung
Buttermelcherstr. 6
Map 3 C3, 6 D5.
Tel 32 60 03 07.

Pacific Times
Baaderstr. 28
Map 3 C3, 6 E5.
Tel 20 23 94 70.

Pusser's
Falkenturmstr. 9.
Tel 22 05 00.

Roxy
Leopoldstr. 48
Map 2 E3.
Tel 34 92 92.

Schumann's
Odeonsplatz 6
Map 4 D2, 6 F3.
Tel 22 90 60.

Spatenhaus an der Oper
Residenzstr. 12
Map 3 C2, 6 D2.
Tel 29 07 060.

Stadtcafé im Stadtmuseum
St-Jakobs-Platz 1
Map 3 B2, 5 C4.
Tel 26 69 49.

Tambosi
Odeonsplatz 18
Map 3 C1, 6 D1.
Tel 29 83 22.

TiefenRausch
Schellingstr. 91
Map 1 C4.
Tel 27 27 20 10.

Tresznjewski
Theresienstr. 72
Map 1 C5.
Tel 28 23 49.

Wiener's Café
Neuturmstr. 2
Tel 29 25 69.

TAKE-AWAYS

Adria
Leopoldstr. 19
Map 2 E3.
Tel 39 65 29.

Nordsee
Viktualienmarkt 10
Map 3 B3.
Leopolstr. 82
Map 2 E3.

Thai Magie
Blumenstr. 1
Map 3 B3, 5 B5.

Wienerwald
Bayerstr. 35.

SHOPS AND MARKETS

Retailers in the Bavarian Alps who cater both to the tourist trade and to the more affluent Bavarians offer for sale virtually everything from the finest luxury goods to local arts and crafts. A particularly ubiquitous Bavarian speciality is sports, hiking and mountaineering equipment, which is displayed for sale in many outlets.

**Logo of the
Loden Frey shop**

There is also a large market for anything in traditional Bavarian style, from beer steins to *Lederhosen* to fine glass and porcelain. An enjoyable way of spending a few hours is to stroll among the stalls in the spa towns selling locally made items. In complete contrast, Munich, one of the most sophisticated European cities, has some very exclusive shops.

The greengrocer's counter in one of Munich's elegant delicatessens

WHERE TO SHOP

Shops ranging from department stores to boutiques to souvenir shops can be found in Munich. All larger towns in the Bavarian Alps have a shopping district, usually pedestrianized.

Also popular are the out-of-town superstores, which attract large numbers of shoppers because of their competitive prices and ease of parking for drivers.

SHOPPING IN MUNICH

Munich's main shopping district is the pedestrianized area of the Old Town around Neuhauser Straße, Kaufinger Straße and the Marienplatz area, where stores and shops of major European retailers are located. This whole area probably has the largest daily turnover in the whole of Germany, and one of the best stores is Ludwig Beck am Rathauseck on Marienplatz.

Around Theatinerstraße, Maximilianstraße and Brienner Straße are exclusive

clothes shops such as Versace, Gucci, Escada and Donna Karan, whose prices are out of the reach of most tourists. Maximilianstraße is also the home of the eccentric Munich couturier Rudolph Moshammer.

In the famous Schwabing district, particularly in the area between Amalienstraße, Schellingstraße and Türkenstraße, exclusive boutiques and tasteful second-hand shops can be found, as well as many bookshops (selling both new and second-hand books) and antique shops.

OPENING HOURS

Shops are legally permitted to open from 6am to 8pm from Monday to Friday, and from 8:30am to 4pm on Saturdays. In practice, most food shops open between 7am and 9am (bakeries opening the earliest), and close at 8pm. Other shops, including supermarkets, are usually open from 9am to 8pm.

Small shops, particularly in more out-of-the-way places, often close for lunch then stay open until 6pm. At railway stations in large towns it is possible to buy food and beverages until 11pm, even on Sunday. Petrol (gas) stations that also sell food and drink are often open until late at night; some open 24 hours.

PAYING

Travellers' cheques and credit cards are accepted in department stores and in larger shops. In Germany the most widely accepted credit card is Euro-card. Somewhat less popular is VISA. In smaller shops cash is preferred.

The showroom of a shop specializing in Nymphenburg porcelain

Advertisement for an exclusive designer fashion shop in Ruhpolding

FOOD AND DRINK

As elsewhere in Europe, food shops have largely been taken over by retail chains. The exceptions are small butcher's shops, bakeries and confectioners. Fruit and vegetables are still sold in markets, with the most famous being the Viktualienmarkt *(see p64)*. A visit to the delicatessens **Dallmayr** and **Käfer** will be memorable.

The decorative entrance to one of Munich's delicatessens

GIFTS AND SOUVENIRS

It is virtually impossible to leave the Bavarian Alps without a souvenir beer mug or a decorative bottle of beer. Particularly suitable as presents are bottles of the local spirits and drinks presented in stoneware bottles, often bearing the portrait of the legendary king Ludwig II.

Tourist resorts are full of souvenir shops. Besides the folksy kitsch there is some good-quality woodcarving, pottery, painted glass and porcelain. Stylized Bavarian costume and accessories made of natural materials are ubiquitous. Conforming to the latest fashion, they are often quite attractive. The best place in Munich for gifts of this type are the **Wallach Haus** and **Loden Frey**.

SPECIALIST SHOPS

Munich boasts several specialist shops of renown. **Sport Scheck** is an outstanding sports shop. The best bookshops include **Geobuch**, which specializes in maps and guidebooks, **Hugendubel** and **Werner**, which sell books on art, architecture and design. **Hieber am Dom** specializes in musical instruments and literature, while **WOM** and **Zauberflöte** sell CDs and cassettes. Lovers of fine antique furniture and paintings should visit the famous antique shop **Bernheimer Fine Old Masters**.

A shop in Augsburg selling pottery and basketware

DIRECTORY

FOOD SHOPS

Dallmayr
Dienerstr. 14–15, Munich.
Map 3 C2, 6 D3.
Tel (089) 21 350.

Käfer
Prinzregentenstr. 73, Munich.
Map 3 F4. *Tel* (089) 41 68 255.

GIFTS AND SOUVENIRS

Loden Frey
Maffeistr. 7, Munich. **Map** 3 B2, 5 C2. *Tel* (089) 21 03 90.

Porzellanmanufaktur Nymphenburg
Odeonsplatz 1, Munich.
Map 3 C1, 6 D1.
Tel (089) 28 24 28.

Radspieler
Hackenstr. 7, Munich. **Map** 3 B2, 5 B4. *Tel* (089) 23 50 980.

Wallach Haus
Residenzstr. 3, Munich.
Map 3 C1, 6 D2.
Tel (089) 22 08 71.

SPECIALIST SHOPS

Bernheimer Fine Old Masters
Brienner Str. 7, Munich.
Map A 15. *Tel* (089) 22 66 72.

Geobuch
Rosental 6, Munich.
Map 3 B2, 5 C4.
Tel (089) 26 50 30.

Hans Goltz
Türkenstr. 54, Munich. **Map** 2 D4.
Tel (089) 28 49 06.

Hieber am Dom
Liebfrauenstr. 1, Munich.
Tel (089) 29 00 800.

Hugendubel
Marienplatz 22, Munich.
Map 3 B2. *Tel* (01801) 48 44 84.

Sport Scheck
Sendlinger Str. 6, Munich.
Map 3 A3. *Tel* (089) 21 660.

Werner
Türkenstr. 24 & 30, Munich.
Map 2 D5. *Tel* (089) 28 10 34.

WOM
Kaufingerstr. 15, Munich.
Map 3 B2, 5 C3.
Tel (089) 26 09 513.

Zauberflöte
Falkenturnstr. 8, Munich.
Map 3 C2. *Tel* (089) 22 51 25.

What to Buy in the Bavarian Alps

Bavarian felt hat with a *Gamsbart*, or feather

Besides a vast range of German and European goods, the visitor to the Bavarian Alps can also purchase local products that make perfect gifts and souvenirs. They are usually inspired by folk traditions, and their artistic merit varies greatly. The sheer quantity of gift-shop kitsch is quite overwhelming, particularly items related to beer-drinking ceremonies and devotional art. However, it is also perfectly possible to find good-quality, tasteful and authentic examples of the arts and crafts of the Bavarian Alps.

Porcelain
Dolls dressed in Bavarian costume make good presents for girls or collectors.

FOLK ART

Many shops selling folk art can be found in the Bavarian Alps. As well as wood carvings, for which Oberammergau is particularly renowned, good-quality paintings and antique items of often striking simplicity are available.

Copy of a Baroque statue

Painting on Glass
Painting on glass is a widespread craft in the region, with the main centre being Murnau. Subjects are usually images of saints or religious scenes depicted in a naïve style.

A 19th-century votive painting

Flat tin figure painted in enamels

GLASS AND CERAMICS

Workshops in the Bavarian Forest region are famous for their glassware *(Waldglas)*. They produce both classic functional items, as well as modern art glass in a range of novel shapes and colours. Folk ceramics include painted pottery and stoneware that characteristically has the colour of grey granite. One of the most prominent centres of ceramic production is Dießen.

Stoneware snuff box

Nymphenburg Porcelain
Usually of a high artistic quality and relatively expensive, hand-painted figurines like this are produced by the famous Nymphenburg porcelain factory.

Plate with the Bavarian coat of arms

Bavarian Waldglas

REGIONAL COSTUME

Bavarian folk costume is attractive and practical in its modern-day form. Usually made of high-quality wool, linen or leather, it gives protection from cold or heat. Recommended for children are the famous Bavarian *Lederhosen*, which are practically dirt-proof but also machine washable should the need arise.

A soft woollen *Janker*

The famous Bavarian *Lederhosen*

A decorated leather belt

Leather Goods

Bavaria is renowned for its high-quality leather goods. The material is surprisingly soft, and the items often have a crude but deliberate old-worldliness about them.

Knitted woollen socks

Decorated hunter's bag

Leather shoes in Bavarian folk style

Silver necklace with colourful pendants

Embroidered tasselled shawl

DRINKING ACCESSORIES

Among the articles most widely produced by the souvenir industry are beer mugs of all descriptions, ranging from simple stoneware vessels to highly colourful mugs decorated with paintings or reliefs and fitted with pewter lids. They are characteristic of Bavaria and make good gifts.

A finely decorated beer bottle

Beer mug with the coat of arms of Bavaria

Collectors' Items

Both beer-related artifacts as well as antique beer mugs and lids are valued items that are bought and sold by international antiques collectors.

Antique beer mug lids

OUTDOOR ACTIVITIES
AND SPECIALIST HOLIDAYS

Munich and Bavaria offer an amazing variety of sporting and leisure activities. Throughout the year active holiday makers head to the region's hills, forests, mountains, rivers and lakes. Various national organisations can provide details on a particular sport and have regional contacts. Cycling,

Taking in the scenery in Berchtesgaden National Park

running and Nordic walking rank highest among the area's most popular sports, while snow sports in the easily accessible Alps keep visitors active during the winter months. During the summer this nation of outdoor lovers flock to the lakes and rivers to swim and sail.

Hiking amongst the spectacular scenery of the Mittenwald Alps

WALKING AND HIKING

Walking and hiking is a popular activity for both young and old. Numerous paths are well preserved and marked along rivers, through forests and up mountains. Every town has its own rambling or hiking club. The foothills of the Alps provide some easy terrain for gentle hikes but the higher you go the more demanding it becomes. Family-friendly trails on higher terrain involve taking a cable car up the mountain. Lenggries near Bad Tölz (see p220) is good for family trails and the **Deutscher Wanderverband** (German hiking Club) and **Deutscher Volkssportverbund e.V.** (German Sports Federation) can provide further details. For information on guided walking tours contact the local tourist office in each area, or the **Verband Deutscher Gebirgs/und Wandervereine e.V.** (German Mountaineering

and Hiking Club) who will direct you to smaller regional clubs. The **Kneipp-Verien München** or **DAV Summit Club** also have regional clubs who organise hikes and tours.

CYCLING

Because cycling is such a popular sport the cycling paths here are excellent. Bikes can be hired in towns and cities throughout the region and there are plenty of bike stands available. Munich is Germany's most bike-friendly city with some 700km (435 miles) of cycle paths. Cycling is one of the best ways to take in the beautiful scenery between Lake Constance and Bad Tölz, and to see the towns and villages of Dachau, Passau, Wasserburg and Bayerischzell. Contact the **Allgemeiner Deutscher Fahrrad Club** (German Cycling Federation) in Munich for details and tips before planning a trip. They

provide tour plans, maps, route suggestions and tips for all over Bavaria. They also give advice on the latest regulations for transporting bikes on trains, which is possible with prior booking and a nominal fee.

WATER SPORTS

If you are in this part of Germany in the warmer months, you simply have to take a dip in one of the lakes or rivers. The water is very clean, safe and totally refreshing. The Strandbad, indicating the beach area, is visible in every lakeside town and denotes free public bathing. Excellent sailing conditions can be found on Starnberger See and Bodensee, and the area near Lindau is famous for its yacht building wharves and sailing clubs. Contact the **Deutscher Segler-Verband** (German Sailing Club) for information on locations, regulations and possibilities

Cyclists touring the beautiful Bavarian countryside

of sailing or hiring a boat. To hire or sail a yacht, you will need a current licence showing your sailing abilities and competence. Canoeing is also popular on the Bavarian rivers, especially on the Altmühl between Gunzenhausen and Kelheim or at Loisach near Garmisch, where the World Wild Water Championships have been held. For further details contact the **Deutscher Kanu-Verband e.V.** (German Canoe Federation) or the **Bayerischer Kanu-Verband** (Bavarian Club).

Canoeing on the popular Altmühl River in Bavaria

Skiing in one of the many resorts in the Bavarian Alps

SKIING AND MOUNTAIN SPORTS

Garmisch Partenkirchen (see p217) is Germany's best ski area, others include Reit im Winkl (see p201). There are plenty of hotels and ski hire companies in these areas and the relevant tourist office can provide further details as well as maps of ski lifts and runs. Skiing is also possible at other Alpine peaks in Lenggries or near Berchtesgaden. Langlauf (cross-country skiing) can be pursued on many well kept routes, marked clearly in towns at the foothills of the Alps. Other enquiries can be directed to the **Deutscher Skiverbandes e.V.** (German Ski Association) who can give tips and suggestions for planned visits or tours. **Schuster** or **Sportscheck**, two large sports department stores in Munich centre, have travel offices that organise skiing trips and can advise on the hiring of equipment and on

ski packages available. Climbing is also big in the mountainous areas. Whichever level you are you can find your match here, especially in the Allgäu. If you want to hire a guide contact the **Verband Deutscher Berg-und Skiführer** (Association of German Mountain and Ski Guides). Climbing walls such as **High-East Kletterhalle** in Munich offer an indoor alternative, or a chance to practice. Further information regarding climbing, or rock formations for example, can be obtained from the German Alpine Association, **Deutsche Alpine Verein** (DAV).

GOLF AND TENNIS

Both golf and tennis are increasing in popularity and several towns have excellent clubs, golf courses and tennis courts. To be allowed on a golf course, you will need to prove proficiency and pre-book, so plan well ahead. Contact the **Deutscher Golf Verband e.V.** for information on courses and rules. Many Bavarian golf enthusiasts head out to the course at Wallgau (see p218) where the conditions are good and the scenery beautiful. Tegernsee and the Bayerischer Wald have a few golf-oriented hotels with special packages.

The **Deutscher Tennis Bund e.V.** has information on local tennis clubs and the procedure for booking a court. Some hotels are geared towards tennis, such as the Tannenhof in Allgäu, the Espacio in Garmisch or the Ödhof Sporthotel in the Bayerischer Wald.

NATIONAL PARKS

The Bayerischer Wald is Germany's highest National Park (see p187). Lying in the area behind Grafenau, it has a wealth of unusual wildlife, forests and rivers. Tours operate within the protected area of the park, but the surrounding forest area has camping sites and hiking routes where you will find people mountain biking and Nordic walking. An all-round outdoor fitness sport that involves walking at a brisk pace with the support of sticks, Nordic walking has increased in popularity over the past few years. For further details contact the **Nordic Walking Association**.

Summer is a good time to visit the park when you can see more of the wildlife and fauna indigenous to the woods and waterways. Be sure to stick to the marked paths and to observe the safety and conservation regulations.

Nordic walking in the peaceful Bayerischer Wald, Lower Bavaria

CAMPING AND CARAVANNING

A great number of Germans head south in the summer months from June to August to the sites at lakesides, forests and riversides throughout Bavaria. The Germans love the great outdoors and for this nation of campers, sites are plentiful and well organised. The majority of families who camp are in caravans, while tents are favoured by the younger generation and foreign tourists. Pitching a tent is highly regulated and allowed only at official camping grounds. The majority of camping sites are privately owned, friendly and offer plenty of extras. Washing facilities are always available, and some sites have shops, a bar and restaurants. Well established and more expensive sites tend to offer group activities, especially for children, and electricity. Campfires are popular and sites have designated areas for them. For details and advice on camping and caravanning, contact the **Deutscher Camping Club e.V.** and also the **Backpacker Network Germany.**

HISTORIC AND SCENIC ROUTES

Travelling along the Alpenstrasse, the German Alpine Road, is a great way to experience the best of the scenery in the Bavarian Alps. The road was built in 1927 and connects Lake Constance with Berchtesgaden. At its

Family fun at one of Germany's well-equipped camp sites

The fairy-tale Linderhof Palace, one of many of Ludwig II's residences

highest point the road reaches 1735m (5690 ft) and is ranked among the world's best scenic routes. Travel between Lindau, Füssen, Oberammergau, Garmisch, Kochel, Chiemsee, Tegernsee, Bad Reichenhall and on to Berchtesgaden. On route take in Linderhof palace and Neuschwannstein castle, the Zugspitze mountain in Garmisch and the salt mines at Berchtesgaden. For more information visit www.alpenstrasse.de

The Romantischestrasse, Romantic Road, also runs through Bavaria between Würzburg and Füssen, with old medieval town centres, churches and the rivers Lech and Danube on route. The Alpine foothills form part of the scenery, as does the Ammersee lake, moors and the Allgäu mountains. There is plenty to enjoy from thermal baths, to tobbogan runs, nature conservation areas and hiking paths. Visit www.romantischestrasse.de for further details.

Steingaden is the point where these two routes intersect and has a health resort as well as a famous pilgrimage and ecclesiastical treasures.

SPECIALIST HOLIDAYS

For the best information on German language courses in Bavaria, contact the **Goethe Institut** in London or Munich. The institute runs its own courses for various lengths of time and from beginner to advanced levels. There are

many additional language schools in Munich, which can be found using the internet. Augsburg also has a small but good language school. To find out more contact **Augsburger Deutschkurse.**

Cooking holidays are increasing in popularity and Bavaria has a few to offer. The holidays give you the opportunity to learn the basics of gourmet cuisine from masterchefs in their own restaurants. Students stay in the hotel itself and partake in cookery lessons on site. Two great places to visit in Bavaria are Heinz Winkler's Residenz hotel and restaurant at Aschau near Chiemsee *(see p267)* and André Greul's Fürstenhof in Landshut *(see p280).*

Although Bavaria is famous for its beer rather than its wines, cookery courses also teach you about great German wines. The stretch of Lake Constance behind Lindau produces several varieties of white wine. The best way to experience the country's offerings is to visit a wine festival, held in many towns towards the end of the summer. For more information visit **Deutsches Weininstitut.**

Another popular holiday activity is horse riding and a weekend of riding can be arranged with one of several private equestrian centres. The Deutsche Reiterliche Vereinigung e.V. can provide information on centres throughout the region.

Wine from the Mosel

SPA VACATIONS

"Wellness" is a term cropping up in many hotels in the countryside. This denotes a spa area for health and wellbeing. It is now possible to take a weekend, or longer stay, to enjoy a variety of spa treatments including water therapy, swimming, steam rooms, massages, exercise routines and walks in the healthy, fresh air. **Deutscher Heilbäderverband e.V.,** the German spa association of spas, has information on hotel spas and packages throughout the region. Towns with the word "Bad" preceding the name signifies a spa town. Here you are guaranteed a longstanding tradition of health regimes, rest and relaxation as well as thermal baths. The **Therme Erding** is a paradise of thermal baths, just outside Munich. For more of a family fun holiday, stay at the watr park at Alpamare *(see p220)*, a spa village rich in mineral water. The park is one of the largest in Germany.

DIRECTORY

GENERAL SPORTING INFORMATION

Deutscher Sportbund
Otto-Fleck-Schneise 12
Frankfurt am Main.
Tel 069 67000.
www.dsb.de

WALKING AND HIKING

DAV Summit Club
Am Perlacher Forst 186
81545 München.
Tel 089 642400.
www.dav-summit-club.de

Deutscher Volks-sportverband e.V.
Fabrikstrasse 8
84053 Altötting.
Tel 08671 96310.

Deutscher Wanderverband
Wilhelmshöher Allee
157–159
34121 Kassel.
Tel 0561 938730.
www.wanderverband.de

Kneipp-Vereim München
Prinz-Ludwig-Strasse 6
80333 München.
Tel 089 283780.

Verband Deutscher Gebirgs/und Wandervereine e.V.
Wilhelmshöher Allee 157–
159 34121 Kassel.
Tel 0561 938730.
www.wanderverband.de

CYCLING

Allgemeiner Deutscher Fahrrad Club (ADFC)
Platenstrasse 4.
Tel 089 773429.
www.adfc.de

WATER SPORTS

Bayerischer Kanu-Verband
Georg-Brauchle-Ring 93
80992 München.
Tel 089 15702418.
www.kanu-bayern.org

Deutscher Kanu-Verband e.V.
www.kanu.de

Deutscher Segler-Verband
Gründgensstr. 18
22309 Hamburg.
Tel 040 6320090.
www.dsv.org

GOLF & TENNIS

Deutscher Golf Verband e.V.
Postfach 2106
65189 Wiesbaden.
Tel 0611 990200.
www.golf.de/dgv

Deutscher Tennis Bund e.V.
Hallerstrasse 89
20149 Hamburg.
Tel 040 411780.
www.dtb-tennis.de

SKIING AND MOUNTAIN SPORTS

Deutsche Alpine Verein (DAV)
Von Kahr Strasse 2–4
80997 München.
Tel 089 140030.
www.alpenverein.de

Deutscher Skiverbandes e.V.
Am Erwin-Himmelseherplatz
Hubertusstrasse 1
82152 Planegg.
Tel 089 857900.
www.ski-online.de

High-East Kletterhalle

Sonnenallee 2 85551
Kirchheim/Heimstetten.
Tel 089 92794796.

Schuster
www.sportschuster.de

Sportscheck
www.sportscheck.com

Verband Deutscher Berg-und Skiführer (VDBS)
Bahnhofstrasse 25
83646 Bad Tölz.
Tel 08041 7938606.
www. bergfuehrer-verband.de

NATIONAL PARKS

Naturpark Bayerischer Wald
Infozentrum 3
94227 Zwiesel.
Tel 09922 802480.
www.bayerischer-wald.de

Nordic Walking Association
www.nordicportal.net

CAMPING AND CARAVANNING

ADAC Camping Referat
Am Westpark 8
Munich. *Tel 089 76760.*

Backpacker Network Germany
Max-Brauer-Allee 277
22769 Hamburg.
Tel 040 43182310. www.
backpackernetwork.de

Deutscher Camping Club e.V.
Mandlstrasse 28
80802 München.
Tel 089 3801420.
www.camping-club.de

SPECIALIST HOLIDAYS

Augsburger Deutschkurse
www.adk-german-courses.com

Goethe Institut
Dachauer Strasse 122
80637 München.
Tel 089 159210.
(UK)
50 Princes Gate
Exhibition Road
London SW7 2PH.
Tel 020 7596 4000.

Deutsche Reiterliche Vereinigung e.V.
Freiherr von Langen-Strasse 13
48231 Warendorf.
Tel 02581 63620.

Deutsches Weininstitut
Gutenbergplatz 3–5
55116 Mainz.
Tel 06131 28290.

SPA VACATIONS

Deutscher Heilbäderverband e.V.
Schumannstrasse 111
53113 Bonn.
Tel 0228 201200.

Therme Erding
Thermenallee 1
85435 Erding.
Tel 08122 229922.
www.therme-erding.de.

SURVIVAL
GUIDE

PRACTICAL INFORMATION

Tourist information logo

Famous for their breathtaking scenery and historic monuments, the Bavarian Alps are the most popular destination for visitors to Germany. Like Munich, the regional capital, this alpine region is well prepared to receive tourists from all over the world. Hotels and catering facilities and an excellent road, rail and public transport network makes travelling in the area a pleasure. The Bavarians are generally friendly and hospitable, although communication may be difficult in smaller towns and villages unless you speak German. This, however, is not a problem in cosmopolitan Munich. The best time to come to the Bavarian Alps is in summer, when the weather is most likely to be good, although out of the high season prices tend to be lower and crowds fewer.

Information plaques on historic buildings

MUSEUMS AND HISTORIC MONUMENTS

Almost every town, city and tourist resort in the Bavarian Alps has its own local history museum (*Heimatmuseum*). Even the more out-of-the-way places can reveal private collections of quality and interest. Bavaria's finest museums are, of course, in Munich.

Most museums in Bavaria are open to the public from 10am to 5pm or 6pm, usually from Tuesday to Sunday. Details of opening hours are given on the relevant pages of this guide. Many state (Bavarian) museums, exhibition halls and castles (not the municipal ones) are free on Sundays. In Munich itself, these include the major museums such as the three Pinakothekes and the Bayerisches Nationalmuseum. Many reductions on the price of admission to museums and historic monuments are available, and information on these can be obtained at tourist offices or hotel reception desks.

Of equally good value is the *CityTourCard*, valid for one or three days for one person or for groups of up to five people (prices range from €9.80 to €48). You can buy a card to cover either just the centre of Munich or the outlying areas of the city as well. The *CityTourCard*, comes with a free map of the city and gives reductions of up to 50% on admission to more than 30 of the city's attractions, which are listed in a leaflet attached to the card. These include entry to museums, theatres, sightseeing tours and discounts on souvenirs. All forms of public transport available are also covered in the cost of the card. The card is available for purchase at all suburban railway stations (S-bahn), underground stations (U-bahn), tram and bus stations and wherever the *CityTourCard* sign is displayed. Selected hotels also sell the card.

Many churches are open to visitors from 8am until the evening service. However, sightseeing is prohibited during religious services.

TOURIST INFORMATION

Tourist information bureaux are generally found in town centres, in main squares and near railway stations. In towns where there is no tourist information bureau, visitors can obtain information at the town hall (*Rathaus*) or civic centre (*Gemeindehaus*). In spa resorts, information is available from the Resort Administration (*Kurverwaltung*). The general rule at information bureaux is: the fewer the tourists, the friendlier and more exhaustive the service.

In addition to free town maps, tourist information bureaux provide a range of brochures on principal local attractions and programmes for local shows and cultural events. They also assist tourists who are seeking accommodation, help to organize guided tours, and provide information on travel and admission reductions.

St-Jakobs-Platz, one of the most popular tourist spots in Munich

STUDENT AND YOUTH TRAVEL

Tourist resorts in the Bavarian Alps take considerable trouble to ensure that young people are offered a wide range of interesting and stimulating entertainment programmes. Information is available at hotel receptions and information points, where programmes of events are usually available.

Young people who possess an International Student Identity Card (ISIC) are entitled to reductions in many cultural institutions. In the larger towns and cities there are special information bureaux for young people, where legal advice and support on such issues as education and employment is also available.

The Olympiapark, offering plenty of activities for children

GUIDED TOURS

Tourist information bureaux can arrange specialized tours conducted by guides who are experts in their field. Many tourist agencies offer coach, walking and cycling tours around Munich and the Bavarian Alps, with transport for walkers and cyclists provided where necessary.

Guides can be hired for tailor-made excursions or as part of a regular organized tour. The guides in Munich can speak up to 20 languages between them.

Schloss Neuschwanstein, one of the most popular tourist sites

EVENTS

All year round, the Bavarian calendar is packed with a variety of lively cultural and sporting events, as well as religious and secular celebrations and festivals. Free programmes of such events are available in all towns, cities and tourist resorts. Information on local entertainment can be found in local newspapers, including free newspapers.

For events in Munich, the monthly *In München* and the magazine *Prinz*, which are available at newspaper kiosks and in bookshops, pubs and cinemas, carry information on all important events as does the yellow monthly programme of events that is available at tourist information bureaux across the city.

DISABLED VISITORS

Almost all modern public buildings have access facilities for disabled visitors, and parking spaces reserved for people with disabilities are increasingly common. Institutions that are unable to provide wheelchair access give assistance in other ways.

Munich's Association for the Disabled has a guide that gives useful information on using the underground and on hotels and restaurants with facilities for the disabled. The guide is available from the Association's main office, located at Schellingstraße 29/31 in Munich.

DIRECTORY

TOURIST INFORMATION BUREAUX

Bayerntouristik Marketing Gmbh
Leopoldstr. 146, Munich.
Map 4 D1. *Tel* (089) 21 23 970.
Fax (089) 21 23 97 99.
www.bayern.by

Tourismusamt München, Rathaus
Marienplatz 8, Munich.
Map 3 B2, 6 D3. *Tel* (089) 22 23 24. *Fax* (089) 23 33 02 33.

Hauptbahnhof
Bahnhofplatz 2, Munich.

Tourismusverband Allgäu/Bayerisch Schwaben
Fuggerstr. 9, Augsburg.
Tel (0821) 45 04 010.
www.allgaeu.de

Tourismusverband München-Oberbayern
Bodenseestr. 113, Munich.
Tel (089) 82 92 180.
Fax (089) 82 92 180
www.blt.de/oberbayern;
www.oberbayern-tourismus.de

Tourismusverband Ostbayern
Luitpoldstr. 20, Regensburg.
Tel (0941) 58 53 90.
Fax (0941) 58 53 939.
www.ostbayern-tourismus.de

INFORMATION FOR YOUNG PEOPLE

Jugendinformationszentrum
Paul-Heyse-Str. 22, Munich.
Tel (089) 51 41 06 60.
www.jiz-muenchen.de

Stadtjugendamt
Prielmayerstr. 1, Munich.
Tel (089) 23 34 95 01.

GUIDED TOURS

Münchner Stadtrundfahrten oHG
Tel (089) 55 02 89 95.

Stattreisen München
Tel (089) 54 40 42 30.

DISABLED VISITORS

Sozialverband Vdk
Schellingstr. 31, Munich.
Map 2 D4. *Tel* (089) 21 170.

A typical newspaper kiosk in Munich

CUSTOMS AND VISA REGULATIONS

The border between Bavaria and Austria is practically non-existent, the only indication of its presence being road signs and some deserted customs buildings. However, travellers crossing the border will need to take their passport with them.

Citizens of countries belonging to the European Union, the US, Canada, Australia, and New Zealand do not require a visa to visit Germany, so long as their stay does not exceed three months' duration. Visitors from South Africa will need a visa. In addition, citizens of many EU countries do not require a passport to enter Germany, although a national ID card with photograph is necessary.

German regulations totally prohibit the importation of firearms, drugs, animals and exotic plants that are under special protection.

Customs limits for travellers from countries outside the EU are 200 cigarettes, or 250g (9oz) of tobacco or 50 cigars, one litre of spirits or two litres of wine. Items for personal use, provided they are not in quantities intended for trade, are not subject to customs duty. Commercial imports must be cleared by Customs.

TAX REFUNDS

All goods sold in Germany are subject to 19 per cent tax *(Mehrwertsteuer)*. Except for citizens of other EU countries, visitors to Germany are entitled to a tax refund on the price of any non-edible goods that are bought in German shops.

Shops with the Tax Free sign will always issue a tax certificate or Tax-Free cheque when the value of the items purchased exceeds a specified total, which is usually around €50. A passport must be shown before a certificate or cheque can be issued. When going through Customs on leaving Germany, the certificate must be stamped. Visitors may be asked to show the goods, which must still be in their original packaging, unopened and unused. The tax is either

Tax-free shopping sign

refunded at the border or will be sent to the address on the envelope containing the cheque.

TIME

Germany is on Central European Time (GMT plus one hour). Clocks move forward one hour on the last Sunday in March and back on the last Sunday in October.

TELEVISION AND RADIO

Domination of the national television broadcasters ARD and ZDF and of the local network – the so-called "third channels" *(Dritte Programme)* – has been broken by cable and satellite television. The Bavarian third channel (BR), which provides local news, is largely linked to the local authorities.

Popular new channels are RTL, SAT1, VOX and Pro Sieben, RTL plus, RTL2 and Arte. Their headquarters are in Munich, which after Cologne is Germany's second most important producer of television programmes.

Most televisions receive at least one English-language channel (CNN or BBC World), as well as the French channel TV5. Bavarian radio stations are Antenne Bayern (101.3 & 102.7 FM), with modern music and news, Bayerischer Rund-funk (91.3 & 93.7 FM), with music and local news, and Klassik Radio Bayern (102.3 & 103.2 FM), with classical music. Traffic news (with reports of delays on motorways and rail-ways at border-crossing points.) is broadcast mainly on Bayern 3. Larger towns in Bavaria have several local radio stations.

Tourists in the formal gardens at Schloss Nymphenburg in Munich

CONSULATES AND EMBASSIES

Many foreign countries have consulates in Munich, although many of them, including the American Consulate, do not issue visas. Visitors who lose their passport or experience any serious problems should turn to their country's consulate for help. The British Embassy and the United States Embassy, together with the embassies of other countries, are located in Berlin.

NEWSPAPERS

Mainstream international newspapers such as the *International Herald Tribune*, *The Guardian*, *Le Monde*, *El País*, *Neue Zürcher Zeitung* and *Corriere della Sera* are usually

Poster advertising one of Munich's major galleries

available at kiosks on the day they are published, while others appear a little later.

The main German daily newspapers are the centre-right *Frankfurter Allgemeine Zeitung*, the centre-left *Süddeutsche Zeitung* and the weekly *Die Zeit* and *Der Spiegel*. *Süddeutsche Zeitung*, which is published in Munich, is issued with a large local supplement.

Newspapers also widely read in Munich are the tabloids *Abendzeitung* and *tz*. These are available from automatic vending machines in the street. In the evenings, papers are distributed in bars and restaurants by news vendors.

Of special interest to tourists are the magazines *Prinz* and *Münchner* (this is offered free of charge) which carry information about events and exhibitions. Throughout the Bavarian Alps local illustrated magazines such as *Allgäu* and *Kempten* are available.

ELECTRICITY

The electrical system in Germany provides 230-volt, 50 Hz AC. Electric plugs are of the two-pin

A newspaper vending machine

European type. UK 230-volt appliances can be plugged into German sockets with an adaptor. US 110-volt appliances will have to be used with a transformer. All hotels in Germany have 230-volt sockets for razors and hairdryers. Certain appliances work on both 110-volt and 230-volt current.

PUBLIC CONVENIENCES

In Bavaria's larger towns and cities, public conveniences can be found without much difficulty and are kept in a good state of cleanliness. They are marked with male and female silhouettes or with the letter D *(Damen)* for Ladies and H *(Herren)* for Gentlemen. Busy parts of cities are well provided with public toilets, although a small payment is usually required. Toilets are also provided in shopping centres, public institutions, hotels and restaurants. In the case of restaurants, if you are not having a meal there, it is courteous to ask permission. For people travelling by car, there are toilets in car parks and at petrol (gas) stations.

DIRECTORY

EMBASSIES

Australia
Wallstr. 76–79,
10179 Berlin.
Tel *(030) 880 08 80.*

Canada
Leipziger Platz 17,
10117 Berlin.
Tel *(030) 20 31 20.*

Republic of Ireland
Friedrichstr. 200,
10117 Berlin.
Tel *(030) 22 07 20.*

New Zealand
Friedrichstr. 60,
10117 Berlin.
Tel *(030) 20 62 10.*

South Africa
Tiergartenstr. 17–18,
10785 Berlin.
Tel *(030) 22 07 30.*

United Kingdom
Embassy
Wilhelmstr. 70,
10117 Berlin.
Tel *(030) 20 45 70.*

Consulate
Bürkleinstr. 10.
80 538 Munich.
Map 4 D2.
Tel *(089) 21 10 90.*

USA
Embassy
Neustädtische Kirchstr. 4-5, 10117 Berlin.
Tel *(030) 83050.*

Consulate
Königinstr.5,
80539 Munich. **Map** 2 E5.
Tel *(089) 288 80.*

CULTURAL INSTITUTES IN MUNICH

Amerikahaus
Karolinenpl. 3.
Map 1 C5, 3 A1.
Tel *(089) 55 25 370.*

Institut Français
Kaulbachstr. 13.
Map 2 E5.
Tel *(089) 28 66 280.*

Italienisches Kulturinstitut
Hermann-Schmid-Str. 8.
Tel *(089) 74 63 210.*

Goethe-Institut
Dachauer Str. 122
Tel *(089) 15 92 10.*

Griechisches Haus
Bergmannstr. 46.
Tel *(089) 50 80 880.*

Security and Health

Logo of the Munich police

Like the rest of Germany, Munich and the Bavarian Alps benefit from a rigorous public safety policy, and are safe areas for travellers. However, police presence is discreet here and the general public fairly conservative. Stations and trains are patrolled by officers of the Border Police *(Bundesgrenzschutz).*

Munich is safer than other large German cities, although, as in all large urban areas, vigilance must be exercised against pickpockets. Tourists who experience problems of any kind should go to the police for help.

Policeman and policewoman

POLICE AND FIRE BRIGADE

The police and fire brigade are state-run services. Police officers wear green uniforms and police vehicles are green and white. Traffic police *(Verkebrspolizei),* who look after safety on the streets, roads and motorways, are distinguished by their white caps. Urban police in navy-blue uniforms are responsible for catching motorists who have parked illegally or who have failed to pay the correct parking fee. The *Kriminalpolizei* are generally dressed in plain clothes. They will produce their identification and insignia as necessary.

For assistance in an emergency, dial 110 for the police or 112 for the fire brigade. You will be asked to give your name, the reason for the call and your location. The fire brigade can also be called by operating special alarms.

PERSONAL PROPERTY

Although theft is not a major problem in Munich, special care should be taken in crowded trains and U-Bahn and S-Bahn stations, in and around the central railway station and around large beer-halls, all of them places where pickpockets operate. The station area is not somewhere to linger, as it is frequented by drug addicts and a few harmless albeit annoying drunks and tramps.

Tourists should take basic safety precautions, such as not carrying large sums of money with them and keeping cameras safe. Most hotels have secure lockers or safes where documents and valuable items can be left. For owners of expensive cars, the extra cost of a guarded car park is worth the peace of mind. Never leave valuables in view when you park your car.

It is advisable to take out comprehensive insurance cover before travelling. Victims of theft should immediately report the crime to the police, who will issue a certificate enabling a claim to be made.

SAFETY IN THE MOUNTAINS

One of the greatest attractions of the Bavarian Alps is the scope that they offer for hiking, skiing and snow-boarding. However, personal safety depends on awareness and preparation. Hikers can easily be misled by fine weather, so that possible dangers are forgotten. For hiking in the mountains, it is essential to take proper hiking-boots and a rucksack with warm clothes and something to eat and drink, and to carry a detailed map, a first-aid kit and a form of identity.

Hikers should plan their route in advance, match its level of difficulty with their own physical condition, and keep to the marked routes. Skiers and snowboarders should beware of avalanches and never use pistes that are closed. For more difficult routes, it is advisable to hire a guide. (Consult the local **Deutscher Alpenverein** office or tourist information bureau.)

The most common type of police car in Munich

Police vans – widely used in Bavarian towns

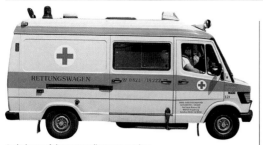

Ambulance of the paramedic rescue services

In the Bavarian Alps there are many mountain shelters where hikers and skiers can rest and eat, and even sleep.

In an emergency, help can be summoned by repeating a sound or light signal six times per minute at one-minute intervals. The response is a signal three times per minute. Mountain rescue teams or emergency services can also be called by telephone.

LOST PROPERTY

Pharmacy logo

If property has been lost, it is worth asking at the local police station or lost property office (**Städtisches Fund- büro**). Lost property offices in smaller towns and spa resorts are often located in the town hall or spa admini- stration building. For items found on trains, there are the **Deutsche Bahn AG Fund- büro** (for Munich) and the **Deutsche Bahn AG Fund-büro Bundesweit** (for all of Germany). The **Regional- verkehr Oberbayern** deals with items found on buses. The central post office has a lost property office for items left in post offices.

INSURANCE

All EU members can receive medical and dental treatment in Germany at a reduced rate. Before travelling, British visitors should obtain the European Health Insurance Card (EHIC) – the form is available from Post Offices – and seek a refund on their return home. It is still advisable to take out some form of health insurance, and visitors from other count- ries should take out insurance. If plans include hiking, skiing

or other sporting activities, make sure that the policy covers the costs of rescue services. Insurance against loss of luggage and holiday cancellation is also advisable.

MEDICAL ASSISTANCE

Germany has one of the best health services in the world. When called, ambulances arrive promptly. Those able to reach a hospital themselves should enter by the entrance marked **Notaufnahme** (Accident and Emergency). Less serious cases can be dealt with in one of the many private clinics. Advice can also be obtained in a pharmacy **(Apotheke)**. Most pharmacies are open until 6pm (some until 8pm), and every area has one all-night pharmacy. The address of the nearest all-night pharmacy is given on the door of each pharmacy. In Munich you can also find the nearest all-night pharmacy by telephoning (01805) 19 12 12.

The window display of a pharmacy in the Bavarian Alps

DIRECTORY

EMERGENCY SERVICES

Police
Tel 110.

Fire brigade
Tel 112.

Ambulance
Tel 19 222.

Emergency Poison Help Line
Tel (089) 19 240.

Confidential Help Line
Tel (089) 56 79 00.

Duty Doctor and Pharmacy Information
Tel (01805) 19 12 12.

LOST PROPERTY

Städtisches Fundbüro
Oetztaler Str. 17, Munich.
Tel (089) 23 39 60 45.
◗ 8am–noon Mon–Fri, 2–6:30pm Tue.

Deutsche Bahn AG Fundbüro
Hauptbahnhof, Munich.
Tel (089) 13 08 66 64.
◗ 7am–11pm Mon–Fri, 7:30am–10:30pm Sat–Sun.

Deutsche Bahn AG Fundbüro Bundesweit
Tel (01805) 99 05 99.

Regionalverkehr Oberbayern (RVO)
Hirtenstr. 24, Munich.
Tel (089) 55 16 40.
◗ 7:30am–3:30pm Mon–Fri.

CREDIT CARDS

American Express
Tel (069) 97 97 15 00.

Diner's Club
Tel (01805) 33 66 95.

EuroCard & MasterCard
Tel (069) 75 76 1000.

VISA
Tel (01803) 61 76 170.

Banks and Local Currency

Logo of the ReiseBank

Although there is no limit to the amount of currency that can be brought in or taken out of Germany, for large amounts of cash a statement of import (or export) may be required by the customs department. Travellers' cheques and credit cards are widely accepted, both of which minimize problems in case of loss or theft. Cash will be needed for small purchases. Foreign currency can be exchanged in banks, at exchange bureaux and at currency exchange machines.

A currency exchange machine on Marienplatz in Munich

CHANGING CURRENCY

Banks in Germany are generally open from 8:30am to 4pm Monday to Friday, but many close early on Wednesdays. Currency can be changed at the larger branches of major banks as well as at bureaux de change, which are located throughout Munich and in larger towns throughout the Bavarian Alps.

Cash can easily be obtained with a cash withdrawal card at an automatic cash machine (ATM). All major banks have automatic cash machines at almost all their branches. The machines are usually located in the lobby, which can be entered after closing time by swiping a cash card. Automatic cash machines are also found in all large shopping centres throughout the Bavarian Alps.

Automatic cash machine

German banks usually charge foreign card-users between €2 and €4 per withdrawal, and card withdrawals are usually the cheapest way of obtaining cash. Changing currency will usually incur higher charges. While the best currency exchange rates are generally found at branches of Sparkasse, the least favourable are usually those offered at airports, in city centres and in most major hotels.

Currency can also be exchanged at automatic currency exchange machines, although these are relatively few. They also only accept banknotes in the most common currencies.

CREDIT CARDS AND TRAVELLERS' CHEQUES

Credit cards can be used to pay bills in most hotels and restaurants, in all department stores and in most shops. Credit cards are not accepted in many smaller shops and restaurants, and usually not for amounts of less than 25 euros.

Travellers' cheques can be used to pay for goods and services, and to settle hotel bills, although it is very often best to pay in cash. Travellers' cheques can be cashed in banks and currency exchange bureaux. It is a best to purchase travellers' cheques in Euro denominations.

DIRECTORY

BANKS IN MUNICH

Bayerische Landesbank
Brienner Str. 18. **Map** 3 B1.
Tel (089) 21 71 01.

Commerzbank
Leopoldstr. 230.
Map 2 F1.
Tel (089) 35 640.

Deutsche Bank
Promenadeplatz 15.
Map 3 B2, 5 C2.
Tel (089) 23 900.

Dresdner Bank
Promenadeplatz 7.
Map 3 B2, 5 C2.
Tel (089) 21 390.

HypoVereinsbank
Kardinal-Faulhaber-Str. 12.
Map 3 B1, B2, 5 C2.
Tel (089) 23 50 790.

Reisebank AG
Hauptbahnhof.
Tel (089) 55 10 80.
Franz-Josef-Strauß Airport.
Tel (089) 97 01 721.

Head office of the Bank of Bavaria, now Hypovereinsbank, in Munich

CURRENCY

The euro (€) is the common currency of the European Union. It went into general circulation on 1 January 2002, initially for twelve participating countries. Germany was one of those twelve countries taking the euro in 2002, with the original currency phased out the same year.

Euro notes are identical throughout the Eurozone countries, each one including designs of fictional architectural structures and monuments. The coins, however, have one side identical (the value side), and one side with an image unique to each country. Notes and coins are exchangeable in each of the participating euro countries.

Euro Bank Notes

Euro bank notes have seven denominations. The €5 note (grey in colour) is the smallest, followed by the €10 note (pink), €20 note (blue), €50 note (orange), €100 note (green), €200 note (yellow) and €500 note (purple). All notes show the stars of the European Union.

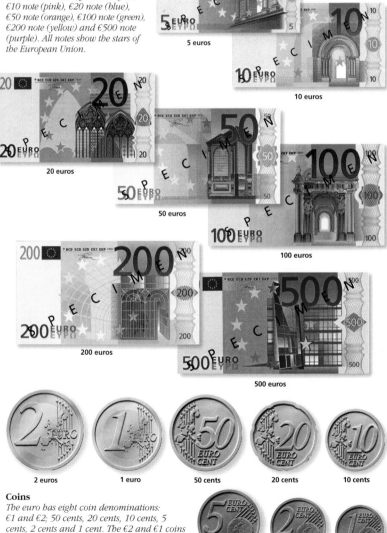

5 euros

10 euros

20 euros

50 euros

100 euros

200 euros

500 euros

2 euros

1 euro

50 cents

20 cents

10 cents

Coins

The euro has eight coin denominations: €1 and €2; 50 cents, 20 cents, 10 cents, 5 cents, 2 cents and 1 cent. The €2 and €1 coins are both silver and gold in colour. The 50-, 20- and 10-cent coins are gold. The 5-, 2- and 1-cent coins are bronze.

5 cents

2 cents

1 cent

Communications

Deutsche Telekom sign

The postal and telecommunications services in Germany are very efficient. Although it may be necessary to queue for a while in the post office, letters and postcards are usually delivered within the country in 24 hours. Telephone boxes can be found on street corners, in stations, and in restaurants and cafés.

Mail boxes (once yellow, but now often grey and pink) are found everywhere, even in the most out-of-the-way corners of the Bavarian Alps.

Colourful chip telephone card (back and front)

USING THE TELEPHONE

As everywhere else in Europe, the market for telephone services in Germany has changed fundamentally in recent times. The introduction of mobile phones has brought about a revolution in telephone usage. Visitors wishing to use their mobile phone in Germany should contact their service provider for information.

Much has also changed in traditional landline phone services, although the principal provider continues to be Deutsche Telekom, which is responsible for all public telephones in Germany. The number of payphones taking coins,

Card-operated telephone sign

rather than cards, is constantly dwindling. If a user inserts too many coins into a payphone, the unused coins will be returned after the call, although change will not be given. A telephone card (costing €6 or €25) gives better value for money. The cards can be bought at post offices and most newsagents. Alternatively, travellers can purchase an international phone card before leaving home. While a phonecard is being used in a public phone, an illuminated display shows the amount of credit remaining on the card.

In many busy areas of towns and cities and at railway stations and in airports public telephones operated

by credit cards can be found. In order to use them it is necessary to dial in a PIN number. Many public phones have their own telephone number. These can receive incoming calls, so that you can be called back if your money or card runs out.

Every public telephone should be equipped with a set of local telephone directories, although, unfortunately, these are often missing. Deutsche Telekom recommends the use of its national information service, although at about 1 per enquiry, using it is expensive.

Charges for local, national and international calls depend on the time of day. It is important to bear in mind that the cost of calls made from hotel rooms is considerably greater than from public telephones.

USING A COIN-OPERATED TELEPHONE

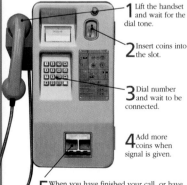

1 Lift the handset and wait for the dial tone.

2 Insert coins into the slot.

3 Dial number and wait to be connected.

4 Add more coins when signal is given.

5 When you have finished your call, or have not been connected, replace the handset. For the return of unused coins, press the button above the slot where you inserted the coins.

USING A CARD-OPERATED TELEPHONE

1 Lift the handset and wait for the dial tone.

2 Choose the appropriate language.

3 Insert the card as instructed. The illuminated display will show the amount of credit remaining.

4 Dial the number and wait to be connected.

5 After finishing the call replace the handset. Withdraw the card by pressing on the green button.

POSTAL SERVICES

Post offices are indicated by the word *"Post"* while mail boxes and the Deutsche Post logo are a distinctive yellow. In large towns post offices are usually open from 8am to 6pm on weekdays and from 8am until noon on Saturdays. Branches with service on Sundays or with longer opening hours can be found at most airports and large railway stations.

Stamps for letters and post-cards can be bought at post offices and from automatic stamp machines, and are sometimes sold along with postcards. Some mailboxes have two slots – for local post and for all other destinations. Collection times are also shown on the mailbox.

Letters sent *Poste Restante* are usually issued from post offices near railway stations. Such correspondence should be marked with the words *"Postlagernde Briefe/ Sendungen"*. In order to collect mail, a passport or other form of identification must be produced.

Just as in other countries, registered mail, telegrams and parcels can be sent from post

Post Office No. 32, at the Central Station in Munich

offices. Besides stamps, post offices sell phone cards, postcards, envelopes and cartons in which to send items by post.

Many former post offices have been converted into service centres offering such facilities as a fax and photocopying service. They also sell books and stationery.

THE INTERNET AND E-MAIL

The internet and e-mail have become increasingly popular and essential as a means of communication, and

they can be especially useful for people who are abroad on holiday or business. As a result, many hotels now offer their guests access to the Internet as well as e-mail facilities. Internet cafés, where online access can be obtained for a small fee, can be found in most towns and cities throughout southern Bavaria, while computers can often be hired by the hour in commercial centres.

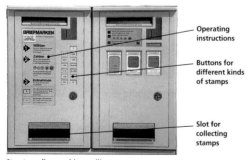

Operating instructions

Buttons for different kinds of stamps

Slot for collecting stamps

Street vending machines selling postage stamps and telephone cards

Collection times

Slot for local letters

Slot for long-distance mail

The most typical style of mail-box seen in Germany

USEFUL TELEPHONE NUMBERS

- National directory enquiries: 11 833.
- International directory enquiries: 11 834.
- To make an international call: dial 00, wait for the dialling tone, then dial country code, area code + number, omitting the first 0.
- Country codes: UK 44; Eire 353; Canada and USA 1; Australia 61; South Africa 27; New Zealand 64.
- Country and area code for Munich: 49 89.

TRAVEL INFORMATION

The Bavarian Alps are situated in the heart of Europe. Thanks to Bavaria's excellent road and rail network, and to Munich's large, modern international airport, reaching the Bavarian Alps – Germany's most popular tourist destination – from anywhere in Europe is fairly straight-forward. Buses are comfortable and effi-

Lufthansa plane

cient and are particularly use-ful in rural areas not served by rail. In Munich – the heart of Bavaria – trams, buses and the U-Bahn and S-Bahn network provide a swift and convenient way of moving around the city. The Bavarian Alps are also a gateway on the route into Italy: roads can become congested at peak holiday times.

ARRIVING BY AIR

Munich's Franz-Josef-Strauß International Airport is Germany's second-busiest after that at Frankfurt am Main. Flying to Munich takes you to the heart of Bavaria. The main airlines providing links between the UK and Bavaria are British Airways and Lufthansa, Germany's national airline. Both operate regular flights from London direct to Munich. The low-cost airline easyJet also serves Munich from London's Stansted airport, with two flights daily.

Direct flights to Germany are usually available from major US cities, including New York (JFK), Washington DC, Boston, Chicago, San Francisco and Los Angeles. Most arrive at Munich or Frankfurt. Although Canada does not have many direct flights to Germany, Air Canada operates regular flights to Frankfurt

from Toronto and Vancouver and, in the summer, to Munich from Montreal and Vancouver.

DBA, Munich airport's home carrier, serves many German destinations, including Berlin and Hamburg, as well as other European destinations, such as Nice in France.

AIR FARES

Scheduled air fares can vary considerably, with possible reductions for children, students, people under the age of 26, elderly people, and groups. The cheapest scheduled ticket is an APEX, to which certain conditions apply. The cheapest fares are often those offered by the new low-cost airlines or by discount agents. Apart from over the Christmas period, some of the cheapest fares are available from November to March, coinciding with the best Alpine skiing conditions.

Flight information board in Munich's airport

GETTING TO MUNICH AIRPORT

Franz-Josef-Strauss International Airport, which opened in 1992, is one of the most modern and important airports in Europe. It is located 28 km (17 miles) from central Munich, and thanks to efficient connec-tions you can get to the city centre in about 45 minutes, although delays can occur on the motorway, especially during the rush hour.

The quickest and most reliable way of getting to and from the airport is by the S-Bahn, whose lines S1 and S8 run from about 4am to 1am (with a service every 20 minutes after 5am). Travellers taking the S1 to the airport should board one of the rear carriages marked *"Flughafen"* (airport), as the train's front carriages are uncoupled at Neufahrn and continue to Freising.

The railway station is situated beneath the airport, and all directions are clearly

Arriving by bus or train, two ways of getting to Munich airport

Inside Terminal 1 at Munich's Franz-Josef-Strauß International Airport

signposted. Rail tickets from Munich to the airport cost €9.60, but if you buy a *Streifenkarte*, for €10, you need to punch only eight of the 10 sections. Children (aged 6–14) pay €1.10 and €1 respectively (for one red section of a child *Streifenkarte*). Groups of up to five people can buy a group ticket *(Gruppenkarte)* for around €17.

Taxi fares from Munich to the airport are relatively high – around €50. An *Airport-Bus* runs between Munich's Central Station and the airport every 20 minutes: the cost is around €10 for adults and €5 for children. The first bus leaves Central Station at 5:10am, and the last at 7:50pm. There are also bus links between the airport and other towns and cities in Bavaria.

The use of luggage trolleys is free in the arrivals lounge, but in the departure lounge the cost is €1.

MUNICH AIRPORT

Passengers waiting for their flights have a wide variety of bars and restaurants to choose from. In addition to fast-food outlets, the airport has good-quality restaurants, as well as cafés and self-service snack bars. It is also home to the world's first airport microbrewery, Airbraeu.

Travellers wishing to shop are catered for with a range of stores selling Bavarian delicacies, as well as clothes, toys and various souvenirs. Terminal 1 has more than 40 retail and restaurant outlets, including a perfumery, a pharmacy, a hairdresser and a post office, as well as bookshops, where foreign newspapers are available. Terminal 2, which opened in June 2003, has more than 110 shops and restaurants over three levels. Names there include Tie Rack, Max Mara and Hermès. All shops in the airport accept the main credit cards, although for small purchases and in snack bars cash payment is required.

Additional facilities include a health centre with a 24-hour service. Some airlines, such as British Airways and Lufthansa, have special check-in desks

Control tower at Munich airport

for passengers arriving late for their flights. Staff at information desks can give further details.

Terminal 1 is in the shape of an elongated rectangle and offers departures and arrival on the same level. The design reflects the style of the early 1990s, in which it was built.

Terminal 2 is centred around the 30-m (100-ft) high check-in area, where ticketing, check-in and security are undertaken for both terminals.

A major attraction is the Besucherpark (visitors' centre), which can be reached from car park P51, or by a two-minute S-Bahn journey (alight at Besucherpark).

In addition to a restaurant and playground, the centre also has a simulator for visitors to experience the sensations of flight, an information point on air-travel technology and a viewing platform where planes can be seen taking off and landing at close quarters.

Travellers needing to spend the night near the airport can stay at one of the hotels nearby, such as the Kempinski Hotel Airport München.

DIRECTORY

Franz-Josef-Strauß Airport
Tel (089) 97 500.
www.munich-airport.de

Air Canada
Tel (069) 27 11 52 30.
www.aircanada.ca

British Airways
Tel (01805) 26 65 22.
www.britishairways.com

Delta Air Lines
Tel (01803) 33 78 80.
www.delta.com

easyJet
Tel (01803) 654 321.
www.easyJet.com

Lufthansa
Tel (0180) 58 38 426.
www.lufthansa.com

Qantas
Tel (01805) 25 06 20.
www.qantas.com.au

United Airlines
Tel (069) 50 07 03 87.
www.united.com

Munich's central railway station

ARRIVING BY TRAIN

The Bavarian Alps are well served by a relatively extensive railway network. Trains are very frequent and delays are a rarity.

Munich has direct connections with most major European cities. Main routes from the United Kingdom are via Dover to Ostend or Harwich to the Hook of Holland. An alternative is to travel to Brussels by Eurostar and pick up an onward connection to Germany from there.

GERMAN TRAINS

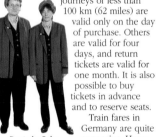

Deutsche Bahn railway workers

German trains, which are operated by **Deutsche Bahn AG**, are comfortable and only crowded during the peak holiday season. The fastest trains, the high-speed InterCity Express (ICE), have air-conditioning and airline-style seats, a bistro and restaurant, card-operated payphones, and newspapers and earphones on sale. Somewhat slower and less expensive are the InterCity (IC) trains and EuroCity (EC), on which a small supplement is payable regardless of the distance travelled. The network also runs slow trains (D). Short-distance links between towns are made by Regional-Express (RE), Regionalbahn (RB) and the suburban S-Bahn trains.

TRAIN TICKETS

Train tickets can be purchased at the ticket offices of railway stations, or at station ticket machines for shorter journeys. Although long queues are rare, it is wise to allow 10–15 minutes for buying a ticket. Tickets for journeys of less than 100 km (62 miles) are valid only on the day of purchase. Others are valid for four days, and return tickets are valid for one month. It is also possible to buy tickets in advance and to reserve seats.

Train fares in Germany are quite expensive. However, a wide range of discounts is available, particularly during the summer season. One way to travel more cheaply is to buy a *Bahn-Card*, which gives a 25 per cent discount. An InterRail card, available to all European citizens, is economical for extensive or frequent rail travel.

For rail travel in Bavaria, the *Bayern-Ticket* offers good value. A one-day ticket, costing €28 at the ticket machines or €30 at the ticket office, can be used by up to five people from Monday to Friday, or by parents with any number of their own children up to the age of 17. These tickets are valid only on RE, RB and S-Bahn trains and time restrictions apply. The *Schönes-Wochenend-Ticket* (SWT), costing €37 from a ticket machine or €39 when bought at a ticket office, also for use only on RE, RB and S-Bahn trains, is valid all day and most of the night on either a Saturday or a Sunday. Both tickets also give free travel on urban transport in Munich.

ARRIVING BY COACH

Munich and other cities in the Bavarian Alps can be reached by coach (long-distance bus). Coaches from Vienna, Zurich or Bozen (Bolzano) terminate at Munich's central station. Routes from the UK are operated by Eurolines.

TRAVELLING BY BUS

Almost all Bavarian towns and villages are connected by a local bus network, particularly in places where there is no railway station. Bus timetables are devised mainly to suit commuters, so that the service is very frequent at peak hours and relatively sparse at weekends and on public holidays.

Most towns have a *Zentraler Omnibus Bahnhof* (ZOB) close to the train station and it is here that most bus services originate and where service timetables and other information can be obtained and tickets purchased.

In rural areas there are many request stops. Here every bus stop has a timetable, and tickets can also be bought from the driver.

Comfortable, long-distance, double-decker coach

A popular way of seeing Bavaria is on a coach tour. Information is available from any tourist information office, hotel or travel agent. A wide range of tours is on offer – from sightseeing tours of Munich to special-interest tours and skiing trips.

BOAT TRIPS

Bavaria's many rivers and lakes make boat trips a great attraction. The most scenic of these are on the region's largest lakes – the Starnberger See, Ammersee, Tegernsee, Chiemsee and Königssee – and on rivers such as the Danube and the Altmühl. Their confluence is the start of canals linking the Rhine and the Main. On many of the smaller lakes, small privately run boats operate, and it is also possible to hire boats there. Rafting is possible on the River Salzach near Burghausen, and particularly on the River Isar. The Isar route covers the stretch of river from Wolfrats-hausen to Thalkirchen, a southern district of Munich. Longer cruises are available on the Danube from Passau to Vienna. This can be pleasantly combined with visits to the historic sights of the Danube valley.

DIRECTORY

Deutsche Bahn AG
Tel Information and reservations 11 861.
www.bahn.de
www.deutsche-bahn.de

RAILWAY STATIONS

Hauptbahnhof
Tel 11 861.

DB-Railwaystation
Tel 11 861.

TRAVEL AGENT

Deutsches Reisebüro (DER)
Promenadeplatz 12, D-80333 Munich.
Tel (089) 21 08 920.
www.der.de

RAFTING ON THE ISAR

Josef Seitner Floßfahrten
Lindenweg 1, D-82515 Wolfratshausen.
Tel (08171) 78 518.

Boats moored at the jetty at Stock am Chiemsee

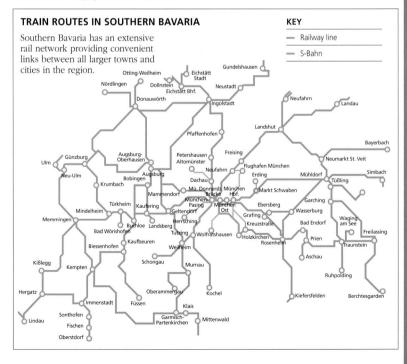

TRAIN ROUTES IN SOUTHERN BAVARIA

Southern Bavaria has an extensive rail network providing convenient links between all larger towns and cities in the region.

KEY
— Railway line
— S-Bahn

Munich's Buses, Trams, U-Bahn and S-Bahn

In addition to its eight underground (U-Bahn) lines, Munich has an extensive network of bus and tram routes. The environs of Munich are connected to the city by the fast suburban overground (S-Bahn) trains, which also serve Munich itself. The city's S-Bahn stations are linked to over 200 bus routes, so that the whole region is well connected by public transport. As all four networks are part of the Münchner Verkehrs- und Tarifverbund (MVV), uniform regulations and fares apply.

One of Munich's trams, bearing the city's coat of arms

TRAVELLING BY BUS AND TRAM

With 61 bus routes and 10 tram routes (as well as four tram light services), overground travel in Munich is easy. For tourists in particular, buses and trams are an attractive alternative to the U-Bahn and S-Bahn networks as they are less crowded and allow passengers to see the city as they travel.

Buses and trams are frequent and punctual. Each stop has a route map giving details of timetables, connections and multiple tickets. Tickets can be purchased at machines situated beside the stops as well as on the buses and trams themselves. To buy a ticket at a machine, press the button to select the appropriate ticket, insert the payment into the slot (accepted coins and notes are listed) and take the ticket, together with any change. When you board the tram or bus, you must validate the ticket by stamping it at the franking machine located just inside the doors. However, in the new-style trams, tickets are sold ready-stamped.

Each bus or tram stop is either announced by a recorded voice (or the driver), or is displayed on a screen. If

in doubt, ask the driver or other passengers.

The city and its environs are divided into four zones, each of which is indicated on maps by a different colour. For tourists, Zone 1 (the white zone) is the most important, because it covers the city centre. Single tickets cost €2.20 for travel within Zone 1, €4.40 for Zone 2, €6.60 for Zone 3 and €8.80 for Zone 4. If you intend to make several journeys, it is cheaper to buy a *Streifenkarte* (strip card), which costs €10. The card is divided into ten sections; you will need two sections for each zone you travel through. The ticket should be folded at the appropriate place and inserted into the franking machine. The last stamp cancels all previous ones. For short journeys (of up to four stops), a *Kurzstrecke* ticket costing €1.10 can be bought. Alternatively, you can frank just one section of a *Streifenkarte*.

For tourists, the best type of ticket is the one-day *Tageskarte*, or the three-day *3-Tageskarte*. Both are available in two forms – for a single person *(Single)* or for

Typical bus stop in Munich

groups of up to five people *(Partner)*. Two children aged 6–14 count as one person. A *Tageskarte* costs €4.80 *(Single)* or €8.50 *(Partner)*, while a *3-Tageskarte* costs €11.80 *(Single)* or €20 *(Partner)*. These tickets are available at tourist information offices, in most hotel receptions, and in travel agents, newsagents and stationers. They are valid from the time they are stamped until 6am the following day.

For visitors staying in Munich for an extended period, a weekly, monthly or even annual *Isarcard* may be more advantageous. The cost depends on the number of "rings", or zones, which will be used. The maximum number of rings is 16, four of which are in the centre of Munich.

A weekly four-ring *Isarcard*, for example, costs €14.60. All *Isarcards* allow any number of the holder's children plus three other children to travel free. They

A long Munich bus, serving one of 82 bus routes in the city

Information panel in one of Munich's U-Bahn stations

are valid after 9am Monday to Friday, and all days Saturday, Sunday and on public holidays.

Children under the age of six travel free. Single tickets for children aged 6–14 cost €.1.10, and a 5-section child's *Streifenkarte* €5 (only one section needs to be franked for travel over any distance). A one-day child's *Tageskarte* valid for the whole public transport network costs €2.30. Young people aged 15–20 need to stamp only one section of their *Streifenkarte* per zone, in effect travelling half-price.

All passengers with valid tickets are entitled to carry one dog free of charge. A child fare must be paid for each additional dog. This does not apply to animals in baskets or carriers.

The Münchner Verkehrs- und Tarifverbund (MVV) also offers various combination tickets, such as the *München Welcome Card (see p284)* and the *Weißblaue Kombikarte*, which includes boat travel on Starnberger See and Ammersee. Full details regarding combination tickets are available at tourist information offices.

THE U-BAHN AND S-BAHN NETWORKS

Munich's underground rail network – the U-Bahn – is a relatively new development in the city's transport system. The first section opened in 1971 and some stretches are still not completed. The S-Bahn, which is a fast suburban train network, coincides in some places with the U-Bahn, which emerges above ground outside the city centre.

Many U-Bahn and S-Bahn stations are decorated with motifs that have some connection with the relevant area of the city above the station. In the U-Bahn station at Königsplatz, for example, the decoration is based on some of the exhibits displayed in the museums on the square.

The fare system on the U-Bahn and S-Bahn is the same as that which applies on Munich's trams and buses. Tickets can be bought at machines or at ticket offices in most stations. Before boarding the

Logo of the S-Bahn suburban network

FRANKING MACHINE

1 The letter E denotes a franking machine outside the entrance to a U-Bahn station

2 Slot for inserting a ticket for it to be stamped

train, tickets must be stamped in a franking machine, which is often located at the top of the stairs leading down to the platform. If you are not travelling yourself but only accompanying someone who holds a valid ticket, you need to buy a platform ticket *(Bahnsteigkarte)*.

Tickets for events such as concerts or football matches often include the price of the fare to the venue on the U-Bahn or S-Bahn. This is stated on the ticket for the event.

The U-Bahn and S-Bahn trains are frequent and reliable, although they are likely to become quite crowded during the morning and evening rush hours. Before boarding an S-Bahn train, check the destination given on the electronic information boards. On the U-Bahn, boarding the wrong train is easy to do because trains travelling in opposite directions come in on either side of one platform. Check the direction *(richtung)* panel as well as the destination to ensure that you board the correct train.

TICKET MACHINE

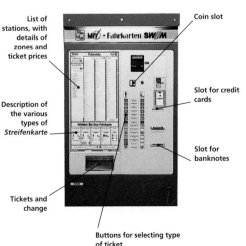

List of stations, with details of zones and ticket prices

Coin slot

Description of the various types of *Streifenkarte*

Slot for credit cards

Tickets and change

Slot for banknotes

Buttons for selecting type of ticket

One of the U-Bahn's blue trains at underground station

Getting around Munich on Foot, by Bicycle, Taxi and Car

Most of Munich's tourist attractions and historic monuments are located in the city centre and distances between them are not far, making it is easy to see Munich on foot. The numerous cafés, squares and parks provide ample opportunity to rest in pleasant surroundings. Because of traffic congestion and parking problems, driving in Munich is a less inviting prospect. Cycling, by contrast, is very popular and bicycles can be hired at one of the many cycle hire points.

A typical Munich street sign

AROUND MUNICH ON FOOT

Exploring Munich on foot is especially interesting and rewarding. Much of the Old Town has been closed to traffic, and only in the main shopping streets do you have to struggle through crowds.

Most of the tourist attractions in the Old Town are within less than 20 minutes' walk of each other and, when venturing further afield, strolling through the city's various districts can be a pleasant experience in itself.

Drivers in Munich are courteous to pedestrians, even though not all pedestrians obey the rules. A basic rule is that pedestrians do not cross the road when a red pedestrian light shows, even if the road is clear. Pedestrian crossings often have a sign saying "Set an example to children". The many cyclists that circulate in the city can be a danger to careless pedestrians. Cyclists using the special cycle lanes can gather considerable speed and pedestrians who stray on to these lanes often receive a severe reprimand or may even find themselves in an unpleasant collision.

Locating a particular address in Munich is straightforward. Street names are posted at junctions and buildings are clearly numbered, with odd and even numbers on opposite sides of the street.

Munich's many parks make walking in the city very attractive. To escape the urban bustle, it is pleasant to walk in the delightful Englischer Garten or the green spaces of Maximilian-anlagen on the river bank, or take a trip to Nymphenburg park or the Botanical Gardens. A cold beer in a beer garden is an excellent reward for the exercise.

BY BICYCLE

Munich is a city of cyclists. Cycle lanes are marked off on pavements (sidewalks) and on the edges of roads. Special bicycle stands can also be found throughout the city and large numbers of bicycles can be seen parked at railway and S-Bahn stations. However, before leaving their bicycle, owners should lock it securely.

Bicycles can be taken on the U-Bahn and S-Bahn, but not on trams or buses.

Sign for a pedestrian zone

Travellers taking their bicycle onto a U-Bahn or S-Bahn train should board at the appropriate door and stand their cycle in the appropriate place (no more than two bicycles are allowed). Bicycles cannot be taken on the U-Bahn or S-Bahn between 6 and 9am and 4 and 6pm Monday to Friday, although this restriction is suspended during school holidays. Taking a bicycle on the U-Bahn or S-Bahn costs €2 or two sections of a *Streifenkarte (see p310)*. The cheapest way is to buy a one-day cycle card for €2.50.

There are bicycle hire points *(Fahrradverleih)* at various places in the city centre as well as at MVV stations and at major tourist spots. Bicycle hire is quite cheap, and cycling in the city is a great pleasure.

Tourist information offices provide cycle maps of Munich and brochures showing the routes of the best cycling tours around the city. MVV also publishes a guide entitled *Radeln mit dem MVV (Cycling with MVV)*, showing 52 cycle routes around the most scenic parts of Munich.

BY TAXI

Taxis in Munich, as elsewhere in Germany, are invariably large cream-coloured cars with a "TAXI" sign on the roof; this is illuminated when the taxi is

Cycling – a quick and popular way of getting around Munich

A taxi in Munich, identifiable by its cream colour and "Taxi" sign

available. Taxis can be hailed on the street or booked by telephone. They can also be picked up at a taxi rank, although these are rare. If the rank is empty, a cab can be called from the telephone there. Taxi ranks together with their telephone numbers are also listed under *"Taxi München AG"* in Yellow Pages *(Gelbe Seiten)*.

The fare is calculated by an illuminated meter on the dashboard. The lowest rates apply during the week, for journeys within the city limits. At night and at weekends the rates are higher. It is customary to give a small tip.

DRIVING IN MUNICH

Munich is at the hub of a network of motorways radiating in many directions. To the south are motorways A8 to Salzburg and A95 to Garmisch Partenkirchen, to the southwest is motorway A96 to Lindau, to the west is motorway A8 to Stuttgart, to the north motorway A9 to Nuremberg, and to the east motorway A95 to Passau.

There is a ring road *(Autobahnring)* around the city, although this is often congested. Munich also has two smaller ring roads, the *Mittlerer Ring* and the *Altstadtring*, which relieve some of the congestion but are themselves often filled to capacity with traffic.

One of the biggest problems for motorists in Munich is finding a parking space. Although there are many multi-storey car parks *(Parkhäuser)*, they are expensive and often full. (The word *"Frei"* indicates that parking spaces are available.) Most on-street parking must be paid for, either by inserting coins into a meter or by buying a pay-and-display ticket. Another problem is that there is a strict time limit for parking in the city centre, one hour often being the maximum time allowed. Parking attendants *(Politessen)* patrol the streets, issuing tickets when cars are illegally parked or parking is unpaid.

Parking rules in Germany are much stricter than in most other European countries. Cars can only be parked in the same direction as the flow of traffic. Parking is forbidden even slightly on the kerb (unless there is a sign or markings allowing this). Some of the strictest penalties are for the unauthorized use of parking spaces reserved for disabled drivers.

For those who are not familiar with the city, driving in Munich can be quite a harrowing experience. The traffic is relatively heavy and although drivers obey regulatons, their driving style is quick and decisive. Visitors are advised to leave their car at their hotel or in the outskirts of the city, and use the excellent public transport system instead.

Parking sign with information

DIRECTORY

BICYCLE HIRE

Aktiv-Rad
Hans-Sachs-Str. 7. **Map** 3 B4.
Tel (089) 26 65 06.

Boots-und Fahrradverleih
Kleinhesseloher See.
Tel (089) 33 83 53.

Call a Bike
Tel (07000) 52 25 522.

Hauptbahnhof, Radius-Tours
Arnulfstr 3.
Tel (089) 59 61 13.

Spurwechsel
Guided bicycle sight-seeing tours
Tel (089) 69 24 699.

TAXIS

Taxi-München
Tel (089) 1 94 10 – switchboard.
Tel (089) 21 610 – bookings.

Pay-and-Display Ticket Machine
Automatic parking-ticket machines like this issue receipts that are placed inside the car windscreen.

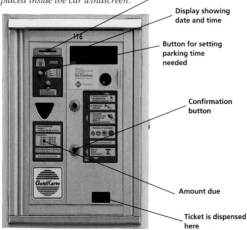

Slot for cards

Display showing date and time

Button for setting parking time needed

Confirmation button

Amount due

Ticket is dispensed here

Travelling by Car

By far the fastest and most comfortable way of travelling around Bavaria is to use the motorways. However, during the holiday season, the Bavarian Alps become a transit route for motorists from northern Europe travelling south to Austria and Italy. To avoid long delays check the holiday calendar in advance, or avoid the motorways altogether. Although it is a little slower, travelling on the well-maintained network of main roads allows visitors to reach interesting places and see the country at a more intimate level.

Road maps sold in bookshops and at newsagents

GETTING TO THE BAVARIAN ALPS

Getting to the Bavarian Alps by car is quite easy. The only problem is that, in the summer months and over public holidays, considerable queues can build up at border crossings into Germany, especially on the frontier with the Czech Republic. However, under normal circumstances, providing that you carry the necessary documents, you should experience a minimum of delay and formalities at border crossings.

Non-EU citizens do not have to make a Customs declaration on arrival but there are limits on the amount of duty-free goods that can be brought in to the country (*see p298*).

WHAT TO TAKE

Visitors travelling by car in Germany must carry a valid driving licence as well as their vehicle's registration document and insurance policy. Before leaving home check with your insurance company whether your policy will cover you in Germany. You will also need to display an environmental badge on your windscreen which can be bought in advance from www.green-zones.eu.

The car must carry a plate indicating country of origin and it must also be equipped with a first-aid kit and a red warning triangle for use in case of breakdown.

ROADS AND MOTORWAYS

Motorways (*Autobahn*) in Germany are toll-free and have regularly spaced petrol stations and facilities with toilets, restaurants and motels. An *Autobahn* is indicated by the letter "A" followed by a number. Some motorway signs also have the letter "E" and a number, indicating that the road crosses the German border. A *Bundesstraße* (main road) is indicated by the letter "B" and a number.

Road signs to the motorway

ROAD SIGNS

In addition to internationally understood road signs, on German roads there are words that clarify the meaning of the sign above. On mountain roads, for example, a warning sign showing a car tyre wrapped in a chain is accompanied by the word *"Schnee"*, which warns about driving without chains when there is snow.

CAR RENTAL

Major international car-rental companies such as **Hertz** and **Avis** have offices in the Bavarian Alps, particularly near railway stations and at airports. They are, however, rivalled, both with regard to price and class of car, by the Munich-based car hire company **Sixt**.

It is sometimes advantageous to rent a car from a smaller agency, particularly after comparing the prices of various companies. Telephone numbers of car rental companies can be found under *"Autovermietung"* in Yellow Pages (*Gelbe Seiten*).

Airlines and railway companies offer a variety of combined tickets that include car rental. This is usually slightly cheaper than booking each separately.

Rates for car rental vary greatly, depending primarily on the model of car chosen. For holidaymakers another option is to rent a camper van (*Wohnmobile*), which outside

One of the many picturesque roads with a view of the Alps

the holiday season can be rented for the price of a medium-sized car and offers a great deal of freedom.

PARKING

Most towns and cities in the Bavarian Alps are crowded during office hours and parking is quite a problem. Town centres are less congested at weekends, when parking is usually free. Tickets issued for illegally parked vehicles usually involve complex procedures that are often more strictly followed in small towns than in cities. Drivers should take special care not to exceed the parking time paid for, as a few minutes' excess can result in a costly fine. Drivers whose car has been towed away should approach the police, who will give instructions on how to proceed.

Sign for a pay-and-display machine

ROADSIDE ASSISTANCE

Germany has an efficient roadside assistance infrastructure. On motorways, emergency telephones (*Notrufsäulen*) are situated at intervals of 1 km (0.62 mile). ADAC, the German motoring association, is the main provider of roadside assistance. Calling for help from a roadside telephone is simple for tourists, as the location is automatically transmitted. ADAC repairmen will try to fix the car by the roadside (this is free for ADAC members), or will tow it to a garage.

When a road accident occurs, the police and an ambulance always attend, with the fire brigade or air ambulance if necessary.

On the approach road to the motorway to Stuttgart is a "pilot station" (*Lotsenstation*) where drivers can obtain information and directions. You can also hire a car with a driver to show you the way.

An ARAL petrol (gas) station, one of the most widely seen in Bavaria

PETROL (GAS) STATIONS

Petrol and diesel stations on motorways are most often located at junctions or at *Rasthöfe* – rest areas with car parks, restaurants, bars, shops and toilets with showers.

The cost of fuel provided by the main petroleum companies (Shell, BP, Aral and DEA) is usually fairly uniform. The cheapest fuel is that sold at petrol stations in shopping centres.

Petrol stations are open until late at night, many of them 24 hours. They also sell motoring accessories, as well as newspapers and refreshments. On lesser roads and in remote or rural areas, petrol stations are likely to be few and far between.

RULES OF THE ROAD

Motorway telephone

Speed limits in Germany are 50 km/h (30 mph) in built-up areas and 100 km/h (62 mph) elsewhere. On motorways there is no speed limit unless this is indicated. When travelling with a caravan or camping trailer outside built-up areas it is 70 km/h (44 mph) and on motorways 100 km/h (62 mph). Speed traps are frequent and fines high. The maximum limit for alcohol in the blood is 0.5 per cent. Seat belts must be worn at all times, children under 12 must travel in the back seats and small children be secured in child seats. The use of mobile phones while driving is restricted to hands-free sets.

DIRECTORY

EMERGENCY NUMBERS

Police
Tel 110.

Fire Brigade
Tel 112.

Ambulance
Tel 19 222.

ROADSIDE ASSISTANCE

ADAC
Tel (0180) 22 22 222.

ACE
Tel (01802) 34 35 36.

Lotsenstation
◻ 7:30am–4:30pm.
Obermenzing (Stuttgart motorway)
Tel (089) 81 12 412.

CAR RENTAL COMPANIES IN MUNICH

Avis
Hauptbahnhof.
Tel (089) 55 02 252.
Fax (089) 55 02 253.
www.avis.com

Europcar
Hauptbahnhof.
Tel (089) 54 90 240.
Fax (089) 54 90 24 66.
www.europcar.de

Hertz
Hauptbahnhof.
Tel (089) 55 02 251.
Fax (089) 55 02 250.
www.hertz.com

Sixt
Hauptbahnhof.
Tel (01805) 25 25 25.
www.sixt.com

General Index

Acknowledgments

Dorling Kindersley would like to thank the following people for their help in preparing this guide:

Additional Photography
Horst Höfler, Katarzyna and Sergiusz Michalscy, Tomasz Myśluk, Werner Nikolai, Ian O'Leary, Gregor M. Schmid, Oda Sternberg, Paweł Wójcik

Additonal Contributor
Susi Cheshire

Publishing Managers
Kate Poole, Helen Townsend

DTP Designers
Jason Little, Conrad Van Dyk

Production
Sarah Dodd

Consultant
Gerhard Bruschke

Fact Checker
Barbara Sobeck

Proofreader
Stewart Wild

Indexer
Hilary Bird

Director of Publishing
Gillian Allan

Editorial and Design Assistance
Emma Anacootee, Sonal Bhatt, Arwen Burnett, Jo Cowen, Marcus Hardy, Juliet Kenny, Delphine Lawrance, Carly Madden, Sam Merrell, Kate Molan, Casper Morris, Marianne Petrou, Dave Pugh, Sands Publishing Solutions, Sadie Smith, Rachel Symons and Karen Villabona.

Picture Research Assistant
Rachel Barber

Special Assistance
The publisher would also like to thank the following for their assistance on the guide:

Anette Alwast, Ingrid Baudrexl-Czuraj, Prof. Dr Adrianowi von Buttlarowi, Tamarze and Jackowi Draberom, Daniel Fink (Pinakothek der Moderne), Erica Gingerich at Munich Airport, Iris and Wolfgangowi Hermannom, Barbarze Januszkiewicz, Irenie Hiemeyer, Aleksandrze Markiewicz German Book Information Centre, Goethe-Institut in Warsaw, Ulliemu Nerdingerowi, Wilhelminie and Wernerowi Nikolai, Dr Elisabeth Pfaud, Margarete Roeck, Dr Thomasowi Weidnerowi and Kartographie Huber (Gerhild Kemper-Wildtraut), Käthe-Kruse-Puppen-Museum in Donauwörth, Kultur- und Ferienland Landsberg am Lech (Ulla Kurz), Kur- und Ferienland Garmisch-Partenkirchen, Kurverwaltung Schwangau, Meteorologisches Institut der Universität München (Heinz Lösslein), Presse-und Öffentlichkeitsarbeit der Stadt Pfaffenhofen an der Ilm Sr. (Elisabeth Benen), Rieskrater-Museum in Nördlingen (Dr Michael Schieber, Monika Spörl), Stadt Donauwörth (Bernhard Kunz, Gudrun Reißer), Steigenberger Drei Mohren (Robert Strohe), Theresienthaler Krystallglasmanufaktur GmbH (Ralph A.W. Wenzel), Tourismus Straubing (Bettina Schauer), Tourist Info Kochel am See (Sabine Rauscher), Touristinformation Stadt Freising (Barabara Sibinger), Verkehrsverband Laufen, Verkehrsverein Lindau (Hans Stübner), Wittelsbacher Ausgleichsfonds, Inventarverwaltung (Andreas von Majewski, Sibille Herz)

Photography Permissions
The publisher would also like to thank all the people and institutions who allowed photographs belonging to them to be reproduced, as well as granting permission to use photographs from their archives:
AB PhotoDesign in Kellberg (Dionys Asenkerschbaumer), Alois Dallmayr in Munich (Patricia Massmann), Alpines Museum in Munich (Ulrike Gehrig), Amt für Tourismus Straubing (Frau Baumhof), Archäologische Staatssammlung in Munich (Dr Dorothea van Endert) Artothek (Jürgen Hinrichs), Augsburger Puppenkiste, Bavaria Filmstadt in Munich, Bayerische Staatsgemäldesammlungen (Prof. Dr Christian Lenz, Christina Schwill, D. Cornelia Syre), Bayerische Verwaltung der Staatlichen Schlösser, Gärten und Seen (Eva Gerum, Michael Teichmann), Bayerisches Nationalmuseum in Munich (Dr Nina Gockerell, Dr Sgoff) Benediktinerabtei Ottobeuren, Bildvorlagen Römerschatz – Gäubodenmuseum in Straubing (Dr Prammer), Bischöfliches Ordinariat Augsburg (Monsignore Josef Heigl), Bischöfliches Ordinariat Passau (Franz Sr. Gabriel) BMW Group Mobile Tradition and.V. (Nikola von Ondarza), Britstock-Ifa in London, Café Luitpold in Munich (Carmen Brenner), Deutsche Bahn (Hans-Joachim Kirsche), Deutsche Press Agentur (Tanja Teichmann), Deutsches Museum in Munich (Marlene Schwarz), Diözesanbauamt Eichstätt (Dr Claudia Grund), Erzbischöfliches Ordinariat München (Dr Norbert Jocher, Dr Hans Ramisch, Hans Rohrmann, Gabriele Skornia), Flash Press Media (Sylwia Wilgocka), Flughafen München GmbH (Wilhelm Hennies, Fr. Kiener), Foto-Production in Gilching (Gregor M. Schmid), Fremden-verkehrsamt in Altötting, Fremdenverkehrsamt in Mühldorf (Peter-Alexander Berger), Galerie im Lenbachhaus in Munich (Daniela Müller), Haus der Bayerischen Geschichte-Bildarchiv in Augsburg (Dr Rudolf Wildmoser), Haus der Kunst in Munich (Claus Vogel), Heimatmuseum der Stadt Bad Tölz, Hilton München Park (Katharina Rösel), Hotel Königshof in Munich (Frieder Lempp), Hotel Residenz Passau (Dieter Austen), Hunsingers Pacific in Munich (M. Hunsinger), Institut für Kunst Geschichte TU in Brunswick 36b, 37c, 37br, 37bl, 39c, 44c, 45c, 49cl, Jura-Museum in Eichstätt (Jutta Streit), Alter Simpl Café in Munich, Kristall Museum Riedenburg, Kurdirektion des Berchtesgadener Land (Vroni Aigner, Birgit Tica), Landeshauptstadt München, Referat für Arbeit und Wirtschaft Fremdenverkehrsamt (Stefan Böttcher), Leopold restaurant in Munich, Marionettenbühne in Munich, Mineralogische Staatssammlung in Munich (Dr G Simon), Münchner Stadtmuseum (Dr Götz), Museum "Reich der Kristalle" in Munich, Neue Messe München GmbH (Julia Spiegelhalder), Nürnberger Bratwurst Glöckl am Dom in Munich (Nadja Beck), Paläontologisches Museum in Munich (Dr H. Mayr), Parkhotel in Donauwörth (Eugen Schuler), Passauer Glasmuseum (Birgitte Holles), Ratskeller München (Renate Werner), SiemensForum in Munich (Dr Marie Schlund), Shop with devotional figures C. Huber in Augsburg, Staatliche Antikensammlungen und Glyptothek (Dr Martin Schulz, Vincent Brickmann), Staatliche Sammlung Ägyptischer Kunst in Munich, Stadt Kempten (Elli Cascio, Marlene Köhler), Stadtarchiv München (Dr Graf), Stadt-bildstelle Augsburg, Stadtmuseum in Munich, Ursulinen-kloster Straubing (Sr. Judith Reis, Oberin), Verkehrsamt der Stadt Nördlingen (Katja Jaumann), Villa Stuck in Munich, ZEFA (Ewa Kozłowska).

Picture Credits
t = top; tl = top left; tc = top centre; tr = top right; c= centre; cb = centre below; ca = centre above; cl = centre left; clb = centre left below; cla = centre left above; cr = centre right; crb = centre right below; cra = centre right above; b = bottom; bl = bottom left; bc = bottom centre; br = bottom right; bra = bottom right above; tla = top left above; tlb = top left below; trb = top right below

The following works of art have been reproduced with the permission of the copyright holders:
Cover of *Der Blaue Reiter* (1912) © ADAGP, Paris and Dacs, London, 2006: 215cr
View of Munich Suburbia (1908) © ADAGP, Paris and Dacs, London, 2006: 105cl
Still Life with Geraniums (1910) Pinakothek der Moderne, © Succession H Matisse/DACS, 2006: 117br

A1 Pix Stefan Herbke 291br
Alamy Images Albaimages/Ronald Weir 11tr; Arco Images 273tl, 290tc; BL Images Ltd 141cr; David Sanger Photography 272cla; FAN travelstock/Jürgen Wackenhut 291tr; Fotosonline/Klaus-Peter Wolf 291cl; imagebroker/ Manfred Bail 141tl; imagebroker/Martin Siepmann 10br; imagebroker/Stephan Goerlich 142 tc; Andre Jenny 140cr; Yadid Levy 140bl; LOOK Die Bildagentur der Fotografen GmbH/Jan Greune 290; nagelestock.com 292tr; Richard Wareham Fotografie 11br; Maximilian Weinzierl 10cl; Christoph Weiser 273c; Westend61/ Franz Faltermaier 290cl
Allianz Arena Munchen Stadion GmbH 143tl
Alois Dallmayr (Munich) 286cl
Alpines Museum (Munich) 89b, 91c
Amt für Kultur und Tourismus (Neuburg) Leander Hopf 168b
Amt für Tourismus Straubing 31t
Archäologische Staatssammlung (Munich) 36b, 107c
Artothek 27tr, 52tr, 119tl, 125t; W. Bahnmüller 43c, 43bl; Bayer & Mitko 119bl, 124b; Joachim Blauel 42tr, 43tc, 43tc, 43tp, 43cl, 43bl, 113c, 118ca, 118cb, 119cra, 119cla, 120b, 121c, 121b, 122tr, 122ca, 123tl, 123crb, 123bl, 124tr, 124cl, 125cl, 125br; Blauel & Gnamm 43bl, 115cra, 117t, 118tr, 118bl, 119br, 120t, 120c, 121t, 122cb, 123trb, 123cla; Sophie-R. Gnamm 92t; Toni Ott 42bl, 42br
Augsburger Puppenkiste 251tr
Bayerische Staatsgemäldesammlungen (Munich) 115t; Neue Pinakothek Munich 122cb
Bayerische Staatsoper Wilfried Hosl 142bl
Bayerische Verwaltung der Staatlichen Schlösser, Gärten und Seen 8–9, 38t, 40t, 46 cl, 47tl, 47tr, 75tl, 132br, 133crb
Bayerisches Nationalmuseum (Munich) 53sca, 108tl, 108tr, 108tla, 108tlb, 108b, 109t, 109ca, 109cb, 109b
Bier und Oktoberfestmuseum 64c
Bildvorlagen Römerschatz-Gäubodenmuseum (Straubing) 35b, 184tl
Bischöfliches Ordinariat Passau 23t, 26tp, 41cl, 188tl, 188tc, 188br, 193tl
BMW Group Mobile Tradition & V. (Munich) 19t, 134tr
Britstock-Ifa Rolf Zschurnack 70
Corbis Zefa/Guenter Rossenbach 11clb; Zefa/Herbert Spichtinger 142cr; Zefa/Wilfried Krecichwost 10tc
Dallmayr 270cl
DCC Europa-Preisträger 292bl
Deutsche Bahn (Berlin) Mann 308tl
Deutsche Presse Agentur (DPA) 19b, 21tl, 28t, 28b, 29t, 29b, 33t, 33b, 49bra, 274tr
Deutsches Historisches Museum (Berlin) 39b, 48c, 49bl
Deutsches Museum (Munich) 12, 94t, 94ca, 94cb, 94b, 95t, 95ca, 95cb, 95b, 96t, 96c, 96b, 97t, 97c, 97b, 170br
Erzbischöfliches Ordinariat München 60b, 61t, 61c, 61bl, 61bc, 61br, 63t
Flash Press Media 48bl
Flughafen München GmbH 306cr, 306bl, 307tl, 307bc
Fremdenverkehrsamt (Altötting) 20tl, 30tr, 195b
Fremdenverkehrsamt (Mühldorf) 28c
Galerie im Lenbachhaus (Munich) 105cla, 105crb, 112cla, 215cr, 218cr
Geisel Privathotels 271tl

Haus der Bayerischen Geschichte Bildarchiv 45t, 48t
Haus der Kunst (Munich) 107t
Horst Höfler 260bl
Hotel Königshof (Munich) 259tl
Hotel Residenz Passau 258bl
Hunsingers Pacific (Munich) 270crb
Jura-Museum (Eichstätt) 164b
Kristall Museum Riedenburg 183trb
Kurdirektion des Berchtesgadener Land 48br, 201bc
Landeshauptstadt München, Referat für Arbeit und Wirtschaft Fremdenverkehrsamt
Bjarne Geiges 275bl
W. Hausmann 50–51
Robert Hetz 49tl
Rudolf Sterlinger 2–3
Marionettenbühne (Munich) 136tl
Katarzyna and Sergiusz Michalscy 17t, 221clb, 244bl
Münchner Stadtmuseum 4t, 5cl, 26cl, 26bl, 65b
Dorothee Jordens-Meintker 34, 44b
Neue Messe München GmbH
Loske 139tr
Werner Nikolai 30b
Nürnberger Bratwurst Glöckl am Dom (Munich) 271cr
Paläontologisches Museum (Munich) 112tr
Parkhotel in Donauwörth 259cl
Passauer Glasmuseum 191c
Pinakothek der Moderne Proust's Armchair, 1978, Alessandro Mendini 116crb; 117br
Ratskeller München 271br
Sea Life München 143cr
Gregor M. Schmid half-title, 86, 158
SiemensForum (Munich)
Bernd Müller 81t
Slips Fashion 140tc
Staatliche Antikensammlungen und Glyptothek (Munich) 52ca, 114c
Staatliche Sammlung Ägyptischer Kunst (Munich) 77cl
Stadt Kempten 237tc, 237bl
Stadtarchiv München 102b
Oda Sternberg 84b
Tomasz MyЕłuk 226tr, 226cl, 227bc
Verkehrsamt der Stadt Nördlingen 13
Villa Stuck (Munich) 15b
Paweł Wójcik 20tl, 23b, 23bl, 29c, 31c, 45bl, 49br, 57clb, 62c, 68tl, 68tr, 72br, 73tl, 78b, 80c, 80b, 82t, 83c, 84t, 85c, 100t, 101t, 103c, 104t, 112cb, 114t, 138tl, 165bl, 182t, 205tr, 205br, 226br, 233tr, 233c, 236tl, 236tr, 236cl, 236br, 258tc, 260c, 286tc, 288tr, 288cla, 288clb, 288cra, 288crb, 288cb, 288bl, 288cb, 289tl, 289tc, 289tr, 289cl, 289c, 289cra, 289crb, 289cr, 289bl, 289bc, 289bca, 289bc, 298c, 300tl, 301bl, 305tc, 310tr, 310clb, 310b, 314c, 315tl, 315dcb
ZEFA 62t, 224; Damm 222; Rossenbach 157tl
Jacket: Front – **Alamy Images:** CoverSpot ca; **DK Images:** Dorota and Mariusz Jarymowicz clb; **Getty Images:** Taylor S Kennedy main image. Back – **Alamy Images:** imagebroker/Martin Siepmann clb; **DK Images:** Dorota and Mariusz Jarymowicz bl, cla, tl. Spine – **Alamy Images:** CoverSpot t; **DK Images:** Dorota and Mariusz Jarymowicz b; **Getty Images:** Taylor S Kennedy tc.

All other images © Dorling Kindersley.
For further information see: www.dkimages.com

SPECIAL EDITIONS OF DK TRAVEL GUIDES

DK Travel Guides can be purchased in bulk quantities at discounted prices for use in promotions or as premiums. We are also able to offer special editions and personalized jackets, corporate imprints, and excerpts from all of our books, tailored specifically to meet your own needs.

To find out more, please contact:
(in the United States) **SpecialSales@dk.com**
(in the UK) **TravelSpecialSales@uk.dk.com**
(in Canada) DK Special Sales at **general@tourmaline.ca**
(in Australia) **business.development@pearson.com.au**